Learning with Computers

Learning with Computers

ALFRED BORK

DIGITAL PRESS

Printed in the U.S.A.

10 9 8 7 6 5 4 3 2

Documentation Number: AX014-DP
ISBN: 0-932376-11-8

This manuscript was created on a DEC Word Processing System and, via a translation program, was typeset on Digital's DECset-8000 Typesetting System.

Library of Congress Cataloging in Publication Data

Bork, Alfred M.
Learning with computers.

1. Computer-assisted instruction. I. Title.
LB1028.5.B615 371.3'9445 81-9695
ISBN 0-932376-11-8 AACR2

Trademarks

Digital Equipment Corporation: DEC, DECUS, PDP, UNIBUS, VAX, DECnet, DECsystem-10, DECSYSTEM-20, DECwriter, DIBOL, EduSystem, IAS, MASSBUS, PDT, RSTS, RSX, VMS, VT.

Speak and Spell is a registered trademark of Texas Instruments.

Monopoly is a registered trademark of Parker Brothers, Inc.

Credits

P. 85 and pp. 94–95, portions from Feynman/Leighton/Sands, *The Feynman Lectures on Physics*, Vol. 1 and Vol. 2. © 1964, California Institute of Technology. Chapters 9 and 19, respectively. Published by Addison-Wesley, Reading, Ma. reprinted by permission of the publisher.

Contents

4 PHYSICS

5 CLASSROOM

6 AUTHORING DIALOGS

7 THE FUTURE

Introduction

This book focuses on the use of the computer as a learning device. It presents a panoramic view, reflecting many different types of usage, but concentrates on a *single* project.

The chapters of the book are based on papers written during the last 10 years, reflecting the work of the Physics Computer Development Project and the Educational Technology Center at Irvine.

Some of the papers used here were co-authored with other individuals. A project such as ours is dependent on insights and works from a great many individuals. In many cases when we develop programs we bring in visitors from other campuses, particularly skilled teachers often with a national reputation in the area involved. Hence, the papers describing these projects often involve those individuals too. We have been fortunate to be able to work with an extremely competent group of teachers.

Changes have been made in the papers to prepare them for this publication. Most of these changes are relatively minor. They fit into several categories. In some cases I have "cancelled" changes made by other editors. Editorial and stylistic changes brought all the information presented up to date. When the original data was no longer applicable or needed to be modified for today's situation, content changes have been made. Thus, although the papers were intitially published over the course of a decade, the information in them, as presented here, corresponds to the January 1981 situation.

The papers have a new set of pictures, photographs from the screen. An attempt has been made to avoid duplication of photographs; the pictures were all taken just for this book by Michael Jones. Occasionally the text has been modified to reflect changes in pictures. All of the pictures are of Tektronix screens. As indicated in some of the papers, our recent work has moved to the new technology found in personal computers. Our initial projects in this direction are not yet complete, so I have used no pictorial examples from personal computers.

It is inevitable that in a collection such as this, compiled from previous papers, there will be repetition. Some ideas, ones that are central to the approach developed in the Educational Technology Center, occur in many papers. No attempt has been made to eliminate such repetition. The reader might take such repetition of details as indicating the importance of the ideas.

Most of the papers are printed in their entirety. Occasionally a section no longer applicable has been deleted. In most cases each paper is self-contained, although a given paper frequently references other papers.

As a guide to the reader, I will describe briefly each of the papers included, proceeding on a chapter-by-chapter basis.

Chapter 1

This chapter is composed of five short papers, written over a considerable period of time. They give an overview of the use of computers in education and a brief introduction to the major future possibilities. In each case the material tries to outline the very important role of the computer in aiding learning, with particular focus on the future. The themes developed here are discussed in more detail in later chapters.

The first very brief paper appeared in a publication of the educational television station in Orange County, California, KOCE, Channel 50 circulated to its subscribers. Hence, it is intended for very general audiences. The provocative title was added by the editor of that journal, and may be slightly misleading, but I have kept it for this presentation.

The second paper was delivered at a NATO Advanced Study Institute in Belgium, an introductory "charge" to the participants in that two-week workshop. I have modified it slightly to make it a little less specialized, as the original form referred to the Institute.

The third paper in this chapter was originally given at one of the Computers in the Undergraduate Curriculum meetings at Dartmouth College. It is the oldest paper in this collection. It is organized in the form of a set of "theses," each with a brief amount of supporting discussion. These theses represent philosophical positions that our group at Irvine has taken from our earliest days. This paper, in its original form, concluded with a discussion of a beginning physics course.

However, the initial presentation was so far in the past that the details of that course do not reflect anything that has happened for many years at Irvine. At that time we had relatively little computer material to use in the course, so the course description is omitted from this presentation. Other papers in this book, particularly in Chapter 3, present more recent activities in our beginning physics course.

The next paper in this first chapter again gives a philosophical basis, concentrating on a number of "myths" in this general area. The paper has stood the test of time. Many of these myths are, unfortunately, still widely held today, some seven years after the paper was written.

The final paper stresses the personal computer, characteristic of our recent work at Irvine.

Chapter 2

This chapter considers the role of graphics, particularly as an aid to learning. Our group at Irvine, from its beginning in 1968, has stressed visual information in the learning process.

The first paper reviews many ways in which graphics can be used to assist the learning process. We have had several other papers on this theme. It should be emphasized that I use the word "graphics" in a wider context than is often the case. Anything associated with the layout of the screen, both pictorial and textual, is considered a graphic component. Our group always argued that pictorial information is critical in the learning process, if we are to reach a very large number of students.

The second, more specialized paper discusses the role of adding graphic capabilities to a particular computer language, APL. This graphic capability was developed by our project at Irvine. The graphic capabilities described later became part of the standard Xerox APL program product. This facility is still one of the few graphic systems supplied as part of a standard language by the vendor. But our interests have moved elsewhere; our current activities concentrate on Pascal. I should also stress that we *never* used APL as a fundamental language for developing computer-based learning material (see Chapter 6 for reasons for this decision). But we have used it as a student programming language in beginning courses and in other ways.

Chapter 3

The papers in this chapter represent discussions of the work and activities of our Center at Irvine. Much of the work was performed before the Educational Technology Center had a formal existence. In the early days of our activities, where we concentrated primarily on physics material, we referred to ourselves informally as the Physics Computer Development Project. More recently, we have been given official status by the Irvine campus of the University of California. The new name reflects the broader nature of our recent activities; many of them are not at the university level, and they cover the full math-science spectrum.

The first section is a list of available dialogs on the Irvine timesharing system. It does not reflect any of our recent work on personal computers. It shows that, even in timesharing, we worked with many different materials that served a variety of pedagogical purposes. Most of this material is still in use by students.

The second paper was initially prepared for a small working conference of the International Federation of Information Processing Societies in London in the summer of 1979. It takes a somewhat more personal stance than many of the other papers. It is a good detailed summary of our first 10 years of activity at Irvine, including information about support received. The projects and products are reviewed in some detail. The paper also presents an overview of our production system for generating computer based-learning material, discussed in more detail in Chapter 6.

The final section reviews the recent projects at Irvine, all using the personal computer.

Chapter 4

Because of my own background, much of the earlier materials developed at the Educational Technology Center at Irvine were in Physics at the beginning college level. Hence, that still represents one of our richest areas, although one that we have moved away from in our newer computer dialogs. This chapter can best be read by someone with science background, although it may be usable for others too. I do not attempt to explain all the physics and mathematics terms used, as they are not essential to the computer details.

Many individual computer dialogs, conversations with the student, are described in this chapter. Many of the interactions described can be followed by those with no science background.

The six papers represent a variety of activities within Physics, often activities that involved other people. The first paper, authored with Herbert Peckham (Gavilan College), reviews using the computer within mechanics with emphasis on the student as programmer. It does not stress the computer dialogs that receive prime attention in much of this book. Some of the materials we have developed in this area are available through CONDUIT.

The next paper, "Two New Graphic Computer Dialogs for Teachers," with Arnold Arons, University of Washington, reflects computer dialogs we developed to aid teachers in learning about the nature of science. This is a theme we have continued in more recent work, not described in this book. The user of these interactive learning dialogs is assumed to be (in the sense of Piaget) concrete operational; the programs attempt to aid the transition toward formal reasoning capabilities. The subject area is Astronomy.

The third and fourth papers are related. They deal with the issues of computer simulations, particularly their role in building student intuition. This is an important goal of many classes, yet one that is neglected in coventional approaches to learning, perhaps because it is very difficult to achieve. The computer can be particularly valuable in providing for each student a wide range of experiences that aid in increasing student insight and intuition, an experiential base for later, more formal learning. This goal is difficult to attain with noncomputer learning aids. We regard these intuition-building computer dialogs to be a very important possibility for the future. But the papers also stress the problems associated with the use of such materials in large classes.

"Computer Dialogs to Aid Formal Reasoning" represents another joint activity with Arnold Arons, one again directed toward aiding students to make the transition to concrete operational to formal operational reasoning in the sense of Jean Piaget. The subject areas of the four dialogs are heat and magnetism, but only the one concerning heat is described in detail. In this dialog the stress is on a series of simple "kitchen physics" experiments. It has proved to be one of our most successful dialogs.

The last paper looks at a dialog in electrostatics for beginning electricity and magnetism, usually in the second quarter or semester of an introductory Physics course. Many authors helped with this dialog. As will be seen in the discussion on writing dialogs in Chapter 6, our standard policy within the Educational Technology Center is to develop dialogs using groups of people. Visitors have often been involved in producing interactive learning material.

Chapter 5

While Chapter 4 considered many applications of the computer in science education, it does not look at the issue of how these applications can fit into a full class structure along with other types of teaching and learning modes. The issue of a "complete set" of learning material, such as that necessary for a class, is a different one from that of a few "tack on" materials to fit into an already existing course. The classroom is the focus of the present chapter.

The first paper looks at the special problem of what computer languages should be used if programming is part of the class situation. The emphasis is on the beginning student in science or engineering. Pascal and APL are recommended. The second paper, related to this, discusses the issue of *learning* to program for beginning students, with emphasis on modes of learning which conserve the student's time. Thus, both of these papers are directed toward the use of the computer as our intellectual tool.

The last two papers are concerned with the computer-based beginning physics course developed at Irvine, looking at various aspects of this course. This course, the beginning mechanics material, was the culmination of much of our early work, combining many of the approaches we had developed for many years. But we also found it necessary in developing the course to develop materials in a new direction (not previously explored), on-line testing. These tests offer immediate aid to students in trouble. So they are an intimate blend of learning and testing, possible only with the computer. We believe that these tests are very powerful and effective learning materials.

The introductory Physics quarter has been taught over a 5 year period at Irvine, and the materials are now in stable condition. Well over 1,000 students have been through the course. However, the dialogs still run in a timesharing environment rather than in our newer personal computer environment. In the winter of 1981 we gave 15,000 tests in 10 weeks to about 300 students.

Chapter 6

This chapter concerns the very important process of producing computer-based learning material. This process is at the heart of the problem of encouraging widespread use of good computer materials. There has already been some description of the full-scale production process developed at Irvine, as the dialogs were being described in earlier papers. For example, the second paper in Chapter 3, has a section discussing the production system at Irvine, as already mentioned. We consider this system, or a similar one, to be the key to our activities at Irvine and the key to eventual successful widespread use of computer-based learning material. Hence, this issue has received special attention for many years in the Educational Technology Center.

The first document gives advice to developers about how to prepare dialog material. The discussion is particularly oriented to *teachers,* addressing the pedagogical problems. It does not concern itself with the problems of getting material running, but rather with the question of how the computer can be used as a learning medium, its advantages and disadvantages, and its common pitfalls. The authors of good material must understand that the computer is *not* a book, *not* a lecture, *not* a film.

The APL paper is something of an aside. Since our group has used APL widely for *student* use, it is sometimes assumed that our authoring structures are based on APL. This has never been the case, although we have employed graphic authoring aids based on APL. This paper, done many years ago, outlines why we do not consider APL as an adequate language for the preparation of dialog materials. Indirectly it states requirements for a suitable programming environment for computer-based learning material.

The next two papers review the production system, outlining the various stages as we have used them at Irvine. Note that neither is a recent paper. We have been following essentially the same strategies at Irvine for some time on a variety of hardware. The emphasis is on a *systems* approach to the problem, determining the various tasks necessary, finding the person best for each, developing a way of doing that task, and constructing "interfaces" between the tasks. In some ways our procedures resemble that of textbook publishing. We have avoided a cottage industry approach where it is assumed that one person carries through all the different activities. Some software details that are no longer relevant have been removed from these papers.

The paper on large-scale production and distribution of computer-aided learning modules is one that looks toward the future, when our current sporadic production will have been extended to much more widespread production all over the country. It outlines some of the issues. The solutions it offers, as the reader can see, are consistent with those of the earlier papers in this chapter. We regard these issues as very important to the future of education.

Finally, the last paper in this chapter argues that the interesting or pedagogical design activity should always be done in small *groups* rather than by individuals. We have always worked with groups of three or four in specifying the material. Most material of this kind has been done by individuals, but we believe that this does not lead to the best possible learning material.

Chapter 7

Anyone who works in the development of computer-based learning material must realize that it is a rapidly changing area. Not only is the equipment improving and decreasing in cost, but techniques for producing good materials are also advancing. Developers cannot ignore the likely evolution of the field, if they expect to develop materials with long-range impact. This chapter tries to review *future* possibilities. Most of the papers in this chapter are recent.

The first paper is concerned with the issue of moving materials from one machine to another, in both the sociological sense and the hardware sense. This brief paper is designed to show that the problem of transportability is a larger problem in terms of its overall dimensions than is usually discussed. On the other hand, I also indicate that I expect the hardware aspects of this problem to be solved primarily by the technology.

The next papers on the personal computer argue for their increasingly important role in the educational system, particularly as compared with elaborate timesharing systems. Some projections about hardware are also made.

The next two papers concern an exciting auxiliary device, one that, combined with computers, will have considerable influence on the educational uses of the computer. This device is the optical videodisc. The term "intelligent videodisc," used in these titles is one that I coined several years ago to indicate this intimate combination of the computer and the videodisc.

The use of computers in learning-at-a-distance environments is just becoming common at the present time. The paper on the extended university argues that they will be particularly useful in this situation. Distance learning is still uncommon in the United States, but we can expect further developments in this direction.

The brief paper reviewing George Leonard's views of the computer in education, as expressed in *Education and Ecstasy,* tries to emphasize the point that in a rapidly moving area such as this, we *must* have visions of the future. Leonard's school of the future is not the only possible vision, but it is an interesting one in terms of the way the educational system is structured. Computers play a major role in this school of the future.

Finally, the book closes with my Millikan Lecturer Award lecture of 1978, "Interactive Learning." This should be considered a summary of the entire book.

I have had the good fortune during this time to have worked with my excellent teachers, colleagues, students, and friends. The project directors and others who have worked with me in developing the potentiality of computers in learning are Richard Ballard, Joseph Marasco, Stephen Franklin, Barry Kurtz, David Trowbridge, Estelle Warner, and Ruth Von Blum. As the papers indicate, this work could not have been done without their aid.

Many undergraduate students have played a very important role in our projects, and I wish particularly to give them full credit. They have consistently performed wonders in programming the computer materials we developed. It has been a pleasure to work with them.

The University of California, Irvine, has offered a good working environment. These people were instrumental in my coming to Irvine: Daniel G. Aldrich, Chancellor; Ralph Gerard, former Dean of the Graduate Division; and Kenneth Ford, Chair of the Physics Department when I arrived.

My wife, Annette, and my daughters, Brenda, Ellen, and Carol, deserve much of the credit for this book.

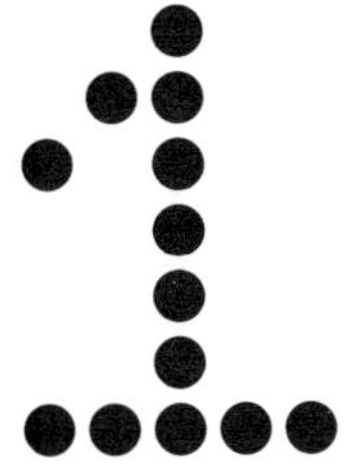

Overview

WILL COMPUTERS REPLACE BOOKS IN AMERICAN EDUCATION?

We are at the brink of a major revolution in ways of learning. Very few people—not even professional educators—understand what is about to happen. The revolution will occur within the next 25 years and will affect our educational system at all levels.

This revolution in the way people learn will be based on the technology of the digital computer. Learning media from other aspects of modern technology will also figure significantly.

A brief review of the history of learning will help explain the situation. The earliest humans learned primarily through experience and interaction with other humans. Until recently in human history, and even now in early childhood, this has been the principal learning mode.

Forum Fifty Magazine, December 1980.

In classical Greece, several new learning modes became prominent. One of these was based on the technology of writing, which was already well developed in Greece. The Greeks realized that written documents could serve as the basis for learning.

The lecture, or group discussion, also seems to have originated in ancient Greece. Perhaps the mode for which Greece is best known is the dialog, exemplified in the works of Plato. Teacher and student worked on a one-to-one basis. The teacher avoided lecturing the student but, by a careful set of questions, led the student to discoveries.

The lecture was a solution to a problem that continues to be of great concern in education: how to accommodate very large numbers of peole who need to learn. The development of printing provided another such mass mode: the textbook. Almost 200 years elapsed from the invention of the printing press until the widespread use of textbooks in school environments.

Why will the computer lead to another major change in education? There are a variety of reasons, some concerning the advantages of the computer as a learning and teaching device and some concerning today's very rapidly decreasing cost of computer technology, a decrease that will continue for many years.

The best way to recognize the computer as an effective learning device is to use some of the best existing examples of computer-aided learning material. The experience is similar to a conversation between two people.

A major advantage of computers is that they make learning an active process, where students play a constant thinking role. This contrasts with large lecture classes where many students struggle to take notes. In a lecture, few students participate actively in the learning process. Most psychologists agree that active learning is superior to passive learning.

A closely related issue is individualization. Each student at a computer display has a unique interactive experience based on the student's past performances or other information. Students can control the pace of learning, which is impossible in the lecture situation. They can review material at their discretion and can be given remedial or more advanced material as appropriate. Students can choose both content and learning sequences.

The fact that the cost of computers is diminishing rapidly is well known. Yet the speed of this decline is startling. The figure often seen in the computer industry is that for equivalent power, computers decrease in cost by about 30% each year. Not all parts of computers are equally affected by this decrease, however. In recent years the most dramatic decreases occurred in computer memory, the section of the computer that stores information and instructions. The reasons for this decrease are twofold. First, we are just beginning to explore a new and exciting technology; we are rapidly becoming more skillful in using this technology. New techniques are appearing frequently and many of these are successful. The second factor in reduced costs is mass production of components.

We can already begin to see the results of lower costs in the appearance of computers for the home market, computers that cost about the same as color TV sets. While these machines lack some capabilities desirable for educational purposes, they are close to providing what we need. Given the rapid pace of development, we can expect their descendants in a few years to offer good environments for learning.

Thus, the combination of increasing educational effectiveness plus decreasing cost of computers will be the primary generator of the educational revolution based on computing and other technologies. It appears likely that computers will soon be more important in our educational process than books, and, indeed, may entirely replace the book medium for many purposes. These changes will have profound effects on our institutions, our teachers, and even our way of life.

COMPUTERS AND THE FUTURE OF EDUCATION

The great physicist, Ernest Rutherford, was once accused by a friend of always being at the crest of a wave. Rutherford is said by C. P. Snow to have replied, "Well, after all, I made the wave, didn't I?" And he did, as he was one of the major early contributors to the revolution in our ideas about the nature of matter that has dominated twentieth century Physics.

Rutherford's wave was not the only wave. At the present time we see the formation of another great wave, the wave that involves the use of the computer in learning. The computer promises to revolutionize education more than any other development of our time. We are the generators of the wave of the future in education.

Eric Ashby, the British technologist, speaks of three great revolutions in human education: the forming of schools, the use of the written medium, and the invention of books. He then goes on to talk about a fourth revolution. This revolution is the improvement in learning to be effected by modern technology—the electronic media and particularly computers[1]. This assessment of the very important value of the computer as a learning device is not unrealistic; we are at one of the great moments in human society.

We each have our current interests and modes of thinking, many of them determined by our present teaching and research situations. But in considering the role of computers in learning, it is particularly important to view the future, to ask what futures are possible. It is only with visions of the future that we can choose our present path, if we are to proceed in the most productive direction.

Furthermore, the computer itself, by its very nature, makes it necessary for us to think about what will be happening in the next few years. No technology is presently more rapidly developing than computer technology. Computers have been a reality in human history only for the past 20 years; for much of that time they were a rare beast. Figures indicate that the technology of computation is still accelerating rapidly in many directions. Large scale integration (LSI) technology is just beginning to influence computer design. So we would experience future shock if we do not consciously adopt a mode of reacting to the future of computers.

Several aspects of the rapid growth of computer technology are important to us in determining the possible futures.

Computer-Based Science Instruction, eds. A. Jones and H. Weinstock, NATO Advanced Studies Institute, August 1976, Nordhoff, Leyden, 1977.

First, we are experiencing rapidly declining computer costs; this decline occurs in a society where inflation is the general rule, and where most other costs of education continue to grow.

The second major important factor is that, because of the newness of computers and because of the rapid change, we are only slowly beginning to understand the full implications of the computer in education, only slowly learning how to utilize this important tool. Everything we do today, even the best, is crude compared to what we will soon be able to do. Every new learning medium has been slow to be adopted, including lectures and books. Hence, current examples of computer-based material should not be considered as models to emulate, but simply as the current state of development, the place from which we can take off to do much more exciting things.

In thinking about models of the future for computer-based learning, we can delineate several interesting possibilities. One important model of the future is described in George Leonard's book, *Education and Ecstasy*[2]. He pictures the school of the year 2001, where the goals of education are fully realized through computer technology. The school accepts students aged 3 through 12; they end up with the background of a typical bachelor's degree from a university at the present time. At the heart of this school is the computer system, offering individualized education to each student. The student displays are large three-dimensional color displays in the basic learning dome. Leonard's descriptions of the student-computer interactions are not that exciting. But the concept portrayed is exciting.

But Leonard's view is not the only possibility. We can see the same technology leading to quite a different situation, in which schools as we know them today, almost cease to exist. We are rapidly approaching the state where computers will be available everywhere, including public libraries and homes. We can, therefore, conceive of an educational future where schools will play a much less important role, even in formal education, than they do at present. The computer in the home and other public locations will become a major distribution mechanism for learning. In both these situations the creation of large quantities of effective computer-based teaching material will be essential.

Another distinction to consider in looking at the future is that of large computer systems versus stand-alone systems. This is not a true dichotomy, because intermediate cases are possible. The most elaborate large system proposed was that suggested by Donald Bitzer of the PLATO Project at the University of Illinois. He suggested a million-terminal educational system, to be based on three communication satellites, to cover the entire United States. At the other end of the scale, and I must confess my prejudices lie in this direction, are the individual stand-alone systems, the personal computers, which contain internally all the computer capability necessary. These systems could, for special purposes, connect to other computers elsewhere.

We can also consider whether the computer is to be used by itself or whether it is to be part of a full multimedia system. So far our computer systems have provided only limited access, and imperfectly, to slides, videotapes, and audio messages. The educational system of the future should consider all of these as part of the learning environment and should provide them along with full computer-based learning facilities.

Another distinction concerns graphic versus nongraphic systems. Iconic representation is important, even vital, in education. Early computer usage was almost entirely nongraphic, although we struggled to obtain graphic capabilities with typewriters and line printers, which were poorly suited to the task. Now inexpensive graphic displays are widely available. It is inconceivable that educational development involving computers will continue in nongraphic ways. Most of the curriculum projects employing computers are working in graphic directions, and this focus is likely to grow. Our graphic capabilities at present are relatively crude, but we can confidently expect that color and full animation will soon be available for widespread educational use.

What do we need to realize the best future possibilities? First, we need the hardware, the equipment to do the job. We are beginning to see the first generation of what will eventually be the final evolution of computer-based learning equipment, with the appearance of personal computers. These systems provide the stand-alone capability described, with higher-level languages an intrinsic part of the machine. But current systems are still only a glimmer of what is possible. Their computational capabilities are still weak, and they do not provide a multimedia environment. One of the most interesting possibilities of the future involves the marriage of personal computer technology with the newly developing videodisc technology. With such a combined system we will be able to provide full multimedia capabilities.

What are the general principles that should guide us in the development of computer-based learning materials? The most important principle at the moment is that we should encourage many modes, many different philosophies, that we should let a thousand flowers bloom. The notion that a "right" way exists to use computers in education, or even a most profitable way, is a false notion, one not borne out by the experiences of the area. The fact that we are beginners in the development of computer-based learning material indicates we must keep the door open to new approaches and we must not freeze our views of the computer's use in education. Thus, discussions about whether we should use the computer only with the students doing their own programming or whether we should use the computer only for drill and practice are misguided. We need a diversity of types of usage. And we should think of this diversity in pedagogical terms, rather than in computer terms.

We can classify types of computer usage in many different ways. I like first to consider the aspects of computer usage where the student is working as a programmer, and then to consider the aspects in which the student is interacting with programs prepared by teachers in advance. Both of these have many subcategories. In the first, we are giving the student an important intellectual tool, an increasingly critical mode for all areas of the future. Computer literacy in the deepest sense makes a strong demand on all liberal education at the present time. Yet we are only beginning to see the types of materials that can integrate computer programming in a large variety of different courses, using it where it is appropriate for each course. Particularly in the sciences, where problem-solving is so critical, we have a new and powerful method of aiding education with the building of problem-solving skills.

The programs we write for students can cover an extremely wide variety of pedagogical types. The computer can be used for on-line testing, particularly in self-paced environments or for on-line homework solving, liberating the resources normally needed in the way of people for grading such activities. It can be used interactively for the activities often done passively in a lecture or reading environment, particularly for the poorer students. It can respond individually to students in ways that cannot be done in a large environment. Computer dialogs can specifically offer aid to increase problem-solving capabilities, working with students on individual problems and developing—through the interaction of those individual problems—general problem-solving skills. We can develop games to motivate students in learning certain areas, and even, with great skill, promote learning with those games. We can bring students to a careful understanding of the phenomena involved in many situations, moving much more slowly than traditional lecture-based courses in responding and letting the student interact with these phenomena. We can create laboratory environments, not to replace the current laboratory environments, but to offer possibilities of experiments that cannot be done ordinarily, and offer possibilities of watching how students progress as they move along. We can offer controllable worlds, worlds that allow the student access to ranges of experience not available in the regular world, similar to the laboratory experiences just described.

This list is not exhaustive, but merely indicates the rich variety of approaches that have already proved successful.

We need to involve as many good teachers as possible in the generation of materials. At a time when teaching is still primarily an art, we must rely very heavily on the intuition of good teachers. A corollary is that we should provide teachers with facilities and modes of working with the computer that they feel to be the most desirable, reacting to individual preferences. That is, we should not force people into a single mode, but let teachers use their own intuitions as to how to best proceed and as to where the computer will be most effective in the learning process. Many current systems are far too restrictive from the standpoint of potential developers of computer-based dialogs.

Currently many dialogs are products of individual teachers, and often do not get used outside the environment in which they are developed. This "cottage industry" stage must be surmounted. We must look to the future where computer-based material is developed and marketed on professional standards, with skilled teachers playing a critical role. We must investigate the organizational structure that makes this possible. The kinds of incentives available for other learning material, particularly books, must be considered with regard to computer-based materials too.

We also need time to learn. Since we are beginners in the process of learning how to use the computer, we can expect that many years will be needed before we are in a position to use this new medium in its most effective fashion. We should not freeze current hardware or software. In this learning process, we cannot afford to be timid, but rather, we must be daring in our approach. We want to employ the computer where it is most effective, not neglecting other approaches to learning. The corollary is that patience is needed!

I started by describing our current wave, the computer as a mediator of learning. I will end with two charges to you. The first is from Frank Herbert's *Children of Dune*[3]:

> "Abandon certainty! That's life's deepest command. That's what life's all about. We're a probe into the unknown, into the uncertainty."

The second is by an American playwright, Tennessee Williams[4]:

> "Make voyages. There is nothing else."

THE COMPUTER IN A RESPONSIVE LEARNING ENVIRONMENT— LET A THOUSAND FLOWERS BLOOM

My tactics in this article are as follows: Like Martin Luther, I will tell you my basic theses.

Thesis I: Different students learn in different ways.

Most teachers would agree, but practically all courses ignore student differences. Most courses are rigidly structured, with only one path to success and only one set of learning materials. An environment truly responsive to students must have a variety of materials and techniques for learning.

Thesis II: We are only beginning the task of learning how to use computers in education.

Dartmouth Conference Proceedings, Conference on Computers in the Undergraduate Curriculum, Dartmouth College, 1971. Section W9, pp. 4-9.

I worry greatly about teachers who feel that they already know all the answers. We have a long way to go, and theoretical analysis will not tell us how to employ computers effectively. Hence, we want to

LUNA, Title Page

maintain flexibility, and we should be prepared for years of trial and error while using computers in learning.

Thesis III: Useful ways to involve computers in learning may depend on the subject matter involved.

What is highly effective in physics may turn out to be useless for literature. This is obvious with computational uses, which are tailored for a specific need. It is less obvious with other types of usage. While techniques may transcend subject matter boundaries, we will continue to need specific techniques for individual areas.

Thesis IV: It is wise to retain all usage modes for computers in every learning situation.

Computational, tutorial, simulatorial, managerial, and other modes as yet unnamed may all prove to be of great importance in education. Further, a mode worthless in one discipline may be valuable in another area.

Thesis V: We should continue to develop ways of learning independent of computers.

Some areas and some students may profit from other techniques. Many powerful learning tools exist. Reading is still important for many students. The film can be used interactively with computers as a very effective learning medium. Furthermore, in some areas, nothing competes in learning effectiveness with the student's experience in working problems.

Thesis VI: The test of all learning is with students—does the material, computer or otherwise, lead to some type of learning for some students?

All educational materials need to be widely used and continually modified on the basis of students' experiences.

(The course description is omitted. Chapters 3 and 4 describe such courses.)

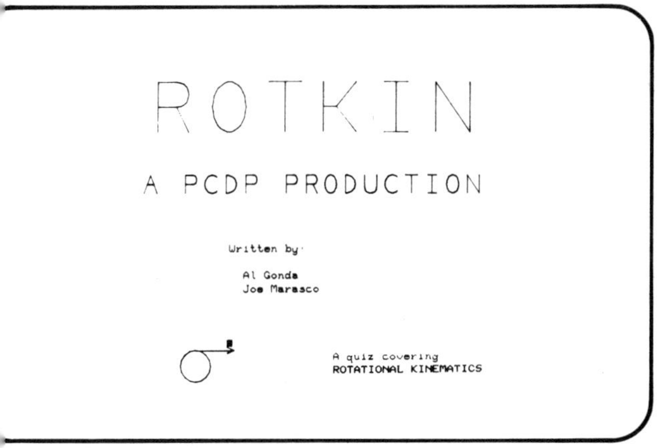

ROTKIN

A PCDP PRODUCTION

Written by:

Al Gonda
Joe Marasco

A quiz covering
ROTATIONAL KINEMATICS

Title Frame for ROTKIN

THE COMPUTER IN TEACHING—WIDELY BELIEVED MYTHS

My plan is to review a number of common myths about the computer in learning. These myths, while not universally believed, are widely held. Within this framework, I will indicate where we are and where we may be going with the computer as a learning aid.

Myth 1: You must choose between direct and adjunct use of the computer.

Literature about the computer in learning has stressed that the computer can be used in two ways. Either students can do their own programming, using the computer as an intellectual tool—sometimes called the adjunct use—or students can interact with teaching programs prepared by others—the direct mainline use. However, much literature tends to go beyond this, stating or implying that a choice must be made between these two. Some major developments in educational computing have chosen between the two uses, making it difficult, either because of equipment or sociopolitical factors, to engage in the other approach. I see no reason why a teacher should be obliged to make this choice. Excellent examples exist of the computer being used both ways, and so neither need be ruled out on philosophical grounds. The same can be said about the many types of dialogs—interactions between teacher and student via the computer. Probably certain types will prove to be efficient for particular subject matter areas, whereas other subject matter areas may require different kinds of dialogs.

ACM SIGCUE *Bulletin*, vol. 7, no. 4.

Myth 2: You must have massive equipment to use the computer in education.

Some of the more interesting teaching applications have come from schools with minimal computer equipment. The idea persists that you can start only at the level of huge installations, but innovative teachers have shown this idea to be wrong many times.

Myth 3: One language is much easier to learn than another.

When students write programs for problems in Physics or Mathematics courses, the questions of which language to use and how students learn that language become important. Arguments are often based on supposed easy learning of one language or another; thus, proponents of BASIC often claim that it is very easy to learn. My own experience indicates that the way the language is taught is much more important than the language itself in determining speed of initial learning. If a reasonable subset is picked, and if reasonable ways are used to introduce the language to students, almost all commonly used languages are relatively easy for beginning students to learn and to use. Differences between initial learning ease have been much exaggerated. But other factors are important.

Myth 4: Computers will not alter institutional structures.

New educational developments are often assumed to fit into existing institutional structures. However, the computer is almost certain to revolutionize the organization of schools and universities. The ability to provide learning materials at any time and at any pace, and provide self-testing features, the ability to respond individually to students, to have access to large amounts of data, all imply that the ways schools operate are likely to change drastically when computers are widely used in learning.

Myth 5: Computers are too expensive to use in teaching.

This issue is one of bookkeeping. With any new technology it is hard to know how to calculate costs, and computer centers in practice do this in quite different ways. (Existing systems quote a wide variety of prices, from $0.25/hour to $50/hour.) Furthermore, it is hard to make comparisons with the costs of other components of education, since these often reflect different bookkeeping practices. It has been claimed, for example, that it costs more than $10 each time a book is checked out of a library. If we regarded this as a direct cost of education, libraries might be considered too expensive; yet almost no institution takes that attitude. Computers are probably now competitive with other learning methods, but this is difficult to demonstrate.

Regardless of what one thinks about the costs today, the future situation is clear: of all the costs involved in the educational process, computer costs are almost the only ones going down. Teachers, books, buildings, and films are going up in cost, while computer costs, because of a rising curve of technological development, are still diminishing dramatically; so the computer will become more and more competitive as a teaching device over the next few years.

Myth 6: We should acquire a "CAI language" that solves our problems.

Many computer center directors take the approach that if some language is available (i.e., on the computer in an operational form) for assisting teachers in developing student-computer dialogs, they have discharged their duties to the teaching community. At one time, COURSEWRITER was highly promoted in this way, and then PLANIT, Tutor, and PILOT.

Experience in many learning applications shows, however, that the availability of a dialog language, no matter how good the language may be, is at best a small part of the process of getting reliable and educationally useful teaching materials on the computer. A production system has many aspects—the way one persuades teachers to write materials; the full facilities provided; the incentives for doing this; the use of secretaries, programmers, artists, and other kinds of auxiliary people; the testing procedures; the gathering of feedback; and the preparation of suitable computer-related text material. These aspects are enormously more important than the question of "special" languages.

Myth 7: PLATO and MITRE are solving all the problems.

The two large-scale projects, with massive government support, are [1973] PLATO at the University of Illinois and the MITRE Corporation project with courseware centered at Brigham Young University. Both are interesting projects. To regard them as exhausting all the possibilities, however, is quite wrong. Many interesting learning materials today could not be run on either of these systems. It would be unfortunate if the success or failure of these two large projects dictated all further educational uses of the computer. In this regard, I agree completely with Arthur Luehrmann's evaluation of these two projects at the 1972 Spring Joint Computer Conference[5]. We need a thousand flowers, not just a few!

Myth 8: Valid educational material can be developed without involving experienced teachers in the area.

Teaching is still teaching whether done by computer or by any other device. Effective educational materials are still coming almost entirely from those who are very much involved in the teaching and learning process. The intellectual structure of every discipline is different, and the tough questions of fundamental goals cannot be resolved in any simple, quick way. While computer scientists and educational psychologists can help develop learning material, they cannot do it alone.

Myth 9: The computer used educationally requires minor amounts of computer resources.

It is often said that student use of computers requires little memory and processor time. While this is the case for some materials, many effective learning programs at Irvine are very long—some are more than 200,000 words in length. And some are extremely demanding of computational and input-output facilities. In a few cases, these demands exceed the abilities of current systems, and so some programs look toward faster systems of the future. Planning for computer uses in learning under the assumption that minimal computer resources are required is dangerous.

We could proceed from these myths to other commonly held misconceptions. But I have indicated some of the more important ones. In spite of these myths, the future is promising for the computer as a learning device.

THE ROLE OF PERSONAL COMPUTER SYSTEMS IN EDUCATION

With Stephen Franklin

While we can view the educational applications of personal computer systems in hardware terms (for example, single user, stand-alone computer systems based, most often, on the newly developed microprocessor technology), for our purposes it is more productive to focus on the mode of use in learning situations implicit in the notion of a personal computer.

The early part of this article will focus more generally on how computers can be utilized for educational purposes. Much of this discussion will apply to timesharing systems even though the importance of such systems in educational environments is likely to decrease dramatically.

We have chosen consciously to use the word "education" in preference to "instruction" because we wish to indicate an outlook that balances consideration of both instructional authority and the learner. As the term "student" may not be appropriate for a person who happens to be using a computer to learn something, we shall refer to people using computers simply as "users" or "learners."

The Association of Educational Data Systems Journal, Vol. 13.

In the next few sections, a descriptive classification of educational uses of computers is given. As with most taxonomies of human activities, this description reflects fundamentally arbitrary distinctions, man-made rather than imposed by external circumstances. Although the categories may be expressed as though they reflect logical dichotomies, they are often not entirely distinct.

One distinction is whether the user programs the computer or simply uses programs written by others. Certain educational modes demand that the user become a programmer of the computer, specifying in some programming language the algorithm to be used to accomplish particular tasks. Often this user employs a standard programming language, writing programs in that language for some special purpose related to education. At other times, the user programs in a highly specialized language developed for particular situations, in which case our "obvious" distinction becomes extremely fuzzy. The fact that almost all programming involves using programs (compilers, interpreters, editors, operating systems) written by others blurs the distinction further. Yet, from the user's point of view, a distinction can be made between programming and not programming.

The Computer as an Object of Study

Computer science has grown as an intellectual discipline as computers have assumed an increasingly important role in our society. We will not enumerate all the areas that computer science has come to encompass. Instead we shall mention three areas that seem to be of particularly broad importance and applicability.

Computer Programming and Problem-Solving

An excellent case can be made for the use of computer programming as a vehicle for the systematic algorithmic expression of the solution of certain problems. The development and refinement of such solutions is a form of training for analytic thinking applicable to broad classes of problems. Even if one does not subscribe to this second statement, one can still appreciate the value of computer programming as training for dealing with abstractions and abstract reasoning. We are encouraged by the increasing availability of courses and curricular material on computer programming.

Social Impact of Computing

The computer is the dominant tool of our time and, as such, is having a profound influence on our society. Knowledge of the technical aspects of computer science does not guarantee understanding the consequences of this technology. But such understanding should be based, in part, on acquaintance with the capabilities and limitations of computers.

Computer Literacy

This area combines elements of the two previous ones. It is concerned with people who will not be computer professionals. In a society where computers are playing an increasingly important role, it is essential that people be acquainted with computers and their capabilities. Computer literacy goes beyond programming, but most computer literacy courses involve some programming efforts on the part of the participants. Computer literacy courses are presently offered primarily at the college level; opinions on how to run such courses vary greatly. It seems inevitable that they will migrate into high school and junior high school curricula.

The Computer as an Intellectual Tool

In this category, the most obvious educational use of computing again involves the user as programmer. However, the user considered in this section is programming not to become acquainted with the computer and its capabilities or as a paradigm for algorithmic thought but because it aids in understanding a subject area that is the focus of interest. A typical activity might be the use of the computer within a Physics course to improve the learner's skill in solving physics problems and even to add new dimensions to problem-solving. Using the computer, we can tackle more realistic and meaningful problems, ones more like those encountered in actual experience than the typical "laundered" textbook problems.

The most dramatic uses of the computer as an intellectual tool are in entirely new approaches to the curriculum. For example, using the computer to provide a numerical approach to differential equations, one can reorganize completely the first quarter course in college Physics; the approach to Newton's laws of motion leads quickly and directly to a student's understanding differential equations and their use in predictive models of physical systems.

Using Programs Prepared by Others

The uses of the computer as an intellectual tool presuppose some programming on the part of the user. However, present computer users and those of the future likely are to be involved primarily with programs written by others. That is, the most common type of computer use in the future (as in the present) is not in writing one's own programs, but in using programs prepared by others. (Even people writing their own programs are almost always doing so using programs written by others.)

As personal computers become more available in educational institutions, in the home market, as part of people's jobs, and in public environments such as libraries, we can confidently expect that the sales of such hardware will depend on very large amounts of materials being prepared for the user, requiring minimal training to use. Many of these materials will be educational in nature and even more will have some educational component, if only to help the user learn how to use the materials.

A wide variety of materials is possible, and schemes for descriptively classifying them vary widely. Some schemes are based primarily on computer considerations, while others are based on educational considerations. We favor the second approach as in the following enumeration of educational uses of the computer that do not require the user to program.

Drill and Practice

While we can debate the importance of practice in learning, almost all conventional educational procedures rely on it to some extent. Thus a student learning calculus, perhaps to use in a Physics course, needs practice in taking the derivatives of common functions. Similarly, few students in elementary school master basic arithmetic without practice. However, when we speak of practice we mean more than the opportunity to work examples; implicit in our use of the term is that the learner receive feedback which tells, at a minimum, when an example has been worked correctly and when a mistake has occurred.

Providing the student with feedback on the correctness of an answer, problem after problem, can be a tedious task for a human. The computer can do this task and more. It can generate a large number of problems of a given type within specifications provided by those responsible for the design of the educational drill and practice. It can also keep records, determining when the student has reached a satisfactory performance level and referring the student to non-computer sources of assistance (such as books, video segments, and people).

A student's tolerance (and need) for routine, repetitious practice may exceed an instructor's (or parent's) available time or patience. Many find that the desire to do something well is, in itself, very compelling (competency motivation). Just the tireless patience of a computer makes drill-and-practice on such a medium valuable.

Moreover, interactive computer-based problems can take on added dimensions. Successive problems can be chosen and presented based on the responses to previous ones. The computer can present problems with missing information or with redundant or contradictory information; the learner must request additional information or ask what of the (contradictory) information is to be discarded.

Drill and Practice with Remediation

An important elaboration of drill and practice material is the provision of remediation tailored to learner difficulties. Remediation sections can be simple, showing how to work a missed problem, or large, complex, interactive learning sequences of the tutorial type we discuss next. Because remediation is intertwined with drill and practice, it can use the data of the problem and the circumstances of the learner's mistake. Incidentally, our choice of the term "remediation" lies in the meaning of the root term "remedy," something that corrects or removes an evil of any kind, and in spite of the condescending connotations that the adjective "remedial" has acquired.

Tutorial Programs

The concept of the tutorial program, a dialog between learner and educational designers of the computer program, is close to the oldest and most personal form of transmitting knowledge, the conversation between an individual and an experienced teacher.

Information, techniques, and attitudes are developed within an environment in which the learner is invited and encouraged to play an active role rather than the passive role of the audience in a lecture or with video material. The term "dialog" is appropriate since well done materials resemble the type of dialog associated with Socrates. The educator is not telling but is leading the learner by means of carefully planned questions, each successive question depending on the learner's previous response.

An important subcategory in Science and Mathematics courses is the notion of an interactive proof. Such proofs, in noninteractive form, occupy much lecture time, with the instructor deriving new results from those already obtained. In interactive computer environments, the users can create the proof insofar as they are able, being offered assistance when needed.

Before leaving this category, note should be taken of a use of computers that bears a superficial resemblance to tutorial programs—the computer as page turner. Certain programs present large chunks of text, asking intermittent questions ("TYPE 1 FOR YES, 0 for NO"), but do not vary the material presented significantly on the basis of the user's responses. While the educational value of such programs is open to discussion, it is clear that the term "dialog" is not appropriate (although some case can be made for "monolog").

Testing

The importance of evaluating student progress is almost universally acknowledged, as is the difficulty and unpleasantness of the task. Part of what computers should be used for is to do what humans do not enjoy doing; therefore, test generation, administration, grading, recording, reporting, and summarizing are tasks appropriate for the computer. As with drill and practice, testing materials can be based on problem generators and other devices for randomizing the materials. Each quiz or test can be unique, allowing a student to take different versions of the quiz several times and students to discuss the quizzes with each other.

While some would insist that the computer is too expensive and important a resource to be "wasted" on interactive testing, we cannot agree. Firstly, testing is an important part of education. Secondly, current economic and technological trends make it clear that the cost of human time is a more important consideration in economic projections than the cost of machine resources. Finally, in this area as in others, the economic reality already often demands that one use the computer because other approaches are unrealistic, inadequate or both.

Testing with Learning

One of the most recent developments in testing, related to the remediation ideas already discussed, is that specific immediate aid can be offered to students having difficulties on an interactive quiz or test, often aid precisely tailored to their difficulties. The interactive test can be an intimate blend of testing and learning, unlike most traditional modes of testing that offer no immediate opportunity to improve. Interactive testing with learning provides students that opportunity at a time when they are most open to taking advantage of it. In our experiences with students, this mode of educational computer usage produces the most favorable student reaction.

Controllable Worlds

The computer can generate rich, creative, manipulatable environments for the learner, environments difficult to manipulate and experiment within the real world, even impossible environments. This type of computer use is *simulation;* we use the computer to model some portion of a real or imaginary world. We prefer the term "controllable worlds" because it stresses the effect rather than the mechanism.

One form of controllable world has the computer duplicating or enhancing a typical laboratory environment. The user is provided with a range of experimental capabilities, with many of the factors that would occur if the experiment were in the laboratory. (One factor missing is the possibility of injury if the experiment is not done correctly.) The user gathers data rapidly in a variety of situations and may be permitted to perform experiments that cannot be done in an ordinary laboratory (e.g., remove gravity). In addition to providing experimental capabilities, this environment allows the student to be guided, at first gently and then perhaps more firmly, into generalizing on the basis of data, and testing the hypotheses formed. Thus we can help every student arrive at the conclusions that were the aim of the materials.

The laboratory environment can be extended greatly. Realms of experiences can be provided that are difficult or impossible to realize in the world as it exists. In as much as experience is the basis for intuition, these controllable worlds can give the user a feel for phenomena and the consequences of theories that was previously available only to the deeply talented or after much study. Thus, the role of the controllable world is extended from that of the ordinary laboratory to that of a tool for building insight and intuition, the basis and inspiration for later formal study. In such a world, the learner can be in complete control, changing variables and studying, with the guidance of the program or auxiliary materials, situations that lead to more secure later knowledge. While building intuition is the avowed goal of many courses, rarely can conventional modes of education address it directly.

Why Use the Computer?

We have discussed some educational uses of the computer; but why the computer is such an effective learning aid and why it will become much more widely used in the future may not be clear.

Much of education during historic times is understandable as a reaction to increasing numbers of people who needed increasing amounts of education. As long as only a few people needed to learn a very limited amount, apprenticeship methods, informal and formal, were satisfactory. But as the number of learners and what they needed to learn increased, learning strategies had to be modified. Most of our current educational methodology at all levels is shaped by the pressure of large numbers. Thus, the lecture, the textbook, and electronic recording and broadcasting media are all mechanisms to disseminate knowledge to large numbers of people. All are essentially one-way media, with communication flowing from the instructional authority to the student; they provide little capability for the authority to respond to individual learners.

Something has been lost in this process. Teachers and students in educational institutions yearn for the situation where they can work together closely. Indeed, great amounts of resources are devoted to making this possible precisely in those situations where the quality of education is perceived to be most critical. Thus, graduate education, at least at the later stages, depends primarily on one-to-one contact. Educational psychologists, even with very diverse views of the learning process, almost all agree that the optimum setting for education is when one excellent teacher works with an individual or a small group.

Perhaps the most well-known attempt to develop an effective small group learning system is the Socratic dialog. Socrates worked usually with three or four students at one time. What modern jargon would call the learning activity was an active conversation in which everyone participated. In no sense did Socrates lecture; Plato often depicts other participants as talking more than Socrates. A major component of most lectures is the conveying of information; Socrates did little of this. Instead he continually queried his students, asking questions that depended on the answers given to earlier questions, always framing new questions for his listeners to react to. There were no time pressures. Presumably, if Socrates engaged in a number of similar dialogs with different people, both the directions these dialogs took and their duration varied considerably.

The computer is the first technological innovation in education that enables us to start moving back, even with a large number of learners, to a situation like that of Socrates where the educator can respond fully to each individual learner.

We do not claim that a computer dialog, even when prepared by a group of excellent teachers, can emulate fully the Socratic situation. But it is the only educational tool with which we can approach that situation with a large number of learners. Each learner can proceed at a different pace and can engage in an individual learning process with educational materials responsive to his or her particular needs. We cannot clone Socrates, but we can use computers to give today's large number of learners more of the type of learning experiences that his students had.

Not all existing computer material reaches these goals; rather, much of it is a poor reflection of what is possible and a better reflection of the shortcomings of our past practices. But we are slowly learning how to create more active, more personalized, more interactive, more effective materials.

Since we wish to focus on the educational advantages, we shall not discuss the economic arguments in favor of educational computing. Such arguments must include assessment of the value of education to our society. The most basic educational advantage we see in the use of computers is that, unlike almost any other medium, the computer provides a vehicle for education that is responsive at all levels to the individual learner.

Because of its unique advantages as a responsive, active learning mechanism, we can use the computer to create more effective educational systems than our present ones. But this future is far from certain. The computer can be used in banal ways or in ways antithetical to the best goals of creative education. Modern educators with a commitment to meeting the needs of the individual learner must play an active role in shaping the future use of computers in education. This effort must take place on all levels.

The Future—Types of Hardware

Educational use of computers in recent years has primarily employed timesharing systems, a central machine providing services simultaneously to many users. Most universities still continue to purchase such systems as the principal vehicle for educational applications. However, the personal computer, a small stand-alone computer used by a single person or a small group will be the focus of future educational activities.

In this discussion, a distinction is made between developmental systems, for the creation of educational materials, and delivery systems on which the learner uses these materials. In the past, the same computer system was often used for both. This situation was more a reflection of the hardware (and the then current understanding of the process of writing programs on one machine to be run on another) than it was of an underlying similarity between what is required for developmental work and for delivery. When we say that personal computers will be the focus of educational activities we are referring to the delivery of educational materials.

The personal computers likely to be the major delivery systems for direct use by learners are not the lowest level of those currently available. These systems, although interesting, have serious deficiencies for educational use. The basic software on minimum systems is more appropriate for the creation of small, simple and limited programs than for designing, writing, and maintaining the complex and extensive educational applications we have discussed. These systems often have poorly designed keyboards (e.g., one popular system has the "stop the world, I want to get off" key immediately above the "return" key). Many support only uppercase letters; many allow few characters per line and few lines per display; many display characters whose graphics quality is exceeded by the scrawl of a first grader. The graphics capabilities are typically crude. (A popular inadequate approach to graphics is to provide a handful of special characters, line segments at different angles.) Their mass storage devices may not provide easy, quick, or reliable storage and transportation for large programs. They most often have fixed character sets, on whose quality we have already commented, and do not allow all the characters needed for education. Few have color capabilities. In addition to their technical shortcomings, the lower level of systems currently available do not come close to the minimum level of visual appeal that one would accept in a book or piece of video material.

But the personal computer situation is changing rapidly. The newer systems are providing more extensive and reliable capabilities. New software systems reflect the understanding of software that has been gained over the past decade. As the market grows and becomes more competitive, we can expect better hardware and software. The rising curve of technology helps in that we are learning to build better computer systems, particularly microcomputer-based systems, at a very rapid rate. This technological advance is reflected in decreasing costs (for fixed capabilities) and increasing capabilities. As mass production of integrated systems becomes the norm, there will be further cost savings. The home computer market will be an important factor. Some estimates predict many millions of computers in homes in the next few years.

The existence of the home market and parents' interest in providing educational opportunities for their children are major reasons supporting our assertion that personal computers will be the focus of future educational activities. Without going into great detail, we can mention a few others. Thanks to declining hardware costs, any institution or individual who starts using computers is more likely to be able to afford a small personal computer than larger, more expensive systems. Many institutions will buy a personal computer, to see how it works out, whereas the institution might not have even made the experiment had it entailed a more substantial initial investment. The small cost of a complete unit also makes buying a system feasible purely to get access to the learning materials that the system supports.

To apply different reasoning in considering why personal computer systems, rather than timesharing systems, are likely to be the focus of educational activities in the future, we turn to a direct comparison.

Personal Computers Versus Timesharing Systems

The personal computer, on occasion connected for a brief period to another system, will be the major educational delivery system of the foreseeable future. Several important considerations make this almost a certainty.

A major issue concerns which type of computer leads to a clear marketing path for large-scale distribution of computer-based educational materials. Many timesharing systems exist, different in hardware and operating systems. These differences affect large complex programs more fundamentally than they affect simple ones. Effective computer-based educational materials are not simple programs; they are complex because learning, even learning simple matters, is a complex process.

For a program to be widely marketed in a timesharing environment, where the hardware is so expensive that it cannot be purchased for a particular use (unless that use is extremely extensive), the vendor must supply the program for a variety of systems. The initial expense and the difficulties of maintaining dozens of versions of a program make this approach unlikely. If we had highly standard languages and highly standard interfaces with operating systems, the problem would not exist. But there is little chance of standardization adequate to meet the needs of large, complex programs.

Most transportability efforts that have assumed standard languages have accommodated only simple programs. In the educational area, CONDUIT is the most extensive effort in this direction. But the programs CONDUIT distributes, although carefully referenced, do not represent the best computer-based learning materials because those materials are not simple to transport. Any organization, commercial or non-profit, restricted to only a few timesharing machines would cut off sizeable portions of the market.

Another approach to using timesharing for delivery has been to employ a communications network, so users at remote sites can access central machines, most often over telephone lines. The economic viability of this approach is far from established. Unless the distance between the local site and the central machine can be bridged by a local telephone call, communications costs exceed the cost of computer services. Another major difficulty with this approach comes with graphic capabilities, capabilities that are essential to full effective educational use of the computer. The rate at which graphics can be displayed in a timesharing system is slow (full animation is impossible). While many timesharing systems have difficulty accommodating even moderate numbers of users at 1200 baud (a minimally acceptable data transmission speed for graphics), experience has taught us that even fewer remote communications links can transmit data reliably at this rate. Thus, complex pictures are often out of the question. We hope that communications costs will drop or that capabilities will improve. While the latter seems likely, the prospects for the former are not bright. Communications cost may not rise and communications capabilities will undoubtedly improve, but the economic-technical prospects in communications cannot compare with those in computers.

If we look at transportability on personal computers, we see a much different situation than with timesharing systems. With personal computers, a program need not work on every machine. The user can buy or lease the hardware along with the course material.

This new marketing concept in computers can be difficult to understand for those with traditional backgrounds. Yet, we can already see successful examples. One is Computer Curriculum Corporation, which leases to school districts systems (hardware and software) covering basic arithmetic and language skills for elementary school children. Currently, this company's system is a timesharing one, and thus the system is leased to serve the entire district rather than an individual school. If an integrated educational package used a personal computer, a school interested in buying a particular set of educational materials initially might buy just one to try the materials, thus, prospective users have a simple entry-level way of trying out the materials over an extended period of time. This entry-level tactic is important as a marketing strategy.

Another approach to transporting software on personal computers is to transport the entire operating system, which is not practical with timesharing systems. An excellent example of this idea is the work done at University of California, San Diego (UCSD), under the direction of Professor Kenneth L. Bowles, in creating a portable operating system using Pascal. The UCSD Pascal system, including its sophisticated screen-oriented editor, runs on many personal computers. Most sophisticated, complex programs depend on features and conventions particular to the operating system in which they run. Rather than confining oneself to programs that do not use these features and thus limiting what one can do, it makes more sense to transport the entire environment in which the program functions.

Another important consideration is the complexity and the concomitant reliability problems of timesharing operating systems as opposed to stand-alone operating systems. General-purpose timesharing systems are among the most complex programs in widescale use. When a timesharing system crashes, every user on the system is affected for the entire period the system is down; on the other hand, a personal computer with problems affects only one user. There is, however, another side to this point. When one finds a "bug" on a timesharing system, one can correct it for everyone. Maintaining and updating software on stand-alone personal computer systems is a less easy procedural problem. Some of the complexity of timesharing systems arises because of the need to support several users simultaneously and because the overhead on such systems, requiring a considerable fraction of the computer, cuts down on what is effectively available to the users. On the other hand, some of the complexity results from the fact that the timesharing system is providing a range of software and capabilities that personal computers do not. Another reason for this complexity is that timesharing systems have complex resource allocation algorithms that provide the flexibility to meet peak demands from users.

System stability over time is another important issue. New versions of operating systems appear, sometimes fixing known bugs and supporting new capabilities. While it is often said that user programs will be unaffected by the change, it is our experience that complex programs have problems with new operating systems. On a good personal computer system, we can continue to run programs under several versions of the operating system, gradually phasing in the changes on a program-by-program or disk-by-disk basis. Thus, we use at Irvine programs using several versions of the UCSD Pascal system.

We already have mentioned the difficulties a timesharing system may have supporting graphics, particularly when the system is being accessed from a remote site. No such problems exist with stand-alone systems; information can flow to the screen as fast as it is generated. One immediate consequence is that simple animation is possible even with minimal personal computers. Such capabilities are just not possible in timesharing systems except in very limited ways.

Timesharing systems, however, currently provide important communications facilities that personal computers do not. On a timesharing system, users can exchange messages, maintain central records, and access central libraries of programs and data; users can maintain and update programs more easily. However, capabilities such as these can be supported on personal computers by having them communicate occasionally and briefly with a large or small central system.

These communications capabilities exemplify an area where timesharing systems have an advantage over personal computers, not for any inherent technical reason but merely because they have been around longer. Better examples might be the richness of software tools (including various text editors and library facilities), different methods of file organization and access, and a broad variety of languages. We can expect such capabilities to be increasingly valuable on small single-user systems. It is even reasonable to demand them!

A totally different area where one might compare timesharing systems and personal computers concerns the internal institutional problems involved in a school's acquiring one or the other. A cooperative interdepartmental effort is usually necessary for a school to acquire a timesharing system, even a small one, of sufficient sophistication to provide some of the advantages we have discussed. These departments must get together on what they want, often accepting undesired compromises of an imposed solution. A similar process even may go on within a department. These political considerations can be reduced to some extent with personal computers. On the other hand, if each individual faculty member chooses a different personal computer, the institution may find that maintenance of these diverse systems and future cooperative action, is impossible. There have been cases where one person's equipment was worthless to anyone else. Some central considerations are still necessary. Personal computers may allow one to avoid some political problems (e.g., the need to find groups of allies), but they are not a panacea.

Some Final Remarks and a Look Ahead

We have focused on the delivery of computer-based educational materials, outlined the variety and possibilities of such materials, and argued that the personal computer is the vehicle that provides for learner access to them. We have not discussed the development process or type of computer system that is a reasonable vehicle for development. Arguments for using personal computers as development systems are less compelling.

It is an accident in past history of computer-based educational materials that development and delivery systems were the same. Many people still assume, implicitly, that this dual-purpose use of the same system will continue. Any careful analysis of the situation suggests that developmental work requires different and more extensive capabilities than are needed in a delivery machine.

Another important issue is the software needed for developmental purposes, both the basic software environment required for work on any complex program and the specialized software needed in creating computer-based educational materials. We present briefly our opinion (prejudices) as revealed in our current work. That work is taking place using the UCSD Pascal system, an effective system for complex programming, including that being considered. Our project is developing special software tools modeled, in part, on our previous (timesharing) production system.

As we anticipate future developments and trends in education, a great many problems are apparent—financial, social, and educational. The educational advantages of the computer, its increasing capabilities and the decreasing cost of computer technology are bright spots. There can be little doubt that the computer will be a major component of all education. The time scale involved probably will be on the order of a quarter of a century but could be significantly less. However, the mere existence of computer technology is not a guarantee that it will be used in creative and constructive ways. The computer is the first technological innovation that allows education of large numbers of people in a manner truly responsive to the individual learner. But only the involvement and commitment of educators of vision can ensure that it is used in that manner.

References

1. Eric Ashby, "Machines, Understanding, and Learning: Reflections on Technology in Education." *The Graduate Journal,* Vol. 7, No. 2 (Austin, Texas, 1967).

2. George Leonard, *Education and Ecstasy* (N.Y.: Delacorte Press, 1968).

3. Frank Herbert, *Children of Dune* (N.Y.: Berkeley Publishing Co., 1976).

4. Tennessee Williams, *Camino Real* (Norfolk, Conn.: New Directions, 1953).

5. Arthur Luehrmann, *SIGCUE Bulletin,* Vol. 6, No. 4 (October 1972) pp. 9–11.

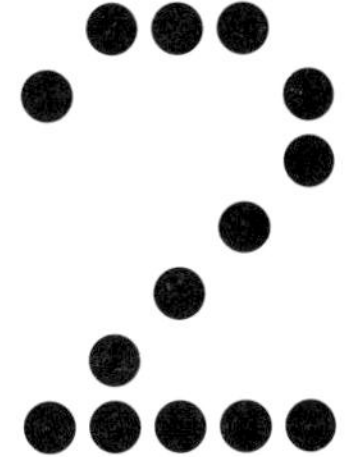

Graphics

LEARNING VIA COMPUTER GRAPHICS

Graphics and Learning

During much of human history we have had only our five senses, used in their direct form, to assist in learning about our world. The invention of writing, and even more of printing, are much newer devices to aid learning. There seems to be no disagreement that the most important sense for learning is the visual sense, perhaps because of the rich complexity of information that can be gathered visually.

Computer-Based Science Instruction, eds. A. Jones and H. Weinstock, NATO Advanced Studies Institute, August 1976, Nordhoff, Leyden, 1977.

We can only stand in amazement at the long, slow learning process that went on in human beings, as they evolved over hundreds of thousands of years, based primarily on vision as the information source. Most of the constructs that we think of as "common sense knowledge"—ways of conceptualizing the ordinary world—developed in this long, slow period of evolution. These constructs were developed by speculation on the basis of information obtained visually.

The invention of language was an important critical new development in learning. Language made it possible for humans to pass on from generation to generation the things that had been learned, and gave continuity to the learning process, a continuity beyond information contained in the genes. It probably played a sizable role in the development and passing on of agricultural knowledge, although watching the examples of how it was done continued to be extremely important. Oral communication also provided a way to learn from someone who was not present, through a third intervening individual. However, at this stage learning still depended primarily on direct contact with the person who had knowledge. The "lecture" developed slowly as a mode of learning.

The invention of writing, and later printing, made it possible to learn from many others. Several hundred years elapsed from the invention of printing to the time it was commonly in use as a learning medium.

Books, even in the earliest time, tended to have illustrations. The printed word was often supplemented by pictorial information. Examination of textbooks reveals that it is still widely the case. We cannot find a textbook in almost any area that does not resort to pictures, sketches, drawings, and other visual imagery. An examination of common beginning college Physics textbooks reveals approximately one illustration per page. If an author were to present a textbook publisher with a manuscript with no drawings or illustrations, the publisher would not publish it. If somehow such a pictureless book were published, it would have little audience.

For a long period, formal education has depended on verbal mechanisms. Such a system tends to be self-supporting; the next generation of teachers were those who were the successes of the system, so they teach primarily with words. It is probable that today's teacher is less skillful in the use of iconic information than the teacher of a hundred years ago. Therefore, a student who can learn if pictorial supplements are provided, but whose grasp of language is weak, is declared to be an inadequate learner. We can no longer afford such an approach; we should work toward providing an optimum learning environment for each student.

Outside of formal learning visual information is often important. One example is the widespread use of graphic design in advertising. Advertising can be regarded as an attempt to "educate" people although not necessarily in directions that we would always approve. The education consists of persuasion to buy a particular product. The ads major industrial companies put in magazines or show on television are developed by extremely sophisticated graphic designers. While we may not agree with the purpose of commercial advertising, we have much to learn about the techniques and devices used. These techniques would be very useful with university students. It is significant that large corporations have had a long working relationship with the best graphic designers of our time: Eliot Noyes and Charles Eames worked for IBM, for example.

Some direct experimental evidence also indicates the importance of pictorial information in learning. The best study is William Huggins and Doris Entwisle, *Iconic Communication: An Annotated Bibliography*[1]. But, as with much educational testing, it is difficult to base the case for graphics purely on such evidence.

How Computer Graphics Can Assist Learning

In this section, I elucidate how graphics can be used in an interactive computer learning environment, with specific examples based on our work at Irvine.

The first distinction suggested is between the two principal aspects of graphics in any type of learning situation. The first role of graphics is as a conveyor of information, an alternate way in which information can be given to the learner, different from the manner information is conveyed through words or numbers. Whether the old saw, "A picture is worth a thousand words," is true or not, we can often approach an idea through a picture in a way that is an alternative to verbal and numerical ways of approaching it; a picture offers information not available in other ways.

A second important aspect of visual information is the motivational aspect. Learning is not an easy activity. The student needs every possible stimulation and aid to make learning as pleasant as possible. Visuals have long been recognized as an important factor in motivating people. We cannot afford to neglect such motivation in student environments.

It would be nice if we could give simple rules about when to use pictures in learning material, computer-based or otherwise. But unfortunately no reliable rules exist. What we do must still depend on the intuition and experiences that a good teacher brings to bear on all learning situations. Starting with excellent teachers who have taught the material and are acquainted with the problems of students is an important and necessary beginning point. Hopefully the teachers have been listening to students, and so have some appreciation of the student's view. Many lecturers unfortunately do not listen to students, and so have a vague view of the effectiveness of the learning approach. Good teachers can use as a guide in graphics their own experiences, particularly experiences about where graphics would be employed in texts and in lectures. At each point, we need to ask if a picture would help some students.

Perhaps the most obvious use of visual information in the sciences comes with graphs. We utilize many ways of representing information in terms of graphs, including bar graphs, simple curves, and surfaces representing mathematical functions. A curve, for example, might represent a known function and give equivalent information to an analytic formulation, perhaps in a way more understandable to many students. Or it may represent information not accessible in any other form and so necessarily presented in graphical form. In any case the graph, as shown in Figures 2-1 and 2-2, is a carrier of information.

Sometimes the information is inherently pictorial. The typical situation might be an orbiting body, such as a planet going around a pair of suns. This is shown in Figures 2-3 and 2-4.

In other cases, we may be dealing with a model that is essentially geometrical, such as the model that explains the phases of the moon, from a dialog called LUNA (Figure 2-5).

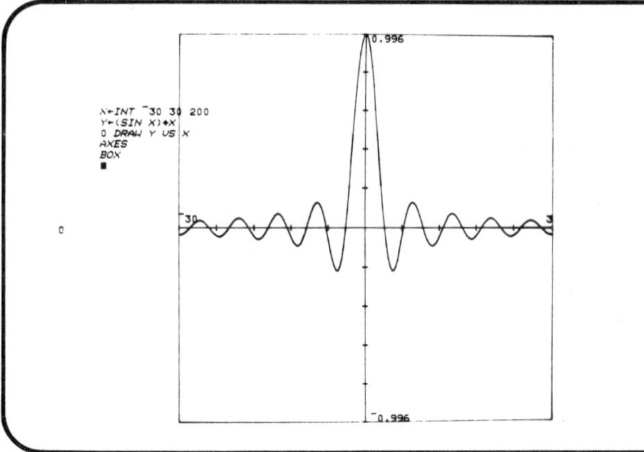

FIGURE 2-1 Plotting a Graph in APL

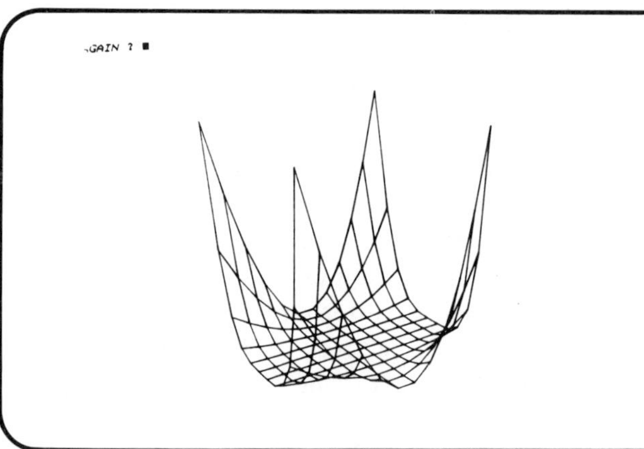

FIGURE 2-2 Surface Plotted in an APL Workspace

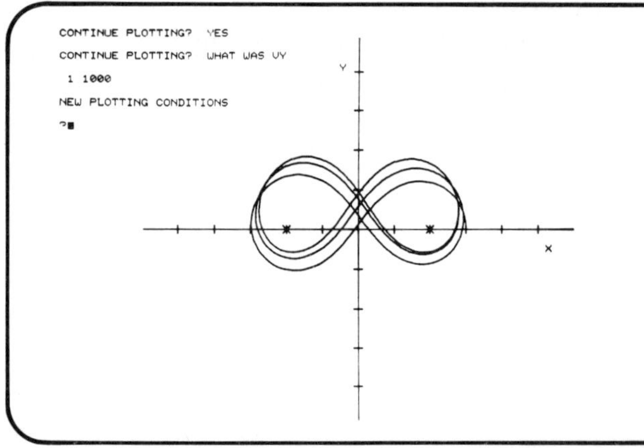

FIGURE 2-3 MOTION—A Planet Moving Around Two Suns

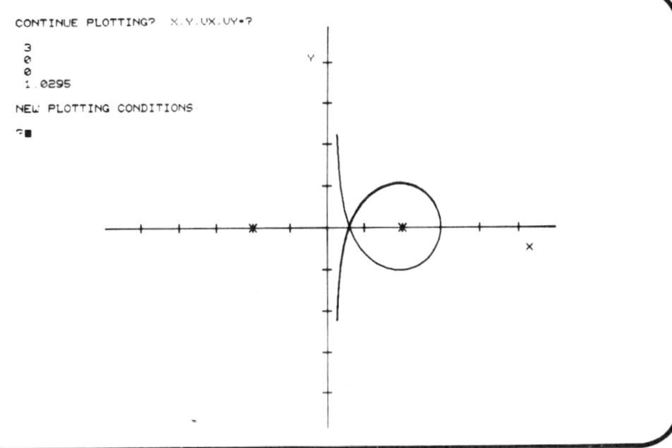

FIGURE 2-4 MOTION—Planet with Two Suns, Different Initial Conditions

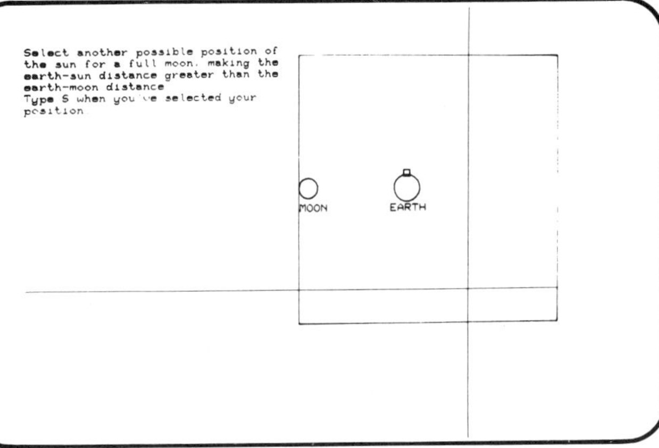

FIGURE 2-5 LUNA—Location of Sun for Full Moon

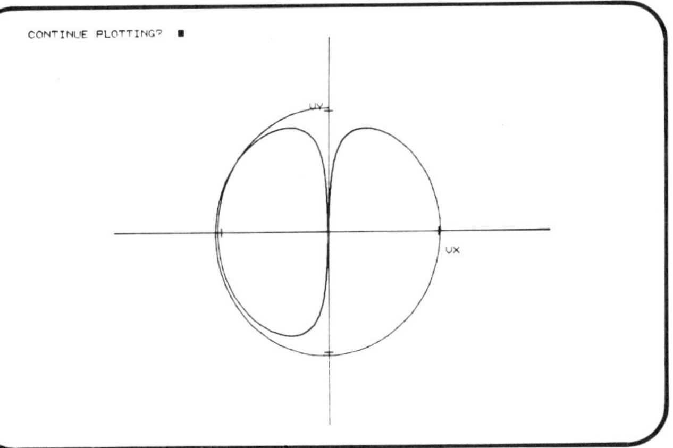

FIGURE 2-6 MOTION—Initial Conditions as in Figure 2-4, Velocity Space

Another place where graphic information can be extremely valuable in learning is in helping students build intuition in physical situations. The pictures showing planetary orbits in a double star system were pictures looking in actual configuration space. But a great many other spaces are important for the scientist in understanding the behavior of this system. One such important space, for example, is *velocity space* where the two components of velocity are plotted against each other. Here the student has no way of "seeing" this except through the computer; so the computer offers unique advantages in constructing a world not realizable in any other way. Each of the pictures, taken from the dialog MOTION, represents the same physical system we already discussed—a planet in a multistar system. But we are plotting different aspects in each case, and so developing intuitions about how that system behaves. We are providing the student with a range of experiences that may aid learning, experiences not available in any other way. (See Figures 2-6 and 2-7.)

Sometimes visual information can add a humorous touch that is difficult to represent in text. Humor is a difficult issue in learning. Undoubtedly it helps, but what is humorous to one person is not necessarily humorous to another. But we can try to make our lessons more interesting in this way. (See Figure 2-8.)

Another important use of pictures in interactive computer dialogs is to support and reinforce the textual material. Thus, the picture may offer information related to that in text, providing an alternate information source or helping to make the text easier. We have a very powerful aid not available in textbook graphics, but which is available in film and video. We do not need to display the whole text and the whole picture at once, but we can interweave the text and parts of the picture, having the pieces come on as appropriate. Thus, we can display a phrase or a sentence, pause briefly (to allow the eye to move), draw some lines in a diagram, display another phrase, draw another line in the diagram. The delays are important, assisting the student with the learning process. While they are not strictly a graphic device, they are a necessary feature of graphic facilities in computer-based learning material. All this is to be contrasted with how this material would be handled in a textbook, where everything—the full text and the pictures—must all be on the page at one time; there is no sense of information evolving in time to aid the student in understanding the phenomenon. Unfortunately, I cannot show pictures to support these ideas, because development in time is essential!

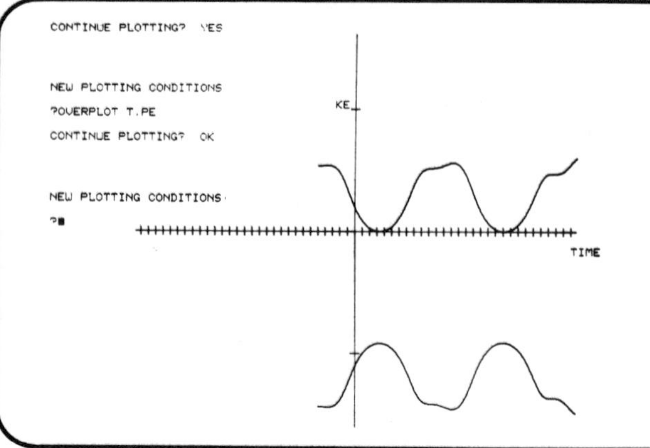

FIGURE 2-7 MOTION—Another Aspect of This Motion, Kinetic and Potential Energy

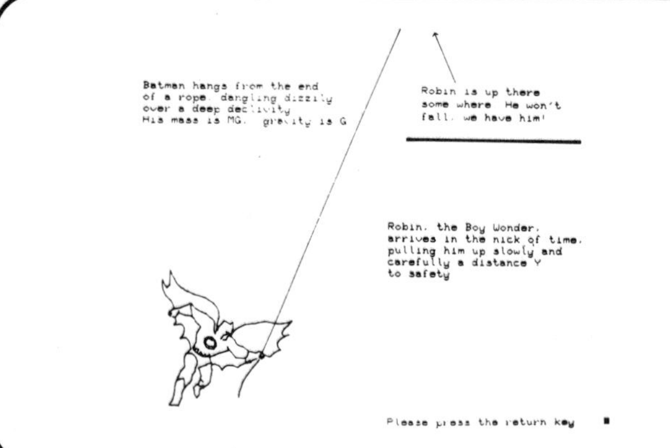

FIGURE 2-8 From the Dialog WORK

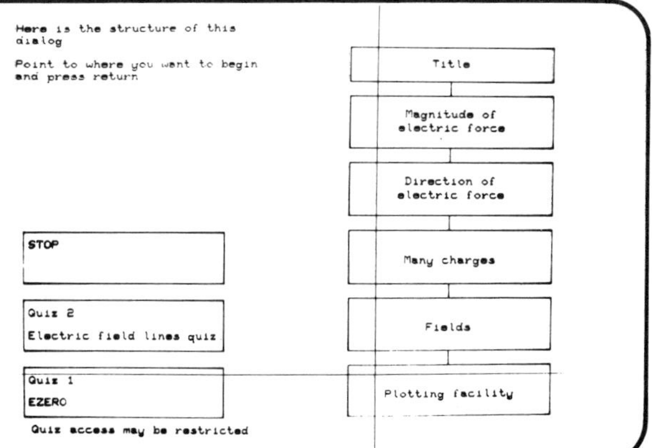

FIGURE 2-9 Map from the FIELD Dialog (Note On-Line Tests)

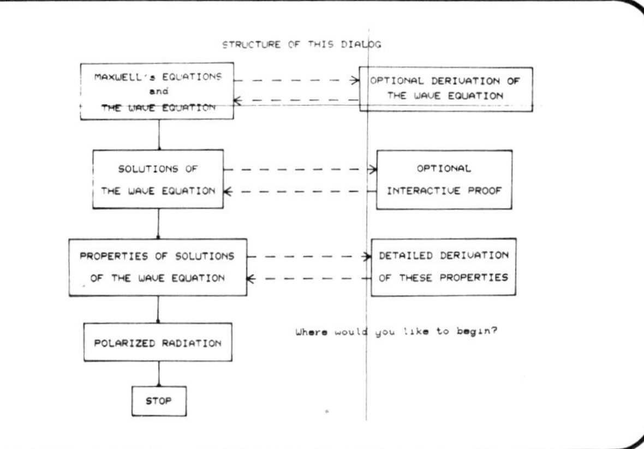

FIGURE 2-10 Map from MAXWELL (Dotted Lines Indicate Optional Material)

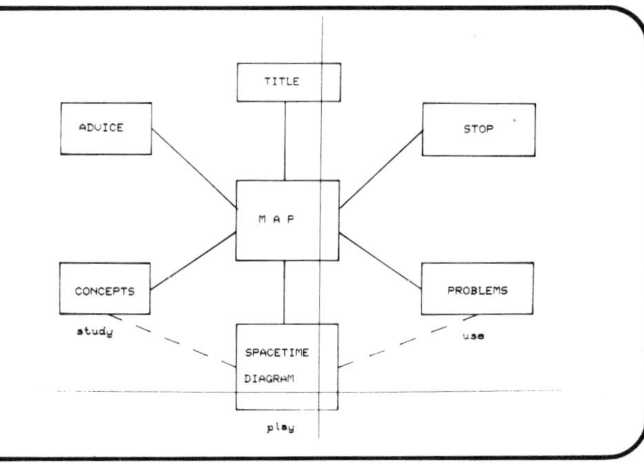

FIGURE 2-11 Introductory Map in SPACE, Reflecting Pedagogical Content

One important use of the visual information is giving students an overall view of the area they are learning or of what facilities are available in the learning material. Textbooks sometimes do this by presenting a chart of the chapter showing which chapters depend on which others. Very elaborate maps can be built showing the organization of particular areas of knowledge. Computer dialogs too can use such information. Three of our dialogs employ maps in different ways. In FIELD, the map shows the major blocks of the program in a linear fashion. For MAXWELL, the map not only shows the major learning blocks, but shows that certain features of the program are optional and may not be desirable for all users. The organization of the map in SPACE is entirely different, showing not the topics contained in the dialog but the pedagogical organization, emphasizing the notion of a free play facility (the space-time diagram)—a set of formal learning concepts and a set of problems that exercise the student's knowledge of the learning concepts. (See Figures 2-9, 2-10, and 2-11.)

Our discussion so far has referred to graphic output. But graphic input is also an important tool. As mentioned, displays will have different facilities for graphic input. Some of the uses are somewhat trivial. Thus, graphic input can be utilized as a substitute for multiple-choice input, where the student points to a choice rather than typing a word or a number. There are advantages where graphic input speeds up the process. (See Figures 2-12 and 2-13.)

In other places, alternatives to graphic input are less pleasant to use. For example, we can enter events on a space-time graph, as in the dialog SPACE (Figure 2-14).

We could have entered the numerical values of the points, but that would have been more time-consuming for the students and would much limit the manipulation of events and world lines in space-time allowed within this dialog. Hence, graphic input plays an important role.

A second place where graphic input is useful is in the sequences from PROJECTILE where we are asking the student to indicate the origin of a co-ordinate system, as shown in Figure 2-15.

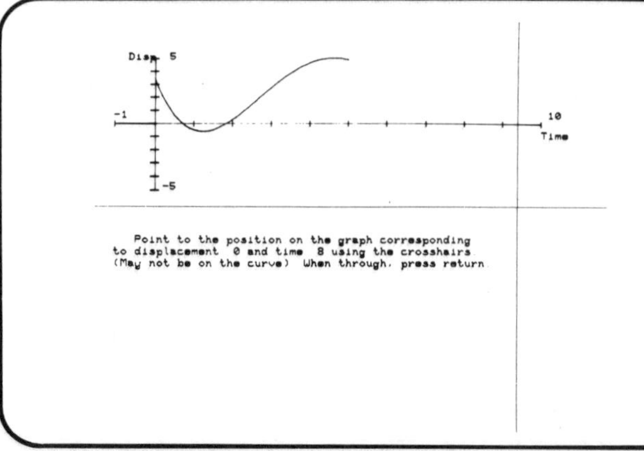

FIGURE 2-12 Example from the Quiz SLOPE, Using the Built-In Pointer

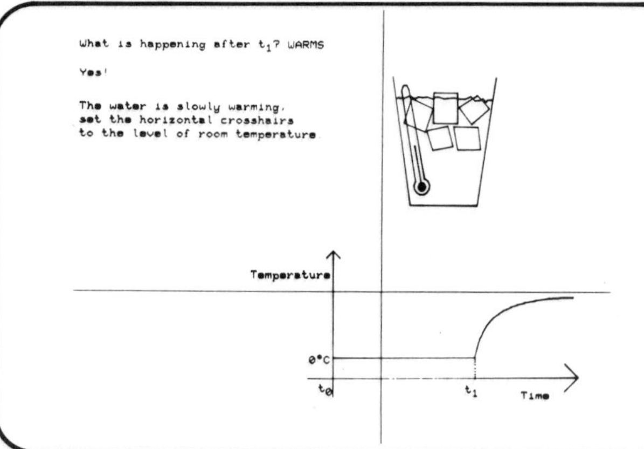

FIGURE 2-13 Graphical Input with Pointer in the Dialog, HEAT

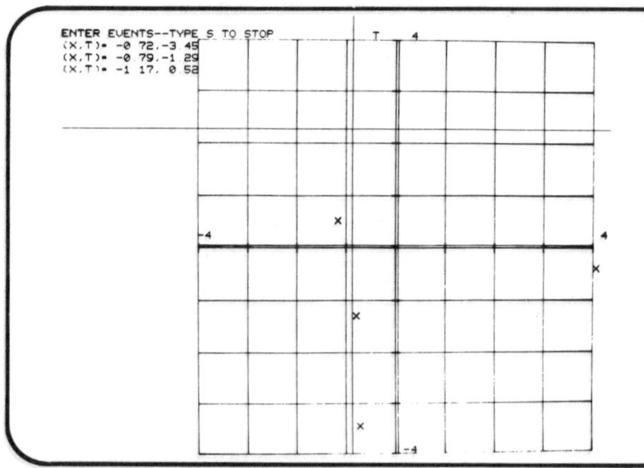

FIGURE 2-14 Entering Events in SPACE, Using Space-Time Diagram

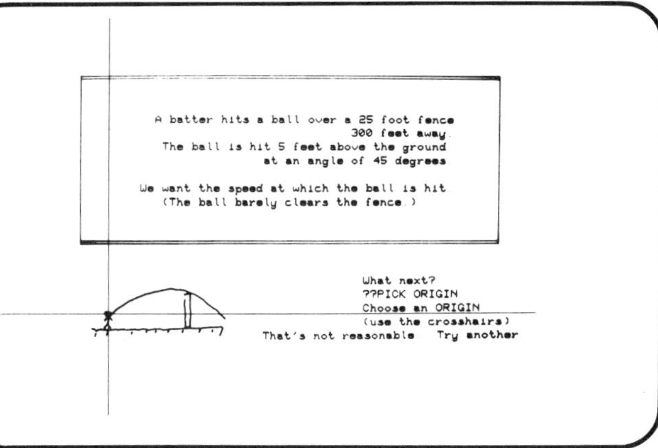

FIGURE 2-15 PROJECTILE—Student Points to Choose an Origin

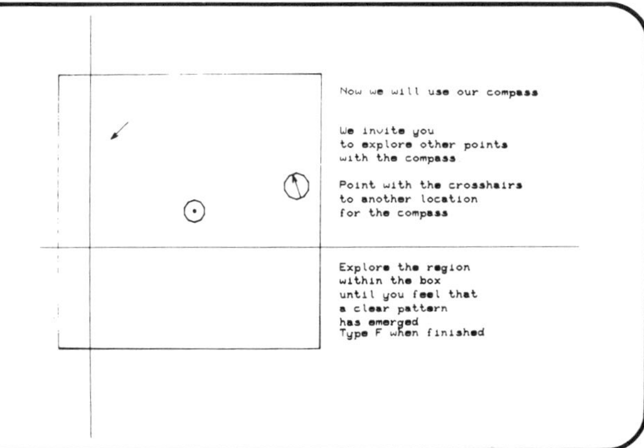

FIGURE 2-16 Initial Sequence Using the Pointer in MFIELD

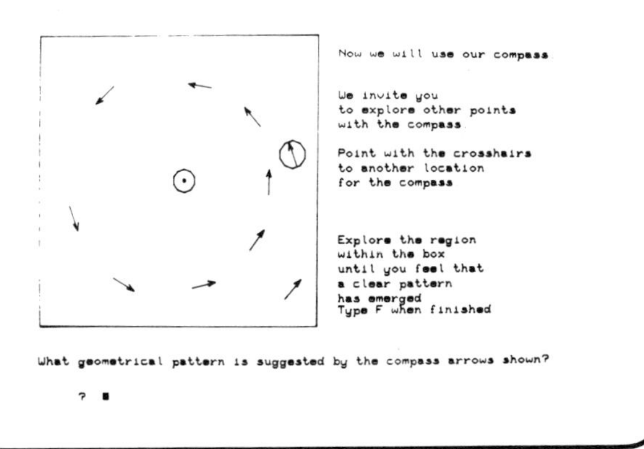

FIGURE 2-17 MFIELD, with Several Compass Locations Showing

The third place where graphic input is a natural mechanism for dealing with the situation is where we allow the student to explore, as in MFIELD. Students are given a "compass" which they can move from place to place. Wherever the compass is placed, the dialog indicates the direction of the magnetic field at that point. So we have an experimental facility. Again positions could be specified by pairs of numbers, but only at a much slower and less natural pace. (See Figures 2-16 and 2-17.)

So far I have been concerned with iconic information in the usual sense, pictorial and graphic information. But text has graphic aspects too, and it is these implications that I would like to consider next. While some of these are not typically thought of as graphic, many are *possible* in a graphic environment.

Perhaps the most obvious example is the use of subscripts and superscripts. Most alphanumeric displays do not have this capability, but on a graphic display allowing us to display a character anywhere on the screen, it is possible to provide subscripts and superscripts. Since they are widely used in mathematics, and thus in all areas of science, the inability to use subscripts and superscripts is a serious handicap for students utilizing computer-based material. Hence, this ability is an advantage of a graphic-based teaching system; we can show formulae in the forms the students usually see. Thus, a dialog, PROJECTILE, writes the formulae like the textbooks, and does not involve learning new notation simply because the medium has changed. (See Figure 2-18.)

A related idea is the ability to display special characters. The best solution to the problem of special characters is not the graphic solution but making the display intelligent enough to understand a character defined in software. But, nevertheless, a graphic display can make available any characters by drawing them. Thus, the presentation of Maxwell's equations uses the same notation that typical textbooks use in writing down these equations, as shown in Figure 2-19.

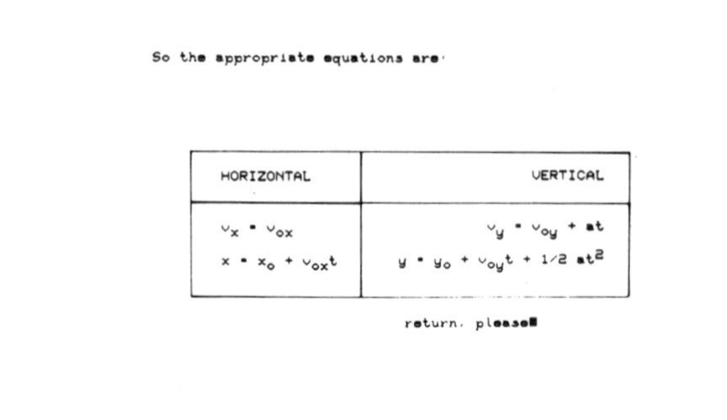

FIGURE 2-18 Equations in the PROJECTILE Quiz Help Sequence

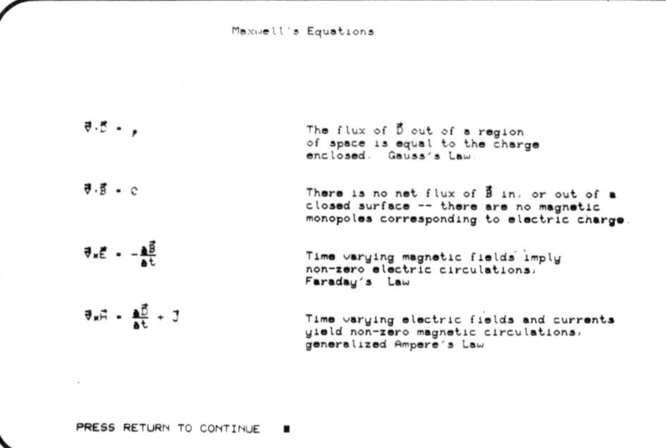

FIGURE 2-19 From the Dialog MAXWELL (See Figure 2-10)

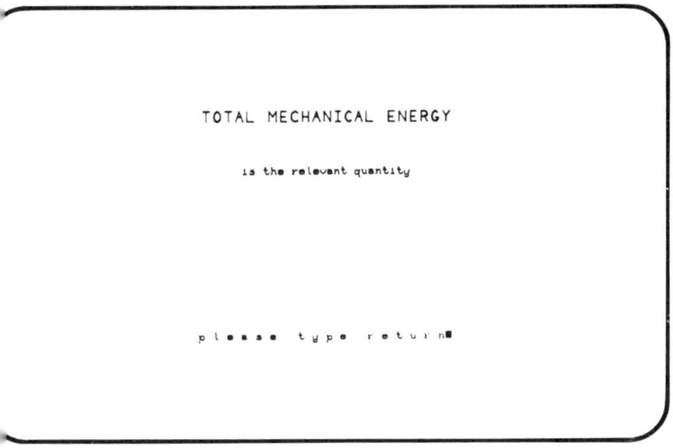

TOTAL MECHANICAL ENERGY
is the relevant quantity
please type return

FIGURE 2-20 Large Letters in the Quiz POT

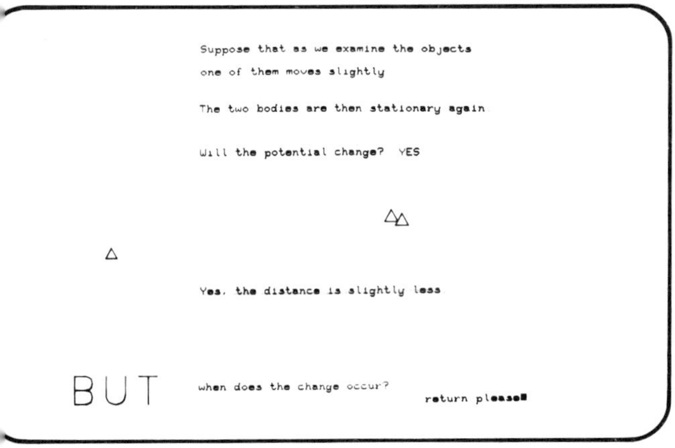

Suppose that as we examine the objects
one of them moves slightly
The two bodies are then stationary again
Will the potential change? YES
Yes, the distance is slightly less
BUT
when does the change occur?
return please

FIGURE 2-21 From the Dialog POTENTIAL

Problem 10
right
6
wrong
3
Your task is to determine the dot product of two 3 dimensional vectors:

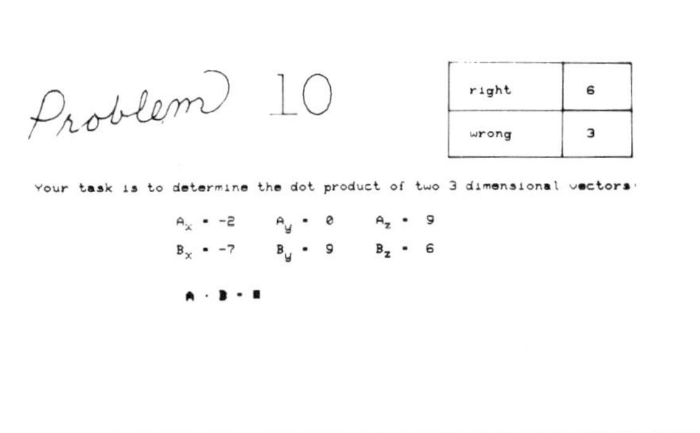

FIGURE 2-22 VECTORS—**A** and **B** in Bold to Indicate Vectors

The use of subscripts, superscripts, and special characters is an obvious graphic device, and one that enhances and eases learning. But many text modes can be employed to aid the student. We can, by the way we handle the textual information, emphasize critical ideas, and we can make the presentation more visually attractive to the student and thus more interesting. The use of italic and underlining in printed material is one such example. But we can see many more examples if we look not at texts but at blackboards after lectures. Here a great variety of different devices are used, all of them usable in a computer graphic environment.

The lecturer may emphasize important ideas by putting them in large letters, making them stand out at that point, and affecting the student's notions. These may be the critical concepts. (See Figure 2-20.) Or they may be in the line of text, but trying to shift the student's attention to a new phase of development, as in POTENTIAL. (See Figure 2-21.)

A similar graphic device is the use of bold letters. In some situations in science bold characters are needed, as with vectors. These too can be added graphically with no difficulty. But bold letters can also provide emphasis. Bold has also a time effect because the letters appear to flash brighter when they are being displayed, at least with certain types of CRT technology. (See Figure 2-22.)

Another related device is that of underlining areas of text to emphasize the important words. This can be done after the text is written to draw the student's eyes back to the material and to point out the critically important ideas. Something like this is used by students when they use transparent color markers in textbooks.

We can increase the student's ability to understand text or make it more interesting. One possibility is to use text as a graphic object, moving it around the page in natural phrases and sentences to assist the student in reading it and to emphasize the important ideas. (See Figures 2-23 and 2-24.)

As shown in the figures, both right and left justification of text material are utilized, and the lines are broken up into their natural pieces. We are not using whatever letters are necessary to fill up the line, but we are aiding student comprehension, assisting the reading process. Delays can be put between phrases to further enhance this aspect. Reading is frequently a serious problem, even with good students. Some students have grown up as quite poor readers, and need all the help we can give them in this direction.

FIGURE 2-23 From the Introduction to the Quiz VECTORS

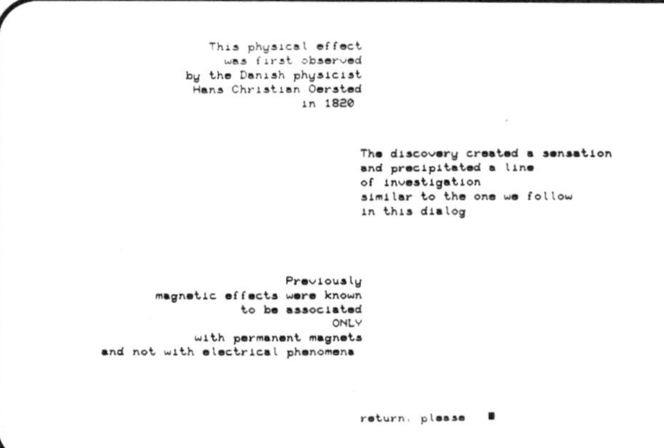

FIGURE 2-24 From the Dialog MFIELD, Showing Various Text Displays

Graphic Hardware

The prospective user of computer graphics in education needs to know something about the hardware available, both now and in the immediate future. In this section, I review some of the parameters involved.

We consider first the display medium, the screen on which the picture appears. The most widely used display technology is the cathode-ray tube, basically the same tube that appears in televison sets. Such tubes can be black and white or color. They can be utilized in two ways. First, points on the screen can be directly addressed. Thus, the computer can tell the display device, "Draw a line from this point to that point," as its basic command.

A second possibility is the raster scan technique used in television sets, with the beam moving across a line and then dropping for the next line.

Cathode-ray tubes differ with regard to how they handle the signal after it is displayed on the face of the tube. In the television-type tubes, the picture quickly fades, and only appears to be persistent because it is written over and over again. Another approach is reflected in the storage tubes. Several storage mechanisms are available; the picture stays until explicitly removed. In some storage mechanisms it is possible to remove part of the picture, but in others the whole screen must be erased to remove anything.

A second display technology is the plasma panel. In such a device, the tube is a grid of many points—500 $\times$ 500 with current technology. By applying a voltage across any of these points it can be "turned on." By appropriate design of circuitry, the plasma panel can store the points, keeping a point after it has been turned on until it is explicitly turned off. The plasma panel received most attention through its development in connection with PLATO, developed by the University of Illinois. Control Data Corporation's version does not use the plasma display.

In considering hardware for displaying graphics, we must also consider screen resolution. Two different issues present themselves: the addressable resolution, the accuracy with which we can address a particular point on the screen, and the observable resolution, the question of when two points or lines will actually appear different on a particular display system. Addressable resolutions differ greatly in displays that are purported to be graphic, going everywhere from relatively crude (100 $\times$ 100) matrices to ones with thousands of values in the x and y directions. A particular application may determine which is most realistic.

The question of just what constitutes a graphic display is not perhaps as clear-cut as we might imagine. A great many systems are either advertised or thought of as graphic. Sometimes any computer with a visual display, as opposed to hard copy, is referred to as a graphic display, even though many of these displays are only capable of displaying characters on the screen. Another compromise is to build into the system a set of small lines and to draw curves by concatenating these small lines. A reasonable definition of a graphic display would be that it is capable of displaying a full line, at a single command, of arbitrary length. The implementation might be at either the hardware or software level. Thus, we ought to be able to say, "Draw a line from here to here." How the machine actually constructs this line—whether it makes it up from a series of small vectors or whether it turns on groups of dots or whether it moves a beam continuously—is a design consideration for the system developer but not a major concern for the user.

Graphic Input

In addition to drawing pictures on the screen, an important component of a graphic display is its ability to enter graphic information. Many devices have been employed for this, most of them in expensive displays.

Perhaps the two oldest and most versatile ways of entering graphic information are with the light pen (a person appears to draw directly on the face of the cathode-ray tube) and with the tablet, again a drawing device. The light pen depends on software to locate the current position of the beam and to relay the information back to the computer. A typical procedure is for a scanning signal to move across the entire face of the tube or some smaller segment of the tube and for a photocell in the light pen to pick up the signal when it appears at the location of the pen. Most cathode-ray tubes have vertical screens, so the user must write in an unnatural position. A tablet is a more natural means of writing, but has the disadvantage that the picture is displayed somewhere other than at the writing location.

Other input devices are in less expensive displays. The "mouse" is one such device. The user rolls the mouse around on a flat surface. As it moves, a cursor on the screen makes corresponding moves, determined by potentiometers within the mouse. A similar device is the "joy stick," again moving a pointing device around on the screen as it moves from one position to another. It is possible to make joy sticks in such a way that the velocity of the device affects the positioning.

Another type of input is through a pointing device, where the user can literally point to a place on the screen. This is convenient for the novice, but offers fairly poor resolution in terms of the regions you can point to. Another inexpensive but versatile device is to build a set of wheels on the displays (or similar devices on personal computers). It is very difficult to draw a circle in such an environment.

Characters

Graphic displays must also display characters. Many options are available. Most displays construct characters by turning on a series of dots in a matrix. Older inexpensive systems used a 5 × 7 dot matrix, which has relatively poor resolution. Seven by nine is a common choice, particularly when both uppercase and lowercase must be generated. Character quality is still much less than print quality.

Dot matrix characters are, at best, crude and do not represent the highest graphic standards, no matter what care is used in their construction unless the matrix is very large. It is possible to display elegant, well-formed characters, and even give the user a choice of character fonts. The work at the Xerox Palo Alto Research Laboratory with the ALTO system illustrates what is possible with contemporary technology. However, commercially available systems currently have inadequate characters.

In addition to the question of how characters are produced, there is the question of which characters are available.

Traditionally, displays have been designed for the standard ASCII sets of characters. A few foreign fonts are also available. But symbol users in many different areas employ a great variety of symbols beyond the ones in standard sets. Some languages, such as APL, demand new symbol sets. The use of a device in another country almost always involves different needs in symbols too, because most languages have symbol requirements of their own. These letters can differ in only minor ways from English, but they can also be extremely different, as in the oriental countries. Special symbols are frequently found; thus, a physics student sees certain standard symbols in textbooks and expects to employ them on the computer. An educational display should have available a full range of characters.

Few commercial systems have a great variety of symbols accessible to the user. Perhaps the most flexible characters are those available with the PLATO displays and with the Terak 8510/a; the computer can load a character or a complete character set. In effect, software tells the display, "When I send you this particular code from now on, turn on this collection of dots, or display this symbol." Thus, users can devise their own symbols. These need not be simply characters in the normal sense, but can be pieces of pictures. A related aspect is that the symbol is designed in such a way that it fills up the entire space—what is normally thought of as the area surrounding the symbol is area that is within the dot matrix of the symbol. Putting this another way, if we turn on all the points in a symbol, and fill the whole screen with this symbol, every point on the screen will be on.

One advantage with graphic displays is that we can, if necessary, draw any character desired, providing the resolution is sufficiently great. But speed may be a limiting factor.

However, no currently available system adequately handles the converse problem of entering a variety of symbols. Usually some unpleasant tactics come in, such as telling the student, "Type *I* whenever you want an integral sign." One inexpensive possibility is to have a series of keyboard overlays showing variable symbols. A better possibility is to have the symbols on the keys change, because they themselves are constructed out of LEDs or plasma panels, but there are technical and financial problems in such a solution.

Auxiliary Devices—Media

The pictures currently seen in graphic displays represent only a piece of the graphic world. Graphics in a general sense includes actual pictures and film or video sequences. Thus, in thinking about computer displays with graphics, we should ask whether such visual facilities are available.

Current systems provide only relatively crude graphic media capabilities. Thus, some systems allow the use of slides, or pictures selected from a microfiche, but only do this in ways that are not convenient from the standpoint of the individual user. The TICCIT system allows limited use of video; built-in tape cassette units are associated with the computer. But most attempts in that direction are still relatively crude. In future educational systems, with videodiscs, we can confidently look forward to full multimedia capability in a form usable by any student.

The circumstances of student use are of supreme importance. The student, using the computer as a learning device, cannot be expected to load various objects into the machine. Systems built around such philosophies have the logistic problems of how students will get access to the necessary microfiche and slides, how they will be instructed in entering this material, and how they will start the unit, and what happens to the slides or microfiche after the session is finished. All the media must be handled on a uniform basis, not on a piecemeal basis.

Graphic Software

The situation with regard to graphic software is unfortunate. Most standard computer languages were developed before graphics were in widespread use and so their design did not reflect graphics. More recent languages, unfortunately, have followed that trend also. These languages supply numerical and alphanumerical output modes, but do not have, as built-in features of the language, graphic output modes. Thus, graphic output must be viewed by the student using these languages as a stepchild. Further, the routines demand greater knowledge of the system, so the novice cannot employ graphics.

The most common graphic software available is in the form of procedures. Often such software is available from the vendor of a graphic display. Graphics in such applications is done by calls to procedures.

In 1968 our project members decided that if adequate access to graphics was to be provided for students, graphics should be a natural part of a language. We decided that APL would be a suitable language to do this, and so we modified the APL available to us to include graphic capability. This is the only APL distributed by a computer vendor that has graphics as a built-in part of the language—few computer languages have this feature at the moment other than the computer-aided learning languages I will discuss.

Input and output in APL is normally done through an operator called quad, with the appearance of a box. Two standard quads exist in APL, quad and quote quad. We added to APL a third quad, quad 0, for graphics. It is used in the same way as the other quads for both input and output. Its only limitation is that not all data is "good" graphic data. If quad 0 receives a $2 \times n$ matrix, it will plot a two-dimensional curve on the screen, while if it receives a $3 \times n$ structure, it will plot a three-dimensional curve, projected onto the surface. But $4 \times n$ is an error.

Recently an attempt has been made to standardize graphic capability through the efforts of SIGRAPH. The resulting "core graphics" procedures have been implemented in several languages. A draft standard also exists from the BASIC standards committee, considering graphic facilities as an inherent part of BASIC.

Major languages for preparing interactive student-computer dialogs have recognized the importance of graphics in learning material. The major projects employ graphics, and so it is not surprising that the software they develop has graphic capabilities. Thus, Tutor (PLATO) and the dialog facilities of the Educational Technnology Center at the University of California, Irvine, both contain a full set of graphic commands as an integral part of the language. Older dialog languages, as with standard languages developed before widespread availability of graphic displays, do not have graphic capability—a serious flaw.

Providing graphic capabilities within a language does not solve the problem of coding interactive computer-based material containing graphics. This mode of working—adding graphic commands to an existing programming language—is inherently noninteractive from a design point of view. First, the programmer writes the code, and then tries it out to see what the visual results look like. To place material on the screen properly, the programmer may resort to graph paper, either explicitly or in terms of thinking about the screen. We should provide a facility more like what a graphic designer uses, where the material can be placed on the screen by pointing, moved around, and adjusted in size and angle until it takes the desired appearance. This facility allows a designer a style like that for layout for a page in a book, or for an advertisement in a magazine.

Given this need, it is not surprising that such facilities have been developed independently both in PLATO and in the Educational Technology Center. I will describe our original approach to the problem. Recent work follows a somewhat different approach.

Since we wanted to work interactively, we picked for our first attempt a language facility that had interactive graphic capability associated with it. As previously indicated, we had added graphic capability to APL. Since APL is a powerful, general-purpose programming language well suited to graphics, we initially developed a new facility within APL; in the past two years we have employed Pascal.

This description makes our approach appear more rational than it was. Our student programmers had been given a program to implement which involved many pictures highly interwoven with textual material. Previous experience indicated that a number of trials were necessary to get the pictures and the text in right relationship to each other. The student programmers developed the first APL-based facility for assisting with this problem. It was gradually refined over several years, and extended to a greater range of dialog facilities. Refinement has led to major expansions in the APL workspace. Functions can be added to the workspace for special purposes. The system is interfaced to a graphic tablet, so input can come not only from constructed graphic items but also from drawn data.

The procedure has several stages. First, there is the design stage. The appropriate pictures and alphanumeric information are placed on the screen and adjusted to give an interesting visual presentation to aid learning. (See Figures 2-25, 2-26, and 2-27 for examples.)

A second stage of the process occurs when the program writes the code or file that produces the display on the screen.

The APL workspace has been converted to different APL systems. It has been one of the major tools developed by the Physics Computer Development Project, the predecessor of the Educational Technology Center, to assist in the preparation of student-computer dialogs, and has proven its value many times over. The new capability in Pascal is still under development.

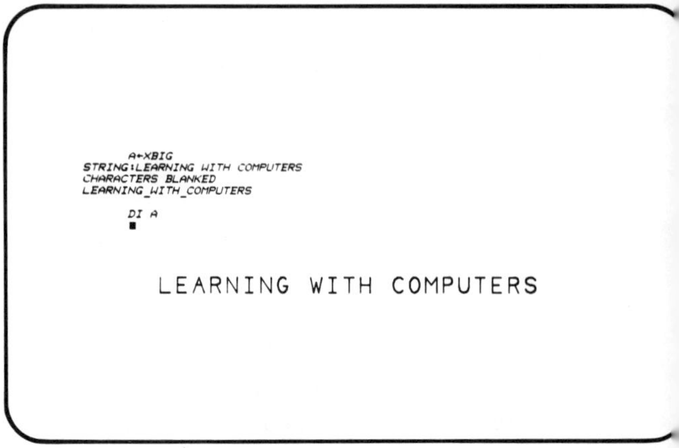

Authoring Graphic Dialogs

The authoring process for computer-based learning material is complicated by graphics. A number of variants are possible, and we need to consider them.

The first question is how authors specify their intents. Basically two types of strategies can be found. One approach assumes that the author will be, at least partially, the programmer of the dialog. Then the author writes the code for graphics as for the rest of the program. This is, as indicated in our discussion of graphic software, not an easy task, and

FIGURE 2-25 Use of the APL Workspace to Create Large Letters

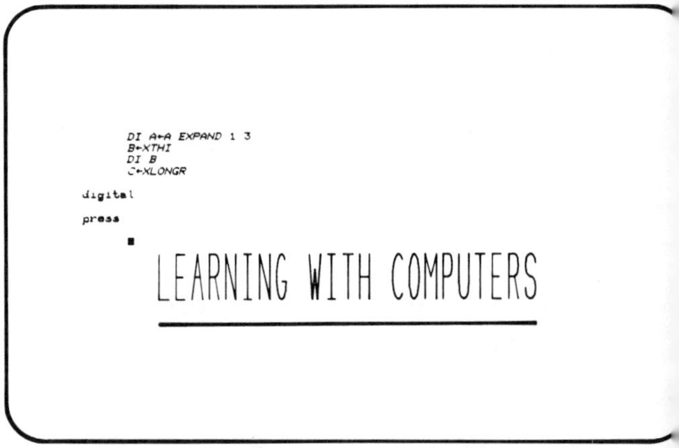

FIGURE 2-26 APL—Changing the Size of the Letters and Underlining Them

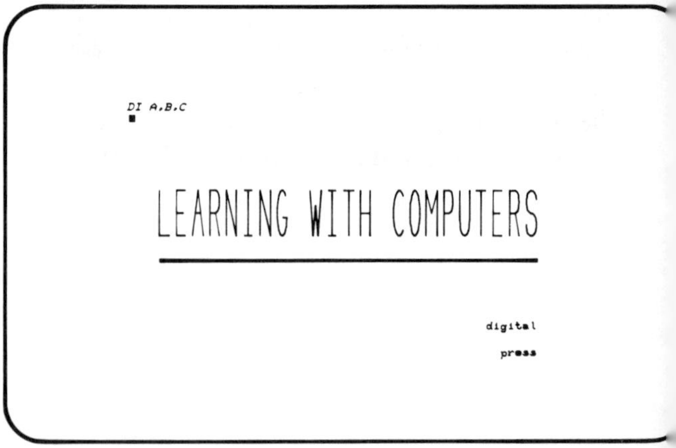

FIGURE 2-27 Final Composition Created in APL

increases the level of sophistication necessary for the author. There are, however, some aids that can be provided for the author's use, such as the graphic design facility just discussed and similar PLATO aids.

The other possibility is for the author to work through a programmer or artist, both for the graphic and nongraphic parts of the dialog. The author specifies the graphic details, by means of sketches and commentary, but leaves implementation to the artist or programmer. This is the strategy we follow at Irvine; I will expand on this through an illustration.

We consider an on-line test in vector analysis at the level required in beginning Physics courses. The form is a series of problems. The graphic information is mostly in the form of vectors, sometimes produced by random numbers generated internally in the program, so that each student will get a unique exam. The pedagogical details were decided on in a series of sessions between Joseph Marasco (University of California, Irvine), John Herman (Western Michigan University), and myself. Typically, we find that a dialog is better when two or three people work together, experienced teachers who can each bring unique knowledge of students to bear. The output was a rough flowchart specifying all pedagogical details.

Our concern is with the graphic details. These are indicated in the flowchart with sketches and comments, particularly with regard to the size of the vectors to be picked. The pictures drawn will often be determined when the student is running the program, when the random variables are chosen.

The flowchart, containing the full pedagogical specifications, goes to the programmer responsible for implementing the graphic code. The programmer knows the details of the language and auxiliary facilities available to carry out the work. This leaves the burden of some of the design considerations to the programmer. The exact location of the textual items and the pictorial information is not fully specified in the flowchart. The programmer is not the best person for screen design. A better possibility would be to employ a graphic designer, serving as an intermediary between the teachers who develop the programs and the programmer.

Future

The computer is a dynamic learning medium, still evolving rapidly. Our discussion of computer graphics for learning has concentrated on the current situation. But many present limitations will soon be overcome by the rapid development of graphic technology. So it is reasonable to ask what is needed for the most effective use of interactive graphics in assisting learning. I examine first the hardware issues, and then the important issues centering around production and distribution of materials.

First, we require cheaper devices. Although the cost of graphic displays has declined dramatically, the expenses are still too great for some contemporary learning environments. With all aspects of computing, including graphics, we can confidently predict a continuing drop in costs.

Color is a clear need. It can play both motivational and informational roles. Animation, in the full sense, is another requirement. We would like to handle special characters adequately for both input and output, and we would like better formed characters. Further, we require, within computer dialogs, full access to a rich range of media, including slides, audio, and video sequences.

Although it might appear that my hardware demands are great, they are all within reasonable reach. Two recent developments are relevant. The first is the continual development of computer technology, particularly large-scale integration. The second is the home videodisc. The intelligent videodisc system, primarily as a stand-alone system, can meet in a reasonable period of time all the hardware goals outlined.

The videodisc would be the medium for transmitting educational material. It would contain the computer code needed for highly interactive graphic programs, video, audio, and slide material. All these ingredients would be randomly accessible under the control of the computer program used where appropriate in the learning sequence. The videodiscs for home television use cost about as much as audio records. A color television set, modified for better resolution, could be the output device. For special purposes, the device might connect to a remote computer, but it would normally function on its own. The videodiscs will provide a product that can be marketed in a fashion similar to books and musical records. Because they are difficult to copy, they will be difficult to pirate.

The hardware and the medium, however, are only part of the problem. As computers become more widely employed in learning, the questions of production and evaluation of computer-based learning material will become of increasing importance.

Many present efforts in improving learning through the use of computers are in the "cottage industry" stage, with individuals working alone or in small groups. Although large organizations for such developments have been proposed in the Carnegie Report on the Fourth Revolution[2], these organizations have not come into existence. We need additional time to learn how to utilize this new medium. We are now beginning to understand the parameters that lead to effective production systems for computer-based dialogs, although more experience is still needed.

The most interesting model for developing instructional material is furnished by The Open University course production. Similar organizations could develop computer-based material, combining the talents of subject matter experts, educators, psychologists, programmers, and graphic designers.

APL AS A LANGUAGE FOR INTERACTIVE COMPUTER GRAPHICS

Introduction

APL is an appropriate language for certain types of interactive computer graphics. A particular implementaion is discussed. Graphics have been implemented in one way or another in dozens of languages before APL, including FORTRAN, LOGO, and EULER-G. APL is well suited for at least one kind of graphic application. In Chapter 6 I discuss the limitations of APL for computer-based learning.

Graphics and High-Level Languages

The creation of a full-scale, general-purpose programming language is not a small task. A growing number of interesting, well thought out, high-level languages are available. These languages, although "general," tend to be specialized toward application. Thus, LISP and PL/1 have a very different community of users, although they are both, in a sense, general purpose; they are optimized toward different applications. Given this thrust, it seems natural that graphics should be available in many high-level languages. A particular language may suit a class of graphic applications. APL is one such high-level language. Adding graphic capability to a language that is little used has a limited influence. If we can work within languages employed in hundreds of installations, greater effect is possible.

Graphic Data

Graphic data can often be viewed as array data, collections of numbers rather than single numbers. Suppose we consider plotting a curve generated by mathematical operations. A curve in many graphic systems will eventually be represented as a series of segments, usually straight lines. Typically, several hundred segments may be present. If the values along the horizontal axis advance with equal increments, the values along the vertical axis determine the curve. Thus, the natural data structure for a curve is an array. We may also have an array for the values along the horizontal axis or a matrix with two rows (or two columns), because the case of equally spaced points is a special one. If we think of three-dimensional plotting, then we are faced with three arrays or perhaps a matrix with three rows or three columns. A complicated picture might be composed of a number of such array structures.

It will come as no surprise to APL users, and even to those who are not strong APL enthusiasts, that APL is a powerful language for the creation and manipulation of collections of numbers. It is one of the few general-purpose programming languages that initially assumed that many calculations involve groups of entities, numbers, or character strings. So powerful built-in mechanisms were developed for creating and manipulating such groups. Hence, the applications program—the program that creates the objects that will be displayed graphically—is often dramatically reduced.

Most computing languages think of every calculation as involving single numbers, rather than thinking of these calculations as involving groups of numbers. Graphics happen to be particularly sensitive to this distinction, and so APL's power with collections of numbers is visible in this type of graphic programming.

So far, I have discussed one type of graphics—curve plotting—in which the data is naturally represented by arrays. In more complex graphic applications, a picture may have identifiable subparts which are separately manipulated. Such data structures are often lists or trees or more elaborate data structures. In this situation, the case for APL as a graphic language is weaker; although lists have been proposed as a data-type for APL, they are not present in common implementations. So the structured data file characteristic of many graphic systems does not have a natural representation in APL. However, if the notion of the structured data file is replaced by the concept of display procedures as the basis of a complex picture, APL function capabilities appear to provide the necessary facilities.

Transformations

Graphic data often undergoes transformations before it is suitable for presentation on the screen. These transformations include placement of the picture on the screen, translation from one point to another, rotation of the picture, restriction of the full picture to some smaller sub-picture, and changes in scale. The picture may be composed of many sub-pictures, and it may be necessary to apply these transformations individually to the sub-parts of the picture. So after graphic data has been generated in the applications program, there is still the problem of transformations. APL, because of its ease in handling matrices, is very suitable for performing these transformations. Likewise, the projections from three-dimensional graphic information on the two-dimensional screen can be viewed as a transformation.

Functions

As indicated, pictures have parts, and these parts often need to be manipulated independently of other parts. Thus, one part of a picture may undergo rotation, while another part stays the way it was.

Therefore, any full graphic facility must have facilities for naming and manipulating individual parts of pictures as well as the total picture. The notion of a subroutine or procedure is critical.

APL's function structure is a viable way of dealing with this problem. It allows us to go in a variety of directions. For example, it would be possible to develop display procedures, in the sense that William Newman has expounded. The availability of both global and local variables, under program control, is also valuable. Arguments can be passed to functions, or they can use data available to a group of procedures. But the scope of variables cannot be controlled as carefully as with modern structured languages such as Pascal.

Examples of an APL Graphic System

After having argued that APL is a reasonable graphic language, at least for several applications, I describe two particular implementations, similar in detail, of a graphic system in APL. Our initial effort provided science-engineering students flexible graphic output from APL programs. Most of this work is curve plotting. We assumed timesharing displays—Tektronix 4013s—with APL capability. The system was initially developed within a Sigma 7 APL developed in the Canadian Defense Research Establishment at Valcartier, DREV APL. Later a very similar set of facilities was added to the Xerox Program Product APL which runs under Control Program V. These two systems are similar, with differences that depend on ease of implementation.

Two different graphic systems were placed in the APL environments. One is based on APL workspace functions, using such common names as DRAW, SCALE, WINDOW, etc. To some extent, the typewriter PLOT function was used as a guide. These workspace functions were designed with the naive user in mind, someone who is not a computer science expert, but needs graphic information (rather than alphanumeric information) as the outcome of calculations. A brief description of these functions follows:

1. DRAW produces a curve, either two- or three-dimensional. The left argument specifies the area of the screen on which the picture is to appear. The right argument is the plotting data. DRAW can use the function VS to combine arrays; or *N*, *N* by 1, 1 by *N*, 2 by *N*, *N* by 2, 3 by *N*, or *N* by 3 arrays can be used as the right argument. The last two cases give three-dimensional perspective plots, the others give two-dimensional plots.

Four numbers determine a rectangular viewing area on the screen, the coordinates of points *A* and *B* in inches from the lower left corner; so DRAW can be preceded by a four-vector, literals or a variable. If the viewing area exceeds the physical bounds of the screen, a "domain error" occurs.

Example (DREV APL):
3 3 6 6 *DRAW Q VS R*

Example (Xerox APL):
3 6 3 6 *DRAW Q VS R*

Q and *R* are vectors of the same length; a 2-dimensional curve appears in a rectangle whose lower left point has coordinates (3,3) in inches, and whose upper right point has coordinate (6,6). *Q* is plotted on the vertical axis, and *R* on the horizontal axis.

If the left argument to DRAW is a scalar, the viewport currently in effect applies; the value of the scalar is ignored.

Example:
0 *DRAW* *C*

If *C* is a 2 by 400 matrix, a curve with 400 points is drawn.

The default viewport for the DRAW workspace is the largest square touching the lower and right edges.

DRAW can specify three-dimensional plotting.

Example (DREV APL):
2 2 6 6 *DRAW VX VS VY VS VZ*

plots the three vectors *VX, VY,* and *VZ* in a viewport. We must have $\rho VX = \rho VY = \rho VZ$. The three-dimensional curve defined by *VX, VY*, and *VZ* is projected onto the two-dimensional screen.

After a DRAW, the alphanumeric cursor goes to the next writeable line. DRAW does not erase the screen, so it can be used to overplot curves.

The viewport can be reset by WINDOW.

Example (Xerox APL):
WINDOW 1.5 3.5 2 6

2. SCALE, NOSCALE, and CENTER determine the placement of the picture within the viewport.

SCALE sets the user coordinates for the smallest and largest value, the corners of the current viewing area. The general form is

SCALE A

For a two-dimensional plot, *A* is a four-element vector; the first two components are the minimum and maximum values of the horizontal variable, and the next two of the vertical variable. For a three-dimensional curve, *A* is a six vector; the last two components determine the scale for the third axis. Data outside these ranges will not be plotted by succeeding DRAW commands.

SCALE and WINDOW data is stored with the workspace, so a DRAW command just after a LOAD will draw the same curve as just before the workspace was saved.

Example:
SCALE ¯1.5 3 ¯1.5 3

The minimum values are −1.5, and the maximum 3, for both variables.

NOSCALE expands the curve to fit the viewport. It has no arguments. CENTER places the origin of the coordinate system in the center of the viewport, and then expands to fit the viewport. It has no arguments.

The default scaling is CENTER.

3. ERASE, HOME, and SET control utility functions on the CRT screen, as in these examples:

ERASE—erases screen, sets cursor at upper left corner

HOME—sets cursor at upper left corner

3.5 SET 6.2—sets the cursor to the position on the screen with measurements in inches.

4. AXES draws axes in the viewport corresponding to current scaling. It has no arguments. The axes are two- and three-dimensional as appropriate, and the end values are shown.

5. DASH causes the next curve only to be dashed.

6. INT establishes an interval of equally spaced values, often useful in plotting.

Example:
A ← *INT* ¯6 6 100

The example sets up a vector of 100 equally spaced values between −6 and 6, and assigns it to *A*.

7. PUT places verbal information at coordinate-defined positions, using the viewing area and scaling in effect.

Example:
2.3 7.1 *PUT 'CURVE A'*.

The example writes the words 'CURVE A' with the "C" at the point with coordinates 2.3, 7.1.

8. GRAPHIC INPUT. Graphic data is entered using the crosshairs, controlled by the horizontal and vertical wheels on the Tektronix 4013 and similar terminals. CURSOR turns on the crosshairs. Any character terminates the input. The *x* and *y* coordinates of the location are returned, using active scaling information. The character is stored.

This is only one possible collection of workspace functions. One of the advantages of APL for graphics is that we could design many different graphic systems within APL, and gain some experience with the relative advantages and disadvantages for different audiences. For example, we could develop a workspace that allows display procedure calls.

APL Primitives for Graphics

At the primitive level, in both of the two APLs, a new operator, quad backspace 0, has been added for graphic input and output. This operator is modeled after the standard input-output operations in APL. It could be thought of conceptually as a shared variable in the sense of IBM APL.

⎕̸0 —quad backspace 0—is the graphic input and output function. Its use for graphic output is in the form

A ← ⎕̸0

The following table shows allowable values of *A* for graphic input:

Two-Dimensional

1. $\rho A = 2\ N$

2. $\rho A = N\ 2$

Two-Dimensional Against Indices

3. $\rho A = N$

4. $\rho A = 1\ N$

5. $\rho A = N\ 1$

Three-Dimensional Plotting

6. $\rho A = 3\ N$

7. $\rho A = N\ 3$

Table 2-1. GRF Calls

GRF Call	Corresponding Function Call	Action Taken
0 ΔGRF 1		Turns off ⎕ input scaling
0 ΔGRF 2		Turns on ⎕input scaling (default)
1 ΔGRF 3		Sets terminal device type=4013
2 ΔGRF ''	WINDOW ''	Sets default window (default)
2 ΔGRF x_1,x_2,y_1,y_2	WINDOW x_1,x_2,y_1,y_2	Sets up given window params
3 ΔGRF ''	SCALE ''	Sets 'transparent' ⎕output scaling and full-screen window
3 ΔGRF x_1,x_2,y_1,y_2	SCALE x_1,x_2,y_1,y_2	Sets x and y limits for fixed two-dimensional scaling
3 ΔGRF x_1,x_2,y_1,y_2,z_1,z_2	SCALE x_1,x_2,y_1,y_2,z_1,z_2	Sets x, y, and z limits for fixed three-dimensional scaling
4 ΔGRF''	SET ''	Restores cursor loc saved by SET x,...
4 ΔGRF x,y	SET x,y	Saves cursor loc; moves it to (x,y)
4 ΔGRF x,y,z	SET x,y,z	Saves cursor loc; moves it to (x,y,z)
5 ΔGRF ''	AXES	Draws axes according to current scaling
6 ΔGRF 1	NOSCALE	Sets noncentered automatic scaling
6 ΔGRF 2	CENTER	Sets centered automatic scaling (default)
6 ΔGRF 3		Fixes current scaling
7 ΔGRF ''	DASH	Specifies next curve to be dashed
8 ΔGRF ''		Erases screen and homes cursor
8 ΔGRF 1	ERASE	Erases screen (cursor homes automatically)
8 ΔGRF 2	HOME	Homes cursor
9 ΔGRF ''	BOX	Draws box according to current window
10 ΔGRF 1		Turns off curve reentrance mode

If a single number is assigned to ⎕ , an ASCII character is sent. The correspondence between integers and control characters is in ascending code order.

Other arguments lead to a DOMAIN ERROR.

If ρA = 2 3, we have a two-dimensional plot of 3 points; if ρA = 3 2, a three-dimensional plot of 2 points. If ρA is 2 1 or 3 1, a point is plotted. If ρA is 1 2, or 1 3, 2 or 3 points are plotted.

⎕ for input turns on the crosshairs and allows a position to be specified by positioning the crosshairs and then striking any key. It returns a three-element vector:

X,Y,CHARACTER CODE

where *X* and *Y* are the coordinates of the selected point and *CHARACTER CODE* is the decimal value of the ASCII code representing the character input.

The *X* and *Y* values returned reflect current scaling.

Graphic input and output do not cover all the needs of graphics in APL. Scaling, rotating, and establishing viewport are also needed. A full graphic system should allow options such as the ability to stop plotting when the curve leaves the viewing area or to continue the plotting if it ever comes back in.

The two different systems described, DREV APL and Xerox APL, have a different but related approach. Within DREV APL, the graphic services are performed by assigning information to a new "output" operator, quad backspace *S*. Quad backspace *S* usually takes a vector argument, with the first element indicating the operation to be performed and the succeeding arguments giving the parameters. Xerox APL employs a built-in intrinsic function, which can be given different names in different workspaces. It is a didactic function, with the left-hand argument describing the operation and the right-hand argument providing data for that operation. Table 2-1 summarizes the situation.

Alternate Approaches

The approach used in the systems described is not unique. Other approaches have been tried. The most widely used is provided by Tektronix for supporting APL graphics on the 4013. The software is mostly in the form of APL functions, with a minimum of additional code at the assembly level, so that it can be used with many different implementations of APL.

One would expect this graphic implementation via APL functions to be much slower; this does turn out to be the case. Depending on the amount of data plotted, CPU time for plotting goes up by a factor of about ten for the Tektronix package as compared with the systems described above. This ratio is not surprising, given the interpretive nature of APL and the bit manipulation aspects of graphics.

Further details are in the Xerox APL Reference Manual[3].

References

1. William Huggins and Doris Entwisle, *Iconic Communication: An Annotated Bibliography* (Baltimore: Johns Hopkins Press, 1974).

2. The Carnegie Commission on Higher Education, *The Fourth Revolution—Instructional Technology in Higher Education* (New York: McGraw-Hill, Inc., 1972).

3. *Xerox APL Language and Operator Reference Manual,* 90 L9 31C, 1975, pp. 163–170.

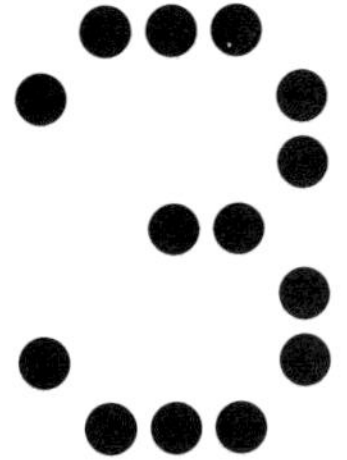

Educational Technology Center at Irvine

COMPUTER DIALOGS FOR STUDENT USE

My purpose is to acquaint you with teaching materials that are available on the Honeywell Sigma 7. Several APL workspaces are also listed.

Calling a Dialog

When you have signed on the Sigma 7, you are at the executive level. To call a dialog, you type its name followed by .PHYSICS; thus, to call the dialog HEAT you type:

HEAT.PHYSICS

followed by a return; you should not type any spaces. This identifies the program as HEAT in the account PHYSICS.

Leaving a Dialog

One possibility to leave a dialog is to type STOP at any input. Another possibility is to press the BREAK key; the computer will query you as to whether you want to continue. If you do not, type NO.

Graphic Dialogs

BLOW; beginning Physics; Alfred Bork. Newton's way into mechanics, via blow-like forces. Allows student to enter any force law, observe results for different times between blows. Shows equal time lines to study equal areas.

BODTEMP; all levels; Frank Potter, Dana Roode. Introduction to human body temperature control. Gives a graphic model of a human body temperature control system. Allows the student to set and change the conditions of the system's environment and observe the effect these changes have on the system.

CHARGE; beginning level; Sun-Yiu Fung, University of California, Riverside. An on-line electrostatic problem. The student queries the computer for the relevant information.

CIRCLE; beginning Physics; Alfred Bork, Martin Katz. An interactive proof of the formulae for uniform circular motion.

CONSERVE; beginning Physics; Noah Sherman, University of Michigan; Alfred Bork. Derivation of conservation of energy for a one-dimensional mechanical system, assuming the laws of motion are known. Introduces kinetic and potential energy. Requires some knowledge of calculus. An interactive proof.

COUPOSC; beginning Physics; Charles Munch, Alfred Bork. Introduction to coupled systems, normal modes, and characteristic frequencies. The system is two masses connected with three springs on an air track. Student sets up the Newtonian equations of motion, and then solves them. Assistance offered where needed. An interactive proof. Approximate time: 2 hours.

ENERGY; beginning Physics; Sun-Yiu Fung, Mark Houston, Leif Erickson, University of California, Riverside. Problem involving energy conservation.

EQAREA; beginning level; Ellen Peterson, Dan Kesler. Newton's proof of the law of equal areas, Proposition 1 in the *Principia.*

EQUIZ; beginning Physics; Sun-Yiu Fung, Mark Houston, Leif Erickson, University of California, Riverside. A quiz on energy.

FERM; beginning Physics; Murray Alexander, de Anza College. An unusual race, based on an optical variational principle. Two players or you can play against yourself.

FIELD; introductory electricity and magnetism; Bruce Rosenblum, University of California, Santa Cruz; Sun-Yiu Fung, University of California, Riverside; Robert Eisberg, University of California, Santa Barbara; Peter Geissler, University of California, Davis; Alfred Bork, Richard Ballard, Thomas Marrs, Joseph Marasco. Introduction to electrostatics and electric fields. One section plots electric field lines and potentials. Includes two on-line quizzes.

FLOAT; beginning level; Arnold Arons, University of Washington. The problem of "weightlessness" in space.

HARMONIC; beginning Physics; Tom Stark, Alfred Bork, Joseph Zeligs, Richard Ellis. An introduction to the harmonic oscillator, both undamped and damped. An interactive proof.

HEAT; high school or beginning college-level Physics; Arnold Arons, University of Washington; Alfred Bork. The study of simple phenomena, leading students to the conclusion that the concept of temperature by itself is insufficient to account for many situations. The new concept of heat is introduced.

HOCKEY; beginning Physics; Robert Eisberg, University of California, Santa Barbara; Peter Geissler, University of California, Davis; Alfred Bork. Introduction to mass and momentum through simulation of collision experiments.

INTEGRAL; introductory electricity and magnetism; Bruce Rosenblum, University of California, Santa Cruz; Thomas Marrs, Mark Geisert. Develops the concepts of line, surface, and volume integrals, leading to Gauss's Law. Students perform simple integrations.

LUNA; elementary level; Arnold Arons, University of Washington; Alfred Bork. The phases of the moon as an example of a scientific model. Ends with a randomly selected quiz.

MAGQ; beginning Physics; Kenneth Ford. Twenty questions that check a student's knowledge of magnetic fields; offers assistance when difficulties appear. A threshold quiz intended to assure a minimum standard of performance for all students in a class.

MAXWELL; intermediate electricity and magnetism; Joseph Marasco, Alfred Bork. Maxwell's equations, plane waves, and polarization.

MFIELD; high school and beginning college; Arnold Arons, University of Washington; Alfred Bork. The first in a three-part series on magnetic phenomena. Field due to a long straight current-carrying wire. Phenomenological approach.

MFIELD2; beginning Physics; Arnold Arons, University of Washington; Alfred Bork. The second in a three-part series on introductory concepts concerning the magnetic field, from a phenomenological point of view. Force on a current carrying wire, and on a charged particle in a magnetic field.

MFIELD3; beginning Physics; Arnold Arons, University of Washington; Alfred Bork. The third in a three-part series on introductory concepts concerning the magnetic field. The concepts of magnetic flux and induced currents and voltages are developed.

MOMENTUM; Robert Eisberg, University of California, Santa Barbara; Alfred Bork. The student is asked to derive, in an interactive proof format, the relation between Newton's third law and conservation of momentum, for a two-body system.

MOTION; beginning, intermediate, or graduate Physics; Richard Ballard, Alfred Bork, John Collins, Charles Munch. One-particle mechanical systems. The user can specify the force law, initial conditions, and constants in the force equation. Plots a wide variety of physical variables in two or three dimensions. An interactive world.

NBODY; introductory and intermediate mechanics; Mark Geisert. Plots orbits of up to ten gravitationally interacting bodies.

PICS; all levels. A dialog for showing picture files on any account. A group of pictures is in PHYSICS.

POTENTIAL; intermediate electricity and magnetism; Alfred Bork. Introduction to retarded potentials, starting from electrostatics.

RAYS; beginning Physics; William Parker, Mark Geisert. Elementary ray optics. Includes reflection, refraction, converging and diverging lenses, microscopes, and telescopes.

ROTATION; beginning Physics; Leroy Price, Dana Roode. A Series of exercises on rotational motion using the definitions of angular displacement, velocity, and acceleration. Hints for a collection of rotation problems. Written supplementary materials are necessary.

SPACE; beginning relativity; Dan Kesler, Alfred Bork, Stefan Demetrescu. Built around an interactive spacetime diagram. Includes problems and concepts. A controllable world.

TARGET; beginning Physics; John Coleman, Alfred Bork. A mass spectrometer. User picks the velocity and the fields to hit the target.

TERRA; elementary level; Arnold Arons, University of Washington; Alfred Bork. The sky as seen from the earth, including standard vocabulary. A preparation for LUNA.

3D; sophomore level; Arthur Luehrmann, Alfred Bork. A unified introduction to the three vector calculus operators, based on a generalization of the concept of derivative.

WORK; beginning Physics; Ronald Blum, Commission on College Physics; Dennis Barrett. Introduction to the concept of work through a series of examples.

APL

The following facilities are available as APL workspaces in the PHYSICS account. They are reached through APL. A DESCRIBE is available for each. Some knowledge of APL is required. All require graphic displays.

CONFORMAL; John Richardson. Conformal mapping from one complex plane to another. Starting function—MAP.

EFIELD; John Richardson. Plots electrostatic fields.

FFT; John Richardson. Displays Fourier transform of a function the student enters, plotting both the original and the transform. The starting function is FTRANS.

SURFACE; John Richardson, Stefan Demetrescu. Plots functions of two variables. The starting function is GRID.

Nongraphic Dialogs

The following is a list of nongraphic dialogs. All are old programs.

BGAME; beginning Physics; John Eastmond, Brigham Young University. Kinematics in the form of a basketball game.

CELLO; beginning Physics; Alfred Bork. Standing waves on a string with fixed ends. Assumes coupled systems, as in COUPOSC, and elementary acquaintance with the one-dimensional classical wave equation. An interactive proof.

COMPLEX; high school or beginning college; Alfred Bork, Lyn Calerdine, William Parker. Complex arithmetic and exponential functions of complex arguments. Offers assistance where that knowledge is weak. Diagnostic-remedial.

COMPTON; beginning or intermediate Physics; Mark Monroe, Alfred Bork. Helps a student who has difficulty working problem 70 in *Spacetime Physics*[1], Taylor-Wheeler, concerning the relativistic Compton effect. Problem assistance dialog.

DOPPLER; beginning or intermediate Physics; Alfred Bork, Mark Monroe. Offers aid to students having problems with problem 75 in *Spacetime Physics*[2], Taylor-Wheeler. The problem concerns the relativistic Doppler effect. Reviews Lorentz transformation for energy-momentum four vector. Problem assistance dialog.

ELEC; beginning Physics; Kenneth Ford, University of Massachusetts, Amherst. Ten simple questions checking knowledge of forces between charged particles and on charged particles in electric fields. Provides guidance to the student having problems. A threshold quiz intended to insure a minimal standard of performance for all students in a class.

KEPLER; beginning Physics; Noah Sherman, University of Michigan. Planetary motion.

MAGM; beginning or intermediate Physics; Alfred Bork, Greg Maxwell. Particle motion in an electromagnetic field. Analytic treatment. An interactive proof.

M3; beginning Physics; John Eastmond, Brigham Young University. Newtonian analysis of a simple 3-mass system.

PLANET; beginning or intermediate Physics; Mark Monroe. The Kepler problem for one body, by analytic methods. The differential equations of motion are solved for inverse square forces. Demands knowledge of calculus.

ROTATE; beginning Physics; Lyn Calerdine. Helps the student derive transformation equations for rotations.

SIGDIG; introductory Physics; Steve Emmerson. Significant figures in measurements.

TRANS; beginning Physics; Lyn Calerdine. Coordinate transformations between two Cartesian systems—translations, reflections, Galilean transformation.

On-Line Quizzes

The following dialogs are intended for use as quizzes. All of them require graphic displays. The quiz part cannot be examined outside of the class situation for which they are intended; however, many of them contain extensive "help sequences" which can be accessed as with any other dialog.

ACCEL; beginning Physics; Alfred Bork, John Herman, Joseph Marasco. Obtaining velocity and position from acceleration.

APLEXP; beginning Physics, computer science; Alfred Bork, Mark Geisert. Recognition of how APL reacts to student inputs. Must be run as an APL workspace.

APLPROG; beginning Physics, computer science; Alfred Bork, Mark Geisert. Checks ability to write an APL program. Must be run as an APL workspace.

APLUSE; beginning Physics, computer science; Alfred Bork, Mark Geisert. Use of APL system commands.

COM; beginning Physics; Stephen Franklin, Al Gonda, Joseph Marasco. Center of mass.

COUP; beginning Physics; Alfred Bork. Coupled systems: equations of motion, normal modes, characteristic frequencies.

DAMP; beginning Physics; Alfred Bork. Damped oscillators. Student must distinguish between underdamped and overdamped systems. A test for the concepts covered in HARMONIC.

EQAR; beginning Physics; Al Gonda, Joseph Marasco, Alfred Bork. Use of the principle of equal areas for central forces.

FORPOT; beginning Physics; Alfred Bork, Stephen Franklin. Forces from potentials and potentials from forces, for one-dimensional mechanical systems.

GRAV; beginning Physics; Alfred Bork, Stephen Franklin. Central forces. Analysis of an APL program for gravitational motion. Alteration of this program for other force laws.

HO; beginning Physics; Alfred Bork, Stephen Franklin, Al Gonda, Joseph Marasco. Checks understanding of an APL program for the oscillator, including changing this program for other one-dimensional systems.

IMPULSE; beginning Physics; Joseph Marasco, Al Gonda. Relations between force, momentum, and impulse.

MOM; beginning Physics; Todd Hopson, Susan Hall, Alfred Bork. Collisions on an air track, analyzed graphically. Extensive help sequence.

MOVE; beginning Physics; Alfred Bork, Stephen Franklin. Newton's graphic use of the first and second laws of motion. Help sequence.

NEWT; beginning Physics; Alfred Bork, Al Gonda, Joseph Marasco. Use of the laws of motion to solve problems involving inclined planes and pulleys. Help sequence.

NRG; beginning Physics; Al Gonda, Joseph Marasco. Conservation of energy concepts.

PEND; beginning Physics; Joseph Marasco, Stephen Franklin, Al Gonda. Motion of a pendulum as an example of an oscillator.

POP; beginning Physics; Joseph Marasco, Alfred Bork, John Herman. Momentum conservation in inelastic collisions. Help sequences.

POT; beginning Physics; Al Gonda, Alfred Bork, John Herman, Richard Ballard, Joseph Marasco. Potential energy as a graphic aid to study motion. Bound and unbound motion. Help sequences.

PROJECTILE; beginning Physics; Al Gonda, Joseph Marasco, Alfred Bork. Problem on projectile motion. Help sequence stresses tactics for problem-solving.

REFRAME; beginning Physics; Joseph Marasco, Al Gonda, Stephen Franklin. Reference systems.

ROTDYN; beginning Physics; Al Gonda, Joseph Marasco. Rotational dynamics.

ROTKIN; beginning Physics; Al Gonda, Joseph Marasco. Rotational kinematics.

SLOPE; beginning Physics; Alfred Bork, Stephen Franklin, Joseph Marasco. Graphic relationships between position, velocity, and acceleration. Help sequence.

SPRING; beginning Physics; Joseph Marasco, Al Gonda, Stephen Franklin. Mass on a spring as an example of a harmonic oscillator.

TWOBOD; beginning Physics; Stephen Franklin, Al Gonda, Joseph Marasco. Newton's third laws are applied to two gravitationally interactive bodies.

VECTORS; beginning Physics; Alfred Bork, John Herman, Joseph Marasco. Checks knowledge of vector manipulation, through the scalar product.

EDUCATIONAL TECHNOLOGY CENTER AT THE UNIVERSITY OF CALIFORNIA, IRVINE

This article describes the history, philosophy, outcomes, and other aspects of the Educational Technology Center at the University of California, Irvine. A major component of this activity was performed by the Physics Computer Development Project.

History

It is difficult to know where to start. I will take a personal point of view. My own interest in computers developed about 1959 when, as a faculty member at the University of Alaska, I attended IBM courses about a new computer, a 1620. This early, now seemingly primitive, machine was one of the first inexpensive machines with a higher-level language, FORTRAN. I participated in early use, working with a graduate student, Harold Leinbach, in developing a program that involves an electron coming through the atmosphere. A group watching the program execute became excited as to how far an electron would penetrate the atmosphere.

IFIPS Conference, London, September 1979. Reprinted by permission, North-Holland Publishing Company.

Soon after that, I began to teach a Physics class in which I saw natural ways to use the computer, making use of the excitement I had observed. This development continued for several years in Alaska until I left in 1962.

After Alaska, I tried to determine to what extent such work was being done elsewhere. I finally received a letter from someone within IBM, later to become a friend. He indicated that he didn't know much about using computers in education but that someone in Alaska was doing it. At this point I decided that I was on to something new!

After spending a year as a National Science Foundation Faculty Fellow at Harvard, working in the history of Physics, I went to Reed College. At Reed, first a 1620 and then an 1130 allowed me to continue working with computers. I was fortunate to be teaching a large Natural Science class for nonmajors; the computer became an adjunct to that class.

The Reed environment was limited to small computers. I made attempts to secure larger interactive systems in Portland, but that seemed to be in the future. Hence, when the opportunity was presented (through Kenneth Ford, then chairman of the Physics Department) to join the faculty at the University of California, Irvine, I moved.

Irvine had committed already in its earliest stages to the importance of the computer as a learning device. It obtained superior support for that purpose from the University of California system-wide.

The Irvine situation was not entirely smooth. I arrived in the middle of a computer crisis. A large joint project between IBM and the University was developing a timesharing system for educational purposes. The system was to be running when I arrived, but early tests showed problems. This and other factors, including resistance from research users, led to a hectic first year. At the end of that year, the IBM equipment left, and we had two new computers, a Honeywell Sigma 7 and a Digital Equipment Corporation PDP-10. I played a role in the choice.

About this time I received the first of a number of grants from the National Science Foundation. Table 3-1 shows the grants received at Irvine. Existence of good timesharing systems plus support from the National Science Foundation allowed me to do many of the things I had been planning.

The fact that we have been supported almost continually for a 10 year period has allowed us to make steady progress. Furthermore, it has led to increased use of computers within classes. For many years, certain beginning Physics and beginning Mathematics classes (discussed in Chapter 5) have given tests on-line; considerable additional material is used in those classes too. These two classes do not cover the complete range of educational usage at Irvine; but much of what happens in other classes is similar to that found in other institutions.

In addition to support from the National Science Foundation and the Fund for the Improvement of Postsecondary Education, we have received several types of support from the University of California. First, my department has been cooperative in allowing our work with computer-based learning materials to be my research activity at the University. This was agreed on before I reached the University. Second, through the Innovative Projects funds of the University, system-wide funds in the University of California that support curriculum development, we have had a series of grants (Table 3-2). While these grants have been smaller than the federal grants, they have been very helpful particularly in providing us capabilities for maintenance of programs.

Another major contribution from the University of California has been computer time. The University receives funds from the Legislature for instructional uses of computing. Irvine has used some of these funds for developmental purposes as well as the more standard uses for class work. Our project has benefited from these funds.

During the 12 years at Irvine, many people have played critical roles. Richard Ballard joined the project in 1970 as a co-director. Joseph Marasco joined the project in 1975 as another co-director. Both have now left; Joseph Marasco still works with us in the design and development of materials even though he has a full-time job elsewhere. Our senior programmer for many years was Estelle Warner. More recently, the people

Table 3-1. Federal Grant Support

Dates	Title	Amount
7-1-69 to 12-31-71	Development of Computer-Based Materials for Teaching Undergraduate Physics (NSF)	$ 350,426
1-17-71 to 9-30-72	College Science Improvement Program Cooperative Projects for Two-Year Colleges (NSF)	56,200
1-1-72 to 6-30-74	Computer-Based Interactive Graphics in Teaching Undergraduate Physics (NSF)	182,000
6-1-74 to 5-31-75	Computer Graphics in Learning (NSF)	213,100
6-1-75 to 5-31-76	Computer Graphics in Learning (NSF)	217,400
6-1-76 to 11-30-77	Computer Graphics in Learning (NSF)	230,433
5-1-77 to 4-30-78	Conference on Educational Applications Intelligent Videodisc Systems (NSF)	17,550
5-21-78 to 11-31-81	A Testing and Tutoring Environment for Large Science Course (CAUSE)	249,000
8-1-79 to 7-31-81	Scientific Literacy in the Public Library (FIPSE)	213,855
1-1-80 to 12-31-81	Development of Reasoning Skills in Early Adolescence (DISE)	179,000
	Total	$1,908,964

Table 3-2. University of California Grants

Dates	Title	Amount
1969/1970	Development of Physics Room at Irvine	$12,000
1972/1973	Development of Motivational and Remedial Units for Use in Beginning Physics Class	10,000
1973/1974	Development of Additional Materials for Physics 1	3,450
1974/1975	Developing Computer Dialogs	6,000
1974/1975	Uses of Irvine Physics Dialogs on Other UC Campuses	30,250
1974/1975	Computer Programs for Instruction of Medical Studies	9,400
1975/1976	Further Development of Instructional Material—Physics 3	3,792
1978/1979	Computer-Based Learning for Beginning Physics	10,448
	Total	$85,340

directly involved are Donald Darling, co-director of our NSF CAUSE grant, from the Mathematics Department at Irvine; Francis Collea, co-director of our NSF DISE grant, from California State University, Fullerton; Stephen Franklin, project director of the NSF CAUSE grant, from the Computing Facility; Barry Kurtz, project director for the FIPSE grant; David Trowbridge, project director for the NSF DISE grant; and Ruth von Blum, evaluator.

Our activities have depended on a very devoted, competent, and hard-working group of student programmers, almost entirely undergraduates, who have worked with the project for many years. Furthermore, visitors—often for extended periods of time—have made major contributions in helping us write programs and in their overall design.

Philosophy

As with any long and extended project, one would expect some changes in the philosophical positions of the project. But these were evolutionary changes, consistent with our earliest philosophy but offering some refinements.

The best source of information about the early philosophy came in speeches given by myself, at the Second Annual Conference on Computers in the Undergraduate Curriculum at Dartmouth in 1971[3] and at a SIGUCC meeting two years later[4].

The Dartmouth speech was one of three keynote speeches. I outlined principles that should guide anyone in the development of computer-aided learning materials, in the form of six "theses." The papers are in Chapter 1. The subtitle of the speech also reflected the project philosophy. It was "Let a Thousand Flowers Bloom." The emphasis was that, at that time, we were very much in a learning mode, understanding how to use computers effectively in learning environments. Therefore, the important thrust was to try many approaches, many modes of computer usage, rather than to focus early on a single approach. At present, everyone is still in this experimentation stage, but we are approaching the end of that period.

The strong emphasis on graphics in the early days of the project has continued. Our earliest grant emphasized graphic capabilities. Visual information plays an extremely important role in the learning process; every learning approach, whether involving computers or not, could normally expect to use graphic information.

This belief in graphics has been reinforced and deepened by our experiences. But graphics has come to take a larger meaning than it had at first. Initially, I had in mind only pictorial information. While this still plays a critical role, we now consider text itself to be a graphic component. The composition of each screen seen by students plays a major role in the effectiveness of the material. I will have more to say about visual design in the developmental process.

The project has never had a doctrinaire attitude toward the way the computer could be used in education, but has argued that many different ways might be usable. We have often been guided by the necessities of classes. One of the dominant aspects of our work in later years, for example, has been the use of interactive, on-line testing. These tests combine learning and testing, offering much help to students in trouble. But we came into this approach only gradually, as we encountered problems with large classes with our computer-based material.

Another shift in outlook was from developing individual pieces of material toward developing a total course. Initially it was the compelling examples that were of most interest to us. Often compelling examples turned out to mean compelling to us, to our evaluators, and to our many visitors rather than to the students. Some of the compelling examples were bombs with students! This pushed us into looking at total class environments.

Another shift came about through external developments. When the project began, an interactive system implied a timesharing system. So naturally, that type of hardware was assumed. The rise, particularly in the last several years, of inexpensive, powerful, stand-alone systems has completely altered the picture. Stand-alones offer tremendous advantages in marketing and delivery of computer-based learning materials. Hence, our recent work is focusing in that direction. While this does not affect the underlying pedagogical philosophy, it does very much affect our attitude toward transportability and related factors.

The project has differed from many other projects on the use of special "CAI" languages. The decision was made in the early days of the project that, because all the ways of using the computer educationally were not known, we would not tie ourselves to any CAI language. Rather, we work within general-purpose languages, exploiting the full capabilities of the computer. As we gained more experience, we would want to do things that we could not conceive of initially; so to begin by designing a language would be a mistake. We have found this to be a very effective position and have maintained it. This issue is further discussed in Chapter 6.

At the present time we are using a new Pascal-based system. The notion of working within very powerful, general-purpose, higher-level languages still seems the best way to proceed; we do not believe that existing CAI languages will survive.

Outcomes of the Project

I discuss the outcomes of our work under five headings—the student-computer dialogs, the use of the computer for problem-solving, course management, the design of full courses, and the Irvine production system.

Student-Computer Dialogs

The major continual activity of the Educational Technology Center has been the preparation of interactive student-computer dialogs, learning conversations between the people who prepare the material and the student. These programs take between 30 minutes and 1 and 1/2 hours of student time for completion. They are often run in a number of sessions and can, at the author's discretion, allow restart at the point reached in the previous session. Programs that provide student facilities are open-ended as to the amount of time involved. Although many of our dialogs have been written by members of the project, visitors often participate.

For convenience, I discuss the dialogs in a variety of categories. They cover a wide spectrum of pedagogical uses, not any single strategy. These categories, as with all human classification systems, furnish no absolute distinctions; often categories are blurred. Several aspects often occur within a single program.

An important early concentration was in interactive proof dialogs. The notion was to let students develop important proofs in the course in an interactive fashion. This is to be contrasted with the student seeing the proof as done by the instructor on the blackboard or as displayed in a textbook, a passive process. Students could better develop capabilities of doing such proofs themselves if they played an active role. Many early dialogs were in this tradition. The earliest dialog, CONSERVE, written by Noah Sherman at the University of Michigan and myself, is an example. A more modern example is MOMENTUM, a joint product of myself and Robert Eisberg of the University of California, Santa Barbara.

A second class of dialogs helps students develop concepts. Our strategy is to avoid the authoritarian approach of many classes where concepts are introduced by fiat. We attempt to convince students that some necessity exists for a concept before the name of the concept is introduced. Thus, in the dialog 3D (Arthur Luehrmann and myself) the notions of divergence, curl, and gradient are arrived at as generalizations on the concept of derivative, before the student has seen the names of these quantities. The FIELD program introduces, with some use of simulation, the notion of electric field, again interactively.

A similar collection of dialogs is concerned with formal reasoning capabilities. We assume that these students are not full formal reasoners, but are reasoning in what Piaget would refer to as concrete modes. This work has been guided by our collaboration with Arnold Arons in the Physics Department at the University of Washington. Six timesharing programs have been written jointly with Arons and myself; Joseph Marasco was also involved in one of these programs, HEAT. Three of the programs concern magnetic fields, and two concern astronomy—the sky as seen from the earth and the phases of the moon. Several are discussed in more detail in Chapter 4.

Laboratory simulations are also useful. We can provide an experimental situation for students similar to experiments that might be carried out in laboratories. But more experiments can be carried out in a short period of time, and students can be immediately queried as to the meaning of the results. The most extensive dialog of this kind is HOCKEY, primarily due to Robert Eisberg. The experiments involve colliding pucks, first in one dimension and then in two dimensions, with three types of collisions considered. The aim is to arrive at the notions of mass, momentum, and conservation of momentum.

Controllable worlds are a type of simulation too but with emphasis on a broader capability than those provided in the laboratory environment. The student can freely manipulate the world. The first controllable world, MOTION, provided a flexible $\mathbf{F} = m\mathbf{a}$ world with the student picking force laws, initial conditions, equation constants, and what to plot. It was developed by Richard Ballard and myself. FIELD provides the ability to plot electrostatic field lines and equipotential lines.

Attempts to produce extensions of this idea were not successful. We tried a range of such simulations that provided much greater flexibility in interacting with students. But in spite of considerable project resources, only one such program reached running form, and this had a limited subject area.

The possibilities with on-line testing were first explored by Stephen Franklin within the precalculus mathematics course. The tests gave a very natural way to conduct a personalized system of instruction course. They relieved instructors of the routine burdens of testing and record-keeping, while providing quick feedback to students.

After our initial experiences with tests, we became more impressed with the possibilities, particularly in combining within tests the learning capabilities we had been providing in our dialogs. The intriguing possibility was to offer direct assistance to students, finding out just what the student errors were and responding immediately with pertinent help. The 27 on-line mechanics tests were developed with this in mind. They cover the first quarter of a beginning science-engineering physics course (several tracks, as discussed in Chapter 5).

These examples do not cover all the possibilities, but they give an impression of the types of materials we have produced. Chapter 4 offers details on some of the dialogs.

Use of the Computer for Problem-Solving

One of the most important aspects of the use of the computer within courses is in providing the ability for students to use this powerful intellectual tool to solve their own problems. The computer thus "expands" the human intellect. This use of the computer allows new approaches to courses that were impossible before the computer existed.

One major question is what computer languages students should use for this problem-solving activity. Project members have developed a continually revised position paper with regard to this issue, appearing later in this volume, in Chapter 5. We felt that the issue of languages should be rationally decided! We should be able to set criteria as to what was desirable, and then compare existing languages against these criteria. The result is that the two choices that are "best" for contemporary science-engineering students are APL and Pascal. The arguments for each are different. The least desirable language for this purpose is BASIC. In most cases, this issue is decided either simply on what is available or on emotional grounds.

In addition to picking the right language, another important overall issue is that of efficient methods of learning the language. If a computer language is to be learned as a part of another course, such as a physics course, learning must be very efficient in terms of student time. Traditionally, university courses have not considered efficient use of student time. Often it is the professor's time that is economized! But student time is an important issue.

We have used two effective ways of teaching languages. The first approach is to start with whole programs, to explain these programs, and then to have the students make modifications. The second approach, which we have used extensively in APL, is the ten-finger approach. The student sits down, gets into APL, and is given (in separate printed material) a series of lines to type. By observing the results of these lines, a controlled discovery process is generated.

Course Management

A major problem in large courses is the bookkeeping problem, the recording of grades, and the compilation of final scores. Many computer systems have been designed to help with pieces or all of this problem. As we moved toward large courses, we became more concerned with course management.

We designed a general course management system with little restriction on the type of course. The same facility works for both a traditional course and for a self-paced mastery course taught through the Personalized System of Instruction (PSI or Keller plan). The course structure, including all the information about what things were within the course, is part of the data base.

An important component of any course management system is the recording of information. This can come directly from the on-line quizzes or through secretaries, instructors, or off-line activities.

Another role of a management system, particularly in a Personalized System of Instruction environment, is control of the quizzes—the question of who can take what quizzes and when. This is a function of course structure, determined by the course instructor. Some modules may depend on other modules and some may not. It may be desirable to impose a time delay after a student has not passed a quiz, before allowing the student to take the quiz over again. It may also be desirable to impose a limit on the number of times a quiz can be taken before the student must see the instructor.

A final aspect of course management is feedback providing information to the instructor and to the student. The instructor needs flexible feedback to spot problems developing in the class. He or she can contact individual students based on this information. Our management system allows these variants, including feedback to aid the instructor in spotting potential problems. See "Course Management System for the Physics 3 Course at Irvine" in Chapter 5.

Full Courses

Development of complete courses puts together the components already discussed and brings in factors that have not been discussed. We have used the computer for courses difficult to offer in other ways.

The major emphasis is to provide greater choices for students. Students should have a variety of choices offered in few traditional courses. The use of the PSI environment, not unique to us, allowed students to choose their pace through the material. A choice in learning materials is also desirable.

A rarer choice that we provide is that of providing different content within the same course. The on-line quizzes covered several contents; no one student took all 27 quizzes. The strategy could be extended to allow several courses within the same administrative format and with the same staff.

In the development of a course, much material is needed besides the dialogs. Module descriptions were prepared for each of the student tracks. For one of the alternate approaches, a full set of notes, begun at Reed College, was further developed while at Irvine. A set of exercises for increasing intuition, used with the controllable world dialogs, was generated. Our philosophy on learning material is to provide a great variety of learning materials associated with each of the units.

The two principal courses developed were the precalculus mathematics course, developed primarily outside the Center but using our software, and the first quarter of the introductory Physics course.

Methods of Implementation

One of our major interests has been the development of an effective production system. By a production system, I refer to the entire process of producing computer-related learning materials. Such a system should be friendly to the various people who work with it, particularly the instructors involved in the project. It should reduce costs as far as possible. It should lead to highly effective material.

Many production systems developed almost without thought. They could be described as cottage industry systems, where the approach was for one person to do all the work. The cottage industry approach, while it may work for early experimental stages, is inappropriate for large-scale production. Furthermore, the whole "lore" that grew up with it, including a collection of special languages, will, we believe, have to be abandoned eventually.

The problem suggested a systems approach, an analysis of the process involved and a structuring of a system to meet the needs. One aspect of such an investigation was examining other models. The most suitable models seemed to be those already used for large-scale production of educational materials. Within academic situations, the work at The Open University in the United Kingdom was particularly interesting, even though it used computers only rarely. The structure of the textbook industry also gives very useful clues.

One important criterion of the production system from the earliest stages was that it should not restrict the materials produced. We felt unhappy with systems where the authors were put in procrustean beds to make later stages of the process easier. The focus should always be on pedagogical or instructional design, and the greatest freedom should be allowed at that stage. Many widely discussed systems impose major restrictions on the teachers developing the learning modules.

We gradually evolved toward a production system involving seven steps. In each of these processes, different people play dominant roles. Some steps are well understood in much of our current activities. Others we believe we understand, but are typically not in a position to carry out fully. In one case, the process is one where much is to be learned. These issues are more extensively discussed in Chapter 6.

The first and focal part of the activity is instructional design, development of the complete pedagogical specification of the materials to run on the computer. Since faculty members are experts on how to promote learning in their subject areas, they must play a major role in this process. Educational psychologists and instructional designers may also be involved. We have found this activity works best in groups of two or three, working intensely. Pleasant environments away from interruptions in the usual university settings and away from telephones, are a necessity. The work is not easy; unlike ordinary teaching activities the teachers must design a whole range of conversations at a single time and must look carefully at what student problems should be considered. The instructors need detailed acquaintance with students to be perceptive in the handling of these problems. They work by creating informal flowcharts, specifying all the decisions to be made, the text, and the drawings. I emphasize that this is the most important stage of the production process.

The second stage in production—the editorial process—is the least understood part. Many book publishers are accustomed to a major editorial role. They may feel uncertain about the present situation because they do not see a clear editorial process. In our recent activities, we have found that people who are familiar with the instructional design of computer materials can take other people's material in flowchart form, and make editorial comments. With the text and visuals, the process is like the editorial process for book-like environments. But when it comes to the question of what decisions are to be made based on student input, the issues become fuzzier. More experience is needed.

The growing importance of visual design in our project has been considered. Early computer material almost entirely ignored this, letting things appear on the screen or page simply where the computer language chose to put them. We have moved consistently toward a conscious control of the design process.

The ideal person to be involved in screen design is a competent graphic designer, a person who might do layout for a magazine ad. For this designer to function effectively, it is necessary to develop specialized software. Our screen design software allows such an individual to sit at a computer screen, to compose a variety of elements, to move them around the screen, to change their size and shape in various ways, and then to tell the program to write the necessary code. Both graphic and alphanumeric aspects are covered; a variety of textual treatments are allowed. Newer developments working with stand-alone systems with selective erase capabilities are bringing in such new possibilities as the ability to control scrolling and formatting within individual areas of the screen while not affecting the rest of the screen.

The next component in the production system is logic design closely related to traditional computer programming activities. This work is done by programmers, either professional programmers or those particularly trained for this purpose. We employ undergraduate students.

The question of language environment for logic design must be considered. In the cottage industry stage, specialized languages were designed with the pious (but unsatisfied) hope that they would be easy to use by ordinary teachers. Such languages as Coursewriter, PILOT, PLANET, and Tutor fit into this category. Others developed query-based systems. We felt that any such language would limit the material produced, and we preferred to stay within powerful, general-purpose computer languages, developing whatever special capabilities were needed within that environment. Thus, if we required new resources, they could be constructed because we were working within a general-purpose language. Our older work used a mixture of assembly language macros for the interaction, FORTRAN for calculation, APL for interactive design, and COBOL for data base management. Our newer work is proceeding within Pascal as a single language for all aspects.

After the program is initially prepared, the next stage is for the individuals involved to sit down together and run the program a few times, suggesting changes. Learning sequences look different on the screen than they do on paper; many new elements come in through a series of reworkings of the program.

Next, student use is essential. No matter how good the designers were, the question of how the material works with actual students is critical. An important point is that the computer can save detailed information, and this can be a powerful aid in improving the dialog.

The next obvious stage is modification of the program based on information obtained. The strategies in the above stages must allow easy modification, often by programmers and graphic designers other than those initially involved. These last several phases may go through a number of cycles with modifications leading to new class use leading to new modifications.

Internal Evaluation

Two types of evaluation will be considered, internal evaluation activities conducted by the Center and external evaluations conducted either with project funds or through independent agencies or individuals. Perhaps the major test of the Irvine materials has been their repeated use in large classes. Unlike projects which develop materials used only in trial classes, we have aimed at dialogs that can be used in large class environments in regular courses, a "true test" of the material. Use with a few students where project members play a major role (either intentionally or unintentionally) does not show whether the materials are adequate for general environments. Our mechanics material has been used for five separate quarters in two beginning Physics courses. Over 1000 students have been involved.

One of our major interests in working with large classes is to see whether the course restructuring ideas, allowing students to choose content, can be carried out in typical large courses. In each of the classes we have offered a variety of choices. We have demonstrated that the instructor can decide for a particular course what the options should be and that students can be sufficiently informed to make choices.

External Evaluation

Several external studies of the project can be mentioned. The most elaborate was conducted by Michael Scriven with funds from our grants from the National Science Foundation. Two major aspects of this study were examination of the course itself while running and an examination of some of the controllable world dialogs. Participating in the study were Jill Larkin and Mark St. John from the Sesame program at Berkeley. The formative study tended to agree with our internal evaluations of the courses' strengths and weaknesses. The material that received the highest rating was the help sequences in the on-line quizzes. Students felt deprived in quizzes that did not have help sequences. On the other hand, the material that still presents the greatest need for improvement is that designed to increase physical intuition. We are rewriting this material based on advice from the evaluators.

Another type of external evaluation could be described as peer review. Several aspects are interesting. We often "exhibit" at national meetings with gratifying results. The project has had a steady group of visitors from all over the world. These visitors have often written glowing descriptions of the project.

A more formal peer review occurred in connection with *Change* magazine's project to identify innovative teaching in the United States[5]. The *Change* project was *not* particularly concerned with computers but rather with excellent courses. It was a discipline-oriented project. In each case, *Change* went to the discipline leaders of education and asked for a selection of projects. *Change* then made a preliminary investigation of these projects and selected typically four projects for major articles in each discipline. Our project was one of the four in the country chosen in Physics.

The Future of Computer-Based Learning

It is important in a dynamic area as computer-based learning to think about the future. We should suggest where developments should take place next to ensure that this learning tool will develop as rapidly and as powerfully as possible. This is particularly critical in an area where large companies will soon be involved in marketing activities. Chapter 7 considers this further.

The following topics indicate important areas. We cannot do all of these within our own project. However, many show directions we would like to pursue.

Research in Learning

We still have much to learn about the learning process and about how the computer can be effectively used in learning. Hence, continued research in computer-aided learning is essential; we have only scratched the surface. The issue of more effective production of material also needs additional work.

I do not believe that all developmental efforts should stop until this research takes place. That would only lead to poorer materials, because others, not always with views we might like, will continue to work.

Personal or Stand-Alone Systems

I have argued in several articles that the future of computer-based learning will be very much dominated by intelligent stand-alone systems, systems which will only on rare occasions converse with another computer elsewhere. These systems will continue to decrease in cost and increase in sophistication for a long period.

Of particular importance will be the increasing number of home computers. I have seen estimates that 800,000 personal computers have already been sold, and projections of a saturation market of 60,000,000 in the United States. This market will continue to grow as large vendors enter it.

The personal computers of today are not entirely suitable for educational purposes. But they are improving rapidly. It is interesting to note that one can buy complete graphic systems (stand-alone computers) for less than one can buy graphic displays. Older graphic displays tended to be ordinary CRT displays with a separate new component to handle graphics. More recent stand-alone devices are integrated designs, so these new systems can realize cost savings because of this approach.

Intelligent Videodisc

Another important hardware factor in the immediate future will be the development and use of what I have termed the "intelligent videodisc" system. The idea is to combine the capabilities of the stand-alone computer and the new optical videodisc systems. The videodisc systems are available for the industrial-educational market and for the home market. Home systems are currently selling for about $700. Chapter 7 gives more details.

The importance of systems for education that combine the computer and the videodisc is that they allow us to bring into the computer-based learning environment a full multimedia capability. Thus, at any point within a learning sequence a slide, video sequence, or audio message can be presented. All of these media and the computer code can be stored on the same inexpensive, long-lasting disc.

The market is a mass market. Discs are expensive in small quantities but become cheap when quantities are large. The discs are easy to handle. Several developmental projects are proceeding, but much additional work is needed. The economic issue of computer alone versus computer plus videodisc must be carefully investigated.

Continual Improvement in Quality

Much effort in the last 20 years has gone into understanding how to use the computer as a learning device. In addition to research, part of this is simply the gaining of experience, the trying of many possibilities.

We still need further experience. Although the materials now available are better and more effective than those of a few years back, they still represent only a glimmering of the future potential. Almost all current modules will look relatively primitive in only a few years, even to our best efforts at this time. Very little that is currently available will find its way into commercial release.

Increased Use

The current use of computer-based learning material in education at any level is almost trivial. Even in universities that claim to be doing much of it, only a few courses are typically involved. The major delivery system in education worldwide is the combination of lecture-textbook, starting at an early age and continuing through graduate school.

In the next few years, we will see a sharp rise of computer-based learning activity, as more effective materials and less expensive machines are available. Increased use will be seen at all levels of education, in both traditional and newly developed nontraditional learning situations.

Further Developments in Production Systems

The development process of computer-based learning materials at Irvine has been described. Further studies of this process and developments of variants are essential for progress. We need to refine our techniques so that effective material can be produced at reasonable cost.

Specific problems exist as already pointed out. For example, the question of how to use editorial services within the process needs further experience.

Large-Scale Production and Distribution

Currently our production and distribution modes for computer-based learning material are almost nonexistent. A few organizations such as CONDUIT are distributing a limited range of materials. All the marketing, production, and distribution mechanisms for established educational media (such as textbooks) do not exist for computer material. Thus, if a mathematics professor is looking for computer-based learning material for either part of a course or an entire course, there is no where to turn at present except in limited areas.

As usage increases and as the commercial vendors see a larger market in the home and schools, we can confidently expect that more material will be available, and that national marketing activities will begin. Interesting questions arise as to which kinds of companies will be involved in this process. A number of existing companies have a stake in the market. One is the textbook publisher. Another is the computer hardware manufacturer.

But new companies may be involved. Several such companies have already come into existence, and more may appear as older companies find that it is hard to adapt to new conditions. The article on large-scale production and distribution, in Chapter 6, discusses these issues.

Changes in Traditional Institutions

As some traditional institutions begin to use the computer more, questions will arise as to how these institutions will change, and also as to what will happen as other institutions, with conservative policies, resist change.

The computer allows new educational possibilities. It allows self-pacing not only within individual courses but within the entire curriculum. Courses need not start on quarter, semester, or term boundaries. Students need not spend a fixed amount of time in either individual courses or in the entire educational program of the institution. With new and powerful learning resources available around the clock and with these resources being individualized so students can move at their own pace, we can expect changes.

Along with these scheduling changes may come changes in the grading system. Many studies have indicated that current normative grades have almost no correlation with any aspect of the student's life after school. While the possibility of grading by competencies completed is new (and so little evidence is available concerning its connection with the real world), it provides new opportunities to make success in school relevant to success in society.

Some institutions will resist changes and will regard the computer as the work of the devil. The interesting question will be whether these organizations will continue to remain competitive, as students become aware of the effectivness of computer-based learning and as society becomes more concerned with the costs of traditional education.

Changes in the Role of Teachers

Teachers are concerned with the effect of the computer on their status. One obvious answer is that the large-scale production of computer-based learning material, already mentioned, will require very large numbers of teachers. Hence, many teachers may shift roles from the deliverer of courses to the designer and developer of materials.

A second role of the teacher will be to respond to learning problems that the computer and other learning media available cannot handle. There will always be need for teacher expertise to determine why the student is not learning in spite of a rich variety of available modes and approaches. I already see such a change developing in my own experiences with classes that depend heavily on the computer. This will mean that the teacher will spend less time in large group environments and more with individual students.

New Institutions

Perhaps the most exciting development in the period ahead will be the rise of new types of educational institutions, some resembling such recent institutions as The Open University in the United Kingdom. Many of these new institutions will capitalize on the computer as a learning device, particularly as the computer becomes more available in public libraries, and other public places such as science museums, shopping centers, airline terminals, and homes. Others may develop from extension services of existing institutions, while some institutions may be entirely new.

New Educational Systems

The rise of new types of institutions, the demise of some of the more traditional institutions, plus the changes in other formal institutions imply massive changes in the educational system—a new system. This is perhaps the most difficult of the changes to foresee, since it depends on so many other factors already introduced. This development will be the capstone of the entire movement.

THE EDUCATIONAL TECHNOLOGY CENTER

This article reports on the Educational Technology Center at the University of California, Irvine. The primary focus of the Center is the use of the computer as a learning aid. The Educational Technology Center started on January 1, 1980, with University funds providing staff support. The Center continues the activities in computer-based learning conducted by the Physics Computer Development Project during the previous 11 years.

Need

The Educational Technology Center was formed because we believe strongly that the next two decades will be a critical period in American education. Such centers are needed to guide us toward a future where the computer will play an extremely important role in education. It is important to develop a number of continuing groups that are not fully dependent on grant funds but have an existence beyond support for particular projects.

National Educational Computing Conference II, *Proceedings*.

We have pursued for some years within the University of California the possibility of one such center. We will provide guidance to others working in this area. The Center will work on a wide range of research and development activities leading to more effective use of the computer and associated technologies in learning.

Current Activities

The Educational Technology Center engages in many activities concerning more effective and more efficient use of information technology in learning, emphasizing the personal computer. Some of the activities will be pure research, while others will have strong applied and developmental components. We shall work closely with individuals and groups elsewhere, as in the past, so that the Center has a nationwide effect beyond its immediate activities, materials, and publicity.

The Center will publish a newsletter reviewing the activities and results of its projects. Although no set schedule is planned, we expect this newsletter to be published three times a year. Anyone interested in receiving the newsletter should write to the Center.

The following list gives the active projects at the Irvine Center. Further information about any activity is available on request.

I. A testing and tutoring environment for large science courses.

   A. Authoring for personal computers

      1. Testing environments
      2. Physics—waves
      3. Statistics

National Science Foundation—Comprehensive Assistance to Undergraduate Science Education (CAUSE).

II. Scientific literacy in the public library.

   A. Public libraries, shopping centers, science museums
   B. Public understanding of science
   C. Personal computers

Fund for the Improvement of Postsecondary Education (FIPSE)

III. Mathematics competency tests for beginning science courses.

University of California/California State University and Colleges.

IV. Biology materials

   A. Ecology

University of California, Irvine, Committee on Instructional Development

V. Development of reasoning skills in early adolescence.

   A. Junior high school students
   B. Transition to formal reasoning
   C. Personal computers

National Science Foundation—Developments in Science Education (DISE)

Production System

In addition to specific products, such as those just mentioned, the Center has developed a production system for generating computer-based learning material. The emphasis is on both efficiency and effectiveness and on techniques that will allow natural extensions to large-scale production of learning modules. The production system is based on a systems analysis of the problem and on our many years of experience in producing a wide range of learning material, as discussed in Chapter 6. Specific details are available from the Educational Technology Center.

Issues for the Future

We can distinguish several very important issues that will shape the future of computer-based learning; these issues indicate directions the Educational Technology Center will pursue. No order of priority is intended in this list.

1. *Full-scale course development.* At present, with a few notable exceptions, computer-based learning materials are supplementary to course structures. Very

few full courses make heavy use of computers to aid learning. We need experience in developing such complete courses and in integrating computer and other learning aids. We need additional experience in computer-aided delivery of such courses.

2. *Expanded acquaintance.* Very few teachers, and even fewer members of the general public, have seen effective computer-based learning material. Often the examples seen have been weak examples; so the learners have formed inaccurate opinions of the value of such material. We need more acquaintance with the full range of possibilities, more computer literacy with a learning emphasis.

3. *Research in learning.* Presently we have conflicting theories about learning. We need to know more about how students learn so that we can develop better learning aids.

4. *Production techniques.* Older strategies for developing materials often were not suited for the large-scale development needed in the years ahead. The types of systems approach followed at Irvine and elsewhere needs further exploration and refinement as the scale of activities increases. We should aim for the best possible materials at the least developmental cost.

5. *Expanding technologies.* Computer and associated technologies are evolving rapidly. We must learn quickly to use an expanding range of capabilities, developing materials that are not immediately outmoded.

6. *The computer as a new interactive medium.* In understanding a new learning medium, we must learn how it differs from older media. For example, reading from computer displays has many differences from reading print medium, but the empirical details are not known.

7. *Dissemination.* New media also demand new modes of dissemination.

8. *New course and institutional structures.* As computers are more widely used, they will have major effects on course and institutional structures.

The Educational Technology Center intends to pursue these and other issues.

References

1. *Spacetime Physics,* Edwin F. Taylor, John Archibald Wheeler (San Francisco: W. H. Freeman and Co., 1963) p. 152.

2. *Spacetime Physics,* Edwin F. Taylor, John Archibald Wheeler (San Francisco: W. H. Freeman and Co., 1963) p. 155.

3. Proceedings, Second Annual Conference on Computers in the Undergraduate Curriculum, Dartmouth, 1971.

4. SIGUCC Meeting, 1973.

5. "Report on Teaching: Analyses of Some of the Most Notable Improvements in American Undergraduate Teaching" *Change*, January 1978.

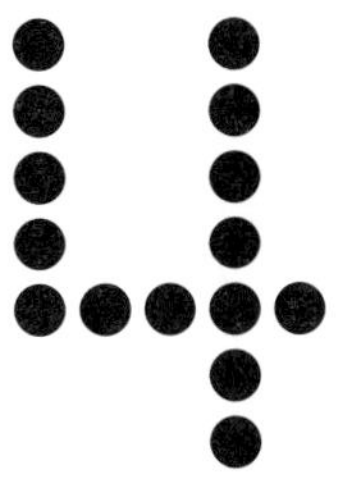

Physics

COMPUTER APPLICATIONS IN MECHANICS

With Herbert Peckham

Abstract

One of the most striking illustrations of how the computer can transform a beginning course into something quite different from that usually encountered, occurs with the early parts of the introductory mechanics.

This article reviews the various ways in which the computer can be used within the mechanics section of a beginning Physics course. While the authors are concerned primarily with the introductory college course, many of the details would be applicable to high school Physics courses.

Reprinted with permission from *Computers and Education,* vol. 3, A. Bork and H. Peckham, "Computer Applications in Mechanics,"

The Great Promise

In all beginning Physics courses, mechanics is based on Newton's laws of motion. These powerful laws, we tell students, enable us to find out how anything moves. Furthermore, mechanics is historically the first successful physical theory, one that served as the model for the development of all the rest of science. The second law is particularly powerful; this relatively simple law predicts correctly an enormous variety of phenomena, ranging from simple motions on the earth to motions of full galaxies. This success is still one of the most impressive results of all science.

In the typical beginning course the progression is like this. First, kinematical notions of position, velocity, and acceleration are defined, sometimes with the aid of calculus. Usually some kinematical problems, such as projectile motion, will be introduced before the Laws of Motion are considered. Then $\mathbf{F} = m\mathbf{a}$ is introduced for the single body point particle system, hopefully with a careful discussion in operational terms of the meaning of mass and force.

But at this point we forget the major promise we made earlier, that this law will be powerful enough to tell us how everything moves. Rather, we consider a series of applications to relatively trivial mechanical systems (masses over pulleys, blocks sliding down inclined planes) or special cases of interesting systems (planets moving in purely circular orbits). Whether the course uses calculus or not, few beginning courses have considered $\mathbf{F} = m\mathbf{a}$ as a differential equation. Yet its full power as a predictive tool, as seen from any intermediate or advanced mechanics course or as seen from its applications in such practical problems as putting a satellite on Mars, demands that it must be used as a differential equation! Thus, we give students the form of the law, but we offer no way to understand how that form leads to predictions in a wide variety of mechanical situations.

Numbers, Numbers, Numbers

The usual reason is that students do not have sufficient mathematical background to treat the laws of motion immediately as differential equations. Hence, this approach is put off to intermediate mechanics, a course with only a small fraction of the students from the beginning course. Thus, the vast majority of the people who take Physics never see the laws of motion in a form where they can really do what they are supposed to do! The few courses, such as the Berkeley Physics mechanics course, that have tried to treat $\mathbf{F} = m\mathbf{a}$ as a differential equation through analytic solutions have proven to be not accessible to the majority of the beginning students.

However, an alternative exists, simple, straightforward, and practical at all beginning levels. We can approach the equations of motion immediately as differential equations if numerical techniques are used. The computer makes this a practical technique from the student point of view.

The idea is not new. There are at least two "classical" references to the use of this tactic, both predating the utilization of computers in teaching physics at the beginning level. The first is in Chalmers Sherwin's book, *Basic Concepts of Physics*[1], the second is in *The Feynman Lectures in Physics*[2]. The Feynman material clearly shows Feynman's own enthusiasm for this procedure. Seldom does one see the writer of a beginning textbook get so enthusiastic about the use of **F** = *m***a**. Thus, Feynman says at the beginning of the chapter[3]:

> ". . . before this chapter we could not calculate how a mass on a spring would move; much less could we calculate the perturbations on the planet Uranus due to Jupiter and Saturn. After this chapter we *will* be able to compute not only the motion of the oscillating mass, but also the perturbations . . ."

At the end of the chapter Feynman once more picks up this enthusiasm[4]:

> "So as we said, we began this chapter not knowing how to calculate even the motion of a mass on a spring. Now, armed with the tremendous power of Newton's laws, we can not only calculate such simple motions but also, given only a machine to handle the arithmetic, even the tremendously complex motions of the planets, to as a high a degree of precision as we wish!"

The exclamation mark is Feynman's own.

The Three Faces

The basis of the numerical method used in both Feynman and Sherwin and most of the computer-based approaches described is the Euler method for solving differential equations. It can be looked at from several points of view.

Feynman considers the method as approximating derivatives by finite differences. Thus, we replace

$$V = DX/DT$$

by

$$\mathbf{V} = \frac{\mathbf{X}_{new} - \mathbf{X}_{old}}{\mathbf{T}_{new} - \mathbf{T}_{old}}$$

Transposing this into a calculational form, we obtain:

$$\mathbf{X}_{new} = \mathbf{X}_{old} + \mathbf{V} \times (t_{new} - t_{old})$$

A similar step can be taken with acceleration, giving the approximate equation

$$\mathbf{V}_{new} = \mathbf{V}_{old} + \mathbf{a} \times (t_{new} - t_{old})$$

Then **F** = *m***a** plays its role; it tells us how to find the acceleration from force; the force generally will be a function of position and velocity.

At least two alternate ways exist to obtain these same equations, the basis for the numerical approach to **F** = *m***a**. One is to start from everyday phenomena. The equation for the new position is one that can easily be explained in terms of simple experience. It says that the new position is equal to the old position plus the velocity times the time interval, just what any American 12-year-old knows about cars.

That is, if you tell a 12-year-old that you are 10 miles away from Los Angeles and traveling away, and that you traveled 30 miles an hour for 3 hours, he or she will know that you are now 100 miles away.

A third approach that arises with these same equations, much rarer in practice, is one that has been followed by one of the authors. It starts with Newton's approach to mechanics, which is geometrical and considers only blow-like forces. The equation for position is a form of Newton's first law, keeping the particle moving along the straight line and covering equal distances and equal times. The second equation (with the replacement of acceleration by force over mass) is the algebraic equivalent of Newton's geometrical use of the second law. This approach has many nice features, including the fact that students have a visual way of thinking about what is happening with the equations.

One benefit of using the computer in the introductory Physics course has not been emphasized enough. The computer can be used to provide insights into mathematics that are difficult to obtain by other means. The idea of a limit, for example, seems to be an elusive one for the beginner. If, however, the student is using the computer to investigate the instantaneous rate of change of position versus time in a physics problem, the notion of the limit becomes quite clear. Or once the student sees sinusoids plotted as the solution to the harmonic oscillator problem, it is certainly much easier to motivate the analytical solution to the differential equation of motion. We have had good results with a motion problem where the force is proportional to velocity. In this problem, students were introduced to the numerical approximation to the derivative, they were able to "discover" that the exponential function is its own derivative. Again, the implications to mathematics classes are obvious. The important point is that students may acquire a better understanding of analytical techniques if they are introduced to them first in a numerical context.

The Student as Computer

With any of these three approaches, the fundamental equation and the essential numerical method is the same. With the plethora of electronic pocket calculators currently available, students can be encouraged, or required, to perform some hand calculations using these results before they go to the computer. This is probably desirable, as it convinces students that they can carry out the computation that the computer is doing.

Such student activity can be encouraged either by means of problems, or perhaps as part of a required assignment in the course. For example, in beginning Physics courses at the University of California, Irvine, one of the on-line quizzes gets the student to make precisely this computation.

Table 4-1 Harmonic Oscillator Program in Five Programming Languages

JOSS

```
1.1   T=0
1.2   X=1
1.3   V=0
1.4   D=.1
1.5   X=X + V*D
1.6   V=V – X*D
1.7   T=T + D
1.8   TYPE T,X
1.9   IF T<3. TO STEP 1.5
```

BASIC

```
110   LET T = 0
120   LET X = 1
130   LET V = 0
140   LET D = .1
150   LET X = X + V*D
160   LET V = V – X*D
170   LET T = T + D
180   PRINT T ; X
190   IF T < 3 THEN 150
200   END
```

FORTRAN

```
      T = 0.
      X = 1.
      V = 0.
      D = .1
10    X = X + V*D
      V = V – X*D
      T = T + D
      WRITE (6.70) T,X
      IF (T – 3.) 10, 10, 14
14    STOP
70    FORMAT (F10.2, F12.4)
      END
```

APL

```
      HARMONIC
[1]   T←0
[2]   X←1
[3]   V←0
[4]   D←0.1
[5]   CALCULATE:X←X + V × D
[6]   V←V – X × D
[7]   T←T + D
[8]   T,X
[9]   →CALCULATE × T < 3
```

PL/1

```
OSCILLATOR: PROCEDURE OPTIONS (MAIN):
      T = 0; X = 1; V = 0; D = .1;
CALCULATE: X = X + V*D; V = V – X*D; T = T + D;
      PUT SKIP DATA (T, X);
      IF T < 3 THEN GO TO CALCULATE;
END OSCILLATOR;
```

Finally, the Computer

As mentioned, the Feynman approach assumes that the students will do hand calculation, perhaps in problems to solve **F**= *m***a** for a variety of problems. But this is tedious, the kind of thing the student will quickly identify as busy work once the basic method is understood in a few calculations. At this point, the student is well motivated to seek aid from a calculational assistant, the computer. The simple program required can be written in almost any standard beginning language. Table 4-1, for example, is a program for the harmonic oscillator, written in five different programming languages.

This is the simplest of all possible calculations for the oscillator, and does not use any fancy tricks to improve things. The early steps are simply setting the initial values for the position and velocity, X and V. D is the time step; from the Newtonian point of view it is the time between successive blows. From the usual numerical approximation point of view it is the finite time step that replaces the "infinitesimal" time of the derivative. The fact that the system is an oscillator enters only in the calculation for the velocity; so we have a general method for solving one-dimensional mechanical problems.

Note that in the above calculation the units have been chosen in "natural" units with $K/m = 1$. Feynman, and some of the other references to be mentioned later, discuss natural units. They are not essential, but they do lead to a simpler calculation and to some insight into the system's behavior. However, some students have difficulty with the notion of switching units to make a particular problem more convenient.

Other Forces

The fact that the force enters into only one line in the program is a clear indication that we have here a general method for solving any one-dimensional problem. Thus, the student can at this point be presented with the whole variety of very interesting physical systems to analyze. These include such things as anharmonic oscillators, with force laws such as

$$F = -k\,X - e\,X^3$$

and damped oscillators (where velocity-dependent terms are added to the oscillator force). In this last case it is possible to consider not only the usual linear damping (in many books mainly because it's a case that can be solved analytically), but we can also investigate nonlinear damping, such as damping which depends on the cube of the velocity. One-dimensional gravitational motion, with (l/r^2) force is also a possibility.

Evan Jones of Sierra College has ingenuously used motion pictures of everyday phenomena to bring liberal arts physics students to grips with forces and accelerations[5]. His films of airplanes taking off and landing, drag races, projectile motion, a sledge hammer driving stakes at a circus, an athlete on a trampoline, etc., are projected frame at a time on a chalk board where position information can be measured. The frame rate of the film gives the time corresponding to each position. Then, computer analysis of position versus time produces the desired accelerations. Jones, in what must certainly be one of the all-time-great physics demonstrations, arranged for a private filming of a belly dancer, the film subsequently being used by his class to study navel forces!

Away from the Line

One-dimensional problems have only a limited interest, as most interesting physical situations concern two- and three-dimensional motion. Hence, the extension of these methods to more dimensions is of great interest.

Luckily, once the basic notions have been developed for the one-dimensional case, little new appears for two and three dimensions. The basic notion is that $\mathbf{F} = m\mathbf{a}$ must hold component by component, as do the definitions of position and velocity. Thus, each of the following vector equations corresponds to two or three component equations, for two or three dimensions.

$$\mathbf{X}_{new} = \mathbf{X}_{old} + \mathbf{V} \times (t_{new} - t_{old})$$

and

$$\mathbf{V}_{new} = \mathbf{V}_{old} + \mathbf{a} \times (t_{new} - t_{old})$$

In BASIC, FORTRAN, and Pascal, this implies variables for each of the components and several equations. In

```
BASIC
100   PRINT "MOTION IN A GRAVITATIONAL FORCE."
110   PRINT "INITIAL X1,X2"
120   INPUT X1,X2
130   IF X1 = 999 THEN 410
140   PRINT "INITIAL VX,VY?"
150   INPUT V1,V2
160   PRINT "FINAL TIME?"
170   INPUT T0
180   LET D = .1
190   LET T = 0
200   LET T9 = .5
210   LET R3 = (X1*X1 + X2*X2)↑1.5
220   LET A1 = -X1/R3
230   LET A2 = -X2/R3
240   LET V1 = V1 + A1*D/2
250   LET V2 = V2 + A2*D/2
260   PRINT "T","X1","X2"
270   LET X1 = X1 + V1*D
280   LET X2 = X2 + V2*D
290   LET R3 = (X1*X1 + X2*X2)↑1.5
300   LET A1 = -X1/R3
310   LET A2 = -X2/R3
320   LET V1 = V1 + A1*D
330   LET V2 = V2 + A2*D
340   LET T = T + D
350   IF T < T9 THEN 270
360   LET T9 = T9 + .5
370   PRINT T,X1,X2
380   IF T < T0 THEN 270
390   PRINT
400   GOTO 110
410   END
```

FIGURE 4-1 BASIC Program for Gravitational Force

```
APL
          ∇GRAVITY(□)∇
          ∇GRAVITY
[1]       'MOTION IN A GRAVITATIONAL FORCE'
[2]       START.
'ENTER INITIAL POSITION'
[3]       X←□
[4]       'ENTER INITIAL VELOCITY'
[5]       V←□
[6]       'ENTER FINAL TIME'
[7]       TFINAL←□
[8]       DT←.1
[9]       T←0
[10]      TPRINT + .2
[11]      A←-X ÷ ((/X × X)*1.5)
[12]      V←V + A × DT*2
[13]      'T      X1      X2"
[14]      LOOP:X←X + V × DT
[15]      A← X ÷ ((+/X × X)*1.5)
[16]      V←V + A × DT
[17]      T←T + DT
[18]      →LOOP× ιT < TPRINT
[19]      TPRINT←TPRINT + .2
[20]      T,X
[21]      →LOOP × ιT < TFINAL
[22]      →START
          ∇
```

FIGURE 4-2 APL Program for Gravitational Force

APL, with vector capability, we write the same equations that were utilized for the one-dimensional case. Figures 4-1, 4-2, and 4-3 are BASIC, APL, and FORTRAN programs respectively for the case of the two-dimensional gravitational motion problem, assuming a single central force varying inversely as the square of the distance from the force center.

One practical problem is easily overcome with proper equipment. The programs shown produce only tables of numbers, giving position and velocity at different times. But large collections of numbers are inpenetrable for the average student. Hence, to get some view of what is happening, graphic presentations are essential. These programs are more informative if students plot curves. Graphic capabilities are an important, almost essential, adjunct to computer facilities for use with programs such as the ones presented.

Unfortunately graphic capabilities are still individualized to particular devices; graphic computer programs are difficult to transport. But only a few lines will be needed to add the graphic code in most systems, so this should not present a difficult task. To give an example of programs with graphic capabilities, we present two programs for gravitational motion. Figure 4-4 uses the APL graphic capability developed at Irvine.

The second program (Figure 4-5) is based on the use of a stand-alone graphic system, the Terak 8510/A using Pascal.

In both cases, the graphic commands are transparent. A possible output of a program of this type is shown in Figure 4-6.

Improving the Calculation

Both of the graphic programs also have a small change which gives an enormous increase in accuracy. This is a precalculation of velocity before the main calculational loop. This initial calculation of the velocity for a half-step interval in time is a common numerical technique.

The Feynman lectures present a good reasonable physical argument. The basic idea is to place the velocities half way between the positions, to improve the computations. Since this is done once at the beginning of the entire computation, very little additional computational load is added for the considerable improvement in accuracy attained. Students are often surprised, when these programs are run against exact solutions, to see how much difference the Feynman half step makes. Other more effective numerical methods are available, but they need not be introduced at this point in the student's education.

Beyond Gravity

A wide variety of interesting, two-dimensional physical systems can be presented to the student, many with interesting physical consequences. Some

```
        FORTRAN
        WRITE(6,102)
102     FORMAT(1X,31HMOTION IN A GRAVITATIONAL FORCE)
        WRITE(6,103)
103     FORMAT(1X,33H      T      X1      X2)
5       READ(5,100)X1,X2,V1,V2,TEND
100     FORMAT(5F10.5)
        IF (X1-999.)10,50,10
10      T = 0.
        TPRIN = .5
        DELT = .1
        RCUBED = (X1*X1 + X2*X2)**1.5
        A1 = -X1/RCUBED
        A2 = -X2/RCUBED
        V1 = V1 + A1*DELT/2.
        V2 = V2 + A2*DELT/2.
        WRITE(6,101)T,X1,X2
20      X1 = X1 + V1*DELT
        X2 = X2 + V2*DELT
        RCUBED = (X1*X1+X2*X2)**1.5
        A1 = -X1/RCUBED
        A2 = -X2/RCUBED
        V1 = V1 + A1*DELT
        V2 = V2 + A2*DELT
        T = T + DELT
        IF (T-TPRIN) 30,40,40
40      TPRIN = TPRIN + .5
        WRITE(6,101)T,X1,X2
101     FORMAT (1X,3F12.5)
30      IF (T-TEND) 20,20,5
50      STOP
        END
```

FIGURE 4-3 FORTRAN Program for Gravitational Force

```
        ∇ORBIT[⎕]∇
        ∇ORBIT
        'MOTION IN A GRAVITATIONAL FORCE'
        SCALE ¯2 2 ¯2 2
        START:
'ENTER INITIAL POSITION'
        X←⎕
        DATA←2 1ρX
        'ENTER INITIAL VELOCITY'
        V←⎕
        'ENTER FINAL TIME'
        TFINAL←⎕
        DT←.1
        T←0
        TPRINT←.2
        A←-X÷((+/X×X)*1.5)
        V←V + A×DT ÷ 2
        ERASE
        LOOP:X←X + V×DT
        A←-X÷((+/X×X)*1.5)
        V←V + A×DT
        T←T + DT
        →LOOP× ιT < TPRINT
        TPRINT←TPRINT + .2
        DATA←DATA,X
        →LOOP × ιT < TFINAL
        CURVE DATA
        →START
        ∇
```

FIGURE 4-4 Graphic Program (APL on the Sigma 7)

```
PROGRAM Orbit;
CONST TimeStep=0.1;
          PrintStep=0.5;
          Half=0.5;
VAR Xposition,Yposition,Xvelocity,Yvelocity,Xacceleration,
       Yacceleration,TimeSoFar,FinalTime,TimeToPrint:REAL;
(*$I GRAPH *) (*Brings in procedures needed for graphics.*)
(* The following variable and procedure declarations for graphics are
   designed to be used on the Terak 8510/a. They will probably not work
   on any other computer without revision. *)
   Screen:PACKED ARRAY[0..239,0..319] OF BOOLEAN;

PROCEDURE InitGraph;
CONST Xoffset=160; Yoffset=120;
VAR I:INTEGER;
BEGIN
   FILLCHAR(Screen,SIZEOF(Screen),CHR(0));
   UNITWRITE(3,Screen,63);
   FOR I:=0 TO 3 DO BEGIN
         Screen[I+Yoffset,Xoffset]:=TRUE;
         Screen[Yoffset,I+Xoffset]:=TRUE;
         Screen[Yoffset-I,Xoffset]:=TRUE;
         Screen[Yoffset,Xoffset-I]:=TRUE   END;
END;
8
PROCEDURE Plot(X,Y:REAL);
CONST Xoffset=160; Yoffset=120;
BEGIN
      IF (Y<11.5) AND (Y>-11.5) AND (X<15.5) AND (X>-15.5) THEN
         Screen[ROUND(Y*10)+Yoffset,ROUND(X*10)+Xoffset]:=TRUE;
END;

(* END of machine dependent graphics routines *)
(*$I GRAPH *) (*Brings in procedures needed for graphics.*)
      PROCEDURE GetParameters(VAR Xposition, Yposition, Xvelocity, Yvelocity,
                                                      FinalTime:REAL);
         PROCEDURE AskParameter(VAR Param:REAL; Message:STRING);
         BEGIN
            WRITE('What is the ',Message,'? ');
            READLN(Param);
         END;
      BEGIN
         AskParameter(Xposition,'initial X position');
         AskParameter(Yposition,'initial Y position');
         AskParameter(Xvelocity,'initial X velocity');
         AskParameter(Yvelocity,'initial Y velocity');
         AskParameter(FinalTime,'final time');
      END;

      PROCEDURE GetAcceleration(VAR Xacceleration,Yacceleration:REAL);
      CONST Rexponent=1.5;
      VAR Rcubed:REAL;
         FUNCTION Power(X,Y:REAL):REAL;
         BEGIN
            IF X>0 THEN Power:=EXP(Y*LN(X))
            ELSE Power:=0;
         END;
      BEGIN
         Rcubed:=Power(SQR(Xposition)+SQR(Yposition),Rexponent);

         Xacceleration:=-Xposition/Rcubed;
         Yacceleration:=-Yposition/Rcubed;
      END;

BEGIN
      PAGE(OUTPUT);
      WRITELN('Motion in a gravitational force.');
      REPEAT
         GetParameters(Xposition,Yposition,Xvelocity,Yvelocity,FinalTime);
         InitGraph; TimeSoFar:=-TimeStep; TimeToPrint:=PrintStep;
         WRITELN('    Time           X            Y');
         REPEAT
            PLOT(Xposition,Yposition); TimeSoFar:=TimeSoFar+TimeStep;
            GetAcceleration(Xacceleration,Yacceleration);
            Xvelocity:=Xvelocity+Xacceleration*TimeStep*Half;
            Yvelocity:=Yvelocity+Yacceleration*TimeStep*Half;
            Xposition:=Xposition+Xvelocity*TimeStep;
            Yposition:=Yposition+Yvelocity*TimeStep;
            IF TimeSoFar>=TimeToPrint THEN BEGIN
               WRITELN(TimeSoFar,'    ',Xposition,'    ',Yposition);
               TimeToPrint:=TimeToPrint+PrintStep END;
      UNTIL TimeSoFar>=FinalTime;
      WRITE('Press RETURN for new parameters, ETX to quit:'); READLN;
      PAGE(OUTPUT);
   UNTIL EOF;
END.
```

FIGURE 4-5 Graphic Program (Terak 8510/A Using Pascal)

are small variants on gravitational motion. There is a perturbation, with the gravitational force augmented by a small perturbing force. There is the satellite drag problem, with the dragging force proportional (in direction and magnitude) to the velocity, or other power of velocity, leading to the interesting satellite drag paradox. There is the question of what would happen if gravity weren't quite an inverse square law, but different slightly from an inverse square law. In all these cases the question of how motions differ with different kinds of initial conditions is of physical interest too. Figure 4-7 shows a "gravitational" motion where the force is not quite an inverse square force.

Force laws, which are very different from the gravitational law, are also of interest. Thus, central forces with positive powers lead to a phenomenon that can be understood easily—the fact that when the powers get higher and higher, we get more and more the effect of a ball bouncing off a spherical shell of radius one: r^5 is a small number when r is less than 1 but is large when r is larger than 1. This phenomenon is illustrated beautifully in Frank Sindon's film, *Force, Mass and Motion*[6] and in Figure 4-8. But students can discover it themselves. All these cases represent only slight changes in the programs already presented.

Two-dimensional motion with *two* fixed gravitational force centers is also within the range of beginning students. If they are to study the situation fully, they will need guidance from the instructor or from instructional materials since a bewildering variety of orbits is possible. We can obtain interesting orbits with cusps; we can even, in this case, obtain an elliptical orbit but only with very specialized initial conditions. Figures 4-9 and 4-10 illustrate such orbits.

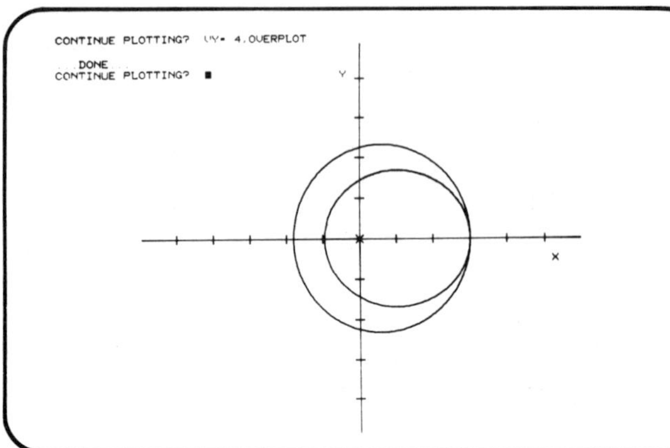
CONTINUE PLOTTING? VY= 4.OVERPLOT
DONE
CONTINUE PLOTTING?
Y
X

FIGURE 4-6 Two Planetary Orbits with Different Initial Velocities, from MOTION

Errors

Typically, beginning students feel nervous about the computational errors that are always present in computer solutions. The fact that these errors can usually be controlled to any desired degree of accuracy usually fails to dispel this sense of uneasiness. A strategy that has been used quite successfully, to dispel the fear of error accumulation and to emphasize physical principles, is to employ conservation laws to the accuracy of the numerical solution. For example, in the undamped harmonic oscillator problem, energy is conserved. Simple program changes enable the total energy to be computed. One caution is that if the Feynman half-step method is used, the velocity contribution to the total energy must be computed at the same times as the position.

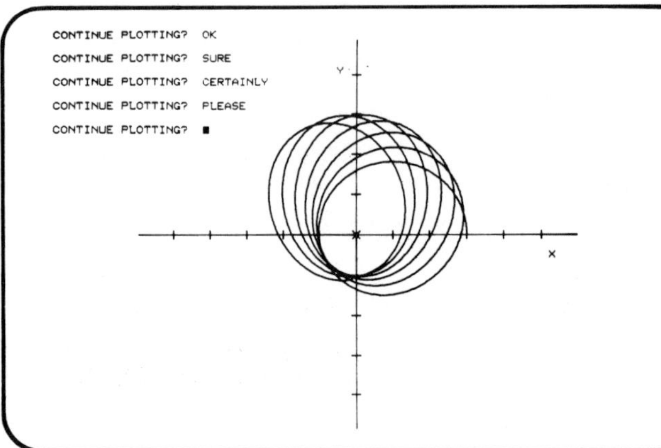
CONTINUE PLOTTING? OK
CONTINUE PLOTTING? SURE
CONTINUE PLOTTING? CERTAINLY
CONTINUE PLOTTING? PLEASE
CONTINUE PLOTTING?
Y
X

FIGURE 4-7 Force Law Differing Slightly from Inverse Square, from MOTION

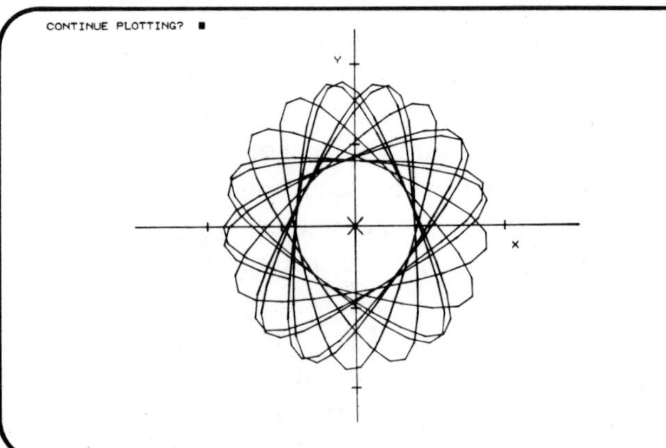
CONTINUE PLOTTING?
Y
X

FIGURE 4-8 Particle Moving Under a Positive Power Force Law, from MOTION

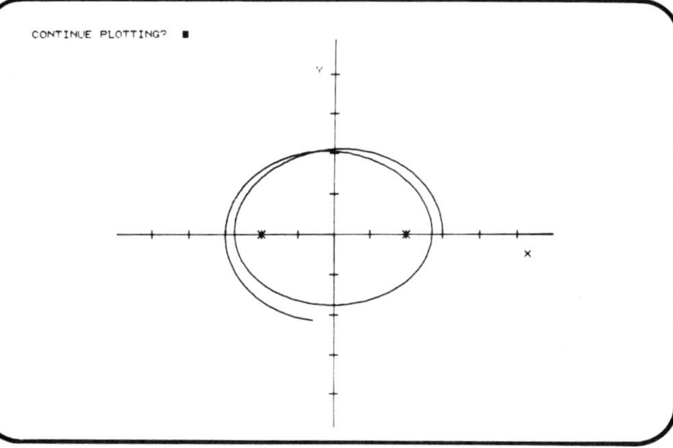

FIGURE 4-9 Almost Elliptical Orbit with Two Suns, from MOTION

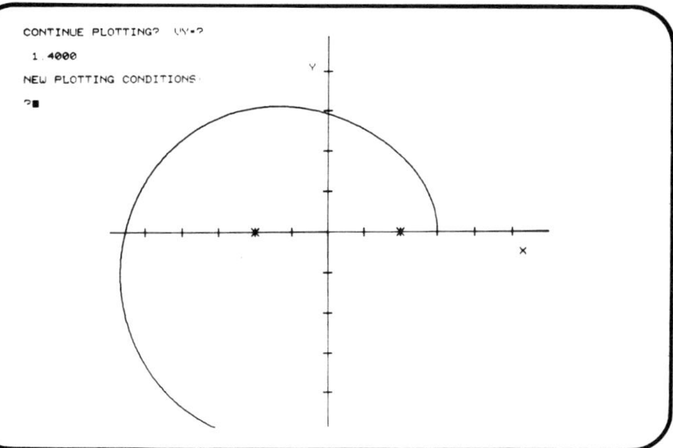

FIGURE 4-10 Plot with Two Suns, Greater Velocity than Figure 4-9

If the student sees that the total energy is almost constant to, say, four significant digits, the computer solution is "precise enough" for most situations. The other conservation laws can be used advantageously in a similar fashion.

Onward

The step to full three-dimensional systems, and multi-particle systems, is conceptually easy at this point. However, the complexity of the problems and the variety of different conditions available probably makes this not advisable for the typical beginning course. Thus, to tell a student, "Investigate the general three-body gravitational problem," is too open-ended a problem for the typical beginning student, although it might furnish a very interesting term project for some students.

Solar Wind

A very interesting two-dimensional problem with rich resources has been discussed by Arthur Luehrmann[7]. The problem is gravitational motion but with a constant force added to the problem. The equations describing the problems are

$$\frac{d^2x}{dt^2} = -x/r^3 + k$$

$$\frac{d^2y}{dt^2} = -y/r^3$$

Without k in the first equation, the problem is the standard gravitational case where length and time have been scaled so that $GM = 1$. However, suppose that the particle is in a circular orbit, and then perturbed with force k which is about 3% of the central force. What will happen to the circular orbit? The result is both surprising and perplexing.

The important point is that a relatively minor change in the description of a problem has produced enormous changes in the resultant phenomena and the mathematics required for analytical solution. Happily, and this is typical of numerical solutions, the appropriate modification of the computer orbital program requires only a small change in a single line of code.

The results cry out for explanation. Luehrmann has posed a number of questions that should be answered. What does increasing or decreasing *k* do to the motion? Can a functional dependence on *k* be found among the observables? Does the effect depend on the initial angular position of the particle in an unperturbed circular orbit? If *k* were turned on slowly, from zero to its full value in the space of several orbits, would that change the effect very much? Is it true that the major axis of the quasi-ellipses is constant or changes? What does a graph of angular momentum versus time look like? What does a graph of "orbital energy" (kinetic energy plus gravitational potential energy) versus time look like? Can the computational algorithm be refined so that the situation can be examined when the particle comes near the center of force? Is the phenomenon characteristic of all central forces, or is it unique to the inverse square force? What if the initial conditions were such that the unperturbed orbit was a fairly long ellipse lying along the horizontal axis? What motion would occur? Instead of plotting x versus y, plot v_x versus v_y. Bearing in mind that force changes the "velocity state," not the "position state," explain why the velocity-space picture is more intuitively clear.

Each of these questions can be the basis for rich and meaningful student exploration. This is not limited to very gifted physics majors by any means. Liberal arts majors can learn a great deal answering the questions from a strictly numerical point of view. At the other end of the spectrum, graduate physics students can be challenged to answer the questions with rigorous and analytical descriptions.

The main point is that the "solar wind" problem and others considered are quite different from the typical, predictable, canned exercises usually encountered by Physics students. The element of the unknown in the problem, the astonishing results that show up initially in the numerical solution, the rich harvest of insights obtained ultimately, all combine to make this the "million dollar problem."

Less is More

The Feynman Lectures contain a most intriguing introduction to the principle of least action. As in the numerical treatment of the orbital problem, Feynman's words display his fascination with this subject[8].

"When I was in high school, my physics teacher—whose name was Mr. Bader—called me down one day after physics class and said, "You look bored; I want to tell you something interesting." Then he told me something which I found absolutely fascinating and have, since then, always found fascinating. Every time the subject comes up, I work on it. In fact, when I began to prepare this lecture I found myself making more analyses on the thing. Instead of worrying about the lecture, I got involved in a new problem. The subject is this—the principle of least action.

"Mr. Bader told me the following: suppose you have a particle (in a gravitational field, for instance) which starts somewhere and moves to some other point by free motion–you throw it, and it goes up and comes down."

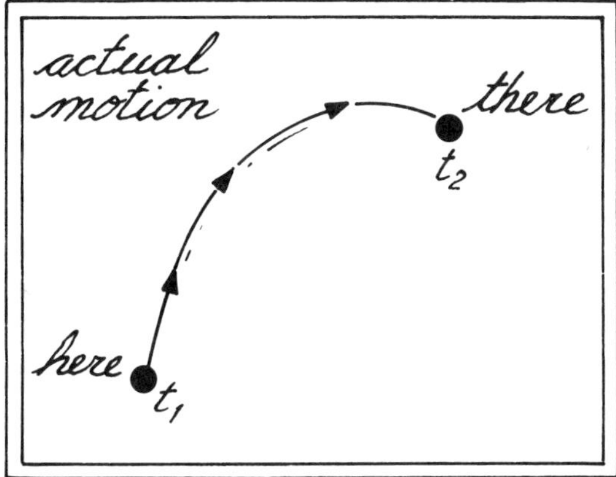

FIGURE 4-11a Possible Particle Path

"It goes from the original place to the final place in a certain amount of time. Now you try a different motion. Suppose that to get from here to there, it went like this:

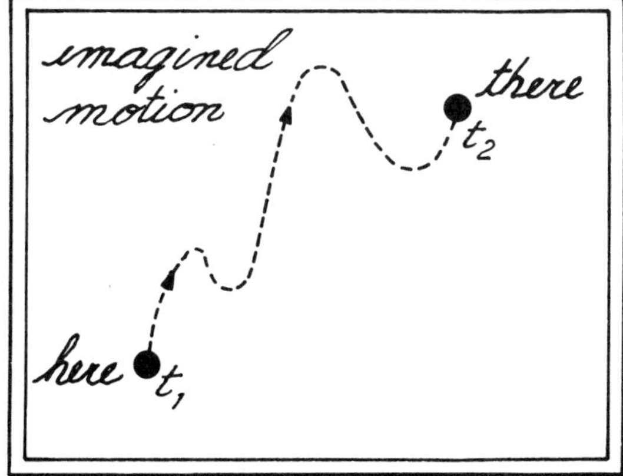

FIGURE 4-11b Another Possible Particle Path

but got there in just the same amount of time. Then he said this: If you calculate the kinetic energy at every moment on the path, take away the potential energy, and integrate it over the time during the whole path, you'll find that the number you'll get is bigger than that for the actual motion."

"In other words, the laws of Newton could be stated not in the form $\mathbf{F} = m\mathbf{a}$ but in the form: the average kinetic energy less the average potential energy is as little as possible for the path of an object going from one point to another."

Of course, the problem is to find the true path given a potential energy function. Later on Feynman suggests one way to to do this[9].

"Problem: Find the true path. Where is it? One way, of course, is to calculate the action for millions and millions of paths and look at which one is lowest. When you find the lowest one, that's the true path."

Then Feynman goes into the calculus of variations to demonstrate that Newton's second law is a consequence of least action.

This derivation assumes a level of mathematical sophistication that excludes most beginning students. However, with the computer we can attack the problem precisely as Feynman first suggests. Many paths can be computed to find the one corresponding to minimum action. Instead of integration, we do a summation of the difference between kinetic energy and potential energy over the range of variables involved. By assuming a trial path, and then perturbing the path in some systematic way to see if the total action is increased or decreased, the path can be "squeezed" into the one corresponding to least action. This is most striking if the process can be viewed on a graphic display device.

The notion of least action via the computer opens up a powerful way to treat mechanics using variational principles. The result is a global view of a problem rather than the local view described by Newton's laws. There are sophisticated ideas contained in the variational method that the beginner rarely sees or appreciates. With such tools, and a minimum of mathematics, the student can "discover" that harmonic motion is a consequence of $V(x) = -kx^2$ or that $V(x) = kx$ leads to parabolic trajectories. The student is not limited to the routine potential functions, but is free to explore the characteristics of any function.

Both the authors have used this method of least action in mechanics[10]. A BASIC program that solves the one-dimensional least action problem for any arbitrary potential function is available from Herbert Peckham.

References to the Numerical Approach

The older, noncomputer-based references, Sherwin and Feynman, have already been mentioned. In addition, class-usable material has been developed along the lines suggested here.

Two monographs are available from CONDUIT, a National Science Foundation sponsored organization[11]. Introductory Computer-Based Mechanics and Introductory Computer-Based Mechanics II. The first of these considers one-dimensional systems and the second considers two-dimensional systems. Various topics are also investigated beyond those discussed and student problems are given. The approach is similar to that in the Feynman material.

Similar material has also been developed by Huggins[12] and Gavenda[13].

A full set of notes for the beginning course is now in use at the University of California, Irvine, prepared by Alfred Bork. Copies of these notes can be obtained from the Physics Department at Irvine, at cost[14]. They follow the Newtonian approach to the use of numerical methods.

Although the references have been to the use of standard digital computers employing standard programming languages, the approach through numerical methods is also possible on programmable calculators. R. Eisberg's supplementary book[15] contains student-oriented material with programs for both Hewlett-Packard and Texas Instrument programmable calculators.

Most of the supplementary books that consider various computer applications in the teaching of Physics include the approach through numerical methods also. See, for example, the books by Alfred Bork[16], Herbert Peckham[17], and John Merrill.[18]

Unfortunately most of these books and monographs are supplementary. In many courses it is difficult to utilize supplementary material, if for no other reason than it much increases student cost. Full-scale beginning Physics textbooks incorporating the ideas reflected in this paper are desirable. Such a textbook would lead to considerable improvement in the way the beginning Physics course is taught. Two textbooks have just been published, and others may soon be available.

TWO NEW GRAPHIC COMPUTER DIALOGS FOR TEACHERS

With Arnold Arons

Introduction

A major problem in teaching science at all levels, particularly pre-university levels, is to bring students to an understanding of the structure of science—the nature of scientific theories, the evidence for these theories, and the mechanism for relating the terms of these theories to experience. Too often science appears to students as a series of pronouncements from on high, somehow magically true, or a series of isolated "facts." Thus, the students in introductory courses are likely to preface something which cannot, they think, be doubted, by the phrase "scientists say . . ."

Some problems at the elementary and high school levels arise because teachers view science in just this way. Thus, the notion that scientific theories require experimental evidence to support them, that we can employ scientific models to make an infinite number of predictions, that theories have logical structure, that operational definitions are needed to connect terms in theories with laboratory experience—all these are notions that are too often foreign to the teacher. Not surprisingly, therefore, the students acquire false notions of the nature of science.

Giving teachers new curriculum material will not necessarily overcome this handicap, even if that material reflects reasonable attitudes, as recent experience clearly indicates. Summer institutes and other retraining programs can reach some small percentage of the teachers involved, but this number is indeed negligible as compared with total national needs. Given the major role of science in shaping contemporary society and given the magnitude of the problem of reaching very large numbers of teachers in the country, the problem is important, but current modes of teacher education and popularizations of science are inadequate to make a large impact.

Computer-student dialogs, interactions of students with a computer program, might assist in this situation. As a first step, to gain experience with the technique, we prepared the pair of computer dialogs described in this paper. The software for creating such interactive student-computer dialogs was developed by the Physics Computer Development Project at Irvine.

The American Journal of Physics, vol. 43, no. 11.

Elementary and high school teachers used these dialogs in institutes at the University of Washington during the summer of 1973. One of the dialogs, LUNA, has been rewritten based on the experience gained. The dialogs require graphic displays which draw pictures under computer control, as pictorial information is an intergral part of the learning experience. Once effective dialogs are available, they could be utilized on a nationwide basis with large numbers of teachers.

The two dialogs are also proving useful for high school and college students. They are self-contained, demanding little previous background. They are in use in several other locations with similar computer equipment. The continually decreasing cost of computers suggests that such material will be much more widely available in the near future.

TERRA

The first of these dialogs for teachers is TERRA. This dialog is a preparation for the second dialog, and may not be needed by everyone. It encourages the teacher-student to think about how the sky looks as viewed from the earth, both during the day and one evening, and over many nights. It introduces requisite vocabulary for use in the later dialog LUNA. An observant teacher, with some knowledge of what happens in the sky, could bypass this dialog.

TERRA draws on information based on observations of the sky during the day and at night. Experience indicates, however, that many teachers, particularly elementary teachers, will have only the vaguest notion of what transpires in the sky. Hence, if the teacher cannot respond to the computer's requests for information, it may be necessary to tell them certain things and persuade them to more active observation of the world around them. We do not introduce terms until the ideas and experiences on which they are based are clear. As with other dialogs, the experience of using the dialog is different for different students.

This dialog deals with operational definition of terms such as "noon," "midnight," "north-south," "vertical," "zenith," "celestial and terrestrial meridians," "celestial and terrestrial poles," and "latitude and longitude."

LUNA

The second of the dialogs for teachers is concerned with developing and understanding a scientific model, the model that accounts for the phases of the moon. The emphasis is on the notion of a *model,* in addition to the formation and use of this particular model. The program is a self-contained, self-study unit, providing both learning material (in the earlier part of the dialog) and a randomly selected quiz at the end of the unit. Teachers recycle through the material if they do not do sufficiently well on the quiz, and then they repeat the quiz. The quiz is selected by the computer from a pool of questions. Thus, the unit is a Personalized System Instruction (PSI) or self-paced unit, with the computer playing the role of tutor both in assisting the student in learning and in giving the unit test at the end.

The opening passage of LUNA is shown in Figure 4-12. LUNA starts by determining if the student is already familiar with the phenomena and the common terminology for describing the phases of the moon, such as crescent, half moon, and full moon. Figures 4-13 and 4-14 show the flavor of the early section. The student input comes each time after the question mark at the beginning of the line. The information, including drawings, is generated by the computer. Different student responses elicit different computer-produced messages and pictures, so one set of samples like this does not by any means exhaust the range of the program.

Quite near the beginning of the program we try to find if teachers already have some notion of the model for the phases of the moon, in terms of the simple geometry involved. We do this by allowing them to point to the sun, using the graphic pointer built into the terminal, in the case where the observer on earth sees a full moon. Figure 4-15 shows how the screen looks to the students when this concept is first presented to them. The observer is represented by the small box on the earth. Several responses are indicated in Figures 4-16 through 4-18.

```
'Till clomb above the eastern bar
The horned Moon, with one bright star
Within the nether tip.'
            Coleridge
            Rime of the Ancient Mariner

What does the term 'horned' or 'crescent'
moon mean to you
?VERY LITTLE

Yes
Here is a picture of a crescent moon
Have you seen a crescent moon?
?■
```

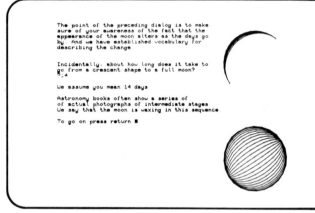

FIGURE 4-12 LUNA—Introductory Frame

```
The point of the preceding dialog is to make
sure of your awareness of the fact that the
appearance of the moon alters as the days go
by. And we have established vocabulary for
describing the change

Incidentally, about how long does it take to
go from a crescent shape to a full moon?
?14

We assume you mean 14 days

Astronomy books often show a series of
of actual photographs of intermediate stages
We say that the moon is waxing in this sequence.

To go on press return ■
```

FIGURE 4-13 LUNA—Early Sequence

```
What is the source of the brightness of the moon?
?THE SUN

Yes, the moon shines by the sun's
reflected light

You've heard from childhood that the
moon shines by reflected light
Why do we believe this?

In the following sequence we will use this
as an hypothesis and build a model of the earth-
moon-sun system. The ability of the model to
account for observed facts and to predict
phenomena not used in building up the model
is what eventually justifies any initial
hypothesis

Except for the case of the full moon,
part of the lunar face is dark rather
than bright. How do you account for the
dark portion?
?SHADOW

Shadow of what?
?■
```

FIGURE 4-14 LUNA—Early Sequence

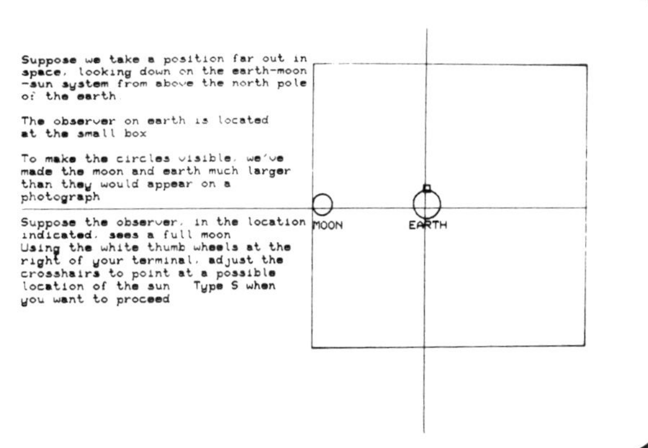

FIGURE 4-15 LUNA—Student Chooses Sun's Location

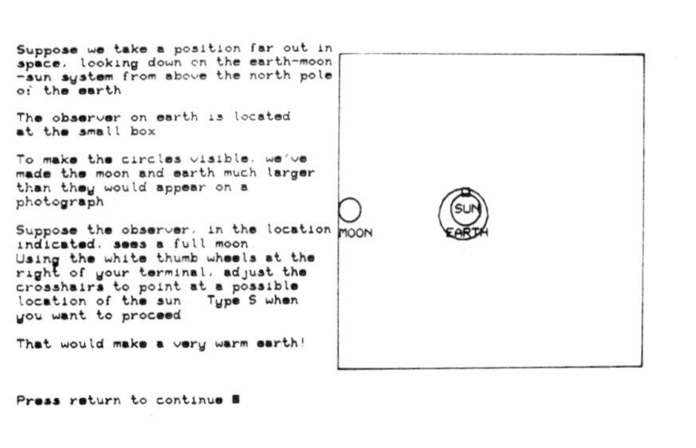

FIGURE 4-16 Response in LUNA. Student Places Sun on Top of Earth

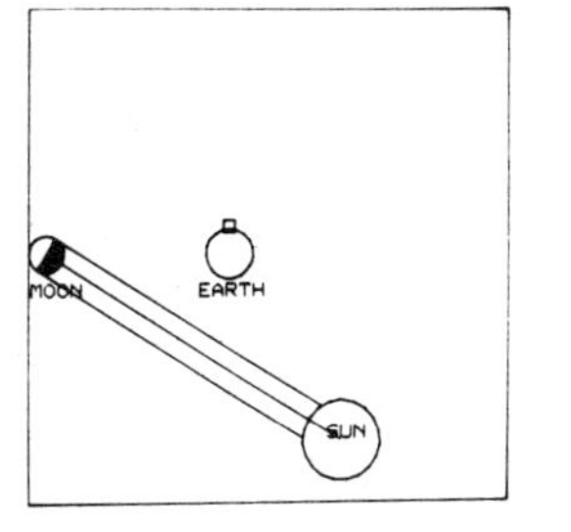

FIGURE 4-17 LUNA, but Not a Full Moon

The program, as always, recognizes not only the correct responses, but also wrong responses that would elicit an immediate comment from an instructor talking directly to the student, carrying on a Socratic dialog.

LUNA continues in the same vein. It covers the full cycle of the moon's waxing and waning. It tries to get students to make the connections, implied by the model, between the rising and setting of the sun and the moon in the various phases. Thus, we stress the predictive power of models. As far as possible, students are urged to generate the necessary connections, often with hints provided in multiple tries; we try to avoid presenting information directly to the students. See Figures 4-19 and 4-20.

Preparation of Dialogs

Since the generation of student-computer dialogs is still a relatively new experience, it seems appropriate to discuss the authoring system used in TERRA and LUNA. Details are presented in Chapter 6.

Work on the two dialogs started during the Christmas vacation in 1972, at the University of California, Irvine. The initial day of our two weeks went into deciding what type of computer material we intended to write. We decided to write the two dialogs indicated. Several other possibilities were actively considered.

We proceeded by generating loose flowcharts showing the form the dialog was to take, indicating the pictures by sketches and verbal descriptions. These hand-drawn charts of pedagogical details were on large sheets of paper. We were working as teachers, deciding what students are likely to respond to a particular question, and what replies should be given for various replies the students might give. One of us worked full time, the other about half time, so about 1 and 1/2 man weeks were needed at this stage for each dialog.

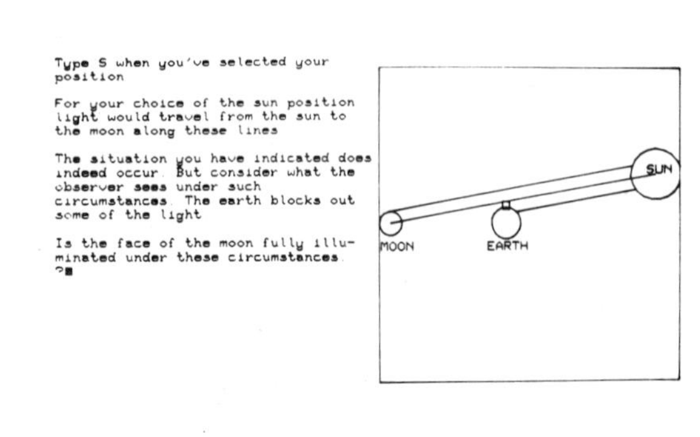

FIGURE 4-18 LUNA, a Partial Eclipse

This way of working produces material in sufficiently good form to go to a secretary or programmer. We had secretaries trained to sit at the display and enter, using the computer editor, much of the code required. The secretary can successfully do about 90% of the typing required, and can do it effectively. We have not found the training of secretaries to be difficult. In this case, the material was typed by Anna Tartaglini of the Irvine Physics Department; she spent about two weeks, interspersed with other work.

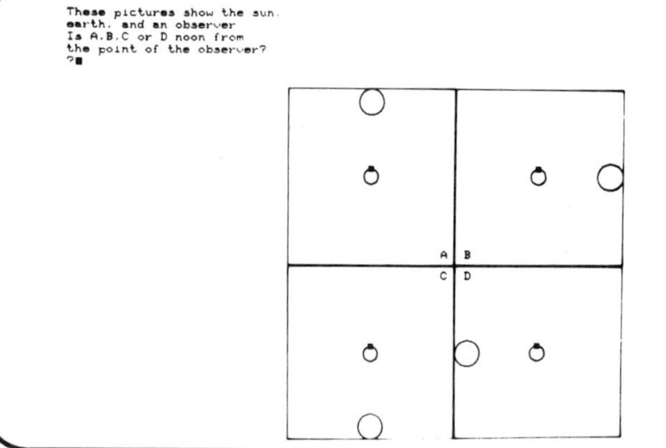

FIGURE 4-19 LUNA, Astronomical Meaning of Noon

In the next stage, the material goes to an undergraduate programmer who fills in the parts the secretary omitted and generates the initial running version. The programmers associated with TERRA were Hal Deering and Dobree Purdy, and John Collins was responsible for LUNA. Although the secretary has done 90% of the typing, this is only about 10% of the coding. The major problem lies with graphics. The programmer must still construct the graphic material in a relatively careful, slow fashion, and this is time-consuming. [Note: The screen design program had not been developed at this time.] The programmer, working with the instructor, can trace down and eliminate many errors. Each dialog required about two weeks of programming time, spread over a period of about two months.

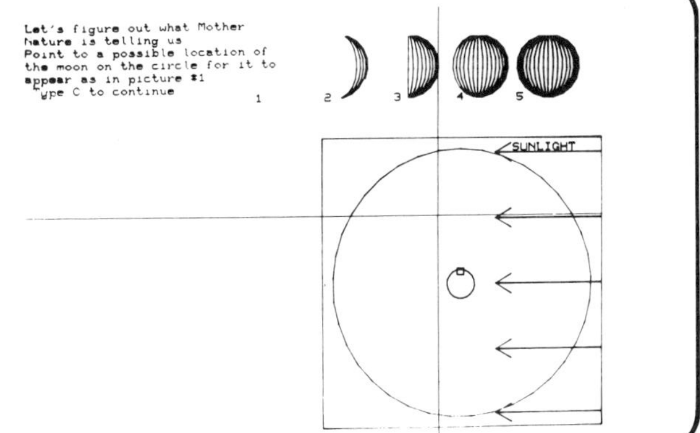

FIGURE 4-20 A Later Sequence in LUNA

The first running versions were available in March. These versions still had problems due to oversights on the part of the authors and programming problems, particularly in constructing the graphic material.

Several students in the elementary education program at Irvine tested the dialogs, running the programs to help us find problems. We also used the programs as demonstrations with visitors and with our own students.

At this point the program is changeable, going through many variations. Some changes are cosmetic such as clearing up places where the writing overlaps the picture—while others uncover programming errors that would make the program unusable with many students. After several months of such testing, a relatively "stable" version was available.

The two programs were first used on a sizable scale with teachers at the University of Washington during the summer of 1973. Two different institutes were involved—one with elementary teachers and one with high school teachers.

Three types of information were secured while using the dialogs with teachers. First, the instructors watched what was happening and talked with the students, and so formed impressions about effectiveness. Second, the teachers commented on the programs; we received detailed written comments from the high school group. Third, the programs gathered information as they were run, storing such information in computer files. What is saved is dependent on the author; we primarily saved information on what responses the computer could not analyze and also information on what parts of the program were used.

This testing revealed weaknesses. One difficulty was the omission of any facility for teachers to review a section after finishing it, even if their grasp might still be shaky. The lengths were a problem. LUNA requires about 90 minutes, TERRA about 60 minutes. Teachers often found the programs exhausting, yet unlike college students who have used dialogs, they were reluctant to use the restart facilities which allow the student to come back in at a later time.

Timing considerations were found to be weak. The computer often pauses to allow time for reading, but the timing of these pauses needed tuning, particularly in changing pages (erasing the screen). Students needed more control over the delays in the program.

A major problem came up for the elementary teachers in the use of LUNA. LUNA was too difficult for many of these teachers, assuming too much background information. On the other hand, LUNA proved reasonbly effective with the high school group. It may be necessary to get students started by personal discussion and holding objects out in three dimensions, and noting the shadows. We did not follow this sequence, but plunged them directly into the dialogs, hoping this would relieve us of the usual start-up.

New Version of LUNA

On the basis of this information, we prepared a second version of LUNA. The programmer was Craig Taylor. In addition to meeting the problems indicated by saved responses, the new version allows the student to review previous material, and it allows student control over the delays. This version is in use by Irvine students. It is particularly popular with students not taking Physics classes, and is employed widely in demonstrating the Physics Computer Development Project material to visitors.

Future Use

Computer dialogs such as TERRA and LUNA are available at only a few schools. Only a few schools are currently dedicating considerable interactive computer use to learning. Hence, developers of such material cannot expect immediate large-scale availability similar to textbook availability, but such availability is likely in the long run. Prices of computers continue to decline, and thus computer-based learning materials will be more and more competitive in cost. The potential, therefore, exists for such dialogs to be used very widely. It is not likely that this potentiality will be realized, however, until a larger body of well-tested dialogs has been developed.

LEARNING WITH COMPUTER SIMULATIONS

In the last 15 years the computer has been used as a learning device in many different ways. One of the modes, representing work by many individuals, is that of computer simulation. While simulations as learning aids exist in a variety of forms, this article considers only computer simulations, describing learning materials that fit under this category and reviewing how these materials can be integrated within a classroom environment. Many of the examples were developed at the Educational Technology Center within the Physics Computer Development Project at the University of California, Irvine; all have been employed in large classes.

It is difficult to define simulation precisely. Computer simulations usually involve modeling aspects of a world—either the experimental world or an imaginary world designed for pedagogical purposes. A wide variety of aspects can be so modeled. We might be considering physical phenomena, predicted by a well-known physical law, or social phenomena such as the economic system of a country.

Based on "Learning with Computer Simulations" appearing in *Computer*, vol. 12, no. 10, pp. 75-84, October 1979.

Computer simulations are not restricted to teaching and learning. Their most common science and engineering application is in research: in designing a new airplane, for example, simulations are used to investigate behaviorial components before the design is frozen and the prototype produced. In pure research, too, computer simulations play a major role. Science instructors are often familiar with this use of computers, even if they have never seen classroom simulations.

Classroom Use

The usefulness of computer simulations in learning has long been recognized. Indeed, according to some proponents, this is the only mode in which computers should be used! I, however, maintain that it is only one of many valuable computer-based learning approaches; the classroom environment presents a full spectrum of possibilities.

Why should we use the computer in a simulation mode with students? First, science or engineering students need to understand computer simulations to become acquainted with this important research tool. However, since most students in beginning courses are non-majors and not all majors become researchers, this reason does not, by itself, justify their widespread use in such courses.

Another value of simulation, quickly apparent in practice, is motivational. Simulations, like the phenomena, can have a strong dramatic component that captures the imagination of the individual interacting with the computer. Most research users of computers, as well as users of computer simulation within classes, can recall examples from their own work where this excitement was present. Whether such motivation extends to most students in a typical beginning course is, however, a more questionable issue that will be touched on later.

A third reason for using computer simulations is to provide students with experiences that may be difficult or impossible to obtain in everyday life. Students cannot experiment directly with the economic system, but in a well-designed simulation, they can experience some of the flavor of that experimentation. Since these experiences—unlike real-life experiences—can be controlled, the students become active participants, not just passive observers.

A final reason—related to the third—concerns the value of increased experience in developing insight and intuition, always a difficult task. This critical component is often missing from learning materials. A typical complaint concerning PhD candidates is that, although they can carry out formula manipulations, they are baffled by simple problems demanding insight. Because advanced work and great scientific developments so often depend on insight and inspired guesses, any method that develops intuition is important in our educational system.

Attitudes Toward Learning Simulations

Since simulations resemble many research calculations, it is not surprising that faculties are easily convinced of their value. In demonstrating a wide range of computer-based learning materials at national meetings, we have found that good simulations appeal to faculty, thus simulations have helped convince teachers of the computer's value in education.

However, in observing classrooms, it quickly becomes apparent that students may not be as entranced as the faculty. The good students are highly motivated, displaying the same level of interest as the faculty. However, repeated experience shows that many students, particularly in introductory courses, do not become that involved with computer simulations.

Sometimes, simulations have proved disappointing just because full consideration was not given to how the materials were used. As will be seen, a variety of proven mechanisms are available. Instructors must consider student attitudes if the material is to see successful classroom use.

Graphics

Early computer-based simulations depended on teletypewriter-like terminals. But simulations, perhaps more than other computer materials, need graphics to realize all the advantages.

Iconic representations are important in learning. If we consider the goal of increasing intuition, greater understanding of phenomena is more likely from graphic presentations than from equivalent collections of numbers. Both kinds of data have their usefulness; it is not a question of choosing one or the other. But graphics enhance the possibility of increasing insight. A variety of graphic presentations is also important; what brings the point across to one student may not, because of differences in learning style, be meaningful to another.

Examples of Simulations

To further define simulations, I will give examples and formulate a tentative classification scheme.

Laboratory Simulations

In its simplest form, a laboratory simulation involves redoing a laboratory experiment on the computer. In other situations, while the experiment could be carried out in the laboratory, the desired degree of student control or guidance could not be obtained without the computer, except in laboratories with only a few students per instructor.

A good example of a laboratory simulation dates from the earliest days of computer-based instruction. One of the first programs for the IBM Coursewriter system was a qualitative analysis program for chemistry. The student, presented with an unknown, could ask for the results of tests on the unknown. In the better versions slides were available; the student could see the colors and other aspects, as well as descriptive information from the computer.

One of the best-known laboratory simulations is the Plato simulation involving the breeding of fruit flies. The student picks two flies to breed and is shown the next generation.

Neither of these examples precisely duplicates an ordinary laboratory. For example, the fruit fly experiment allows "breeding" many generations on a greatly accelerated time scale. Altering the time scale is often of importance in computer simulations. The next two simulations could be done in the laboratory, but the computer dialogs go beyond what might be possible in a typical large beginning laboratory environment.

ROPEGAME

The first of these laboratory creations is a controlled-discovery experiment called ROPEGAME. An important physical aspect of waves, the $(x - vt)$ dependence, is the result the student "discovers." As seen in Figure 4-21, students are told that a disturbance exists in the rope and that, if they specify a position and a time, the computer will tell them the rope's displacement at that place and time.

At first, only this simple "measurement" facility is available. To ensure independent investigation by each student in a large class, the details of the disturbance are picked randomly each time the program is run; each student works with a "different" disturbance in the rope. The form of the wave is always a sum of two Gaussians, with both a positive and a negative peak.

If the program were a "pure" simulation, this measurement capability would be the only facility available, but in ROPEGAME other processes take place. The computer keeps full records of just which measurements the student has made, and uses this information in progressing through the material. Early in the procedure (Figure 4-22), the computer looks at the data to see if the student has determined any place as nonzero disturbance. This nonzero region is restricted to a finite range in both position and time. If no disturbance has been observed, the computer will generate, partially randomly, values where the disturbance is nonzero.

Later in ROPEGAME the computer checks the student's strategy. Given two independent variables, the position of the rope and the time of the observation, a reasonable strategy is to hold one of the variables fixed for a series of measurements, varying only the other. But not all students will realize that this is the

```
        The physical system we will explore is an
        extremely long rope with a disturbance in
        it  If you tell me a  POSITION  along the
        rope  and a  TIME.  I  will give you  the
        DISTURBANCE. the displacement from equil-
        ibrium  Your job is  to find out  what is
        happening in the rope

      I will eventually TURN-THE-TABLES. giving you
      information and asking you to predict values

      Position is in meters and time is in seconds
                         You needn't enter units

TIME= 67         POSITION= 34        DISTURBANCE =   0

TIME= 29         POSITION= 78        DISTURBANCE =   0

TIME= 67         POSITION= 98        DISTURBANCE =   0

TIME= ■
```

FIGURE 4-21 Introduction to ROPEGAME

```
JUST TO CONVINCE YOU THAT THE DISPLACEMENT
IS NOT ALWAYS ZERO. HERE ARE SOME POSITION
AND TIMES AT WHICH THE DISPLACEMENT IS
DISTINCTLY NON-ZERO

TIME=      2.55    POSITION=  7.37    DISPLACEMENT=  0.21
TIME=     -1.65    POSITION= -4.55    DISPLACEMENT=  0.13
TIME=      0.11    POSITION=  1.20    DISPLACEMENT= -0.07
TIME=     -3.43    POSITION= -9.94    DISPLACEMENT=  0.17

GRAPHS OR SKETCHES MIGHT BE USEFUL

TIME= ■
```

FIGURE 4-22 ROPEGAME Aid to Student Who has not Found Nonzero Displacement

```
YOU MAY HAVE SOME IDEA OF HOW THE ROPE IS
BEHAVING. AT THIS POINT I WILL CHANGE THE
RULES OF THE GAME  FOR

     MEASUREMENT             TYPE M
   TURN-THE-TABLES           TYPE T
LIST OF MEASUREMENTS         TYPE L
   GRAPHIC DISPLAY           TYPE G

DON'T BE DISTURBED IF YOU CAN'T TURN THE
TABLES AT FIRST--I WILL GIVE YOU OTHER CHANCES.

MEASURE? LIST? TURN? GRAPH?   ■
```

FIGURE 4-23 Facilities Available to Student in ROPEGAME

```
YOU KNOW ALREADY THAT AT T = -1.65 AND AT  X = -4.55
     THE DISTURBANCE =    0.13

AT T =   1.02  THE DISPLACEMENT IS TO BE THE SAME
WHAT VALUE OF POSITION MAKES THIS THE CASE?
?7

TRY ONCE MORE  ACCURACY  1
?■
```

FIGURE 4-24 Turn the Table Predictions Required in ROPEGAME

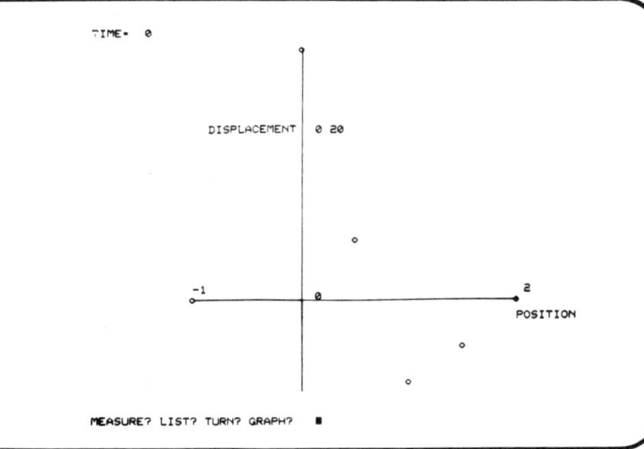

FIGURE 4-25 Graphic Display of Data Generated by ROPEGAME

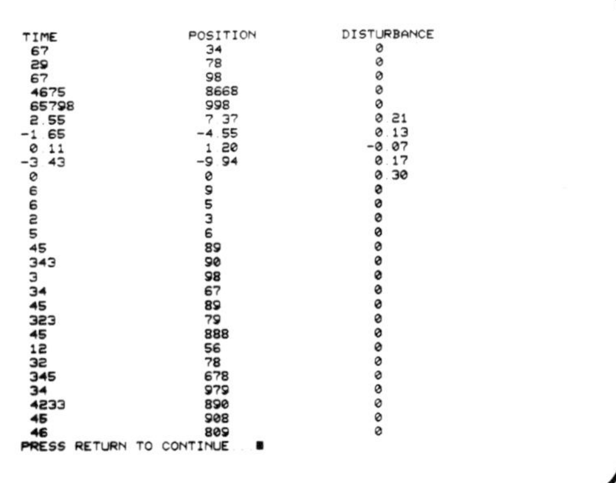

TIME	POSITION	DISTURBANCE
67	34	0
29	78	0
67	98	0
4675	8668	0
65798	998	0
2.55	7.37	0.21
-1.65	-4.55	0.13
0.11	1.20	-0.07
-3.43	-9.94	0.17
0	0	0.30
6	9	0
6	5	0
2	3	0
5	6	0
45	89	0
343	90	0
3	98	0
34	67	0
45	89	0
323	79	0
45	888	0
12	56	0
32	78	0
345	678	0
34	979	0
4233	890	0
45	908	0
46	809	0

PRESS RETURN TO CONTINUE ... ■

FIGURE 4-26 Data Provided by ROPEGAME on Request

way to proceed; some students need guidance and the program provides it, aiding their understanding of how to work in situations with several independent variables. If students have already picked a good strategy, the program suggests that they are proceeding reasonably. (See Figure 4-23.)

Students have a goal (Figure 4-24). They must eventually predict what is happening in the rope. Actual numerical predictions are required, with details generated randomly. The student can attempt predictions a number of times. Indeed, the wise student will try the prediction quickly to determine what type of prediction is required. Both numeric and graphic summaries are available to the student (Figures 4-25 and 4-26).

If students have not tried prediction after a long sequence of measurements, the computer persuades them to do so.

The object of the simulation is to develop understanding of the wave phenomenon, the $(x - vt)$ dependence of the traveling pulse to the extent of making detailed numerical predictions. This relationship never appears explicitly. Students may run the dialog a number of times to make the discovery; credit is typically given only after successful completion.

ROPEGAME was developed by Alfred Bork and John Robson of the University of Arizona.

HOCKEY

A quite different use of laboratory simulation, aimed at motivating and elucidating important concepts in physics, is furnished by the Irvine dialog HOCKEY. HOCKEY simulates colliding pucks on air tracks and air tables, frictionless one- and two-dimensional environments. The concepts considered are mass and momentum. The student "discovers" momentum conservation.

After preliminary material the student is presented with a one-dimensional collision of two identical pucks. The student sees (Figure 4-27) a visual stroboscopic presentation of the collision and receives data on velocities before and after collision.

Following several computer-generated experiments, students are allowed to do their own experiments, entering values of velocity before the collision. Again the computer shows both the collision and the velocity values. After several trials the data gained in these simulated experiments is displayed in tabular form (Figure 4-28). The student is asked to make generalizations about what happens to the velocity.

Different types of one-dimensional collisions (elastic, partially elastic, and nonelastic) are considered. Then two-dimensional collisions are investigated.

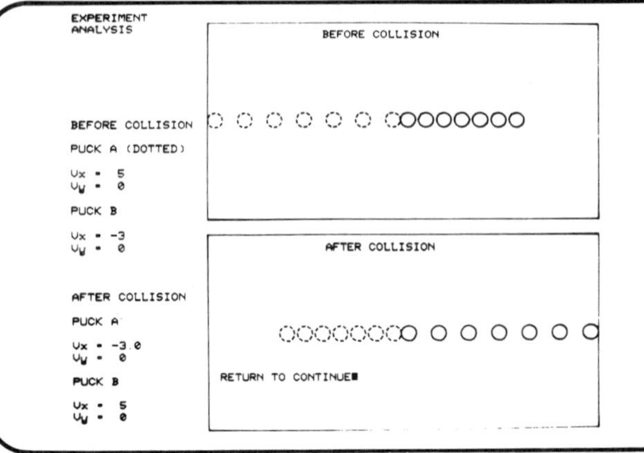

FIGURE 4-27 One-Dimensional Collision in HOCKEY

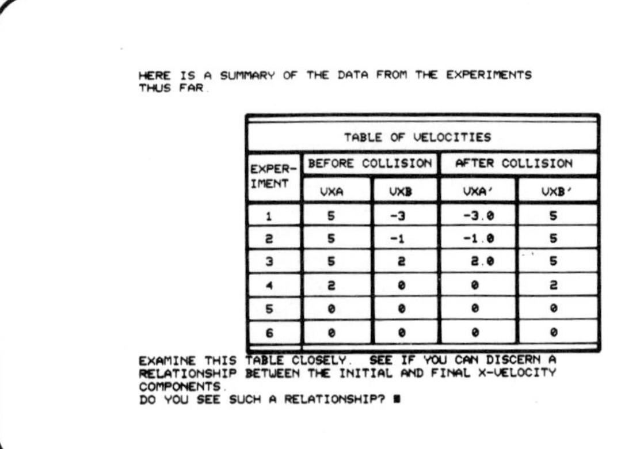
HERE IS A SUMMARY OF THE DATA FROM THE EXPERIMENTS THUS FAR.

TABLE OF VELOCITIES

EXPER-IMENT	BEFORE COLLISION		AFTER COLLISION	
	VXA	VXB	VXA'	VXB'
1	5	-3	-3.0	5
2	5	-1	-1.0	5
3	5	2	2.0	5
4	2	0	0	2
5	0	0	0	0
6	0	0	0	0

EXAMINE THIS TABLE CLOSELY. SEE IF YOU CAN DISCERN A RELATIONSHIP BETWEEN THE INITIAL AND FINAL X-VELOCITY COMPONENTS.
DO YOU SEE SUCH A RELATIONSHIP?

FIGURE 4-28 Table of Student's Data Presented in HOCKEY

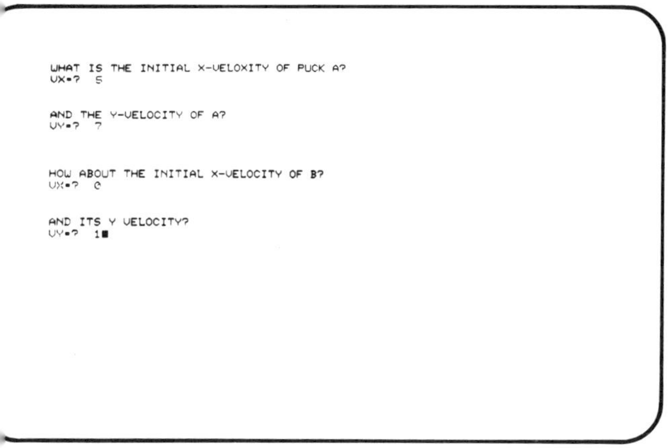

```
WHAT IS THE INITIAL X-VELOXITY OF PUCK A?
UX=? 5

AND THE Y-VELOCITY OF A?
UY=? 7

HOW ABOUT THE INITIAL X-VELOCITY OF B?
UX=? 0

AND ITS Y VELOCITY?
UY=? 1■
```

FIGURE 4-29 Student Entering Data for a Two-Dimensional Collision in HOCKEY

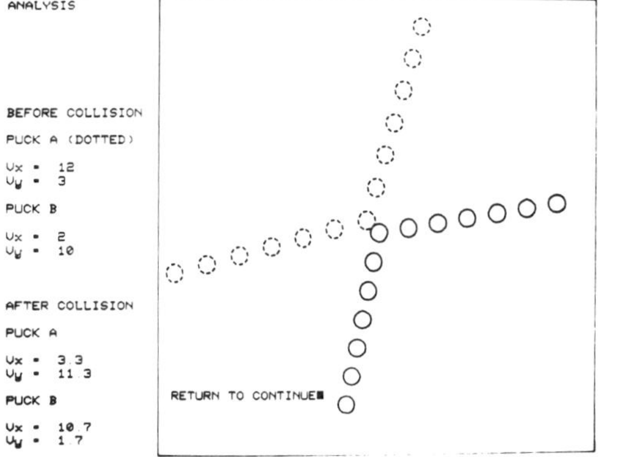

FIGURE 4-30 Display of a Two-Dimensional Collision in HOCKEY

The concept of mass is approached by doubling the initial puck, making one of the pucks twice the mass of the other (though this terminology is not used at this point). If the student is unable to make the generalizations desired, help is given; eventually, it may be necessary to reveal the generalization so that the student can proceed. (See Figures 4-29 and 4-30.)

HOCKEY is primarily the work of Robert Eisberg of the University of California, Santa Barbara.

Controllable Worlds

An extension of laboratory-like simulations, controllable-world simulations provide a richer collection of phenomena, beyond what is practical in ordinary laboratories. The world presented to the student may not be the world we find by experiment, but may be a specially devised world developed for pedagogical purposes.

To use these simulations successfully, great attention must be given to the form of the interaction. The student must, without much previous experience, be able to move freely within the world of phenomena presented, making choices in an easy and natural fashion. That is, the student should be able to play with the phenomena.

MOTION

The first controllable world developed in our project at Irvine was MOTION, an **F** = *m***a** world developed by Richard Ballard and the author. The phenomena presented are all derivable from Newton's laws of mechanics.

The student begins by picking a force law. A wide variety of forces are available (Figure 4-31) and the student can move to a different force at any time. Since the program recognizes variants, natural language descriptions can be used in selecting a force. A vague description often leads to further questioning (Figure 4-32). If the student hesitates, the program offers menus of possibilities, first in general terms and then in detail.

Once students have decided on a force law, they are asked what they would like to do next. The program does not "drive" the student; rather, it persuades students to take an active lead.

After the student picks a force law, the computer sets values for constants in the equations, initial conditions, and variables to be plotted. If a student types only PLOT, or some equivalent, a curve with labeled axes appears. The student can query about variables and change any quantity by entering equations. Variables are identified because the equations are displayed to the student. Thus, in the equation of a gravitational central force, the power is given by a variable *N*, present to –2. The student who wants to see what would happen if gravity were not quite an inverse square can type $N = -2.1$ and the value will be changed.

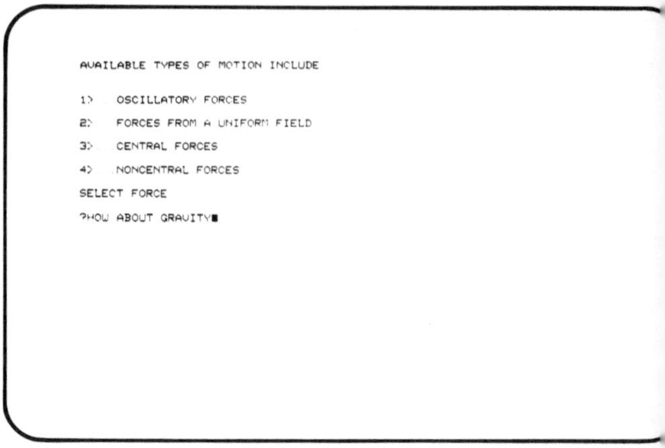

```
AVAILABLE TYPES OF MOTION INCLUDE

1>   OSCILLATORY FORCES
2>   FORCES FROM A UNIFORM FIELD
3>   CENTRAL FORCES
4>   NONCENTRAL FORCES
SELECT FORCE
?HOW ABOUT GRAVITY■
```

FIGURE 4-31 Forces Available in the Dialog MOTION

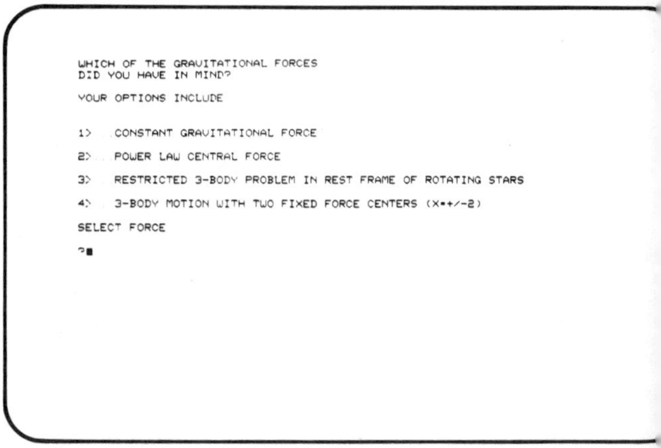

```
WHICH OF THE GRAVITATIONAL FORCES
DID YOU HAVE IN MIND?
YOUR OPTIONS INCLUDE

1>   CONSTANT GRAVITATIONAL FORCE
2>   POWER LAW CENTRAL FORCE
3>   RESTRICTED 3-BODY PROBLEM IN REST FRAME OF ROTATING STARS
4>   3-BODY MOTION WITH TWO FIXED FORCE CENTERS (X=+/-2)
SELECT FORCE
?■
```

FIGURE 4-32 MOTION—Reply when Student Requests "Gravity"

In MOTION, the student can plot any two or any three physically meaningful mechanical variables against each other. The variables available are position, velocity, force, and acceleration components and their magnitudes: the energy—kinetic, potential, or total; the angular momentum components and

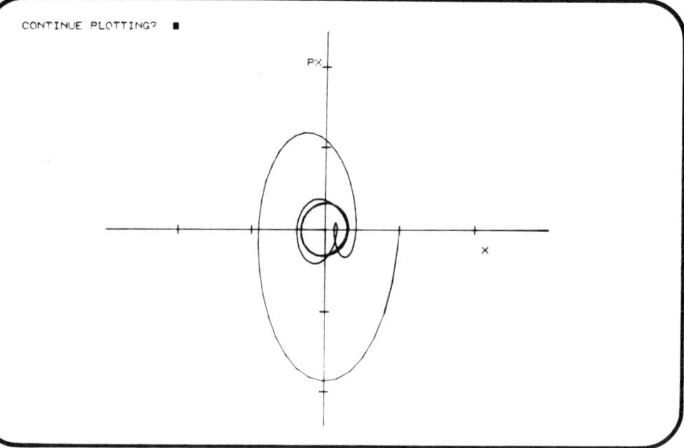

FIGURE 4-33 MOTION—Position Versus Momentum for a Damped-Driven Oscillator

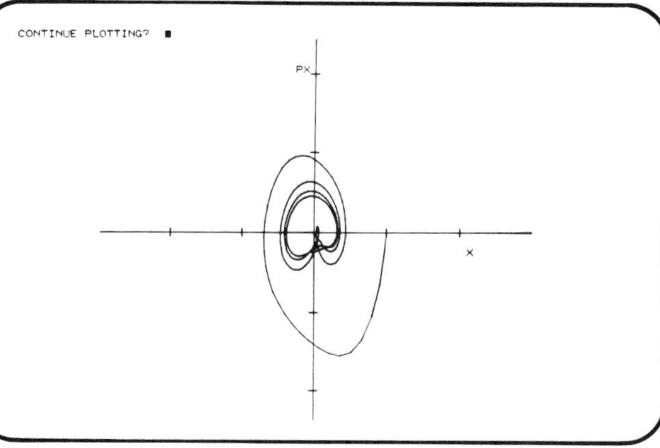

FIGURE 4-34 MOTION—As in Figure 4-33, but Nonlinear Damping

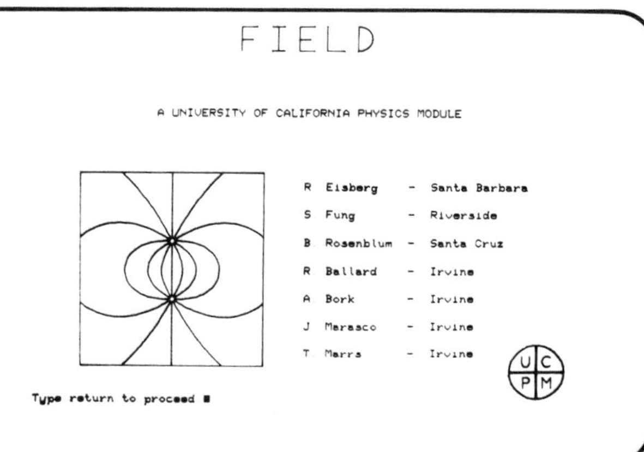

FIGURE 4-35 Title Sequence from FIELD—More Authors Than Usual!

magnitude; and the time. Figures 4-33 and 4-34 show phase space plots, position versus momentum, for a damped driven oscillator. The distinction between transient and steady state solutions is clear. Figure 4-33 shows linear damping; Figure 4-34 shows damping proportional to the cube of the velocity.

MOTION is further discussed in the next article. Although it was our original intent, we have not added instructional sequences to MOTION. However, the next two examples provide both the controllable world and the associated pedagogical material.

FIELD

This dialog is an electrostatics learning module, prepared by a group of University of California faculty members in a university-sponsored project to encourage intercampus cooperation. As with our other dialogs, the title screen (Figure 4-35) indicates the authors.

FIELD is "map-driven." It has a central map showing the major areas (Figure 2-9 in Chapter 2). The student can return to this map at any input by typing MAP. Thus, the learner can control sequencing of the material.

The map provides a browsing capability for the person who is examining it, e.g., an instructor considering using it. This map is content-oriented in contrast to the map in the next simulation, where the emphasis is on structure.

The map for FIELD shows three aspects of the program. First, FIELD contains learning sequences for electrostatics, including the concepts of electric field and field lines. Second, the dialog has a *facility,* a plotting capability that allows the student to place charges where desired and then plots field lines (Figure 4-36) and equipotential lines (Figure 4-37). As with other facilities, it is flexible, allowing a number of student variants. The plotting facility is the only part of FIELD that is a controllable world.

The third component, two quizzes, reviews electrostatics. One involves the straightforward use of Coulomb's law in the form typical in beginning Physics courses (Figures 4-38 and 4-39). The other quiz verifies that the student understands field line diagrams (Figures 4-40, 4-41, and 4-42). Thus, it is closely related to both the teaching sequences about field lines and to the plotting facility that draws such lines, reinforcing both and showing the student weaknesses in understanding FIELD is further discussed on pages 135–140.

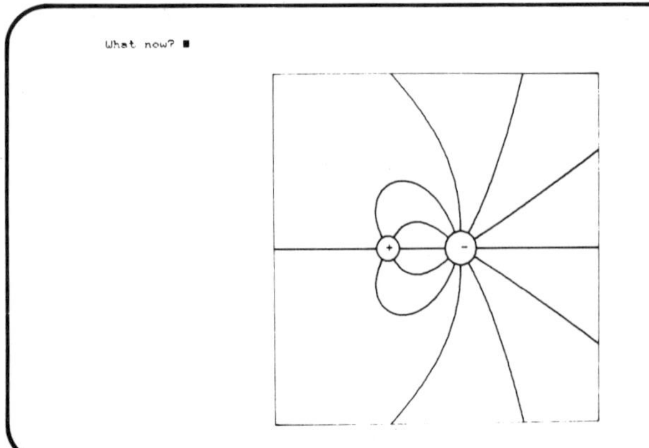

FIGURE 4-36 Field Line Plot from FIELD, Two Unequal Charges

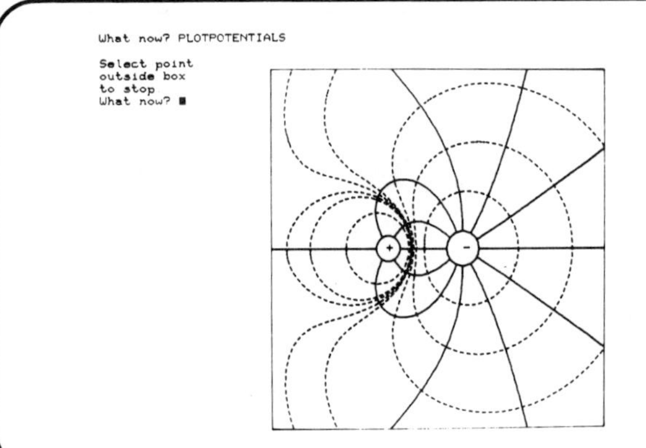

FIGURE 4-37 Equipotential Lines Added to Previous Plot

SPACE

The last example of a controllable world is a relativity dialog, SPACE. The map for SPACE is different than that for FIELD. Rather than section content, it shows the program's pedagogical strategy, adapted from Jean Piaget and Robert Karplus.

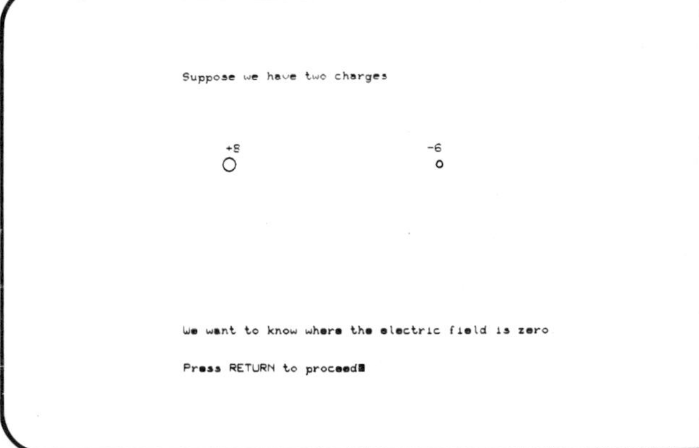

FIGURE 4-38 First Quiz in FIELD

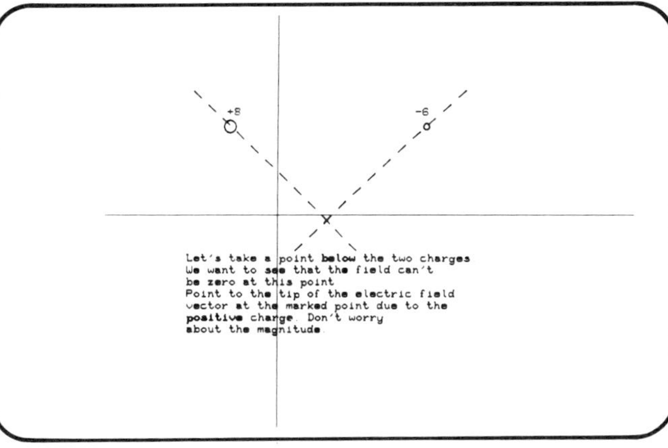

FIGURE 4-39 First Quiz in FIELD, Help Sequence

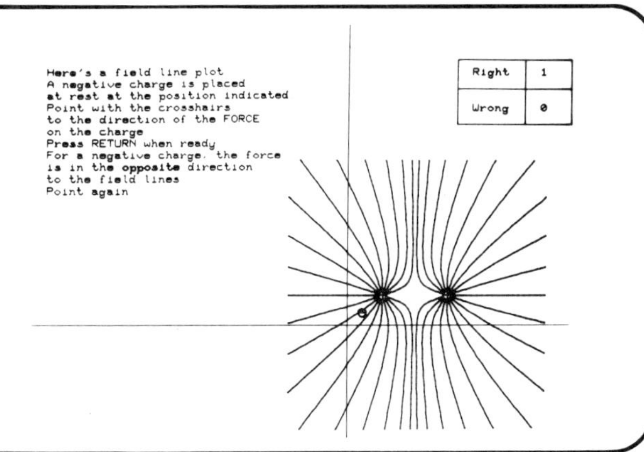

FIGURE 4-40 FIELD, Second Quiz—Force on Charged Particle

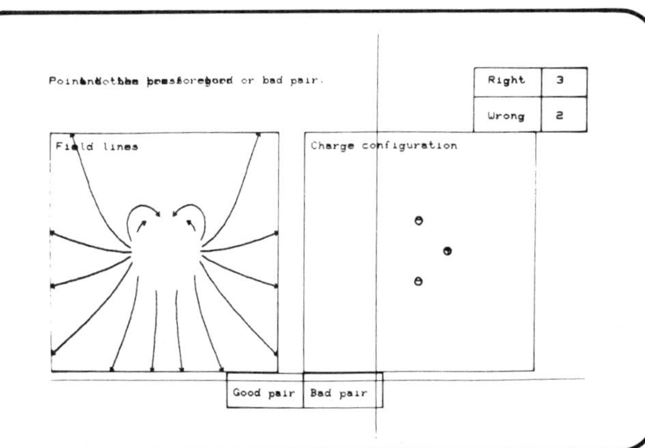

FIGURE 4-41 FIELD, Second Quiz—What Charges Produce The Field Shown?

The three principal sections of SPACE are: (1) concept sequences, where the student learns particular concepts dealing with relativity; (2) problem sequences, where students demonstrate that they can use the knowledge about relativity they have acquired; and (3) a space-time diagram. The space-time diagram allows students to specify events and world lines (Figures 4-43 and 4-44), and then to perform Lorentz transformations (Figure 4-45) on these world lines. The space-time diagram is the controllable world; but to make this simulation a more useful teaching and learning device, it is embedded in the context of the concepts and problems.

Earlier work on relativistic simulation was carried out by Edwin Taylor at the Massachusetts Institute of Technology and Tim Kelley at Oregon State University and Southern Oregon College. SPACE profited from these approaches.

Problem Simulations

In another type of simulation, the problem simulation, a computer program simulates a class of problems—sometimes a very wide class of problems. Problem simulations can either assist students in learning how to solve problems, such as some of the more elaborate heuristic programs available from the artificial intelligence community, or can serve as the basis for on-line tests. The following example, concerning projectile motion, is one of the on-line tests in the beginning course at Irvine.

The dialog chooses randomly between one of the five basic types of projectile motion problems. (These problems are fundamentally identical from the instructor's point of view, but seem different to the student.) In a second random choice, the program determines which variables are known or unknown. Finally, it picks the values of the known variables within specifications provided by the instructor. Thus, the program simulates almost any projectile motion problem that might occur in a textbook or on an exam. Figures 4-46 and 4-47 show two sample problems.

Games

A common type of simulation is the game. While the game may not differ from other simulations, its presentation does. With games we rely on the fact that most people enjoy them.

The motivational value of games is easily seen, but their pedagogical usefulness is often questioned. As one observes students using games, via computer or other simulations that are reportedly learning activities, one cannot help but notice that the games function primarily as entertainments and only slightly, if at all, as learning experiences. Furthermore, the proponents of games seldom relate them to instructional objectives.

Motivation is an important factor, not to be belittled. However, if the game is not related to other learning experiences and tests in the course, it is likely to be of little

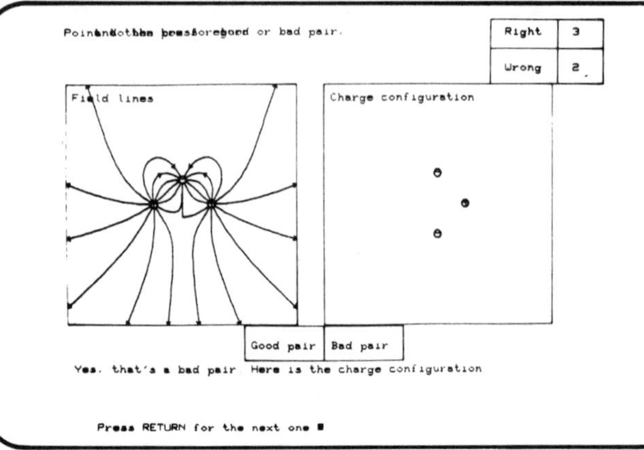

FIGURE 4-42 FIELD, Second Quiz—Response to Previous Question

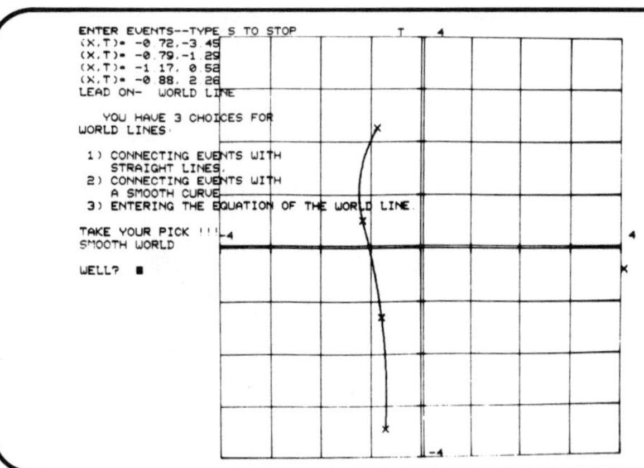

FIGURE 4-43 Entering World Lines in SPACE (See Figure 2-14)

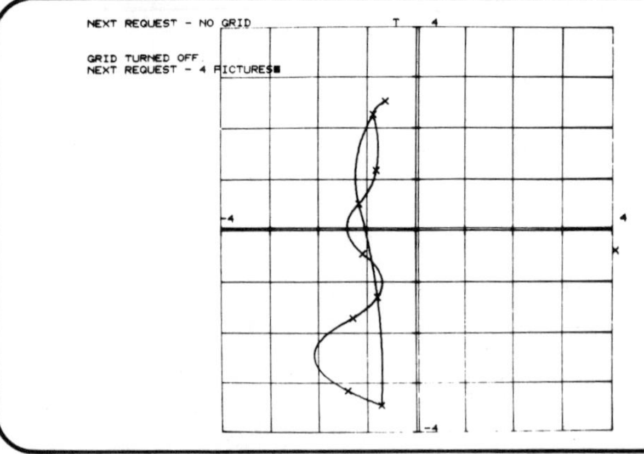

FIGURE 4-44 SPACE with Several World Lines

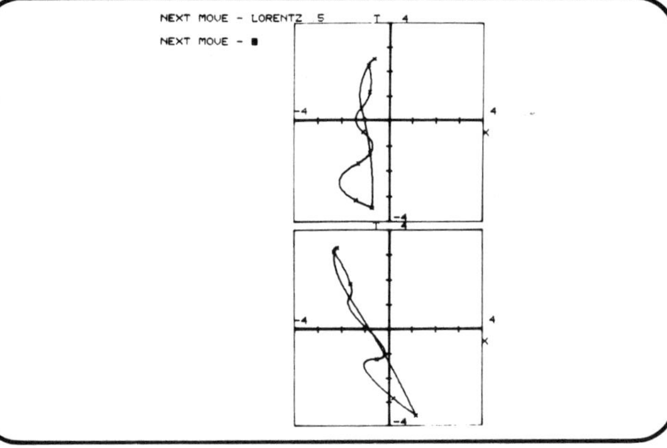

FIGURE 4-45 SPACE, showing Lorentz Transformation of Space-Time

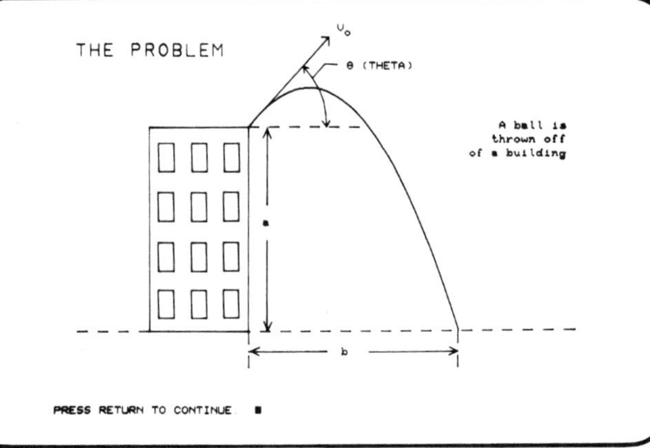

FIGURE 4-46 Problem Generated by the Quiz PROJECTILE

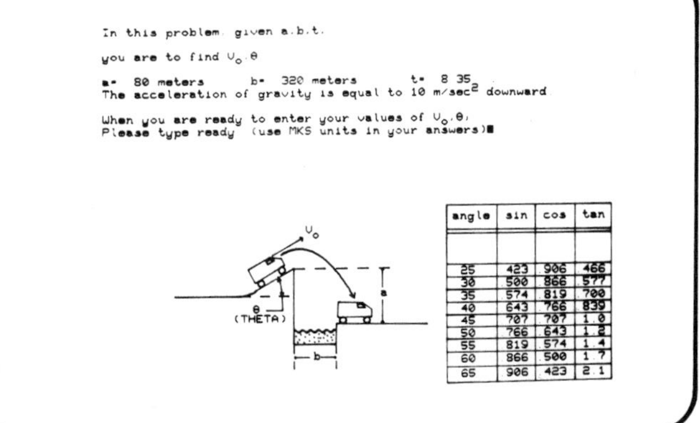

FIGURE 4-47 Different PROJECTILE Problem, Showing Numerical Information Also

value pedagogically. Developing an interesting game that provides some learning experience is a much more difficult task than developing a game that is merely intriguing.

Problems in Using Simulations

Simulations are not an unmixed blessing. Often, they are highly appealing to the instructor and colleagues, but unless they have entertainment value as games, they may be far less appealing to the students.

The major difficulty with simulations is that they often have no relationship to other course components. Simulations of this type will often be heavily used by more motivated students in the class, but may be completely ignored by average students. It is critical, as with any learning material, to integrate simulations into full modules or full courses. Unless the simulation is part of the curriculum, in some way that has been carefully developed, it is not likely to prove valuable for the class as a whole.

A critical first step in employing a simulation in a course is a comprehensive determination of course objectives—not only the simple ideas, behavioral objectives, but also the underlying goals. Many science and engineering courses, regardless of any other stated objectives, are very much concerned with the art of problem-solving, getting students to solve increasingly difficult problems.

A thorough examination of what the course is intended to accomplish is essential in developing a course or integrating new material, such as simulation, into an existing course. Unfortunately this development seldom takes place. Perhaps the only really thorough course developments are those that have been undertaken at such institutions as The Open University and the University of Mid-America. But even in an individual course taught by a single instructor, some reasonable attempts in this direction should be made.

When these objectives have been defined, the next stage is to ask how a computer program, a simulation, or some other computer learning aid, can help achieve the objectives. Such an aid might not be effective for all students, since students have different learning styles. In this regard, particular attention needs to be given to the majority of the students. Motivated students will learn with almost any method and seldom require the individualized attention needed by students who have trouble learning with conventional modes.

To say "average" or "poor" gives the wrong impression. Students may be average only because their modes of learning are not the highly verbally-oriented (lecture-textbook) modes assumed in large beginning classes today. They may require different approaches. Or they may need help, not provided by the course materials, to overcome an inadequate background. These students might become "good" students in more suitable learning environments.

From the student point of view, the course objectives are best defined by the problems, quizzes, and tests that structure the course. Thus, the question of whether a particular simulation helps with the course can be answered by determining whether it aids many students either directly, by giving credit for completion or indirectly, by making it more likely that the student will do well on the quizzes and tests.

The simulation should become part of the class grading structure, since this structure motivates the work of many students. One would like to think that students do not worry about grades, and for some students and some schools that deemphasize grades, that is indeed the case. But for the vast majority of students, grades are an influential factor in classroom performance.

Another possibility is to have testing or homework depend directly on the use of the simulation. If an important objective, such as the building up of student intuition, is associated with the simulation, then the instructor wants to be sure that the students have mastered the material. The only way to let students know that they have the necessary competency, or to let the instructor know it, is to require testing based on the simulation. The test on field lines in FIELD, mentioned above, is one example.

Another strategy is reflected in several of the examples given. In SPACE and in FIELD the simulation is embedded within a wider learning context. Thus, the simulation is not an isolated event, but is a meaningful part of an instructional unit. Future programs should be able to exploit this feature more than our present one,

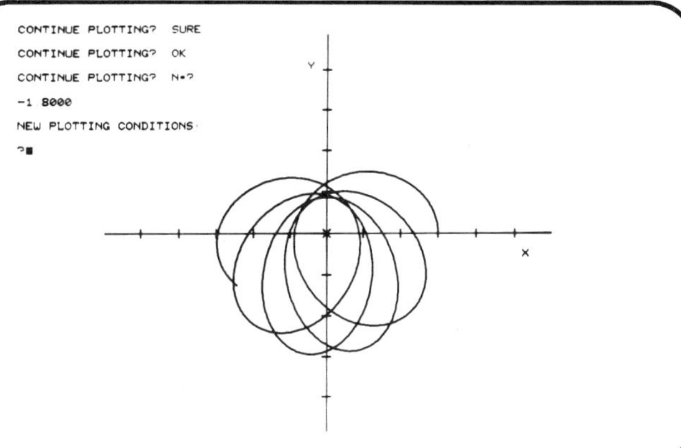
CONTINUE PLOTTING? SURE
CONTINUE PLOTTING? OK
CONTINUE PLOTTING? N=?
-1.8000
NEW PLOTTING CONDITIONS
?
Y
X

FIGURE 4-48 MOTION—Inverse 1.8 Power Force

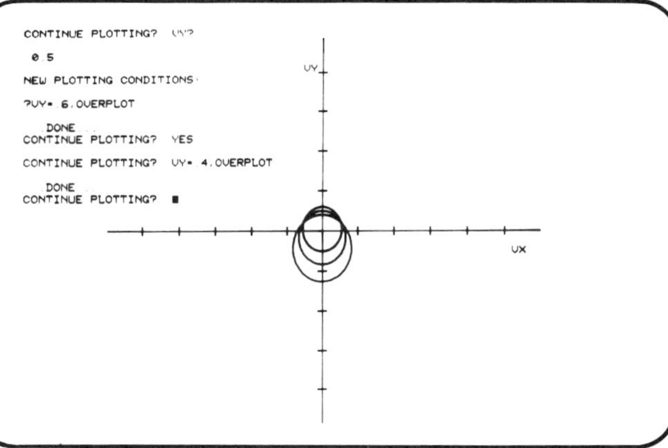
CONTINUE PLOTTING? VY?
0.5
NEW PLOTTING CONDITIONS
?VY= .6,OVERPLOT
DONE
CONTINUE PLOTTING? YES
CONTINUE PLOTTING? VY= .4,OVERPLOT
DONE
CONTINUE PLOTTING?
VY
VX

FIGURE 4-49 MOTION—Inverse Square Force, Circles in Velocity Space

making it possible for the student not only to observe the experiences desired but to freely question the program about the details of what is happening or about related materials.

A third way of integrating the simulation within a course structure is provided by auxiliary material, usually printed material that aids the student in using the simulation. Such materials developed at Irvine are called computer exercises, oriented toward building intuition. The exercises can be a required part of the course or they can be optional.

Typical computer exercises are three- or four-page documents, a student workbook; the student must fill in blanks. The material is used with a controllable world. Consider one of the exercises for use with MOTION, on gravitational motion. First, the student is given guidance in entering MOTION and picking the appropriate force law—an inverse square force, initially for a single particle. The first task the student is assigned is to investigate how varying the initial conditions affects the orbits. Students will see that both closed and unclosed orbits exist, and that the closed orbits are ellipses. (Some students will already know this and will assume that the oval figure they see is an ellipse.)

Then the exercise questions what would happen if gravity were not quite an inverse square force. Since students can change all the equation constants in MOTION, they can type in $N = -1.8$. An orbit that was initially an ellipse becomes a nonclosed orbit (Figure 4-48). The ellipse appears to recess slowly as time elapses. The exercise then introduces an abstract space, velocity space (x component of velocity versus y component of velocity), and queries the student as to what the closed orbits look like when plotted in velocity space. The curves for inverse square force are immediately recognizable as circles (Figure 4-49), and the question is raised, although not necessarily answered, as to why the curves in velocity space are circular. Only the better students pursue the full details, but every student gains a range of experiences with gravitational force. The computer exercises are currently being rewritten, based on advice from the project evaluation.

The Future of Simulations

Although classroom simulations present more difficulties than many teachers expect, they are nevertheless a useful educational tool. It seems reasonable to predict that their use will increase, as we gain experience in pedagogically effective methods of presentation.

Several capabilities not yet common are likely to be important. The first is color. Color systems now exist and are declining rapidly in cost, but we have yet to see widespread use of color in effective computer-based learning. The importance of color becomes immediately apparent as soon as one starts designing simulations. Consider, for example, some noncomputer simulations, such as Monopoly™ and other board games; color plays an almost constant role. The fact that color usually has not been available in computer-based materials is an accident of the technology. We can expect it to make an important contribution soon.

Animation is another feature currently missing from most simulations. Full animation in a timesharing environment requires either much faster communication rates than those currently used for most learning situations, or much more intelligent displays. Stand-alone personal systems, which avoid communication problems, offer a more likely approach. Our work at Irvine is moving toward such systems; limited but useful animation is possible on such inexpensive stand-alones as the Terak 8510/a.

Another restriction is calculational capability. If one wants to simulate a quantum mechanical world, the world of atomic and nuclear structure, the calculations are massive; even large-scale timesharing systems cannot process them rapidly enough to maintain an interactive environment. The speed of current computer equipment denies us a wide range of simulations. But this limitation, too, will diminish as computer technology progresses.

Much more attention must be given to integrating simulations into the course as a whole or into learning sequences independent of courses. Progress has been made, but much work remains before we can realize the full potential of simulations. Since simulations represent only one mode of computer-aided learning materials, they should not be considered in isolation. At present, the total impact of computers on educational structures is small; only a few courses at any level employ computers, and even fewer employ them in any fundamental or extensive manner. But this situation, too, will change. Within the next 25 years the computer will become increasingly important and even dominant in many areas. It should be an exciting time.

COMPUTERS AS AN AID TO INCREASING PHYSICAL INTUITION

Experience and Learning

One of the features of early childhood education is that children start school with a large amount of free-form experience related to topics to be studied. This experience can later be increased in the classroom through various formal activities.

Consider the learning of addition. When children begin to learn addition, they have already been playing with objects such as blocks for a long time. The notion of adding one collection of blocks to another collection of blocks is not a new idea, because previous play with blocks has already provided a range of unconnected experiences that the teacher can draw on. The addition of two lengths provides another set of such experience. The role of such experience in education, both formal and informal, is well established.

The American Journal of Physics, vol. 46, no. 8.

However, as education moves to more and more abstract ideas, students' experiences relevant to what is to be learned become fewer and fewer. This is particularly a problem in the physical sciences as material becomes more abstract and mathematical in upper division and graduate courses.

We can ask how to provide such experiences to science students at the university level, even though everyday life does not provide them. A strategy developed at the University of California, Irvine, uses the computer, in the form of "controllable worlds," with printed auxiliary material, to generate for each student individually experiences that may be useful in learning physics and in promoting physical intuition.

An important goal of the activities is to increase insight about the behavior of physical systems, insight that could be gained only through such detailed experience. The goal is to make this experience available and accessible to all beginning Physics students, providing them with a larger and richer perspective.

Most Physics teachers would see such increased insight as very important. A complaint often registered at doctoral examinations is that some graduate students can carry out the mathematical manipulations, even for very advanced problems, but have little physical intuition as to what is happening. Such insight is critical for successful research, and so courses should consider how to assist students in this regard.

"Intuition" can have a variety of meanings. One way of gaining intuition is to observe the actual system; thus the student might manipulate a mass moving on the end of a spring, with a driving force, to develop insight on driven oscillators. But many aspects of the motion important to the physics are hard to "see" directly; thus the distinction between transient and steady-state behavior is difficult to observe directly. But if we can "see" the system move in "phase" space, position versus momentum, we can develop a better "feel" for the transition to steady state. Our direct experience is connected with configuration space; but other space, in a sense just as "real" as configuration space, is accessible through a graphic computer system.

An insight is not something that can be fully discussed in rational terms. Edward G. Boring[19] discusses an insight into the solution to a simple puzzle as follows:

> "Take a simple controlled insight of seeing how the ring puzzle is solved. Who is there, that has had that insight, and can say how it occurred? At one moment you are frustrated. Then if you are a visualizer, there is a breathless instant in which you see the loop being pulled through the hole and you wonder if that might not carry the solution, and then suddenly, you see that it is the solution, that the ring can pass around the loop if the loop is brought through the hole to the ring. But to know all that is not to say how insight occurs, much less to say why. There is still an adventitious leap from nothing to something, an unconscious leap whose continuity and causes remain hidden in the nervous system."

We can help the potential physicist develop better insight through the computer experiences described in this paper.

Simulations and Controllable Worlds

The form of computer program best able to provide experiences and so provide a chance to increase intuition is the simulation. The computer models certain aspects of the world or of an imaginary world created by the teacher for pedagogical purposes.

Existing simulations, while appealing to the teacher, often do not serve students well. The first problem is that the programmer or teacher often fails to consider adequately how the simulation is to be employed with the expected student population. Because of the nature of simulation, students will have to enter some information into the program.

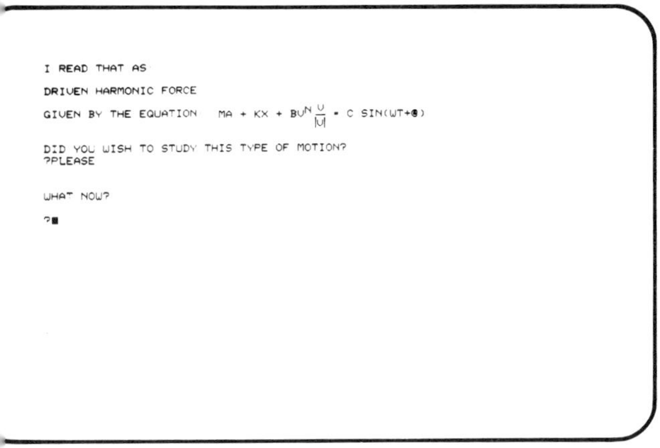

```
I READ THAT AS

DRIVEN HARMONIC FORCE

GIVEN BY THE EQUATION   MA + KX + BV^N V/|V| = C SIN(WT+θ)

DID YOU WISH TO STUDY THIS TYPE OF MOTION?
?PLEASE

WHAT NOW?

?■
```

FIGURE 4-50 MOTION—Student Requests Driven Oscillator

Teachers tend to assume that students will furnish all this input, just as a teacher would do in a similar research application. Sometimes students are expected to enter long lists of numbers, using auxiliary printed materials to know which number goes with which variable. Such an approach is undesirable. But even if students provide input in response to computer requests, with students having natural ways of entering the desired information, they are often asked for information they do not understand. Thus, in a simulation of gravitational motion, if students are asked for initial conditions, they are not likely to know what ranges of initial conditions produce useful results. So they tend to enter random values.

When we first began designing such simulations at Irvine, we were concerned with how they were going to interface with the average student. My colleague, Richard Ballard, and I worked on a simulation we had been discussing for some time, a Newtonian mechanical world called MOTION. Instead of asking students for all the parameters, unknown to them initially, we take the opposite tack, starting any given mechanical situation with a completely loaded set of parameters that would already produce interesting curves. We call such simulations, oriented to students, controllable worlds.

Thus students could begin immediately examining a motion, one that was interesting enough to have been selected by the instructor for just this purpose. Then students could be provided with facilities for changing all the conditions, facilities that react in a natural way to a wide variety of student requests. Experiences in using MOTION over the last few years indicate that we have been successful in this quest.

The following sequence from MOTION gives some notion of the simulation and its student interface. The student has chosen to work with a driven oscillator, and is reasonably well motivated to study the system. The student has requested the driven oscillator. The computer shows the equation of motion for the oscillator, as indicated in Figure 4-50. The equation of motion displayed on the screen contains a number of parameters such as the mass and spring constant. As with the initial conditions, these parameters will have initial preset values; when the student types PLOT, a curve immediately appears on the screen. In the case of the driven oscillator the default curve, a plot of position versus time, is shown in Figure 4-51.

The student can query about current values of constants or initial conditions. Figure 4-52 shows one such query. The student can change these values by entering small equations and can then replot. In Figure 4-53, the spring constant is altered, and the new curve appears over the previous curve.

An important motivation for our developing a program such as MOTION was to allow students a quicker access to abstract spaces important in physics. While students have seen moving objects, they have not in any literal sense gained direct experience in such spaces as phase space. These spaces often provide new and instructive views about the behavior of mechanical systems.

The student can plot a wide variety of spaces in MOTION. The question of which space is plotted initially, as in this example, is determined by the program authors. In Figure 4-54, the student requests a plot of the magnitude of velocity versus time.

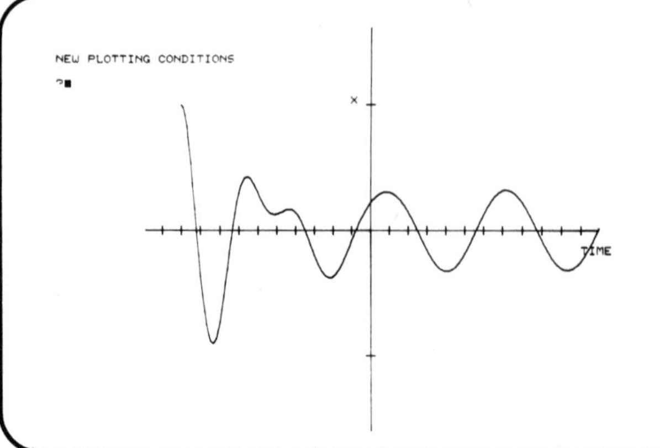

FIGURE 4-51 Initial Driven Oscillator Position-Time Plot, MOTION

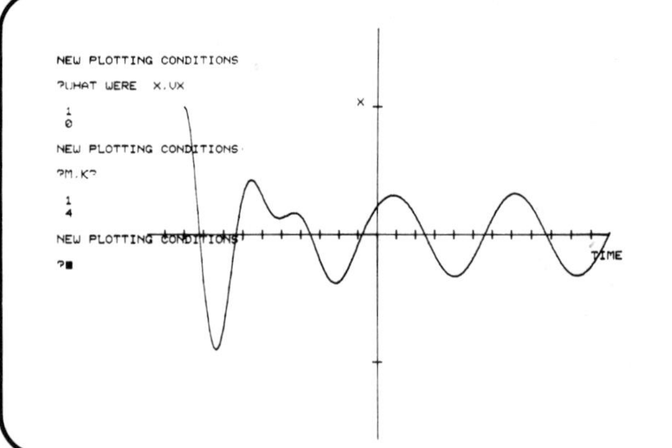

FIGURE 4-52 MOTION—Student Asks for Initial Position, Velocity, Mass, and Spring Constant

Problems with Controllable Worlds

Several problems occur with students' use of controllable worlds. These problems can limit the effectiveness of such programs, particularly in large classes.

First, how are students to learn to use the facility? As students gain more freedom to move around within the program, instructions for employing this freedom can become correspondingly more complex. Programs can do some self-teaching, with initial directions or by offering help when students enter responses that cannot be analyzed. Auxiliary printed guides to the program may be provided to students in the developer's classes, provided the instructor can be certain that everyone has such

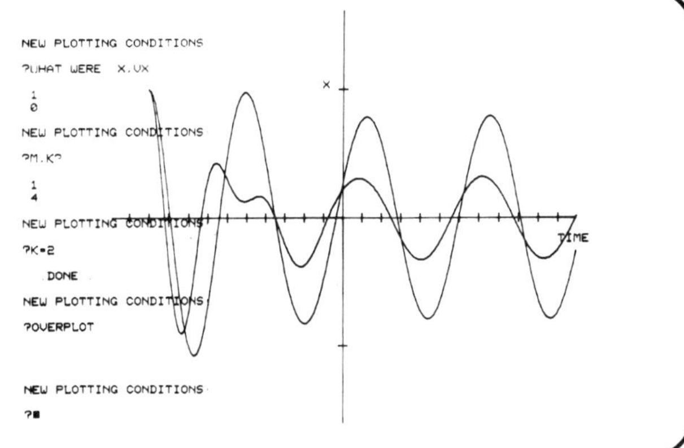

FIGURE 4-53 Student Changes Spring Constant (Driven Oscillator, MOTION)

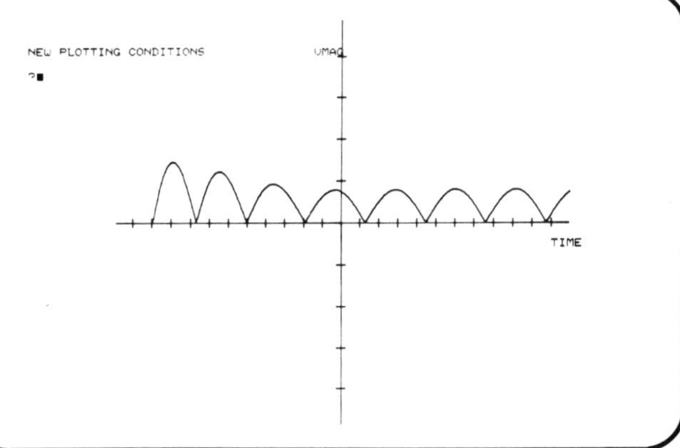

FIGURE 4-54 MOTION—Driven Oscillator, Magnitude of Velocity Versus Time

material. Auxiliary learning aids such as slide-tape shows can also be provided, but only when it is clear in just which rooms the material will be utilized. We have such auxiliary aids for MOTION at Irvine to aid students.

A second problem concerns motivation. While faculty members and highly motivated students will often become entranced with a program such as MOTION, regarding this as a unique and interesting experience, not all students in a typical large beginning course are similarly motivated! Student motivation is almost entirely lacking in the dominant beginning Physics courses in most universities today, Premedical Physics. In these courses we have a captive audience; most students would omit the course were it not required by the medical schools.

The question of how to persuade the average student to employ computer-based simulations designed to increase experiences is one that must be answered. It does not suffice to design materials appealing to the instructor and to the motivated students. We employ these materials with all students, if we consider these intuition-building materials to be useful to all students.

Poorly motivated students will use the controllable world experience only when they are related to the performance criteria of the course. Students quickly determine that some of the activities in courses are relevant to doing well on tests (and thus to making a good grade), while others are not. Students with little direct motivation to learn Physics may nevertheless be highly motivated toward making a good grade. Premedical students must make good grades in Physics if they are to get into medical school. So we can expect students to employ the simulations if such employment affects grades.

Computer Exercises

To resolve some of these problems, we have experimented at Irvine with a different way of using controllable worlds. The basic tactic is to provide the student with a workbook, a series of computer "exercises" at various points during the course. The following lists the currently available computer exercises, with an indication of the computer dialogs needed.

1. Motion with blows—BLOW

2. Exploring oscillators—MOTION

3. Gravitational motion—MOTION

4. Exploring energy—MOTION

5. More about oscillators—MOTION

6. Electromagnetic fields—FIELD

7. Electrostatic potentials—FIELD

8. Charged particle in electromagnetic field—MOTION

As mentioned, new exercises are under preparation.

To be sure students use this material, as already suggested, it must be integrated into the class program. In our class, students handed in exercises as they completed corresponding units in the course.

The computer exercises provide guidance for using the associated dialogs. Thus they avoid simply putting students into the program and leaving them to their own resources. Students are told what to type, particularly in the early parts of the exercise. Students have considerable freedom to explore the situation, because the questions asked are very open-ended. They are usually of the type "Describe what you see in such and such a case," or "Describe what happens." Students are encouraged to experiment freely, but we provide a basic set of experiences for all.

The student material in the next section, from the gravitational exercise, gives a better idea of the computer exercises. Students hand in this questionnaire, with material filled in.

Exploring Gravitational Motion

The following material is based on the use of dialog MOTION. The purpose is to gain further experience with gravitational motion.

1. Log on, enter MOTION, and choose INVERSE SQUARE force. The initial PLOT is for $X = 3$, $Y = 0$, $VX = 0$, $VY = -0.5$.

2. OVERPLOT with VY values from 0.4 to 1, in steps of 0.1. Describe the results. Are there different types of orbits? (You may want to alter your viewpoint with CLOSER or BACK.)

3. Set $VY = 0.5$. Then PLOT T,X and OVERPLOT T,Y. Do the resulting curves resemble any functions you are acquainted with?

4. Now study the system point in velocity space. That is, PLOT *VX VS VY* for the range of initial conditions suggested in step 2 above. What orbits do you find?

5. Now you are to see what would happen if gravitational force were not quite inverse square. Ask for the EQUATION again; the power is N. Set $N = -1.9$. Return to plotting the X–Y space, investigating a range of values around –2. You may want to continue plotting each orbit. What can you say about the results? What happens for values less than 2? Greater than 2?

6. What happens in step 5 if we examine behavior in velocity space?

7. Now consider the case of two gravitational force centers, as if you had two fixed suns. Request TWO FORCE CENTERS at any input. The initial conditions will be reset. Determine them by typing $X,Y,VX,VY = ?$ PLOT the orbit. Discuss the possibility of life on a planet with such an orbit.

8. See if you can find velocities that give closed (repeated) orbits. What velocities do this? Sketch the orbits.

COMPUTER DIALOGS TO AID FORMAL REASONING

With Arnold Arons

Abstract

This article describes six computer dialogs which, as one principal purpose, assist students in making the transition to formal reasoning.

Effective teaching and learning in any level depends on appreciation and understanding of the patterns of intellectual growth in students; as students progress from early childhood to maturity, intellectual growth and development takes place. Even casual observations show that intellectual skills realizable by many adults are not realizable by a young child.

One of the serious students of such development, conducting many empirical studies, is the French-Swiss psychologist, Jean Piaget. Based on his studies of children, he outlined a series of stages leading to the fully mature student who is capable of formal abstract reasoning. These ideas have influenced important curriculum development projects in the United States such as the Science Curriculum Improvement Study, directed by Robert Karplus at the Lawrence Hall of Science, University of California, Berkeley.

National Educational Computing Conference 1979, *Proceedings*.

It has only been within the past few years that such concepts have been applied to university education. Piaget represented the final transition from concrete operational reasoning to formal reasoning as occurring at about age 14. Recently a number of surveys examining American college students have determined, much to the surprise of many, that half of all college students are not capable of all aspects of reasoning. Furthermore, this ratio does not seem to change during the four years of university life.

This failure to attain full reasoning capability presents two problems. One is the immediate problem of the person teaching college courses. Most college courses assume the attributes of formal reasoning. It is, therefore, not surprising that many students have difficulty with these courses. An even greater problem is suggested when we realize that our university students go out into society as educated individuals. These concrete thinkers can only be described as intellectually crippled.

This brief introduction to the problem is not intended to be exhaustive. The reader is referred to these references if further details are needed[20, 21].

Enter the Computer

It is our thesis that interactive student-computer dialogs, with the students interacting on a one-to-one or small-group basis with computer programs prepared by good teachers, can be an extremely important step to solving the problems just raised. In this section we elucidate the reasons why the computer is an appropriate tool.

First, it should be noted that few current university teachers, or teachers at any level, are aware of the problems suggested. Thus, it is unlikely that our teachers will react without either special material or additional training. The problem of providing aid to students in reasoning cannot be expected to come primarily from the existing teaching community unless a sizable effort is made.

Individuals in various parts of the country are reporting success in aiding students in making this important progression. These teachers impact only the local region, although their effects are expanded by talks at national meetings. These effects have also been extended by the development, with the cooperation of the American Association of Physics Teachers, of a transportable workshop for instructors. But primarily the experts have only a local effect, not a national one.

The next point is the increasing evidence that the computer can be an effective learning tool. Indeed, particularly in the sciences, this realization is gaining such common acceptance at the present time that little more need be said. Perhaps the best sources of information are the proceedings of the Conference on Computers in the Undergraduate Curriculum[22] for the last 10 years. Another interesting information source is the articles in *Change* magazine[23] on innovative teaching projects in the United States (prepared with a grant from the Fund for the Improvement of Post Secondary Education). While this project was not directly concerned with computers, nevertheless, some of the courses described in the *Change* article do involve computers within course material.

It is not hard to see why the computer is turning out to be a very effective learning medium. The computer can make the learning experience an active experience, an experience where the student is constantly participating in the learning process. The situation resembles that seen in a Socratic dialog, with the computer asking questions and the student responding in everyday language. This is to be contrasted with the lecture environment where the student is usually in a passive or receptive mode.

The computer provides an individualized and personalized learning medium, not possible within most mass instructional environments. The program pays careful attention to what the student is typing and behaves uniquely for each student. Not all existing material is fully personalized. But enough material exists to show that individualized interactive capability is possible and practical.

Another factor always important when considering computers is the rapidly decreasing cost in this area. Inexpensive, stand-alone, home systems are already available, and costs will continue to decline.

The Dialogs

The six dialogs described were developed by the authors in two Christmas sessions at the University of California, Irvine. Each occupies approximately an hour's time for the "average" student, but the deviation is great. The dialogs are as follows:

1. *TERRA*—A dialog for discussing the sky as seen from the earth.

2. *LUNA*—A study of the phases of the moon, with emphasis on the notion of scientific models and deductions from them.

3. *HEAT*—An introduction to the concept of heat through a series of simple everyday concrete experiences.

4. *MFIELD*—An introduction to magnetic fields, treating the field due to a long, straight wire, again staying close to the observable phenomena.

5. *MFIELD2*—An extension of the previous dialog to consider the force between current carrying wires.

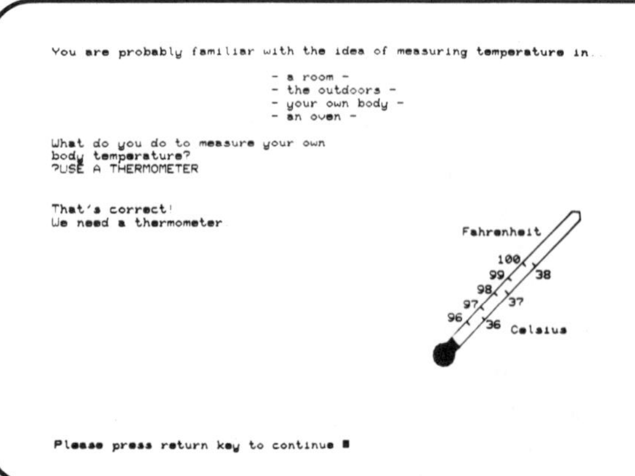

FIGURE 4-55 From HEAT, Taking Temperature

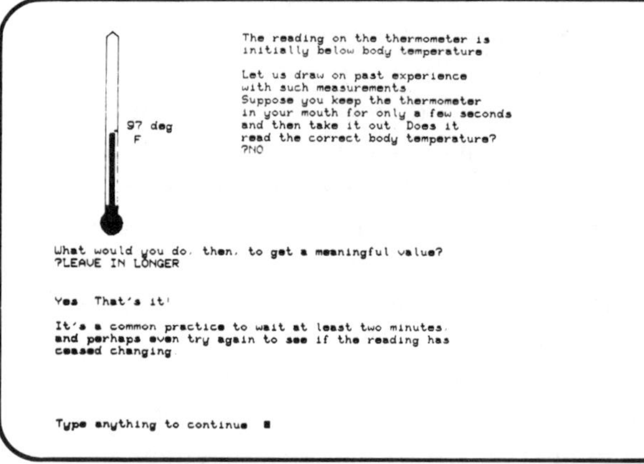

FIGURE 4-56 Further Details on Taking Temperature from HEAT

6. *MFIELD3*—Again an extension of the magnetic field ideas, this time to magnetic induction.

LUNA and TERRA are discussed in "Two New Graphic Computer Dialogs for Teachers" earlier in this chapter. Space does not permit any full description, so we will present one dialog, hoping to show the flavor of some of the others. The dialog we consider is HEAT.

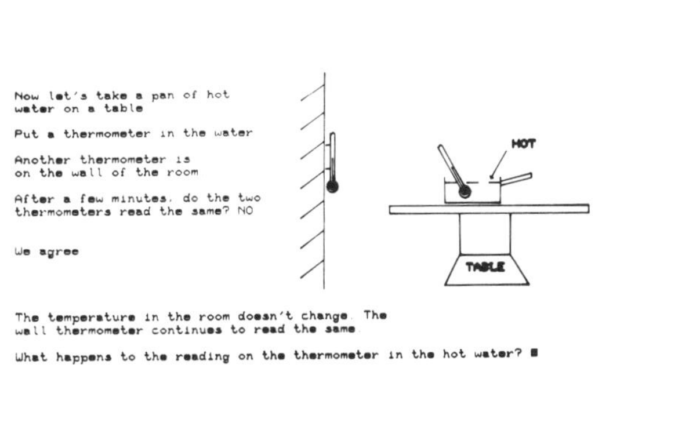

FIGURE 4-57 HEAT, Second Sequence—Hot Water Cooling on a Table

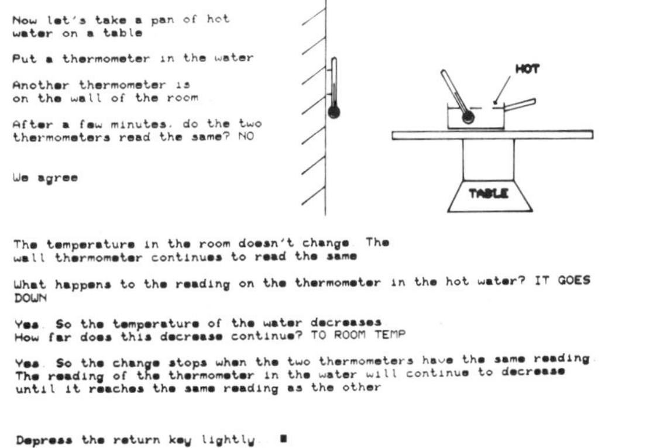

FIGURE 4-58 HEAT, Second Sequence, Continued

Heat

HEAT follows the principles suggested—introducing abstract ideas, heat transfer and heat, through a series of concrete experiences. The experiences are all simple kitchen physics. They involve only thermometers as a measuring device. Hot water, cold water, ice cubes, vacuum bottles, burners, all enter the discussion. The everyday experiences that students have already had with such phenomena are the source of background information for the dialog. Thus, it is expected that students will know that a pot of hot water left on a table for a long period of time will cool down.

The first situation is that of taking one's own temperature, shown in Figures 4-55 and 4-56.

Even 10 year old children have no problem answering this question, at least in our society where taking one's temperature is a critical part of growing up! The student is queried about some of the details of the operation; in any approach to an operational definition it is desirable for students to think about the full situation, a measuring device, in this case the thermometer, and a stated procedure for the use of that device.

The next stage involves a pan of hot water on a table, cooling off, again an everyday phenomenon familiar to most students (Figures 4-57 and 4-58). We are working toward the notion of equilibrium, getting the student to realize and say that the process will continue until the water reaches room temperature. Again thermometers play an important role as measuring devices, complementing the verbal statement of what happens. The next sequence involves a pan of cold water.

Now we introduce the notion that the cooling rate may be influenced by various factors by introducing the notion of putting water both on the table and in vacuum bottles, hot and cold (Figure 4-59).

Again the vacuum bottle is a common device in our society. In each case we are drawing on the student's past experiences. If, however, a program such as this was developed for a less affluent society where vacuum bottles were not an everyday phenomenon, then we would need to follow a different procedure. It is worth pointing out, therefore, that material of this kind may have cultural dependences, and so cannot be assumed to be universal.

The situation discussed in the next stage (Figures 4-60 and 4-61) is a glass of water containing ice cubes. Some time goes into getting the student to elucidate what happens in this situation, verbally and with graphic aids.

The graphic displays might have to be modified for certain types of students, those at a stage where graphic information is not an understandable process.

It is now that we begin to suggest what we have been driving at. Up to this point, the student is seeing one simple experiment after another, based on everyday experiences, and talking about what is happening. Now we have sufficient evidence gathered in this slow, careful way to begin to draw conclusions.

After the verbal ideas, the dialog goes through yet more experiments, now in the mode of testing how the model works with other phenomena beside those already experienced. Thus, the mode is a classical, scientific approach, developing ideas and then seeing if the ideas work in new experimental situations. Eventually some mathematical notation appears. Several points later in the dialog are illustrated in Figures 4-62, 4-63, and 4-64.

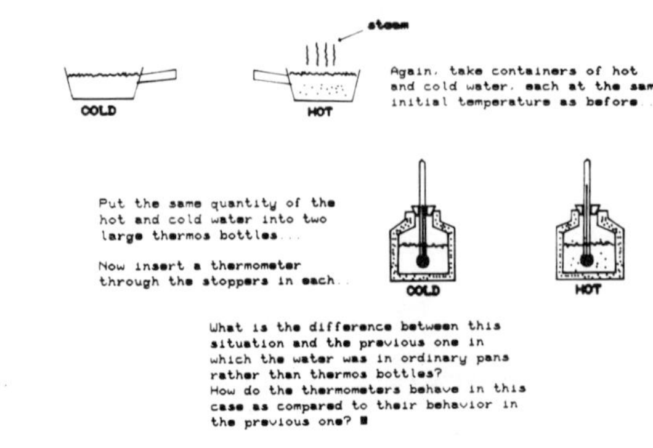

FIGURE 4-59 HEAT, Different Rates of Cooling and Heating

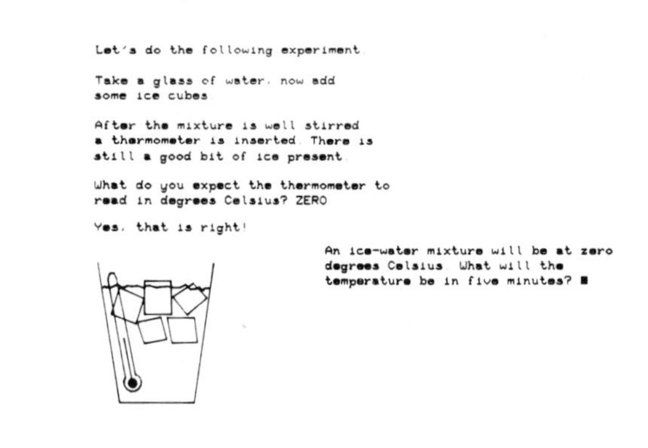

FIGURE 4-60 HEAT, More Kitchen Physics with Ice in Water

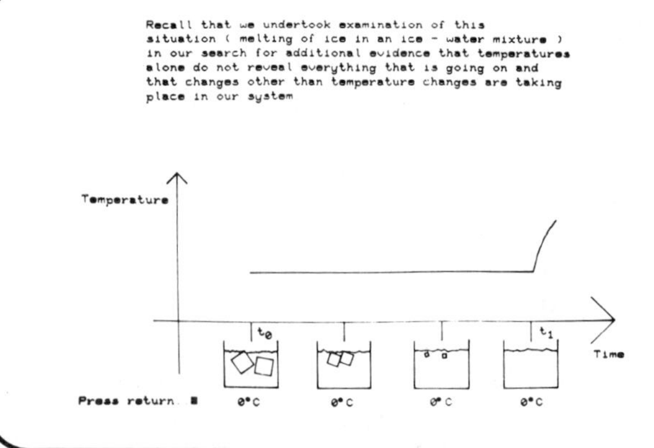

FIGURE 4-61 HEAT, Still Ice and Water (See Figure 2-13 Also)

Suppose we put a burner under a container holding the ice - water mixture
In these circumstances we say that heat is being transferred from the ____________ to the ______________

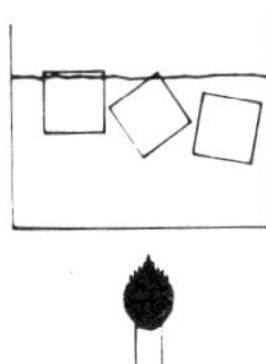

FIGURE 4-62 More from HEAT. Student Enters Missing Words

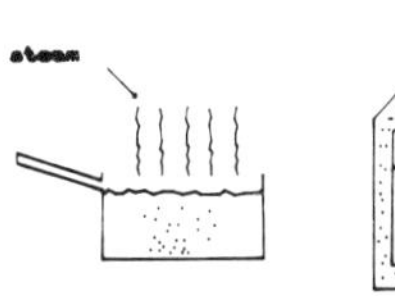

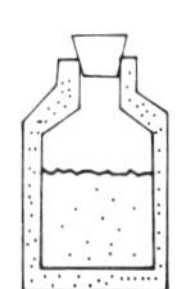

Recall the experiment discussed earlier in which a pan of hot water was exposed in a room while the same amount of water at the same initial temperature was placed in a thermos bottle in the same room. We agreed that the water in the thermos eventually cools down to room temperature as does the water in the pan.

In terms of the concept of TRANSFER of HEAT describe the interactions which occurs in each of these instances. Heat is transferred from the ____________ to the ______________

FIGURE 4-63 Further Sequence in HEAT, Using the New Concept

There is another useful way of saying the same thing - a way we will want to use later. Think of the CHANGE in temperature which takes place in each of the two quantities of water.
Sample A changes by the amount

$$\Delta T_a = T_{final} - T_a$$

Sample B changes by the amount

$$\Delta T_b = $$

FIGURE 4-64 HEAT Sequence Later in the Dialog

As with any such treatment, we are only showing a small fragment of HEAT. For a full experience, the reader should gain access and run the program.

Final Comments

These dialogs are accessible via telephone lines to others having access to Tektronix graphic displays in the 4010 series.

These few computer dialogs suggest very interesting directions for the future. The problem raised, that of students who have not reached their full intellectual development, is a serious one in our society. More programs of this kind, available in a wide variety of environments, could have a major national impact on the intellectual life of the country. We would like, for example, to develop futher material specifically for the public library and science museum environments. [Note: Such development is now underway.] They could also be widely used in such environments as shopping centers and airports. Computer dialogs have sufficient appeal to compete well with other activities in those environments.

Often too the subject matter content could be important. Thus, we can conceive of the same type of programs in such areas as energy conservation, helping people become full formal reasoners and helping them understand the notions of energy and the importance in our society of reasonable use of energy.

The three magnetic field dialogs were the product of the two authors. HEAT involved a third member of the University of California, Irvine group, Joseph Marasco, codirector of the Physics Computer Development Project. The student programmer on the magnetic field dialogs was Martin Katz, and the student programmer for HEAT was Tod Hopson. The programming activities were managed by our senior programmer, Estelle Warner.

Programming of the dialogs, done by student programmers, took approximately three man weeks for each. However, as the students did not work a 40-hour week, this was spread over a longer period of time. This includes time for the extensive revision that characterize the earlier development of such products.

Much of the interactive design of the material, the composition of how graphics and text look on the screen, was done using an extensive screen design capability developed within the University of California, Irvine, over the last several years. Almost all of the above individuals have played major roles in the design of that product. The programmer for the design facility was Mark Geisert.

A COMPUTER-BASED LEARNING AID IN ELECTRICITY AND MAGNETISM

Introduction

A multicampus grant to four University of California campuses (Irvine, Santa Cruz, Riverside, and Davis) from University of California instructional improvement funds allowed faculty members on other campuses to work with us at Irvine in the development of computer dialogs. The electrostatic dialog being discussed, FIELD, involved the following people: Robert Eisberg (Santa Barbara), Bruce Rosenblum (Santa Cruz), Sun-Yiu Fung (Riverside), Richard Ballard (Irvine), Joseph Marasco (Irvine), and Alfred Bork (Irvine). It was developed in stages over a year, and only gradually reached the form described.

Structure and Capabilities

FIELD is concerned with electrostatics as it is taught in beginning Physics courses. It is organized around a central map, a guide to the use of the program. Students return to the map at any input by typing MAP. (See the earlier Figure 2-9.)

Four basic facilities are provided. First, learning sequences develop the fundamental ideas of electrostatics. Second, a plotting capability allows students to plot electric field and equipotential lines. Third, two quizzes or tests check the student's knowledge of ideas developed within the dialog. Finally, the map allows the student to exit.

The map provides a high degree of learner control, including the opportunity to browse through various sections of the program. Access to the quiz sections of the program is controlled by a course management system to protect quiz security. Other sections of the dialog are freely available.

Learning Sequences

The dialog provides learning facilities for students studying electrostatics. The five divisions are: the magnitude of the force between charges, the direction of the force, the force on several charges, the notion of electric fields, and the notion of

Proceedings of the 16th Annual Convention, Association for Educational Data Systems, Atlanta, 1978.

electric field lines. Early sequences assume that the student has little background with this material. Through the map, students move rapidly if they are already familiar with the basic ideas.

As with other computer dialogs developed at Irvine, the student engages in a "conversation" with the computer. Typically the computer presents information—verbally and pictorially—and asks questions. FIELD stresses graphic learning modes. The student types responses, which are analyzed by the program. Depending on the responses, the computer goes off in a number of directions.

We attempt to deal with as wide a range of student input as possible. Some unique capabilities are based on the fact that an accurate pointing device is available for use on the displays, Tektronix 4013s.

We used great care in building toward the fundamental idea of electric field; this powerful idea—critical in modern science—is often ill understood by students in beginning Physics courses. In introducing the idea, we incorporated several small simulations within the computer dialog. Courses often talk about the use of unit test charges, and we used that concept as a gateway to the field notion. We have the advantage that we can "provide" charges, simulated on the computer, let students put them at any location, and then show the force on unit charges. (Figures 4-65 and 4-66 show several examples.)

We start the sequence about electric field with two given charges, present on the screen, and allow the student many opportunities to move the test charge to new locations; we show the force at each location. Then, to emphasize that it is not critical that we know where the charges are, we cover up the region with charges. Again the student is provided with a unit test charge. Thus, the notion is built up, through actual experience rather than by just verbal discussion, that a force acts on the test charge no matter where it is is placed (Figure 4-67). This notion leads to the concept of electric field.

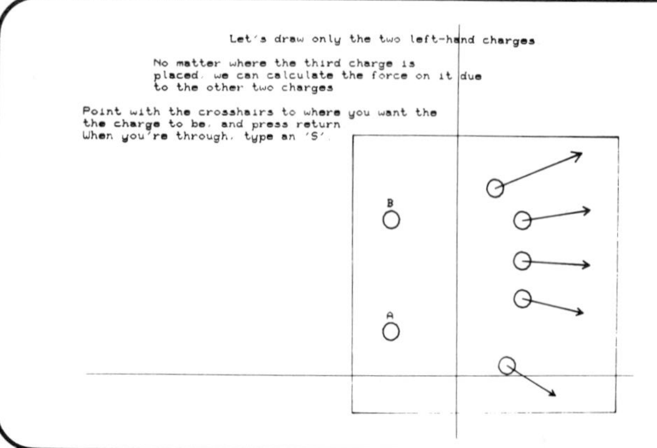

FIGURE 4-65 FIELD, Instructional Sequence Providing Unit Charge Capability

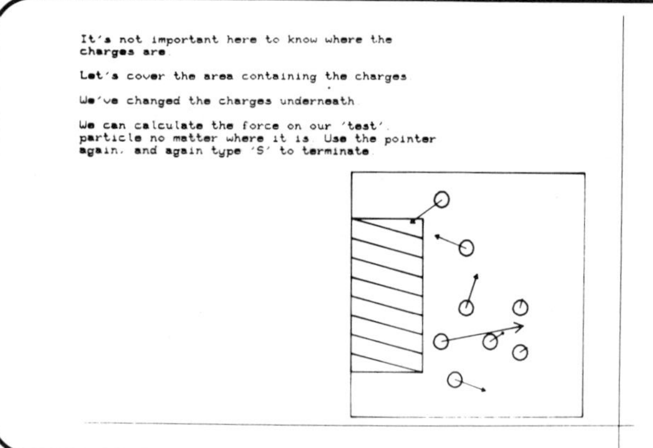

FIGURE 4-66 FIELD, Another Unit Charge Capability

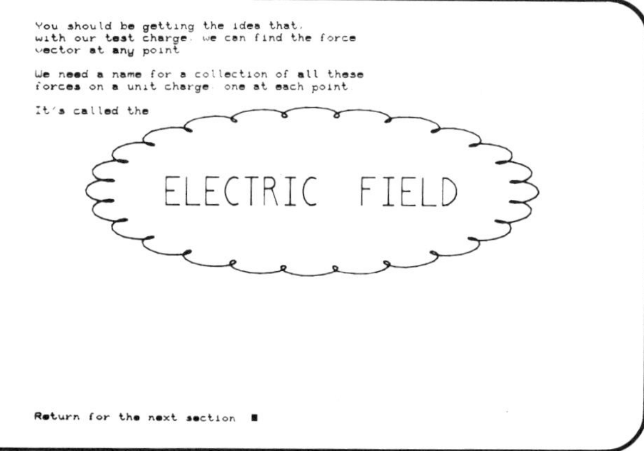

You should be getting the idea that, with our test charge, we can find the force vector at any point
We need a name for a collection of all these forces on a unit charge, one at each point
It's called the
ELECTRIC FIELD
Return for the next section

FIGURE 4-67 FIELD, the Notion of Electric Field

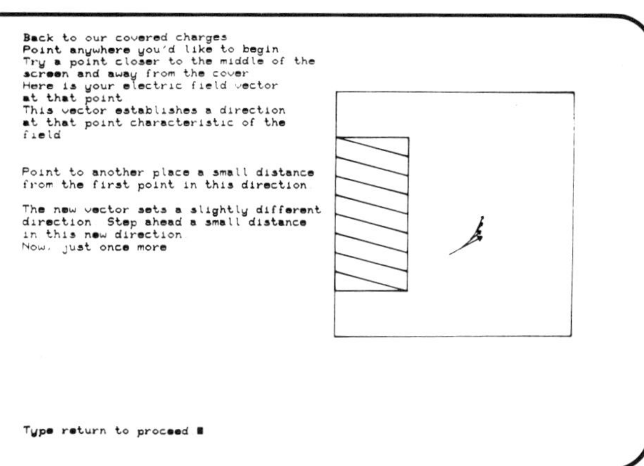

Back to our covered charges
Point anywhere you'd like to begin
Try a point closer to the middle of the screen and away from the cover
Here is your electric field vector at that point
This vector establishes a direction at that point characteristic of the field
Point to another place a small distance from the first point in this direction
The new vector sets a slightly different direction. Step ahead a small distance in this new direction
Now, just once more
Type return to proceed

FIGURE 4-68 FIELD, Developing the Notion of Field Line

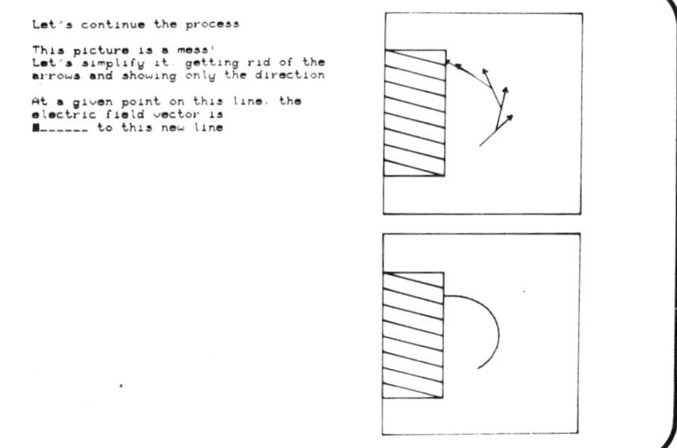

Let's continue the process
This picture is a mess!
Let's simplify it, getting rid of the arrows and showing only the direction
At a given point on this line, the electric field vector is
_______ to this new line

FIGURE 4-69 FIELD, Continual Development of the Field Line Idea

The next critical idea developed with the dialog is that of electric field lines. These visual representations of the electric field offer an important technique for gaining insight into electric field. Field line plots are used in almost every beginning textbook. Students often do not understand these field line diagrams. It is of central importance in the present computer learning material that this notion be explained very clearly, that we provide practice for students in using the notion, and that, as will be seen later, we test to see that the concept is understood (Figure 4-68 and 4-69).

The path introducing field lines is similar to that in most courses; but we provide an active experience for students rather than a passive experience. The student, with the use of the pointer, uses a test charge to "follow" a field line. The student relates field lines to the location of charges and to the signs of charges.

Field Line Plotting

One of the major roles the computer can play in beginning science or mathematics courses is assisting students in building intuition by providing rich and varied experiences for the student not available in the ordinary world. We have developed a number of such controllable worlds, providing the student flexible capabilities for gaining such experience. The calculational capability of the computer is important.

The plotting capabilities of FIELD allow the student to place charges of any magnitude at any location on the screen. Then the student can request a field line plot based on the charges just specified, as in Figures 4-70 and 4-71. Charges can be added or removed as desired.

The student can also explore an interesting region by requesting that a field line be drawn through a designated point, using the pointing device. Thus, in a region where the field is zero it is interesting to note the pattern of field lines as they "avoid" the region.

The program also plots equipotential lines, another view of the electric field in the region. In Figures 4-72 and 4-73 equipotential lines are added. These are shown as dotted lines, to distinguish them from the field lines. The pointing mechanism specifies where the lines are to be drawn; so the drawing is under student control.

Great care is taken in computing field lines and equipotential lines. (A Hamming predictor corrector procedure solves the differential equations.) It was pointed out to the author by Tim Kelley of Southern Oregon College, that simple integration techniques for electric field lines often lead to noticeably incorrect results. Hence, a sophisticated technique such as that employed in FIELD is required.

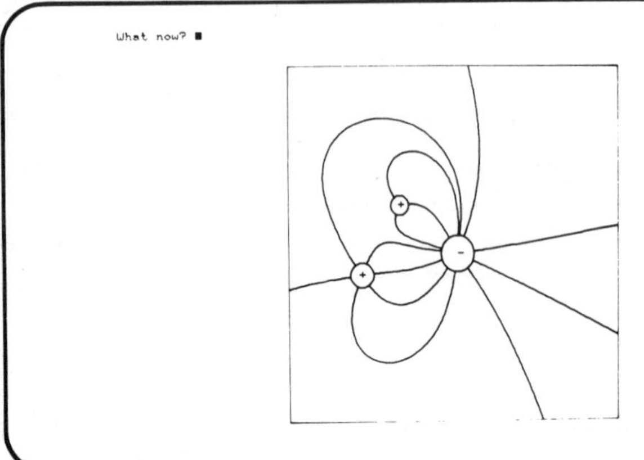

FIGURE 4-70 Plotting Facility from FIELD for Building Intuition. Student Picks Charges.

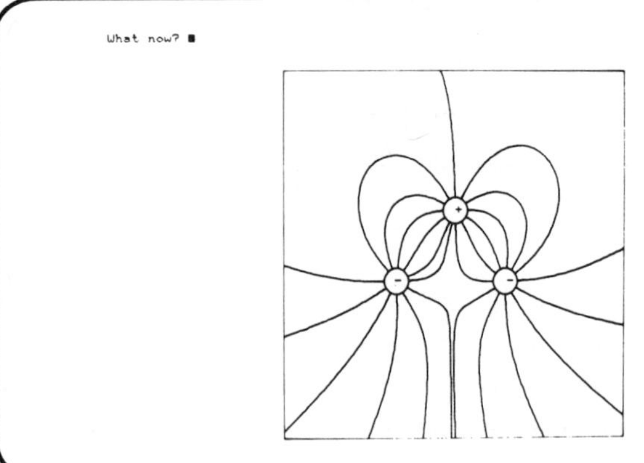

FIGURE 4-71 Another Example of Plotting Field Lines from FIELD

Quizzes

Two quizzes are available within FIELD. They do not cover all aspects of the learning material; at some future time it may be possible to add quizzes.

These quizzes are taken directly at the display. They tie in with a full course management system, controlling access to the tests and recording results. These tests are typically used in a self-paced, mastery

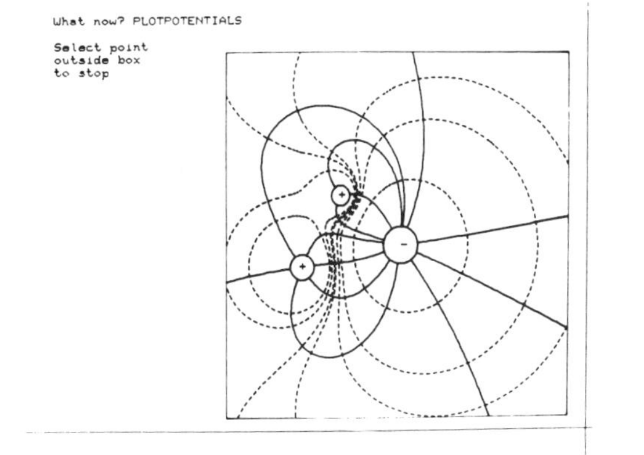

FIGURE 4-72 Equipotential Lines Added to the Field Lines of Figure 4-70

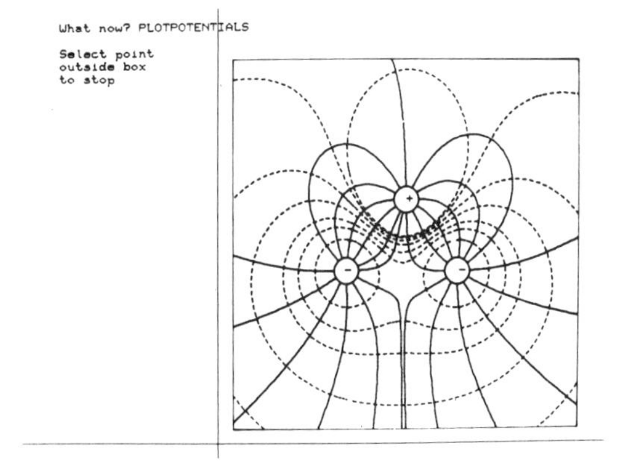

FIGURE 4-73 Equipotential Lines Added to the Field Lines of Figure 4-71

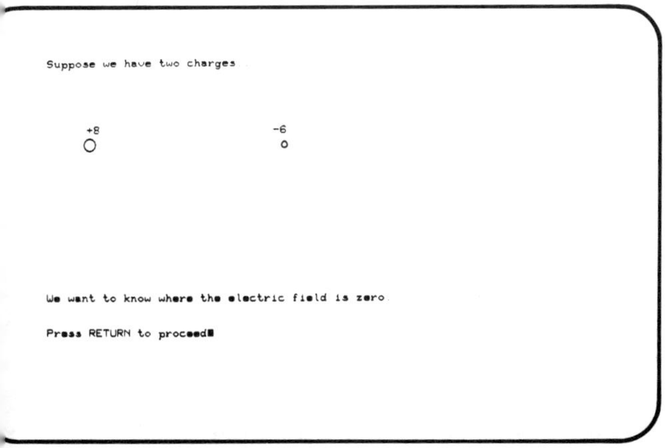

Suppose we have two charges

+8 -6

We want to know where the electric field is zero

Press RETURN to proceed

FIGURE 4-74 First Quiz in FIELD

learning environment. The student who does not pass a test on a first occasion studies further and takes the test again. Twelve hours must elapse between successive attempts of the same test by the same student. Each test is unique; a variety of techniques generate different questions for each student. Tests take a maximum of 40 minutes. As with other self-paced environments, students cannot take a given test until they have completed earlier required tests. All these facets of access and record-keeping are controlled by the computer. The next chapter contains a complete description of the course management system.

The first test concerns the basic notions of electrostatics with regard to forces and fields (Figures 4-74 and 4-75). The student is given two charges of different magnitude. The problem is to find where the field is zero. As with many of our other tests, an optional help sequence is provided.

The second test is not often seen in the usual beginning course. It is illustrated in Figures 4-76, 4-77, and 4-78. In this test, we determine whether a student understands the concept of electric field lines. We check to see whether the notion of the direction of the field line is associated in the student's mind with the direction of the field at the same location, and we check to see whether the student has reasonable views as to the density of field lines and the strength of the electric field. Primarily, however, we see if the student can relate electric field line patterns to the charges that produce these patterns. Thus, in one sequence electric field line plots are presented with a "hole" in the middle, with the charges, and the field lines close to the charges, missing. Various charge configurations are presented as possibilities, and the student is asked in turn whether each charge configuration agrees with the field line pattern. As with other aspects of the quizzes, these patterns are picked randomly from a large collection.

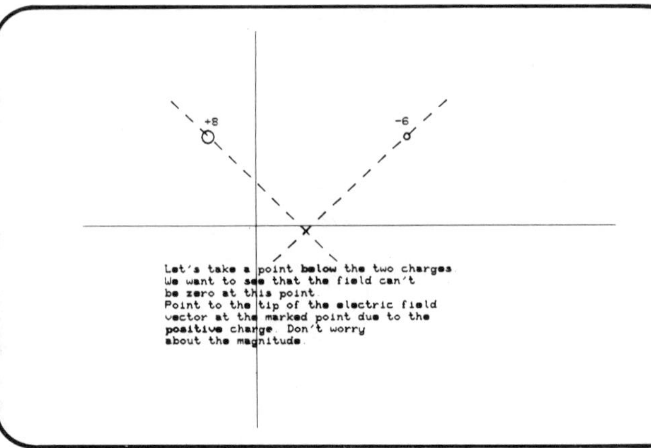

FIGURE 4-75 First Quiz in FIELD, Help Sequence

Environment

This dialog runs on a medium-scale timesharing system, a Honeywell Sigma 7. About 25 Tektronix 4013 displays are available; the computer and the displays are shared with educational, research, and administrative activities. The underlying software was developed within the Physics Computer Development Project.

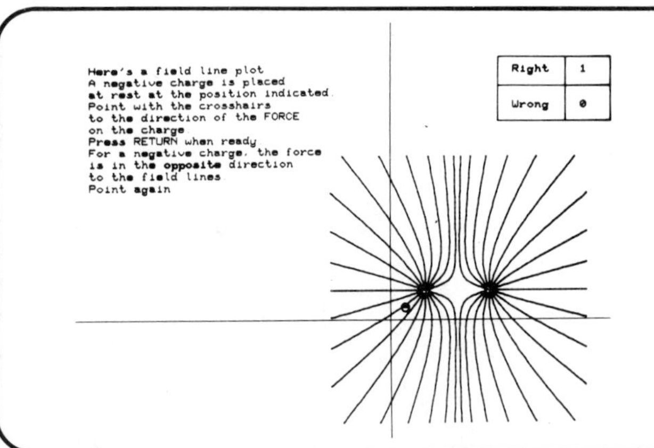

FIGURE 4-76 FIELD, Second Quiz—Force on a Charged Particle

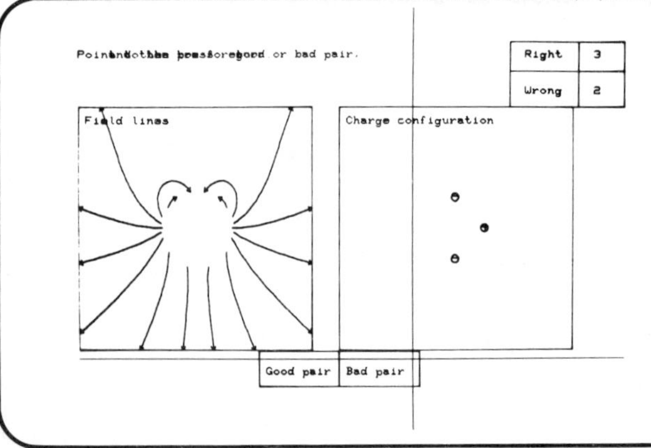

FIGURE 4-77 FIELD, Second Quiz—What Charges Produce The Field Shown?

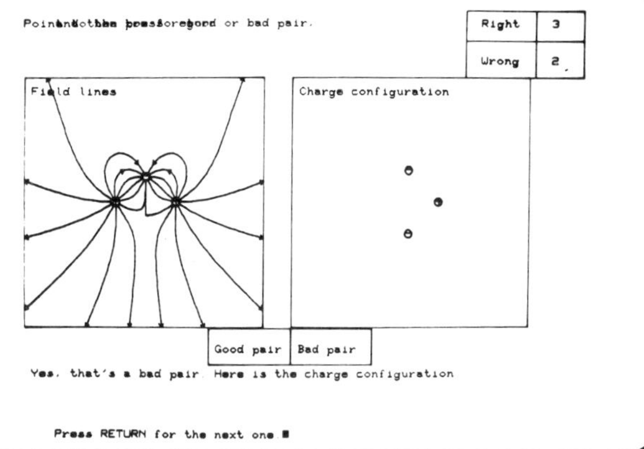

FIGURE 4-78 FIELD, Second Quiz—Response to Previous Question

References

1. Chalmers Sherwin, *Basic Concepts of Physics* (New York: Holt, Rinehart and Winston, 1961).

2. R. Feynman, *The Feynman Lectures on Physics, Vol. 1* (Reading, MA: Addison-Wesley, 1964), Chapter 9.

3. *Ibid.*, p. 9-1.

4. *Ibid.*, p. 9-9.

5. E. Jones, Sierra College, Rocklin, CA 95677.

6. Available from Bell Telephone Laboratories.

7. A.W. Luehrmann, *American Journal of Physics,* Vol. 42, No. 361 (1974).

8. R. Feynman, *The Feynman Lectures on Physics, Vol. 2* (Reading, MA: Addison-Wesley, 1964), p. 19-1.

9. *Ibid.*, p. 19-3.

10. Alfred Bork and A. Zellweger, *American Journal of Physics,* Vol. 37, No. 386 (1969).

11. CONDUIT can be reached at the Computer Center of the University of Iowa, Iowa City 52242. In addition to a complete list of available modules, a periodical (*Pipeline*) is available.

12. E.R. Huggins, Department of Physics and Astronomy, Dartmouth College, Hanover, New Hampshire 03755.

13. J.D. Gavenda, Department of Physics, University of Texas, Austin 78712.

14. Alfred Bork, *Notions about Motion,* University of California, Irvine 92717. Mimeographed notes.

15. R. Eisberg, *Applied Mathematical Physics with Programmable Pocket Calculators* (New York: McGraw-Hill, 1976).

16. Alfred Bork, *FORTRAN for Physics* (Reading, MA: Addison-Wesley, 1967).

17. Herbert Peckham, *Computers, BASIC, and Physics* (Reading, MA: Addison-Wesley, 1971).

18. John Merrill, *Using Computers in Physics* (Boston: Houghton Mifflin, 1976).

19. Edwin G. Boring, *History, Psychology, and Science: Selected Papers,* edited by R.I. Watson and D.T. Campbell (New York: John Wiley & Sons, 1963), p. 46.

20. A. Arons, "Cultivating the Capacity for Formal Reasoning: Objectives and Procedures in an Introductory Physical Science Course," *American Journal of Physics,* Vol. 44 (1976), pp. 834–838.

21. A. Arons, "Some Thoughts on Reasoning Capacities Implicitly Expected of College Students," *Proceedings of the Conference on Cognitive Process Instruction,* University of Massachusetts, Amherst: June 1978.

22. Conference on Computers in the Undergraduate Curriculum. The Proceedings are available from the computer center of the University of Iowa.

23. "Report on Teaching: Analyses of Some of the Most Notable Improvements in American Undergraduate Education," *Change.* Report 1, March 1976; Report 2, July 1976; Report 3, January 1977; Report 4, July 1977; Report 5, January 1978; Report 6, August 1978.

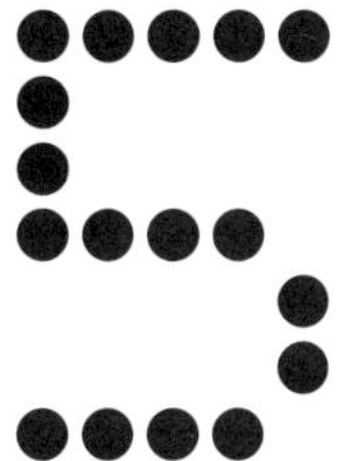

Classroom

SCIENCE TEACHING AND COMPUTER LANGUAGES

Abstract

An evaluation is made of the suitability of various programming languages for use with beginning Science students. Primary emphasis is on computational languages with the students doing their own programming. Among the factors for choosing between the languages considered are ease of initial learning, procedure capabilities, editing facilities, files, ability to meet growing needs, debugging facilities, and array capabilities. Some consideration is also given to dialog languages, for writing teaching conversations and simulations. It is argued that the existing general-purpose languages are desirable for this task. Consideration is also given to graphic developments.

Recently, computers have been used increasingly for learning in Science and in other areas. In some (but not all) modes of usage, the student is employing standard computer languages. Teachers should be concerned about which computers and which languages they should suggest within courses. Traditionally, the decisions about computers available on campus have been made by other computer users, particularly researchers and computer theoreticians. But as computers become more and more widely used in the classroom, teachers should rightfully play some role in the selection of computers. Further, as small stand-alone (one-on-one) systems become more widely used, the instructor may have a larger, often dominant, role in such selection.

A personal element is inherent in these comments on computer languages; the choice is partially a matter of taste, as with all teaching. However, certain languages do have objective advantages and disadvantages. I shall omit many languages which, while perhaps desirable, are available only on a limited basis. The computational languages discussed are widely available and are likely to be available during the next few years. However, not all are available on all computers. No dialog software is as widely available as the computational languages, so our discussion there is oriented toward the types of language capabilities available.

The reader should understand that I am expressing a view about which computer languages are best for various purposes. I do not suggest that teachers should do no computer work within Science teaching if they cannot use the languages I favor. Even the least desirable languages for particular applications are often quite powerful and useful; for many problems it scarcely matters which language is used. Thus, although I will argue against FORTRAN and BASIC as languages of choice for most purposes in Science teaching, they should be employed within classes if, as often happens, they are the only languages available.

Motivation for Computers in the Classroom

At least three factors motivate the use of computers within Science classes.

First, successful Science students will eventually use computers in their research. The computer is a vastly important research tool with great potentialities even outside science. But the computer can harm Science if used improperly. Just as students learn to use essential pieces of laboratory equipment, Science courses are increasingly concerned with the early introduction of computers in a subject matter context. The goal is to display to students the strengths and weaknesses of numerical and symbolic approaches in addition to the purely analytical approach common in undergraduate courses. I call this factor the tool use of computers, as a computer becomes one tool students acquire for their mathematical arsenal during undergraduate and graduate preparation, one of the most important tools of modern science. John Kemeny, President of Dartmouth College, has argued that the computer is so essential in everyone's education that colleges and universities that do not provide adequate student computer facilities should not be accredited. Such usage should be part of any undergraduate curriculum.

The second use of computers in Science classes is in instruction. More and more, the computer is found to be valuable as an aid in learning Science. The student interacts with programs particularly designed to help in learning the important aspects of the area. This use is complementary to the tool use of computers. When the computer is a computational device, we are close to the tool use, because the student is using the computer as a computer. But in dialog or tutorial use, the student needs to know little about operational details of the computer.

A third role that computers play in classes is motivational. Computers can stimulate student interest in the subject.

I assume Science teachers, outside of Computer Science teachers, are not primarily interested in preparing students to become computer experts, so their use of the computer is not motivated by such a desire.

Computational Languages

When scientists consider preparing students for later use of computers (the tool aspect), they tend to gravitate toward FORTRAN. FORTRAN is the most commonly used language for scientific calculation. Most sizable computers come with FORTRAN compilers. It is more nearly a universal language than any other language available, although FORTRAN does often vary significantly from machine to machine. Nevertheless, I believe that teaching only FORTRAN, given other choices, is probably a mistake, even from the tool aspect.

One would have to be a soothsayer to predict the history of computer languages in the next few years. No area of contemporary endeavor is more dynamic and changing than that of computers, with continual growth in new machines and new languages.

Even for the scientist interested in computers solely as a calculational tool, the environment is changing. In this changing environment I cannot envision FORTRAN as a long-term future language for scientific computation. It seems reasonable to predict a slow and steady decline in the importance of FORTRAN relative to other languages used for similar purposes, such as Pascal or Ada.

FORTRAN was the first widely used formula-oriented language and had enormous success. It did more to ease the task of scientific computation than any single development in the computer field. Nevertheless, FORTRAN is over 20 years old, and showing signs of age. It has gone through a series of elaborations, some not necessarily consistent with the original formulation of the language. Some of the original features were related to the structure of the IBM 704, the machine for which it was initially implemented. Thus, FORTRAN is an old and creaky language.

What are the restrictions and limitations of FORTRAN? The control structures, which allow the programmer to set up programming loops, and IF and computed GOTO statements in FORTRAN, are cruder in form and less powerful than those that exist in more recent languages such as ALGOL, PL/1, and Pascal. The standard input-output facilities in FORTRAN are inflexible; writing FORMAT statements is a chore for the beginning FORTRAN programmer, and sometimes even a bother to experienced programmers. Evidence to support this is found in the large number of FORTRAN installations that have implemented format-free forms of input and output. Furthermore, FORTRAN considered large collections of numbers, arrays, and matrices, only as an afterthought; thus only individual numbers in arrays can be directly referenced. Much scientific computation is oriented toward collections of numbers, and some newer languages have more elaborate and far-reaching ways of handling them, as we will note.

The ability to control what happens during error conditions was not built into FORTRAN. The interrupt system, used in most modern computers in error control, did not exist in the early days of FORTRAN, so FORTRAN does not allow the user to decide in his or her program how to handle error conditions which generate interrupts. Similarly, FORTRAN does not allow the user control over usage of fast memory, varying in different parts of the program.

FORTRAN is weak in string manipulating facilities, because its original design contemplated only numerical calculations. Further, these facilities tend to be machine-dependent. While symbol manipulation represents only a small fraction of scientific computation, the use of on-line symbol manipulation is likely to increase; students should at least become aware of the possibilities.

The fact that FORTRAN is now the most common language might be viewed as a sufficient reason for teaching it in Science courses. It may not continue to be as widely utilized as it is today; when many present students are using computers in later research, they will be employing other languages. In general, the argument for teaching whatever exists today seems weak. If this had been done in the late 1950's, for example, students would have learned computing techniques and languages that would not have been useful in their later professional careers; they would have stayed with desk calculators, or they would have worked in machine languages. The teacher must make reasonable projections about the state of the world when students will be out of school.

Recent languages are more rational than FORTRAN, primarily because of later design; they could profit from experience with FORTRAN. Control statements may be more natural and richer, and programs can assume a natural structure.

ALGOL was defined in 1958 and 1960. Although ALGOL 60 compilers exist on many computers, including IBM machines, it is not popular in the United States, and one cannot see promise of its increase. Recently Pascal, an ALGOL relative with simplifications, because of its inherent structured-programming capabilities, has grown rapidly in popularity, particularly in Computer Science departments.

PL/1 exists primarily on IBM computers. A few other manufacturers have PL/1 subsets. Although PL/1 has been vigorously attacked and is not an "idea" language, it has advantages over FORTRAN for many scientific computations. Debugging with PL/1 should be easier than with FORTRAN because of such built-in debugging facilities such as the ON conditions, allowing the user to control error situations. Furthermore, being a more recent language, PL/1 allows the user the full facilities of the computer in ways that are difficult with FORTRAN. Thus, a job can be divided into a number of sub-jobs, to be executed independently, perhaps even simultaneously, and storage of variables can be controlled by the programmer during the course of the program. PL/1 users also have more control over how their numbers are handled internally, useful in sensitive calculations.

BASIC was first developed at Dartmouth College. It is similar to JOSS, an older language, in many ways. General Electric's BASIC service quickly became the major force in this market, and later competitors felt that they had to offer similar service. BASIC is widely implemented, available on most timesharing and stand-alone systems. BASIC was initially a simple language designed for ease of use with unsophisticated beginning students. Gradually it has been extended; these additions differ from implementation to implementation. Some BASIC implementations use compilers and do not have immediate commands. Many forms of BASIC have string manipulating facilities, but they differ in detail. Many types of BASIC allow subroutines (procedures) only in in-line coding. Most types of BASIC have simple but powerful matrix operations. Standardization efforts are currently underway, but the proposed full standard differs considerably from existing BASIC implementations.

Another conversational language, APL, is an outgrowth of a book by K. E. Iverson, *A Programming Language* [1], initially at IBM's Watson Research Center. It is widely available on IBM computers.

Implementations now exist, among others, for Honeywell, Digital, Burroughs, Hewlett-Packard, and Control Data computers. Compared to other languages, APL has extremely powerful array and matrix manipulating facilities. Although the beginner can use a subset that resembles other languages, APL has many unique operators for handling collections of numbers. APL functions most efficiently when calculations are arranged to use these operators. It has both direct execution and a function mode.

APL functions are a subroutining facility. Users do not have the full control of storage the PL/1 user has, but they have some control over which variables are known to which pieces of the program. The string processing facilities are relatively elaborate, and the language has a well-worked-out philosophy of workspaces for system library and student storage. A standards committee for APL has been formed.

Pascal is, of all the languages mentioned, growing most rapidly. Until recently most of this growth was stimulated by Computer Science departments. Now Pascal is available on home computers. Its strengths are those of structured programming—when used correctly, it leads to programs that have fewer errors, are readable, and are easy to modify. A Pascal relative, Ada, developed by the Department of Defense, may well become of increasing importance in the next few years.

Conversation Language Criteria

What are the criteria that might help the teacher choose among languages? Reasonable standards for such evaluation can be formulated, and we can consider the available languages with regard to these standards. The results are a function of both the language and the implementation. I shall refer to the languages as supplied with the machines or as generally available. Some deficiencies can be overcome by skillful programs, but most teachers and students will work chiefly with what is provided.

First, the language should be easily learned by the beginner. This is not simply a function of the language, but depends heavily on how the language is taught. Those who learned computer languages by the older grammatical techniques are amazed to find how quickly students can learn today. An interactive environment where the beginner can play in a structured way with the language at the console provides a particularly rapid way for developing programming skill.

Although some differences are discernable in ease of initial learning of languages, these differences are small. I would contend that within the environment of the Science class, most students can learn enough about any of these languages to work elementary problems in about 5 hours of student time. The beginner need not, and in most cases should not, learn all features of a language before starting to use it.

Nevertheless, some advantages are inherent in learning one system rather than another. A language that has direct or immediate statements can typically be learned faster than a language that runs only a complete program. In this mode individual statements, not full programs, can be executed immediately as soon as they are typed in; so the student can readily learn the effect of the statement. Some types of FORTRAN and BASIC as well as APL have such capabilities. On the other hand, many varieties of BASIC, FORTRAN, Pascal, and PL/1 do not have immediate commands, and so are slightly harder to learn from this viewpoint.

FORTRAN presents additional problems for beginners because of its "unnatural" IF statement, which in its elementary form is not intelligible unless explained, and its FORMAT statements; most of the other languages provide simple methods of input and output.

APL offers two difficulties for the novice. First, it has a different precedence rule for operators than students are (perhaps) accustomed to from ordinary algebra: every operator operates on everything to its right; so "2 – 3 – 4," typed in, leads to the response "3." This deviation from usual precedence, valuable for the advanced user because of the many operations in APL, can be controlled by parentheses.

The second problem for beginners in APL concerns the branching statements, which are very powerful but do not have the simple mnemonic form of JOSS and BASIC branching facilities; a few minutes more are needed to teach elementary branching in APL functions. The right-pointing arrow is the basis of branching, but the branching location is computed. Because of the array facilities, fewer branching statements are needed.

These difficulties with FORTRAN and APL are minor. After using many languages with students, I believe that the few conveniences for the beginning learner in one or the other are minor considerations in choosing a language. The differences in initial learning are often over exaggerated; any languages can be quickly learned if one takes a reasonable beginning subset. The way the language is introduced to the student is a greater factor; the traditional lecture approach, based on discussing the grammar of the language, is slower than learning directly at the student station.

Editing facilities can ease the student's approach. Many students do not type well, so a convenient editing system can circumvent great frustration over typing errors. Further, programs of any complexity seldom run when first written, so they must be debugged and corrected. While editors are not considered to be part of the language, they do heavily influence the ease of using the language.

Conversational editing facilities vary enormously from implementation to implementation. At least three aspects of editing are important.

First, almost all interactive languages allow editing at the line level, replacing a line in a program with a new line, adding lines at any place in the program, and deleting lines. Most facilities for line editing are roughly similar.

Second, facilities for correcting errors on the line currently being typed may not be present, and they can differ in convenience for the beginning user. These allow cancelling individual letters or retyping the line, if errors are noted before the line is completed.

Third, not all systems allow editing within a line after it has been entered, particularly for lines already in files. Powerful editors allow flexible modification of programs stored in the computer. The use of an editing systm to change previously entered material is a very personal matter.

The APL editing system is based on putting slashes, for deletion, or a number, for the number of spaces to be inserted, under the line to be edited. The programmer then places these inserted characters within a newly typed line supplied by the system. Spaces are provided, and the typing element or alphanumeric cursor is conveniently placed. A small change within a complex line is easy with such a system. But most APL editing systems provide no fast way of making systematic changes in many statements.

Two types of editors are in common use. Older editors, assuming printed output, are often line-oriented—lines are numbered, and these numbers specify where changes are to be made. Newer editors, assuming television-like displays, are screen-oriented; the user points to the location where something is to happen. Almost all word processing systems have editors of this second type. The University of California, San Diego, Pascal system has an excellent screen-oriented editor.

Many implementations of the languages mentioned have no within-line editing. Particularly for programs where individual lines become very complex, this lack can be a severe handicap. Some other systems have powerful but very difficult editing systems, almost impossible for use by anyone other than a dedicated professional. Only personal experience can indicate which editing system is most desirable for student use, but the question is important. Prospective purchasers or leasees should "experiment" in some detail with the machines considered so that they can form their own judgment with regard to editors.

Science students are beginners at the terminal for only a brief period. They may then face a long career, both in and out of school, of increasingly active computer use. The opposite side to the question of how quickly the student learns a language is the question of whether the language affords an opportunity for growth in knowledge and use of computers. Some implementations of BASIC are simple to learn, but after learning the elementary material, little else is available. Some languages have a rich superstructure, which is not necessary for beginning users but is available as the users develop and write more sophisticated programs. PL/1, APL, and Pascal exemplify this richness. Languages should encourage student growth toward making better and better use of the computer facility.

An issue related to growth is whether a student can emerge from a language. Given the dynamic nature of computers, most languages will eventually die and be replaced by newer and more effective languages. Furthermore, as students reach more difficult problems, they will want to use specialized languages adapted toward these problems. Hence, the question of how quickly students can make the transition from their first language to a new language is important. I have had examples of good students, brought up on BASIC in high school, who have had psychological problems in switching to a more powerful language. This experience may represent a chance occurrence, or it may be a phenomenon observable for all languages. But I have not personally seen it with other languages. As experience develops with languages, we should keep close contact with "changeability." A person can become accustomed to a language so that it is a "pacifier," a retreat in moments of crisis. Perhaps a multilanguage approach right from the beginning will prevent students from becoming too tied down to one language. There are no perfect languages, so students must be adaptable.

The student also finds it very useful to have effective disc storage of programs between sessions. The facilities for disc storage depend on the hardware and implementation rather than on the language; costs for disc storage vary widely. The availability of convenient and easy-to-use system library facilities on disc is important for class use, because the student can be relieved of the burdens of writing minor associated programs or can be supplied some programs by the instructor. Library program availability and usability vary among systems. Protection features, which allow the instructor to control who has access to files, are useful for timesharing systems. A valuable feature is the automatic save in some timesharing systems; if the user loses connection with the central computer because of device or line failure, whatever he or she is currently working on will be available for the next session. So an entire session of work will not be wiped out by a mishap. This facility exists in APL; it is a valuable user-oriented facility that should be present in all timesharing systems. In a stand-alone system, the existence of floppy discs will accomplish these same purposes; storage on audio cassettes is inadequate for most use.

The language's attitude toward procedures, chunks of self-contained code, is important. The ability to conceptualize a large problem as a series of solvable subproblems, making little problems out of a big problem, is often a critical stage in the solution of any problem, computer or otherwise. A language that naturally pushes students toward this point of view, in an early stage, is desirable. BASIC is perhaps the weakest in this regard, as procedures are possible only by in-line coding in many types of BASIC; this is pedagogically unsatisfactory. FORTRAN, PL/1, APL, and Pascal provide for subprograms.

Programs of any complexity almost never work when first entered. An important part of using the computer for the Science student (or anyone) is debugging, finding and correcting programming errors. Interactive systems are powerful for debugging, giving fast feedback and allowing immediate correcting and rerunning. In correcting code, the editing system, already mentioned, is of great importance. The system facilities can ease the task of finding and correcting errors.

When a program malfunctions, the first concern may be what has happened during the calculation. What statement is currently being executed? What are the current values of the variables? Particularly if no printout has occurred, the user may want to know the values of certain variables. Languages that provide immediate commands, commands executed right away, are convenient for this; as soon as the program stops, the student can determine values of critical variables. Implementations that can only run whole programs do not offer a facility for determining the values of variables on the spur of the moment, an annoyance when things are not going well. But special debugging facilities may be provided.

Several other facilities are effective in debugging. One such facility is *tracing,* the ability to require that each time a statement is executed, the value assigned is printed, and the ability to see the order of statement execution. While all languages discussed allow tracing through the insertion of temporary statements in the program, removable after the program is running, only APL typically has a built-in tracing mechanism, allowing the user to specify lines to trace. A similar facility is the *stop* or *breakpoint,* allowing the user to request pauses after certain points. APL is again the only language that normally has such a facility, although it may be available in some implementations of other languages. Powerful debuggers are available on several systems.

The power of the language in handling vectors, matrices, and arrays should be considered, particularly as the students become more advanced. It is often profitable and desirable to think of an operation as involving the manipulation of collections of numbers rather than, as with most computer languages, thinking of the operation as manipulating individual numbers. Everyday ways of thinking of such calculations as averaging are typically based on viewing the operator as working on a collection of numbers. Many scientific languages have natural facilities for handling collections. Most forms of BASIC have a simple but effective collection of special matrix handling operations. PL/l also has some facilities of this kind. The ability to define new data-types in Pascal is very useful in this connection. APL has an extremely powerful and versatile set of operations for collections of numbers in many dimensions. Many of the APL functions are directed toward specifying operations on collections of numbers or on string arrays.

Computer journals recently have carried many articles concerning an aspect of languages and the use of them called "structured programming." The claims of structured programming are that this approach will lead to programs that have fewer initial errors, are easier to read and modify, and require less debugging. The approach is not yet widely known in the scientific community, but is becoming so.

Some aspects of structured programming are hardly new, but simply represent good programming and problem-solving practice. Thus, the notion that one can break the initial task into a group of subtasks, and then program the subtasks, already mentioned in connection with procedures, is an important aspect of structured programming; there it is often referred to as "topdown programming." Languages with good subroutine structure will be more useful in this environment.

Another important aspect of the structured-programming approach is the availability of rich control structures. This emphasis on control structure is coupled usually with the statement that many of the errors in programming come from indiscriminate use of GOTO statements, unrestricted branches to another point in the program. Some advocates of structured programming have gone so far as to remove the GOTO statements entirely from certain languages.

A number of languages have been developed specifically to meet the requirements of structured programming. Undoubtedly the most successful of these languages is Pascal, now seeing rapidly increased usage throughout the world. Pascal requires explicit declarations by the programmer as to the type of each variable used in the program, thus making certain that no wrong implicit assumptions by the user occur. It contains a rich collection of control statements. Richer forms of Pascal have been augmented to include string and graphic capabilities. The possible future importance of Ada has been mentioned.

Conclusions—Computational Languages

Based on these criteria, APL and Pascal are superior as computational languages for use with Science students. Ada may soon be a contender. BASIC and FORTRAN are the least desirable languages for student use. The reader should remember that many of these aspects depend on the implementation of the language, and that any of these languages can be employed.

Dialog Languages

A special problem arises with computer languages for preparing material for student-computer interaction. The student in this mode interacts with a program already in the computer, and so has only indirect access to the facilities of the computer. A sizable effort is being expended in this area.

Review articles list 30 or 40 languages designed for dialog preparation. Most are in extremely limited use; many have never been used by anyone except their original developers! Few dialog languages could claim to have national use; one exception is IBM Coursewriter, one of the first such languages. Little material is available in any of them; unfortunately more energy has gone into developing languages than developing viable learning sequences.

The use of, and development of, specialized languages for dialogs at this time is, I believe, a mistake. Most of these languages have extremely limited use; no "universal" dialog language exists. Often the languages do not support such important features as graphics. Furthermore, material developed is often presented in a form almost unusable outside the original environment. Many of these languages and approaches are based on a particular teaching or learning strategy, and as the teacher may not care to follow this approach, these impose a severe limitation; the teacher should retain control over the learning process.

Although many specialized languages have been developed, it is possible to write student-computer interactive programs in existing general-purpose languages. Languages already employed include APL, PL/1, FORTRAN, SNOBOL, and Pascal. Most of these languages are flexible enough so that with only minor additions (usually in the form of procedures written by the user), we can handle all dialog material. They do not prejudice the instructional form of this material, but allow instructors to pick their own methods. Furthermore, general-purpose languages are much more widely available than specialized languages, so dialogs written in them have a greater chance of being usable elsewhere. Programmers also have a greater chance of already being familiar with general-purpose languages. APL has problems, as discussed in a later section. Pascal is the best choice.

LEARNING TO PROGRAM FOR THE SCIENCE STUDENT

As computers are utilized increasingly in learning Science, students (and instructors) are faced more and more with the question of learning the programming languages necessary to use the computer. At first glance, this task may appear formidable; but rapid and effective ways exist for learning how to use standard programming languages. Because of their background, Science students have special advantages. My experience is with Physics, but the situation is not too different for Science students in other areas.

Separate Programming Courses

One can learn how to program in many ways. We can profitably distinguish three possibilities: learning from courses set up particularly to teach programming, learning directly within a Science or other course, and learning through self-study. The natural inclination of many teachers is to assume that the student needs a course devoted exclusively or primarily to programming, but this does *not* turn out to be the case. Learning to program within a modern computer environment, either in or out of a formal course, is a relatively simple task for the Science-oriented student and can be accomplished within the Science course or through self-study.

It is not necessarily bad for the student to take a separate programming course. A beginning programming course could, and *should,* offer far more to a student than just learning a language. It should teach the student much about the nature of structured programming and of the algorithmic approach to problem-solving. Useful far beyond the writing of computer coding, it can give insight into computer hardware, and it can also provide useful numerical and symbolic techniques that the student can extend as needs expand. However, if the course available to the student does *nothing* but teach how to write programs, it is an inefficient use of the student's time, spending more time than is necessary to accomplish this task.

Such programming courses work under handicaps. First, little common background among the students exists; therefore, problem assignments that require students to write other than trivial programming are almost impossible. Such problems as the solutions of quadratic equations appear frequently. These tasks are often *not* the type of problem that the student should solve with a computer.

Furthermore, the mathematical talents and insights of the students in the course may cover a wide range, and this may imply an approach that is too simplistic for the Science student.

Computer Availability

Although the student or teacher must usually accept whatever computer facilities are available, in some situations a choice between batch (delayed response) and interactive (instant response) may exist.

The interactive environment provides a very efficient way of learning a language. The student can get large amounts of practice in a relatively small time if sufficient computer access is available. Even more importantly, students can obtain instant error messages, correcting almost immediately the troubles that occur. This rapid feedback is a powerful learning device. The programming language and the implementation existing on a particular machine take over some of the role of teaching the material, providing the language is well implemented. (Later on, I will point to a method of learning a language that systematizes this approach.) Interaction implies either a personal computer or a timeshared system.

On the other hand, the batch computer, with jobs originating on cards, implies a more laborious approach, particularly if a long delay occurs between the time the student submits the program and the time output is available. Many batch systems offer priority to small student jobs, as compared to research jobs. But batch facilities tend to discourage efficient student learning.

What Not To Do

Whether the programming student is considering a separate programming course or learning programming within a Science course, or progressing on one's own, a number of general points can be made. We will start with some comments about "what not to do."

A common but ineffective way of teaching programming languages in classes and in books is what might be described as the "grammatical" approach, the logical step-by-step exposition of the grammar of the computer language. Thus, many FORTRAN courses start by defining integer and real variables, assignment statements, and the like. This approach appeals to teachers who are logically oriented; they order the grammar in a "logical" fashion as the basis for the course. But a difference exists between a logical approach and a pedagogical approach, a way of bringing students quickly to using the language. In the logical approach, students take a long time to get to the point where they *can* write programs, and they do not gain much feel for the art of programming, because they spend so much of their time on the rules of grammar. At one time this strategy was widely used in the teaching of foreign languages; but now it has been largely discredited. However, many, perhaps even most, approaches to teaching programming languages still proceed in this manner.

The latter point is made, in a different context, in the Kingsley Amis novel, *I Want It Now* [2]: "I was like someone who knows exactly how a railway engine's put together, and who can put his finger immediately on any part you care to name with his eyes shut, but who it's never occurred to that the point of the bloody thing is that it pulls trains."

Another fallacy in teaching beginning programming is the belief that a student must learn *all* about the language, must learn the *full* language. It is sufficient for the beginning student to absorb only a subset oriented toward particular needs. With modern and complex languages, such as PL/1, APL, or Pascal, the task of learning the whole language and using all the facilities wisely may be formidable and even frightening to beginning students. But they can learn a subset much more quickly. Then, as needs increase, they can learn more of the language.

It is not reasonable to ignore the background and training of the student. For the Science student, the most profitable approach in learning about computers is through a subject area. Working within Physics or some other scientific discipline, the student is presented with subject-motivated problems that demand the use of the computer and, therefore, motivate the learning of programming languages and demonstrate the relevance of computing in the area involved. The material is not motivated by the general idea that one "should" learn to program, but by the needs of the area. So the tool is not learned abstractly, but rather in a subject matter context. This not only provides a powerful motivation for learning, but it gives the student understanding as to where the computer can be effectively used.

Positive Advice

One important clue to the learning of programming languages comes from the experiences with the audiolingual method of teaching foreign languages. This method starts beginning students with whole dialogs, conversations that they memorize and learn to pronounce correctly, without worrying too much about grammatical details or the meaning of individual words. Thus, from the very beginning, they focus on the language where it will actually be used—at the whole sentence or collection of sentences level.

The corresponding unit for most computer programming languages is the single program; the "whole program" approach in learning a computer language, introducing students to the language through showing them initially complete programs, is analogous to the audiolingual method for a foreign language. Just as with French dialogs, we begin with short (but meaningful) programs, related to the subject matter with which the student is working.

If students find that they must work with a grammatically oriented book, they should move quickly to the writing and running of programs, getting away from pure reading as soon as possible.

It is important even from the beginning that problems be realistic, leading to programs one would actually run on a computer. If a task would be much more quickly accomplished by small hand calculation, the student loses any sense of what is appropriate and important for computer calculation. In Physics, for example, simple numerical solutions of differential equations, which can be done in very small programs, constitute a useful way to begin. Classical mechanics, beginning with the harmonic oscillator and gravitational problems, has been shown by many examples to be an area of Physics where one can successfully combine a high level of Physics with the learning of a programming language.

While initial programs may be provided by the instructor, perhaps in printed form, students should move as rapidly as possible into their own programs. One technique is that of assigning first tasks that involve relatively small modifications of the initially supplied programs. Thus, the student does not have to grapple with all the details of a full and complex program but can begin to learn by changing existing programs only slightly. These changes would depend on the subject. To expand the suggestion of the harmonic oscillator, the program could be modified to treat the motion of other one-dimensional systems. For example, it can be extended into a program for the damped harmonic oscillators; only a few statements in the total program must be changed, and the student can work with these rather than be faced immediately with the task of writing a completely new program.

Something is to be said for the student initially learning not one programming language but two (or more) contrasting programming languages. Programming languages have a problem common to all languages, including natural languages: When students are familiar with only one language, they do not understand that language as fully as they might because they have nothing to contrast it with. A person who knows a variety of languages can see what features are common and what features are different. So by simultaneously studying two or more programming languages, a student can acquire a better feeling for the programming situation.

If two languages are taught, it is wise to pick languages that have substantial differences in outlook or structure. For example, we could combine an algebraic language, such as APL or Pascal, with a language oriented toward string manipulation, such as SNOBOL. Or we could teach a structured language such as Pascal with an array-oriented language such as APL. This multi-language approach offers insight into programming not available if we stay with a single language. Experience indicates that students do not find this a confusing situation. They can distinguish which language they are using and can effectively learn to use both languages at the same time.

Ten-Finger Exercise

One way of learning a programming language, while not applicable in all situations, has proved to be effective at the University of California, Irvine. This method of teaching presumes an interactive environment and a language with "immediate" facilities, so that individual statements, rather than whole programs, can be executed in the language. APL, JOSS, some forms of BASIC, and some forms of Pascal are so implemented.

We have called this approach the "Ten-Finger Exercise" way. The student receives little or no advance instruction in the language. Furthermore, he or she does not have manuals and textbooks, at least at first. What students have is a sheet that tells them what to type; they are told to type each line, and then press the return key. Students usually get some reply each time from the computer, showing what the computer "does." The sentences they type are ordered to elucidate the facilities of the language. Occasionally, also on a printed page, students will be asked a question, just to make sure they have picked up whatever point is being made. They quickly learn that they can do additional experimentation of the same type.

Thus, the student sees no didactic material, encounters no grammatical information, hears no lectures about the language, but does learn to use it by interacting with the language interpreter or compiler. This technique can be compared to a biologist's learning about a strange animal by giving it selective stimuli and watching its behavior in response to those stimuli. The success of the technique depends on the teacher formulating a reasonable progression to move a learner through the language. One does not start with the difficult ideas; rather, with the simple ones. Considerable experience is needed to guide the student through the likely difficulties.

The languages learned in this way at Irvine include APL, BASIC, and a variant of JOSS. In the APL material, when the student types $2 + 3$ and presses return, the computer immediately types 5. They quickly get the idea that the computer is doing the arithmetic they ask it to and they learn how to instruct the computer to do such calculations.

Even the error messages in the system are useful in this mode of teaching. Material can be consciously planned so that occasionally a student *will* get an error message, learning what cannot be done as well as what can be done.

This "Ten-Finger Exercise" approach has been used successfully with both high school students and college students. For example, in a high school group of mixed ninth- to eleventh-grade students, chosen because of their interest in science, a group of students learned a usable subset of APL in only four hours of time, all spent using the "Ten-Finger Exercise." In addition to teaching the language rapidly, this strategy gives students the idea that they can, by experimentation, continue to grow in knowledge of the language.

MODES OF COMPUTER USAGE IN SCIENCE

With Joseph Marasco

Computers can enter into courses in a variety of ways. They can be present only in small additional units, not affecting the main flow of the course, or they can, at the other extreme, alter the course greatly, providing a type of learning not available without the computer. Most current examples fit near the first extreme, but eventually radical alterations will be the order of the day.

This article describes a *beginning Physics course* where the computer makes a sizable difference, as seen by the student. The course could not exist in its present form without heavy access to computing capability, and without considerable preparation of computer-based material. Many different modes of computer usage are involved.

Reprinted by permission of *T.H.E. Journal*, vol. 4, no. 2.

Brief Description of the Course

The first quarter of a Physics sequence, the course was initially taken primarily by Biology majors at the Univerity of California, Irvine. Most of the students were juniors and seniors, with medicine as their career goal. Almost all of the 300 students had two quarters of Calculus, which was required in the Irvine Biology curriculum. However, Calculus was taken several years ago in many cases; students were not necessarily strong mathematically. More recently, we have used the material for freshmen Science-Engineering students.

Self-Pacing and Student Choice

The course is taught in the Personalized System of Instruction (PSI) or Keller plan mode. Students have control over the time sequence of their progress through the course. That is, the pace through the course is not lockstep, determined in advance by the instructor, but can be different for each student. The material is divided into eight units for 10 weeks. Unit descriptions and other study aids, including notes, are available for purchase.

In each unit, learning objectives are carefully specified. Students show that they understand the unit by passing a test on that unit. Passing in most PSI courses, including the present one, is at the 100% level, except for minor errors not related to the objective. If the test is not passed, it is taken again; there are many versions of each test.

PSI courses are widely available, although they represent a small fraction of the total in higher education. Many variants exist. The use of computers in such courses is relatively rare.

The PSI stucture gives students control over pacing, within limitations. But most PSI courses have a single fixed track of subject matter, with some possible options. We provide the student with a choice of content. Rather than push each student through the same course, we allow each student to choose between several different tracks. The chart shows the tracks available.

unit tests - computer dialogs and exercises

a1 ACCEL MOVE EQAR Blows exercise (hand in)	C1 SLOPE VECTORS
a2 APLUSE APLEXP (APL workspace) APLPROG (APL workspace)	C2 PROJECTILE POP
a3 HO SLOPE Oscillator exercise (hand in)	C3 IMPULSE NEWT
a4 GRAV Gravity exercise (hand in)	C4 NRG FORPOT
a5 POT POTFOR Exploring energy	C5 ROTKIN ROTDYN
a6 MOM POP	C6 EQAR TWOBOD Gravity exercise (hand in)
a7 DAMP More oscillator exercise (hand in)	C7 PEND SPRING Oscillator exercise (hand in)
a8 COUP	C8 COM REFRAME

Two sets of learning materials are involved: the units A1 through A8 and the units C1 through C8. The "C" units (C stands for "conventional") are based on a standard textbook for such a course. The "A" units (the "alternate" track) follow notes developed by Alfred Bork. Computer programming is an integral part of the "A" units. In unit A2 students learn APL. Notes are sold at cost, as are unit descriptions for the "C" units.

Student Programming

The two sets of units are distinctly different, although both cover Newtonian mechanics. The utilization of the computer in the "A" units allows students to consider the laws of motion as differential equations, using numerical methods. The "C" units follow the conventional approach of treating mechanics problems that can be handled without the use of differential equations (blocks sliding down inclined planes, masses over pulleys). The "A" unit problems consider more interesting physical situations, such as the motion of a planet around a sun, even in cases where the orbit is not circular.

The material used to teach APL programming was developed by Alfred Bork, Stephen Franklin, Mark Geisert, and Ed Reidel. Its strategy is to put students in APL and ask them to type line after line, as described earlier in this chapter. At each line, the student observes the output of APL, and so learns how this strange animal—the computer plus APL—responds to the stimuli. The experiences are structured, so the student encounters the typical difficulties in learning in APL in a reasonable order. Thus, everything is found through personal discovery. The student document also gives programming and debugging advice, enough to get started with the practical considerations of programming.

The simple Euler approximation is employed in the alternate track for the $\mathbf{F} = m\mathbf{a}$ differential equation in mechanics. Two sets of learning materials are available in the student packets to pursue this approach; each contains the same APL programs. The necessary APL programs are presented first in nongraphic forms and then in graphic forms. Students are urged to use the graphic capabilities, even from their earliest attempts, and the APL learning material introduces graphic capability.

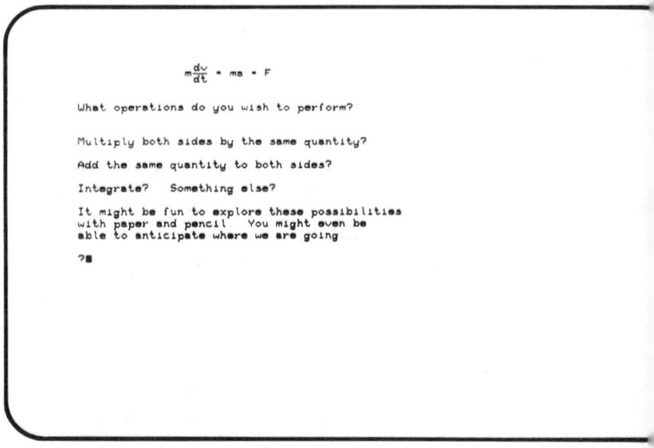

```
m dv/dt = ma = F

What operations do you wish to perform?

Multiply both sides by the same quantity?

Add the same quantity to both sides?

Integrate?   Something else?

It might be fun to explore these possibilities
with paper and pencil   You might even be
able to anticipate where we are going

?■
```

FIGURE 5-1 Early Sequence From CONSERVE

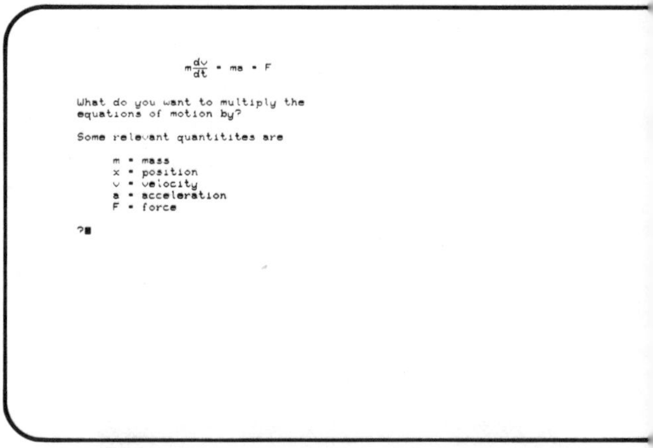

```
m dv/dt = ma = F

What do you want to multiply the
equations of motion by?

Some relevant quantitites are

     m = mass
     x = position
     v = velocity
     a = acceleration
     F = force

?■
```

FIGURE 5-2 From the Interactive Proof Dialog, CONSERVE

Computer Aiding of Intuition

The second mode of computer use is aimed at increasing student intuition concerning the behavior of mechanical systems, a difficult goal to attain in standard learning environments. Typical courses either depend on the laboratory to accomplish this or ignore the problem entirely. But the motions that can be viewed in a laboratory are restricted; they do not include the full range of forces and initial conditions that can be discussed with the theory of mechanics.

We developed many years ago, with National Science Foundation support, programs designed to build insight into the behavior of physical systems, particularly mechanical systems. Until the 1976 course, these student-computer dialogs were used on a free basis, although several courses had assignments based on them.

We prepared student guides to structure these experiences concerning the nature of motion, and therefore aid all students rather than a few. These guides show how

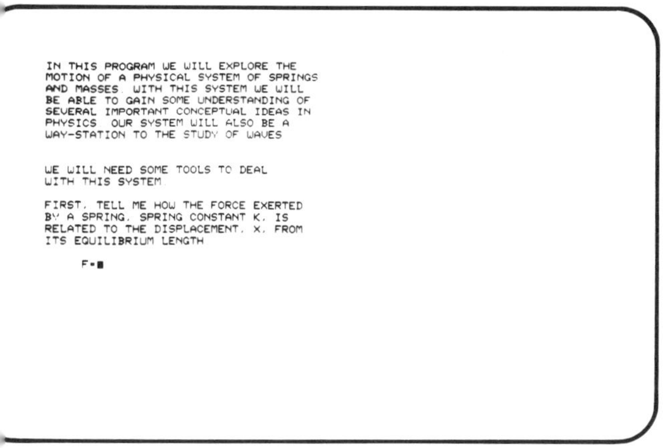

```
IN THIS PROGRAM WE WILL EXPLORE THE
MOTION OF A PHYSICAL SYSTEM OF SPRINGS
AND MASSES. WITH THIS SYSTEM WE WILL
BE ABLE TO GAIN SOME UNDERSTANDING OF
SEVERAL IMPORTANT CONCEPTUAL IDEAS IN
PHYSICS. OUR SYSTEM WILL ALSO BE A
WAY-STATION TO THE STUDY OF WAVES

WE WILL NEED SOME TOOLS TO DEAL
WITH THIS SYSTEM.

FIRST, TELL ME HOW THE FORCE EXERTED
BY A SPRING, SPRING CONSTANT K, IS
RELATED TO THE DISPLACEMENT, X, FROM
ITS EQUILIBRIUM LENGTH

     F=■
```

FIGURE 5-3 First Sequence in the Interactive Proof Dialog, COUPOSC

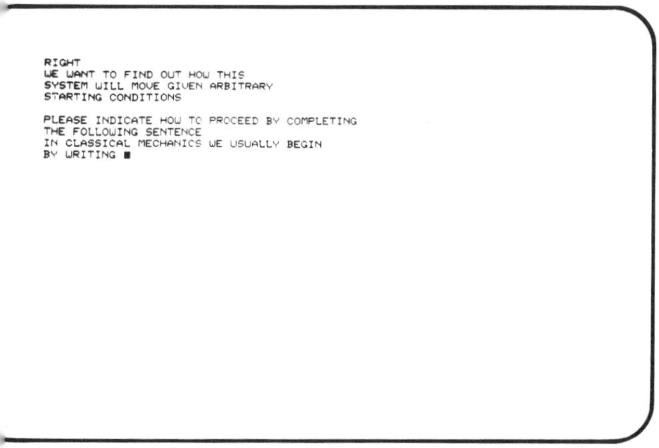

```
RIGHT
WE WANT TO FIND OUT HOW THIS
SYSTEM WILL MOVE GIVEN ARBITRARY
STARTING CONDITIONS

PLEASE INDICATE HOW TO PROCEED BY COMPLETING
THE FOLLOWING SENTENCE
IN CLASSICAL MECHANICS WE USUALLY BEGIN
BY WRITING ■
```

FIGURE 5-4 Also From COUPOSC

to get into the programs and suggest problems to investigate. Students write the results of the investigations on the guides; these are handed in as part of the material necessary to complete the unit. A complete collection of these guides is available from the Irvine Physics Department.

Interactive Learning

The third mode is the use of interactive computer-based teaching programs, the computer dialogs developed in the Physics Computer Development Project at Irvine. These programs, at their best, represent an individualized mode of teaching difficult to match except in one-to-one teaching situations. The computer holds a conversation with the student, responding immediately to problems.

We do not have computer dialogs that cover every aspect of the Physics course, but we do have a body of highly useful materials. The use of graphics is an important aspect of making these dialogs effective learning modes.

The following list gives brief descriptions of the dialogs for mechanics.

CIRCLE—Derivation of the relations between velocity and acceleration for a particle moving uniformly in a circle.

COMPLEX—A review of complex numbers through imaginary exponentials.

CONSERVE—The student derives, with possible help from the computer, the principle of conservation of energy for a one-dimensional mechanical system. The concept of potential energy is introduced. (See Figures 5-1 and 5-2.)

COUPOSC—Properties of coupled systems. The system is that of two masses and three springs on an air track. Students enter the equations of motion for the system; they are given considerable help if difficulties arise. Then the problem is to solve the equations of motion. The dialog introduces the concepts of normal modes and characteristic frequencies. (See Figures 5-3 and 5-4.)

EQAREA—An interactive derivation of the Law of Equal Areas, following the approach in Proposition 1 in Newton's *Principia.*

HARMONIC—An interactive derivation of the motion of damped oscillators. Distinguishes between underdamped, overdamped, and critically damped oscillators.

HOCKEY—Introduces the notions of momentum, mass, and momentum conservation through simulations of puck collisions on an air table.

LUNA—The notion of a theory or model. LUNA uses the phases of the moon, and the predictions that can be made from the model, as its general prototype of a scientific model.

MOMENTUM—An interactive derivation of the logical relationships between Newton's third law and the principle of conservation of momentum. (See Figures 5-5, 5-6, and 5-7.)

MOTION—A versatile mechanical simulation. The student can change force laws, initial conditions, and the plotting spaces, and can work in either two or three dimensions.

NBODY—Simulates an *N* body gravitational system, displaying the orbits of the bodies.

ROTATION—A series of problems of rotational motion.

TERRA—The sky as seen from the earth.

FLOAT—The effect of the earth's motion on the weight of an object on the earth. (See Figure 5-8.)

WORK—A light introduction to the concept of work.

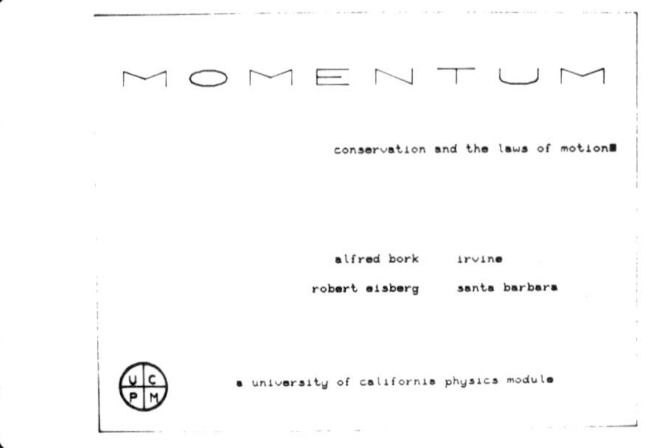

FIGURE 5-5 MOMENTUM—An Interactive Proof—Title Page

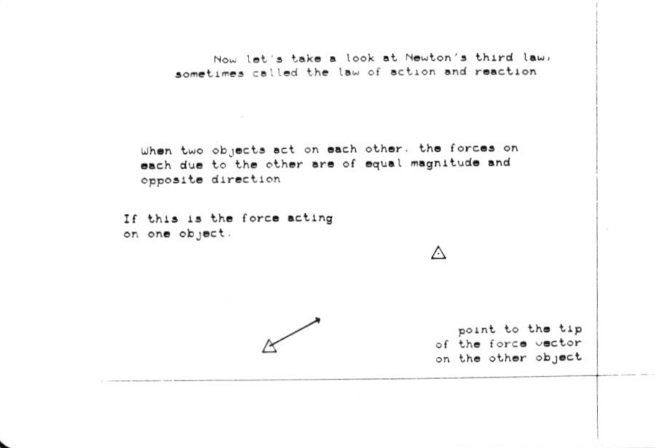

FIGURE 5-6 Reviewing Student's Knowledge of the Third Law in MOMENTUM

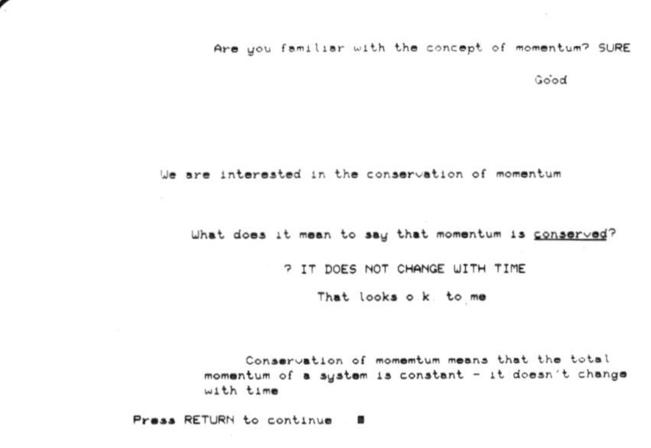

FIGURE 5-7 Checking Student's Background in MOMENTUM

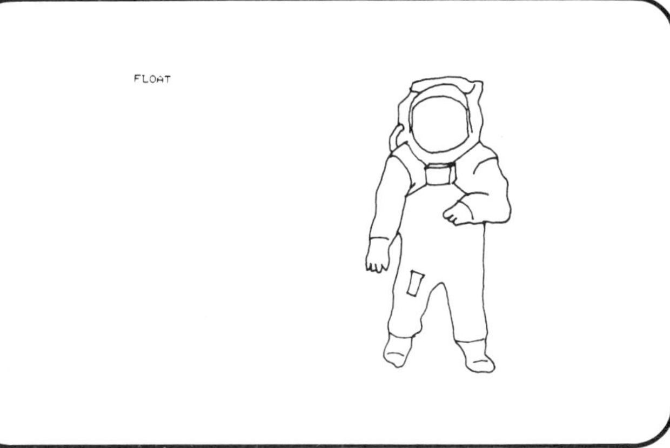

FIGURE 5-8 From the Dialog FLOAT

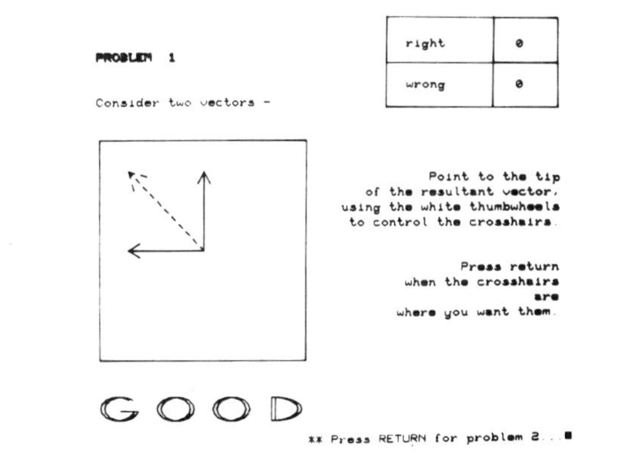

FIGURE 5-9 Problem 1 from the Interactive Quiz VECTORS

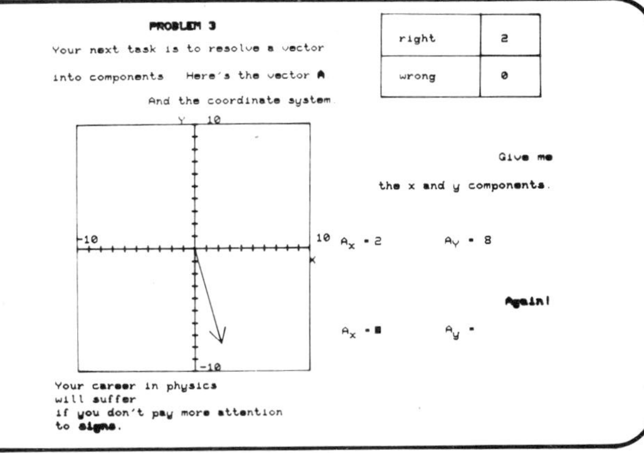

FIGURE 5-10 Problem 3 from VECTORS (Note Help Sequence)

On-Line Testing

In typical PSI environments, unit tests are written and graded, if possible, immediately by student proctors. Hopefully the student receives quick feedback about the areas requiring further study; in practice the amount, quality, and timing of feedback varies considerably depending on the abilities and number of the proctors and the number taking the tests simultaneously.

In 1975–76, Physics 3A employed graduate assistants as proctors for the unit tests. Given departmental resources available, we were often not able to grade the tests immediately. The atmosphere of the testing room was hectic, with many students waiting in long lines. Furthermore, students complained, justifiably, that proctors had different standards as to what constituted the "almost perfect" passing score. Even though we discussed with the proctors what "minor errors" should be overlooked, grading was not uniform, as one would expect. These factors affected student morale. Hence, we decided to use on-line tests.

The tests have a 40-minute time limit. If students do not pass tests, they repeat them until they demonstrate that they understand the unit. Each test is unique; each time the student requests a test, he or she will get a different variant. If the student does not pass the test, he or she cannot take it again for 12 hours; further study is suggested.

The tests are more than tests; they offer considerable learning material. First, many contain extensive help sequences independent of the test; the student can view these sections first. The help sequence does not count as part of the student's time in taking the tests, and it is always accessible. Second, while the test is proceeding, the student receives immediate aid and assistance when problems arise due to lack of understanding. Thus, feedback is much more rapid and relevant than in other learning modes.

The tests are individually prepared and do not follow an "item bank" strategy sometimes found in on-line computer testing. A great variety of modes are used. For a review of the types of structures employed, and for a general discussion of the advantages of this type of interactive testing the reader is referred to a paper by Joseph Marasco and Stephen Franklin[3], who played instrumental roles in the preparation of the tests. Two quizzes are illustrated here: VECTORS (Figures 5-9 to 5-12) early in the conventional track, and COUP (Figures 5-13 to 5-16) late in the alternate track.

Course Management

The final aspect of computer use is the course management system. Control over taking tests (the question as to whether the student is allowed to take a particular test), the record-keeping (the information about failure and passage), and recording information about what the student did are all part of the course management system.

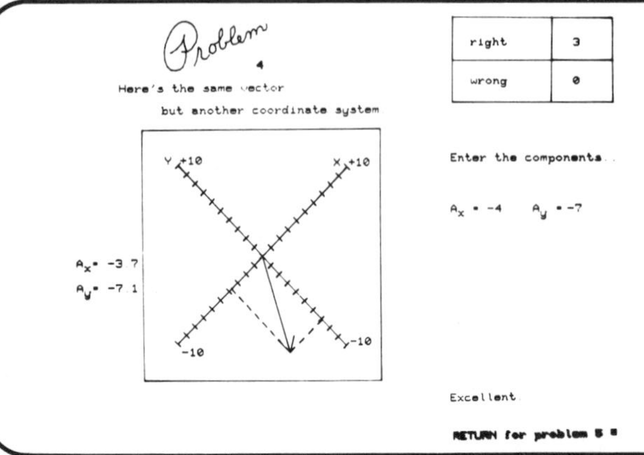

FIGURE 5-11 Problem 4 from VECTORS, with Response

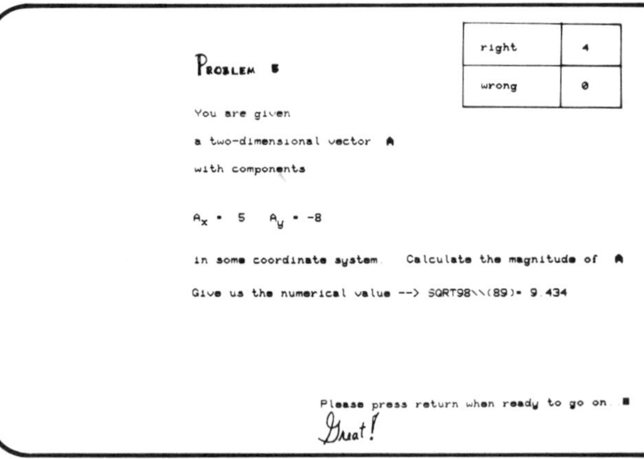

FIGURE 5-12 From VECTORS (Note Calculational Aids)

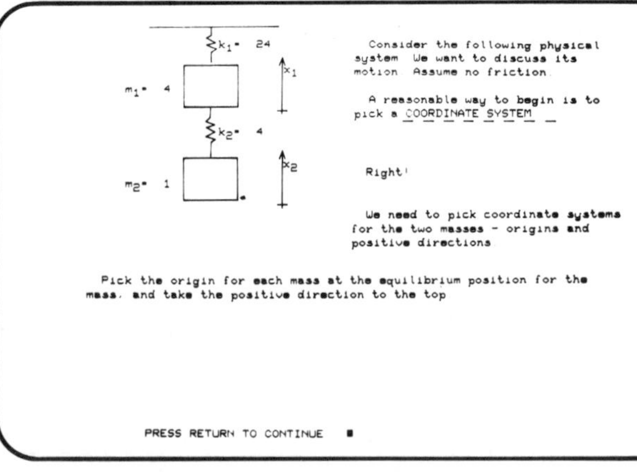

FIGURE 5-13 Introduction to Quiz COUP, on Coupled Systems

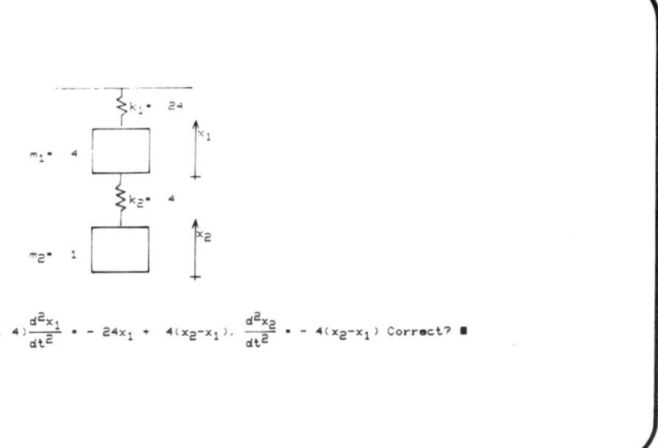

FIGURE 5-14 COUP, Querying about Equations of Motion

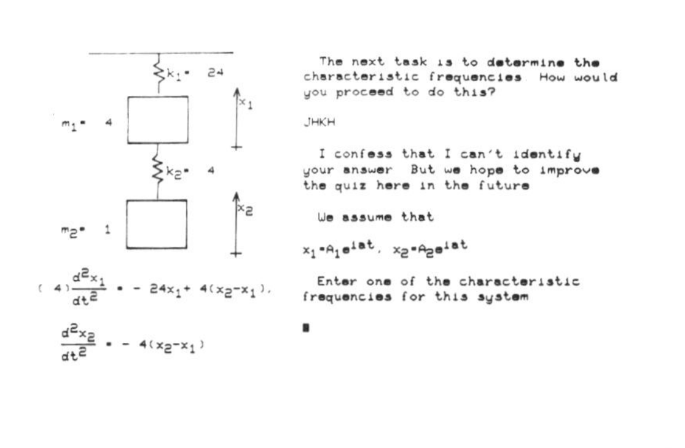

FIGURE 5-15 COUP, Asking for Characteristic Frequencies

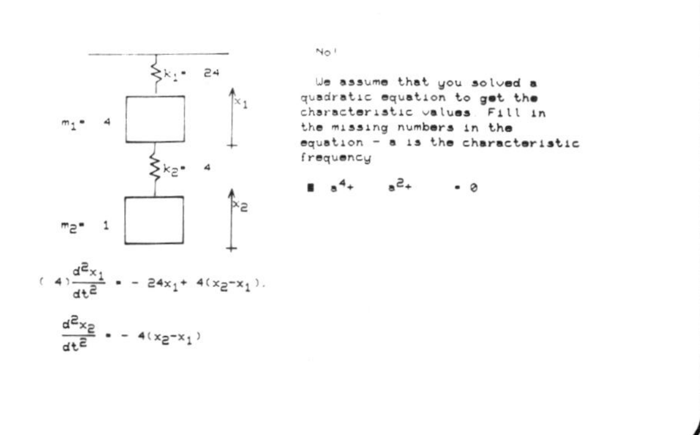

FIGURE 5-16 COUP, Response to Student with Incorrect Characteristic Frequencies

At the heart of the system is a data base of student records, maintained in a CODASYL environment. The data base contains general information about the student plus complete information about his or her progress in the course. A variety of auxiliary files are also maintained in the system. The next article gives further details concerning the course management system.

The course management system helps the student, the instructor, and the course secretary. The instructor is in a position to obtain detailed information about students, designed to assist in the overall management of the course. One typical problem in PSI courses is that of procrastination, particularly in the early days when students may be relatively uncertain about their responsibilities in the course. The course management system periodically provides the instructor lists of people who are behind, and letters are then sent out to those students reminding them that they are in danger. The instructor also obtains information about overall performance in each of the tests, so class problems and test weaknesses can be quickly spotted and remedied.

Resources

We employ in the course approximately 100,000 terminal minutes per month, about two hours per student per week. In the winter of 1980 we gave about 15,000 quizzes.

COURSE MANAGEMENT SYSTEM FOR PHYSICS 3 COURSE AT IRVINE

With Jeff East and Joseph Marasco

The Course

The course considered, described in the last article, is a Calculus-based Introduction to Physics. Two things distinguish this course from most others. For the first quarter (which deals with mechanics), the course is self-paced and multi-tracked. Students have some control of the speed with which they move through the material (self-pacing) and some control of the content. Not all students see the same material, and students may see topics at different times.

The variety allowed students increases the complexity of record-keeping. Students indicate progress by passing quizzes (typically several per unit). By the middle of the course, students are in as many as ten different units. Furthermore, since students often have to take a given quiz several times before passing it, multiple versions of quizzes are required, as well as records of which version of the quiz the student has already seen.

Proceedings of the 1977 Conference on Computers in the Undergraduate Curriculum - CCUC8, Michigan State University.

We decided after an initial offering of the course that traditional methods of administering, grading, and keeping track of the quizzes were grossly insufficient and that much could be gained by going to a system where all the quizzes were given on-line. Every student receives a unique quiz on each attempt. For pedagogical as well as practical reasons, we wanted to control access to the quizzes; for example, we wanted students to wait a fixed time before retrying a quiz. This paper describes the computer-based system designed and implemented to handle the problem.

The System—An Overview

We will first attempt to describe the system in general, showing the relationship of the various components. We will then talk in more detail about aspects of interfacing with existing software.

Figure 5-17 shows the structure of the course management system. The principal file is the Extended Data Management System (EDMS) data base, the data management system. (This file may be found near the center of the figure.) The data base contains all the student records

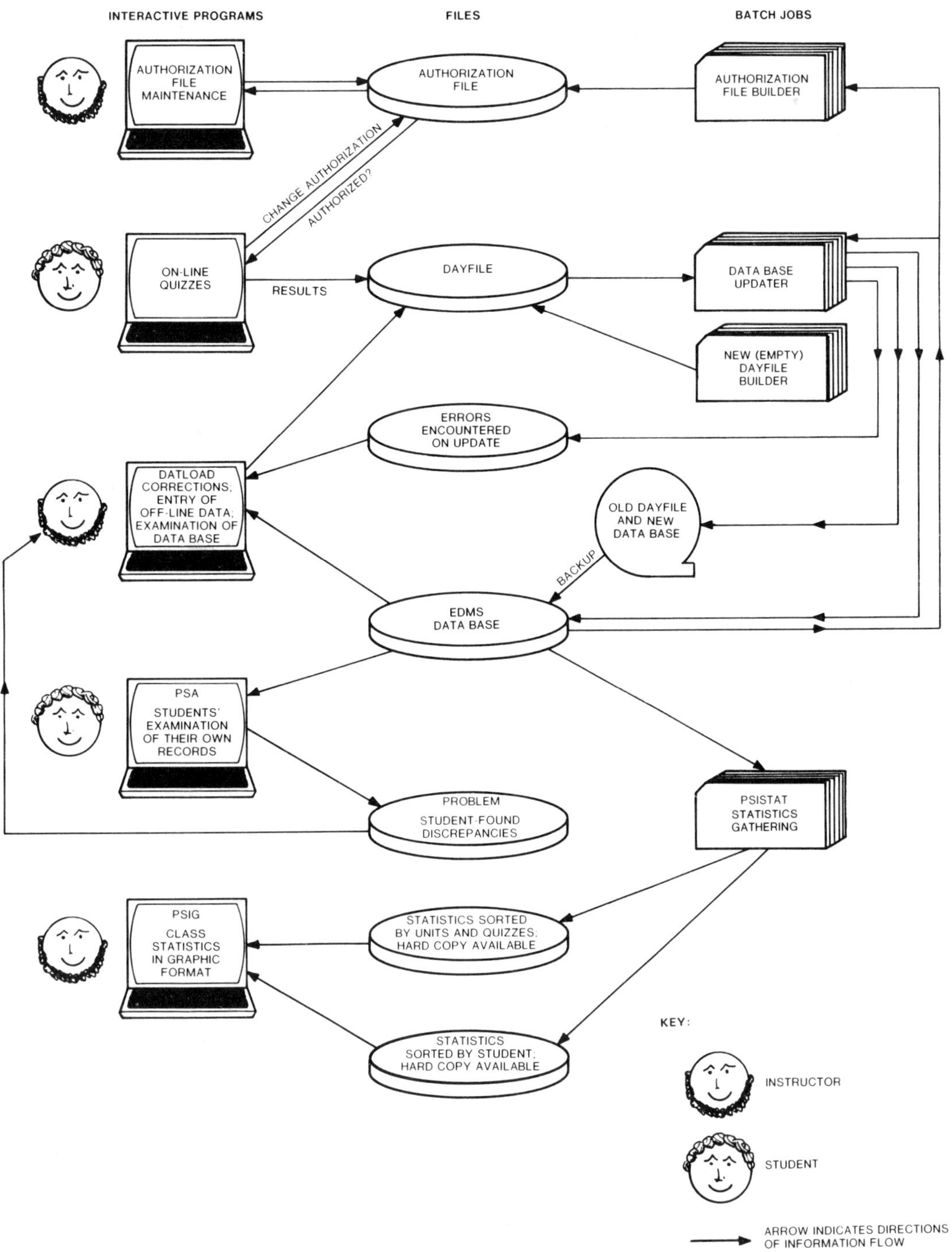

FIGURE 5-17 Structure of the Irvine Course Management System

for the course; a complete description of its network structure is beyond the scope of this paper but is available on request. One of our guiding design principles was that, although the data base could be examined at any time, we wished to update it only once a day. This criterion grew out of cost and security considerations.

How does the EDMS data base get updated? Working backwards on Figure 5-17, we see that a batch job reads a file (the DAYFILE) and then updates the data base. (This and several affiliated jobs are run by our computer center as part of the end-of-day procedures.) As indicated in the figure, any errors or anomalies encountered during the update are written out to a file; the old DAYFILE and the entire new data base are copied to tape as a backup. A fresh (empty) DAYFILE is created for the next day, as well as something called an authorization file. This entire process is called "updating the data base," and it occurs every 24 hours.

Crucial to the above process is the notion of the DAYFILE. Two types of user programs write on the DAYFILE. First, all the on-line quizzes write their results onto it. Second, the instructor using a supplied program can enter off-line results and make corrections. Note that both the quizzes and the instructor program just mentioned are interactive, on-line programs available at all times. The instructor's program, available to other authorized persons, is a restricted access program. A student's complete record may be accessed. Figure 5-18 is a typical example. Material entered by both these methods shows up in the data base the next day, after the data base has been updated.

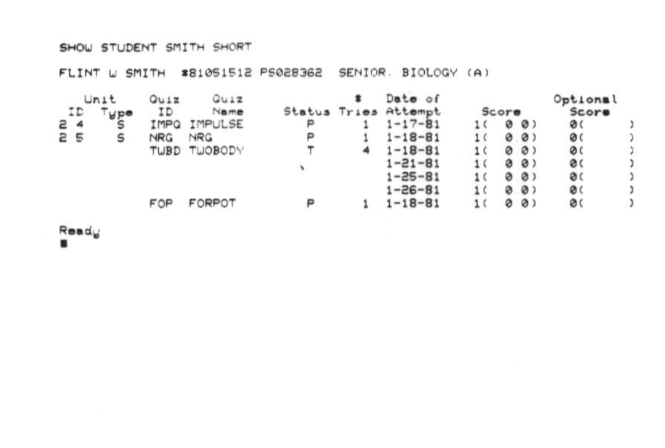

```
SHOW STUDENT SMITH SHORT

FLINT W SMITH  #81051512 PS028362  SENIOR. BIOLOGY (A)

   Unit      Quiz    Quiz                   #    Date of                 Optional
 ID   Type    ID     Name          Status Tries  Attempt      Score        Score
2 4     S    IMPQ IMPULSE             P      1   1-17-81     1(  0 0)     0(      )
2 5     S    NRG  NRG                 P      1   1-18-81     1(  0 0)     0(      )
             TWBD TWOBODY             T      4   1-18-81     1(  0 0)     0(      )
                                                 1-21-81     1(  0 0)     0(      )
                                                 1-25-81     1(  0 0)     0(      )
                                                 1-26-81     1(  0 0)     0(      )
             FOP  FORPOT              P      1   1-18-81     1(  0 0)     0(      )

Ready
■
```

FIGURE 5-18 Partial Student Record in Course Data Base

How does all this appear to students? Their perception of the system may be through two channels—the first being the quizzes themselves. They are allowed to take quizzes based on previous performance: quizzes become authorized progressively. Hence, there is a quiz-authorization file (see Figure 5-17 again) which permits student entry to a given quiz. Passing a quiz may open other quizzes, so the quizzes write on as well as read from the quiz authorization file. This file is recreated each time the data base is updated; an on-line maintenance program allows the instructor to take special action.

The second program accessible to students in some years allows them to examine their own records. We have not employed this program in recent years.

The only remaining part of Figure 5-17 yet unexplained concerns the gathering of statistics. A batch job reads from the data base and writes two summary files, one showing the status of each student and one reviewing each unit and quiz. This batch job is typically run once a week. Hard copy of these statistics is available from the line printer. In addition, a graphics display program uses the information in the summary files to construct histograms and scatter plots for the course. A map showing the progress of the students through the course can also be generated.

Some Further Details

To monitor student progress through the course and to gather meaningful statistics, new procedures to use within quizzes were implemented to supplement the collection available in our software. We will describe the three principal instructions to show the relative ease with which we were able to add these features to our existing system.

The first new facility is used at the beginning of a quiz. It performs several important functions. It marks the point at which an instructional segment shifts from being a conversation-like dialog—hence, freely accessible—to a quiz segment. This procedure first searches the class authorization file to see if the student can take the quiz. If the account from which the query originated is not listed in the authorization file, a search is then made in a privileged user file. Listed are the accounts of instructional personnel who need quiz access for reference or demonstration purposes. If the account number is not found in either the authorization file or the privilege file, access is denied and a message is sent to the user. The procedure also sets the time limit allowed for the quiz, does some bookkeeping with the authorization file to indicate the quiz has been attempted, and sets a flag indicating whether the user was authorized or privileged. No further records are kept for privileged users. We talk only to the authorization file and not to the DAYFILE.

A second procedure aids in keeping detailed records of student progress through the quizzes. Each quiz has this instruction embedded at crucial branching points. By writing a unique identifier for each occurrence, we save the student's path through the exam: what problems students attempted, what problems they successfully completed, and how many attempts they made on each segment. Clearly this is a large amount of data—a "map" of a single student's progress through a single quiz can consist of ten or more records. Considering that we administer over 10,000 quizzes in one quarter, the question arises as to where to store all this data. We choose not to keep this in the data base but to use our nightly archival tape save of the DAYFILE.

Finally, we have a closing procedure. Under normal circumstances, each quiz ends with a call to this capability. Depending on arguments set by the quiz, the procedure records the result in the DAYFILE: Pass, No Pass, or No Pass/Time Limit Exceeded. Modifications when necessary are made in the authorization file. A message indicating the action taken is sent to the student. In the case of an abortive exit—the student breaks out of the program or shuts off the display—our software allows us to get control and execute the bookkeeping operations.

Improvements

The system worked quite well initially during the fall of 1976. Over 10,000 on-line quizzes and several hundred off-line exercises were entered, as well as scores for optional units and the final exam.

More than 300 students were enrolled initially in the course and about 275 completed it. In spite of the usual number of system problems, the data base survived intact.

Nonetheless, we discovered problems, and revised the course management system. While most of these are particular to our way of doing things, they may be generic in that newcomers may commit the same oversights we did.

One of the things that became painfully obvious as the quarter wore on was that our method of handling the diagnostic messages from the updates was poor. That file was overwritten each night, making it necessary for someone to examine it every morning before it was overwritten the following night. As in any large system where there are many principal users, it becomes imperative to have a good way of recording actions taken so as to ensure that all students are being taken care of and that things are being done in a uniform way.

Another flaw was the initial system of only allowing students to go on to the next unit after all material was completed in the present one. While this worked well for the on-line materials, problems arose for the off-line assignments. Students who previously had waited up to a week to have homeworks graded in other courses became impatient when an assignment handed in did not appear the next day in the data base, allowing them to proceed. This was not a fault of the computer or the data base; the weak link was the time needed to grade and record the work. To combat this problem, our ever-efficient students started to hand in this work very early. Unfortunately, we were then caught in our own net for the opposite reason; the work belonged to the next unit and hence was rejected by the data base because it was too early.

The moral of the story is that a system should be no more rigid than you really want it to be. In our next iteration we implemented two types of units: one that has a strict time sequence and one that can be done any time.

A final observation concerns sociological effects. Expectations were very definitely raised as to our ability to respond to any and all problems that arose. Since students had virtually 24-hour access to the quizzes, they sometimes expected that someone would always be there in case of problems. We were highly visible, accessible, and eager to iron out the minor difficulties that came up, yet in some instances, students felt frustrated that we were not doing more. The fact that more attention was being paid to them than in most traditionally-structured courses seemed to be little remembered by a usual minority of the class. But this problem has vanished in recent years.

References

1. K. E. Iverson, *A Programming Language* (New York: John Wiley & Sons, 1962).

2. Kingsley Amis, *I Want It Now* (New York: Harcourt, Brace & World, 1968).

3. Joseph Marasco and Stephen Franklin, "Interactive Computer-Based Testing," *Journal of College Science Teaching,* Vol. 7, No. 1 (September 1977).

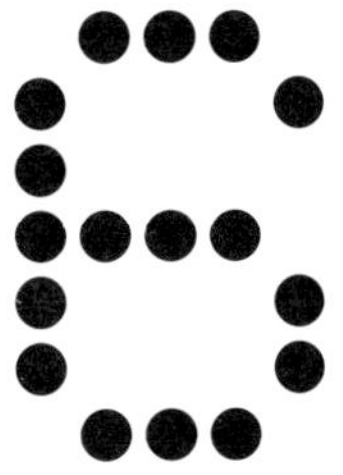

Authoring Dialogs

PREPARING STUDENT-COMPUTER DIALOGS—ADVICE TO TEACHERS

A computer dialog is a "conversation" between a student and a teacher, where the student is at a computer display and the teacher is conducting the dialog through the medium of a computer program. Typically such a dialog follows a pattern like this: First, something will be typed to the student, possibly some information. Then the student will be asked to reply, or perhaps to ask a question. Several modes of reply are available. Depending on what the student types, a number of things might be displayed next. See Figures 6-1, 6-2, and 6-3 for examples.

If you have access to dialogs, you should examine a variety of such dialogs. Experience in running good dialogs is the best way to develop a quick appreciation of what is possible.

In this article, I offer advice to those preparing such student-computer dialogs, with emphasis on the novice. Writing a

Reprinted by permission of the publisher, Teachers College Press. From Robert Taylor, ed., *The Computer for School: Tutor, Tool, and Tutee.*

dialog is only a partially understood process at present, so any advice is subjective and should not be taken too seriously! We all have much to learn about the educational use of computers.

Nevertheless, some useful experience can be brought to the attention of the teacher who is designing such material. This article attempts to do this, using experience in the Educational Technology Center and the Physics Computer Development Project at the University of California, Irvine, as the basis.

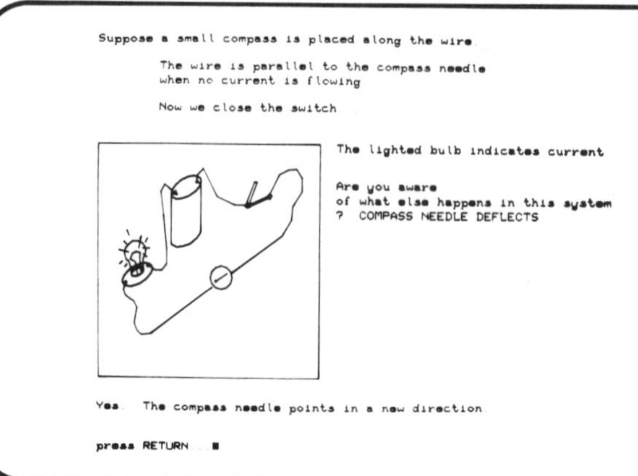

FIGURE 6-1 Dialog MFIELD, Introductory Frame

Getting Started

The critical decision the dialog writer must face is what to write dialogs about. The burden of educational proof is upon the dialog writer, who cannot assume that simply putting standard existing material into interactive dialog form in trivial ways will improve the learning environment. Furthermore, the preparation of extensive dialogs can be a lengthy job, putting a premium on a wise choice of subject and approach for a dialog. If other media are also possible, the problem is to select the best medium or media for the purpose at hand.

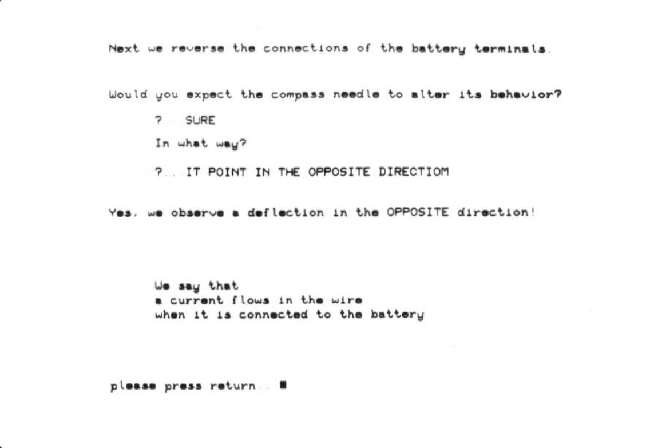

FIGURE 6-2 MFIELD, The Next Step

One way to approach the problem of preparing dialogs is to ask how you could, within the teaching of a particular subject area, gain unusual leverage with computer dialogs. Where can the computer have maximum learning impact? The answer to this question might be different for different areas and could only be given by someone with an extensive knowledge of both subject and pedagogy. It is very

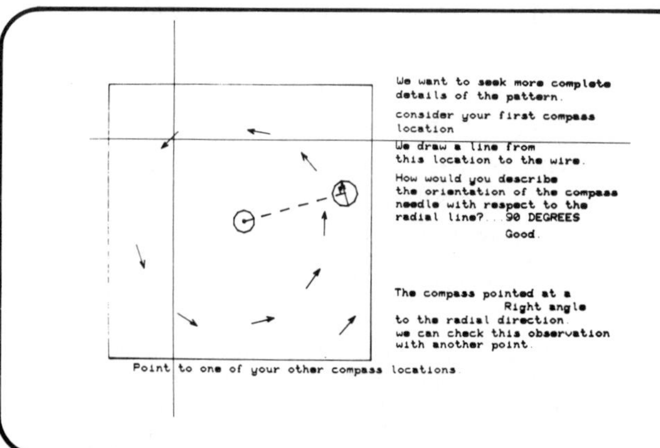

FIGURE 6-3 From MFIELD, Using the Pointer to Choose a New Location

important to ask the question and to concentrate dialog efforts in areas and approaches that look promising for this technique. The dialog is not a lecture or a book, and we must seek the appropriate use of this new medium.

It is reasonable to consult with colleagues about where the effort should be concentrated. Often such a question leads to a fundamental rethinking of the area involved, a reconsideration of deep educational objectives. This approach implies formulation of goals and objectives desired in the unit or course under development. Given this powerful new learning device, it may be possible to learn important ideas at an earlier stage in the student's education; examination of the topics and technique stressed in more advanced courses may be useful at this stage. Some tasks previously considered very difficult or almost impossible can be learned using the computer.

Ideally this process should also consider the other educational media available for learning the specific objective. It is beyond the scope of this book to discuss the full problem of course and curriculum design. To take an entirely new approach to a course rather than simply an approach that adds on existing material is highly desirable, but it is a difficult and expensive process. Instructional design is an extensive science in itself, and one that many teachers may be unwilling to approach simply because there is much to learn. For full curriculum development it is essential, and for maximum impact of the computer such development is necessary.

Everyone will have different views about the best approaches for course design and instructional development. The views presented here are modeled after the activities of The Open University. While The Open University courses have used computers only in minimal ways, their general approach to course design combines both the research information and practical considerations in a very desirable blend. In the United States, the University of Mid-America has also engaged in similar developments.

Goals

Goals can be short-term or long-term. In preparing any activities for learning, we should decide what we are trying to do; we should specify our learning objectives.

If we consider a Science course, the student may need to learn factual information—the standard theories that already exist in the area, the mathematical techniques that go along with these theories, etc. But our interest in learning Science is not archival, intended to persuade people to look admiringly at these lovely mental structures of the past. Rather, we hope to prepare people who can proceed to use this information, modestly or in great creative leaps beyond the present *status quo.* Learning factual material is one task, but being able to use it is often a different matter. The moment of truth for students in a Science course comes when they must work difficult problems, which demand that they obtain new information from the information and techniques presented. The long-range goal of most Science courses is to teach people to make these developments themselves.

Learning to tackle difficult problems successfully is a hard task. The heuristic strategies involved in problem-solving, for example, are seldom discussed with students (a glowing exception is George Polya's book, *How to Solve It*[1], recommended for both teachers and students).

The dialog writer should keep in mind long-range learning goals, and stress them in whatever way possible. They are very easily ignored because they pose far greater difficulties than the mere presentation of information. Although these comments on goals are directed toward Science, the consideration is important in all curriculum development.

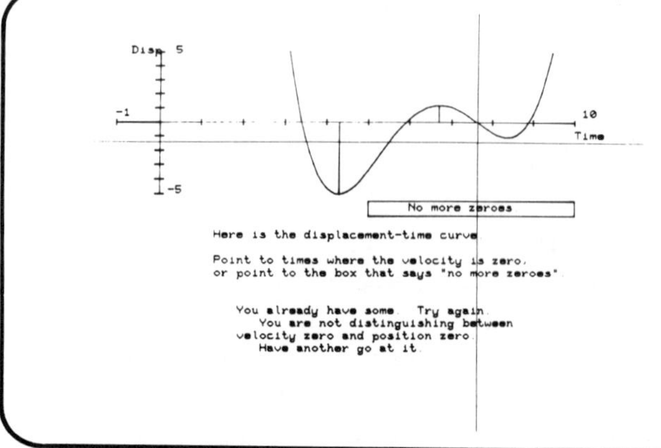

FIGURE 6-4 From SLOPE, Showing Several Pointing Responses

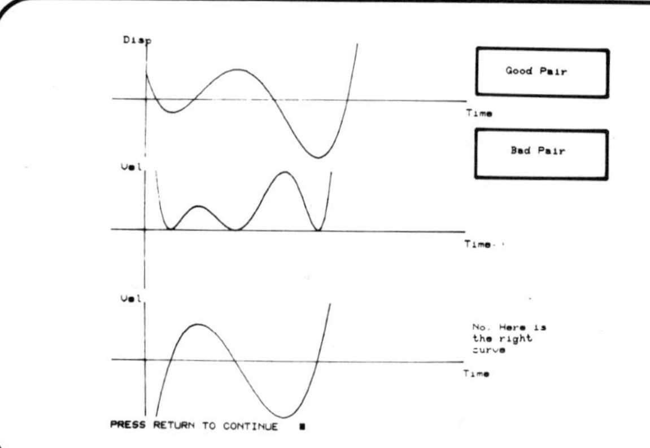

FIGURE 6-5 Quiz SLOPE Showing Response to an Incorrect Answer

Types of Dialogs

A dialog that recreates a book, a printed program text, or some other teaching method, is not likely to have long survival value. Perhaps when the cost of computer usage is less than it is today, and when we become more knowledgeable in the use of computers, the computer may replace the text in many situations, but this is a little in the future.

I will not attempt a full classification of the many types of student-computer dialogs. Several types lend themselves to the beginner. The developer need not use any of the types described.

In recent years the most powerful of our computer applications at Irvine, in terms of both our judgment and reactions of students, have been the on-line tests. The advantage of the on-line tests are that they

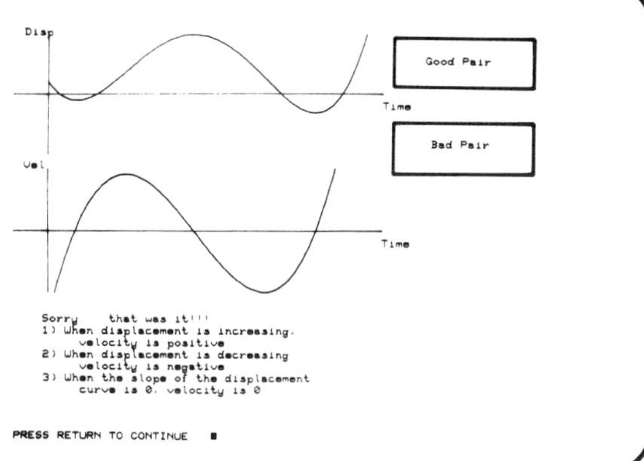
Disp
Good Pair
Time
Bad Pair
Vel
Time
Sorry that was it!!!
1) When displacement is increasing,
velocity is positive
2) When displacement is decreasing
velocity is negative
3) When the slope of the displacement
curve is 0, velocity is 0
PRESS RETURN TO CONTINUE

FIGURE 6-6 SLOPE, Another Type of Response to an Incorrect Answer

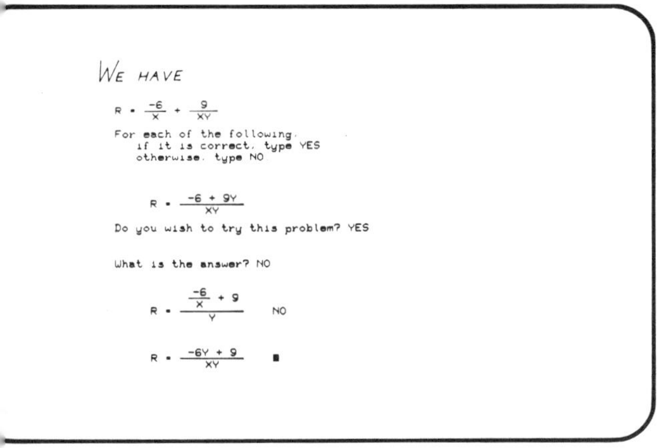

WE HAVE

$$R = \frac{-6}{X} + \frac{9}{XY}$$

For each of the following,
if it is correct, type YES
otherwise, type NO

$$R = \frac{-6 + 9Y}{XY}$$

Do you wish to try this problem? YES

What is the answer? NO

$$R = \frac{\frac{-6}{X} + 9}{Y} \quad \text{NO}$$

$$R = \frac{-6Y + 9}{XY}$$

FIGURE 6-7 Multiple Choice Question in a Mathematics Competency Test

can not only offer immediate feedback to the student as to whether the student has answered correctly but can also offer immediate and highly relevant aid. Thus, we can diagnose, in many cases, exactly what problems students have and immediately show what went wrong with their attempts to solve a problem. Typically this use has taken place in a Personalized System of Instruction environment, stressing mastery learning, but it can be done anywhere.

Thus, this material serves both a teaching and testing function. When coupled with a full course management system, it can be a driving force for the entire course. Figures 6-4, 6-5, and 6-6 illustrate an on-line test, SLOPE.

A class of powerful dialogs are the remedial dialogs that determine the student's weaknesses in an area, and give assistance just where needed. These can occur within an on-line test or as a separate program. One useful procedure is to begin by assuming that the student knows the area, giving a series of questions to selectively test the student's knowledge, perhaps by working examples. These problems need not be difficult; if they are to be repeated an infinite set can be "generated" by means of a problem-generating dialog sequence. Students will only be sent into the remedial parts of the dialog if they cannot handle these problems after several attempts (to allow for typing errors). This approach has the advantage that students receive assistance only where they are weak, so the program can be highly responsive to individual needs. An example from a math competency test is seen in Figure 6-7.

One variant is a dialog that assists students who have trouble working a problem, finding where the trouble occurs and giving help. Figures 6-8, 6-9, and 6-10 illustrate the process; the pictures are from the help sequence in SLOPE.

Another area of the sciences where we think that dialog material is usually effective is that of the interactive proof or problem. The idea is to allow students to attempt to prove important results, partially on their own, making choices and guesses along the way, perhaps in response to suggestions in the program. The process of developing difficult proofs can be made an active process rather than the passive one (for most students) of listening to a lecture or reading a text. The students attempt to make the decisions rather than just seeing the decisions the instructor makes. So, hopefully, the students learn something of the art of proving substantial results. Figures 6-11, 6-12, and 6-13 are from a dialog on momentum conservation.

Similarly, a problem at the computer has advantages over a textbook problem. You can, for example, make students ask for relevant information rather than giving it all in advance as in the typical textbook. (See Figure 6-14.) Students must, therefore, decide what information is relevant, necessary in the "real world" outside the textbook environment.

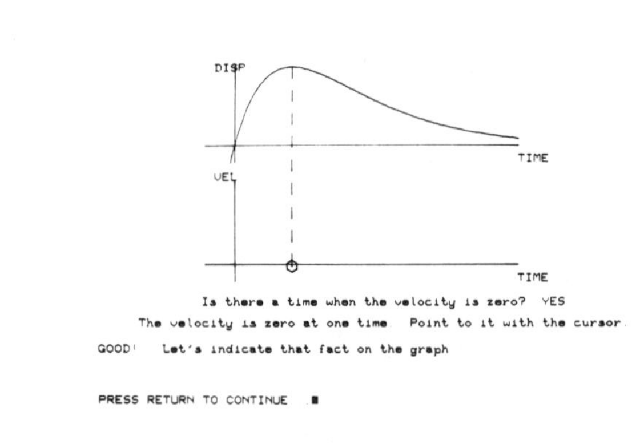

FIGURE 6-8 Early in the Help Sequence for the Quiz SLOPE

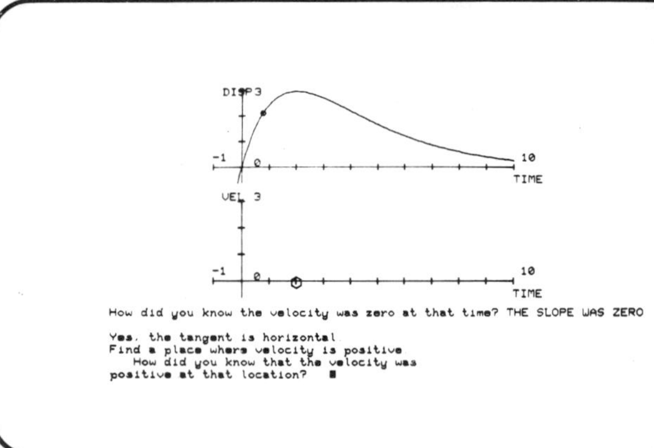

FIGURE 6-9 Help Sequence in SLOPE. Constructing Velocity-Time Curve

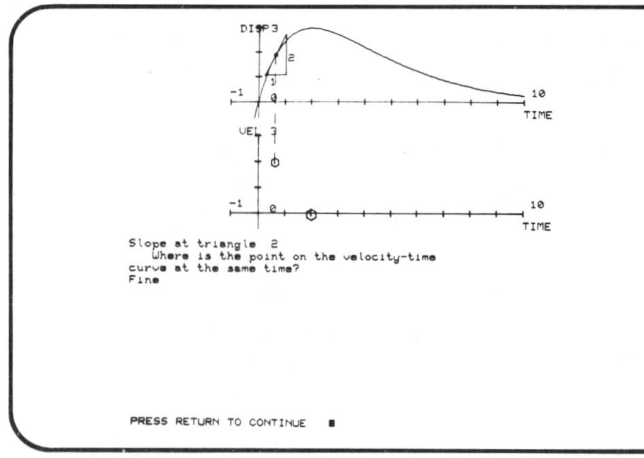

FIGURE 6-10 Help Sequence in SLOPE

We'll pursue two proofs to show the interconections here.

One is.

Newton's second law | and | Newton's third law | implies | Momentum conser- vation

and the other is.

Newton's second law | and | Momentum conser- vation | implies | Newton's third law

In the process we'll also consider some interesting restrictions to the validity of the third law

Press RETURN to continue ■

FIGURE 6-11 MOMENTUM, Frame Outlining the Two Proofs

We begin by writing Newton's laws for each body

$F_1 = \frac{d}{dt}P_1$ $F_2 = \frac{d}{dt}P_2$

F_1 and F_2 are the forces on each particle

What do you want to do with these equations? ■

FIGURE 6-12 MOMENTUM, Student Query

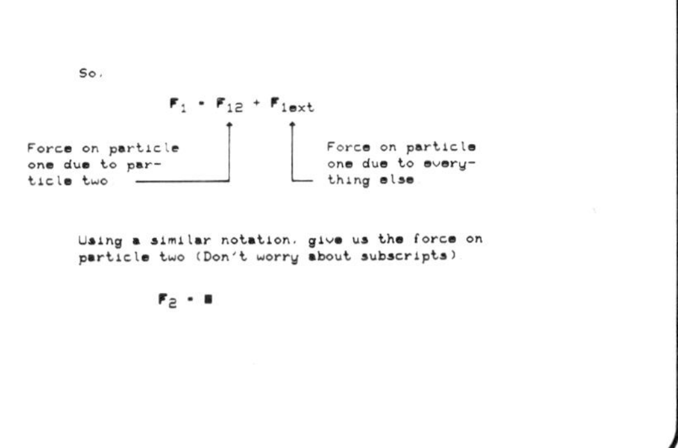

So.
$F_1 = F_{12} + F_{1ext}$
Force on particle one due to par- ticle two
Force on particle one due to every- thing else
Using a similar notation, give us the force on particle two (Don't worry about subscripts)
$F_2 =$ ■

FIGURE 6-13 MOMENTUM, Internal and External Force on a Particle

Another possibility is to present an investigative facility or interactive world for student use. In such an environment students can explore freely, gaining experiences that may not normally be available in any other way. Such a world can be used either freely or as part of an author-structured experience, perhaps a controlled experiment with the computer showing what the student is doing and offering advice where appropriate. Figure 6-15 is a three-dimensional motion around two fixed suns.

One of the principal values of the interactive world dialog is that it provides the possibility of building up student intuition and insight into the way things behave, often by providing a wide range of experiences to the student. Such intuition is an important aspect of learning, and one that is ofen difficult to accomplish within the traditional course.

We are often criticized for producing students who know how to carry out the mathematical manipulations in Science courses, but who are unable to intuit beyond the formal derivations. So dialogs providing experience are useful. However, to use such programs in this fashion demands various auxiliary material. See "Computers as an Aid to Increasing Physical Intuition" in Chapter 4 for examples and further details.

Many other types of student-computer dialogs are also possible.

Mechanism

How should the dialog writer work? As with matters of style, this is very individualistic and will heavily depend on facilities available. If you must work in one way, because that is all that is available, you may want to skip this section. All that is attempted is to mention and comment on some of the possibilities.

Should you work alone or with others? Our experience is that it is highly desirable to work in groups of about three. A single person will miss many possibilities, while a large group tends to spend time in debate, accomplishing little. Work with someone with similar views of the learning process. It is very desirable that one member of the group have previous experience in preparing dialogs. This is discussed further in "Single Versus Multiple Authorship" at the end of this chapter.

After the basic area has been chosen, the authors should prepare an outline of the "mainline" approach, showing the material to be covered. A one-page outline, plus a more detailed treatment, is often a useful beginning. If mathematical derivations are involved, these should be fully worked out in advance, allowing for all the reasonable variants likely to occur with the students using the dialog.

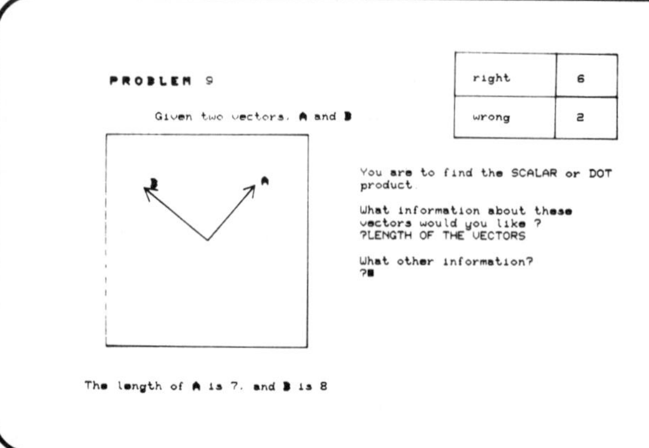

FIGURE 6-14 From VECTORS. Student Requests Relevant Information

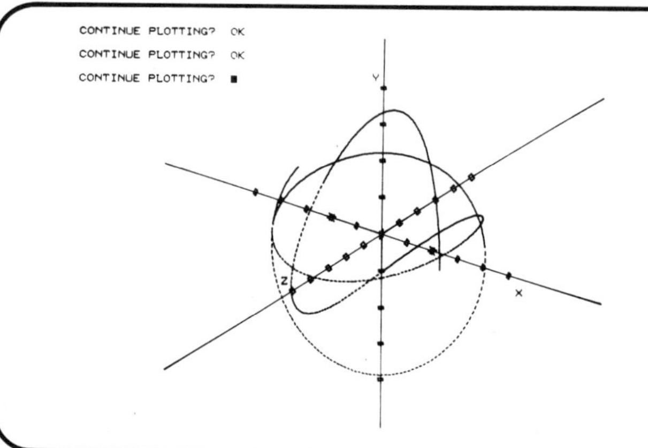

FIGURE 6-15 Gravitational Motion, Two Suns. Orbit Dotted When y Is Negative

Some authors will develop the mainline material almost fully in preparing the dialog, developing the messages that will be typed to the student who is answering correctly in full detail. Then they will go back and fill in "bad" branches or other mainlines. However, some teachers prefer to work on a "frame-by-frame" basis, outlining the principal development briefly, and then going sequentially through the program branches.

My own preference is very much for the second style. The psychological advantage of this approach is that it continually obliges the teacher to think how to respond to students who are confused or who do not know what they are doing. The mainline approach may lead the authors to be impatient in filling in the details. Dealing with the troubled student, giving full aid, is the most important aspect of the dialog; the very good student does not need much assistance in learning.

Another aspect of the mechanism of dialog preparation is the author's relation to the computer programming language or languages involved in the final preparation of the material. A good many variants are possible. First, there is what might be termed the "Coursewriter approach," the one the original developers of the Coursewriter language at IBM seemed to have in mind. The teachers work directly with a computer language (Coursewriter, in the original variant) in writing the dialog, writing statements in that language as they think through the learning sequence.

Many such languages intended for computer-aided learning exist, but most have seen little usage in developing large collections of student-usable materials; Coursewriter and Tutor are the two major exceptions. These languages claim to be easy to use for the novice, but the non-programmer does not necessarily agree with this. Training for reasonable use of the language is non-trivial; a recent estimate from Europe suggested 500 hours to learn Tutor. Further, these languages often restrict the resources available to the author. Most of the languages, including Tutor and Coursewriter, are old and so do not conform to the best standards of modern programming.

A second approach is for teachers to develop the dialog in a (modified) flowchart form, in a way that does not depend on the details of computer mechanisms to be used. (A variant on this approach is to use decision tables.) The teacher sketches out the conversation by a series of boxes, lines, and other graphic aids, showing what to "say" to the student, what responses to handle, the messages typed or displayed for each response, and the record-keeping desired. The following flowchart (Figure 6-16), a fragment, illustrates the process.

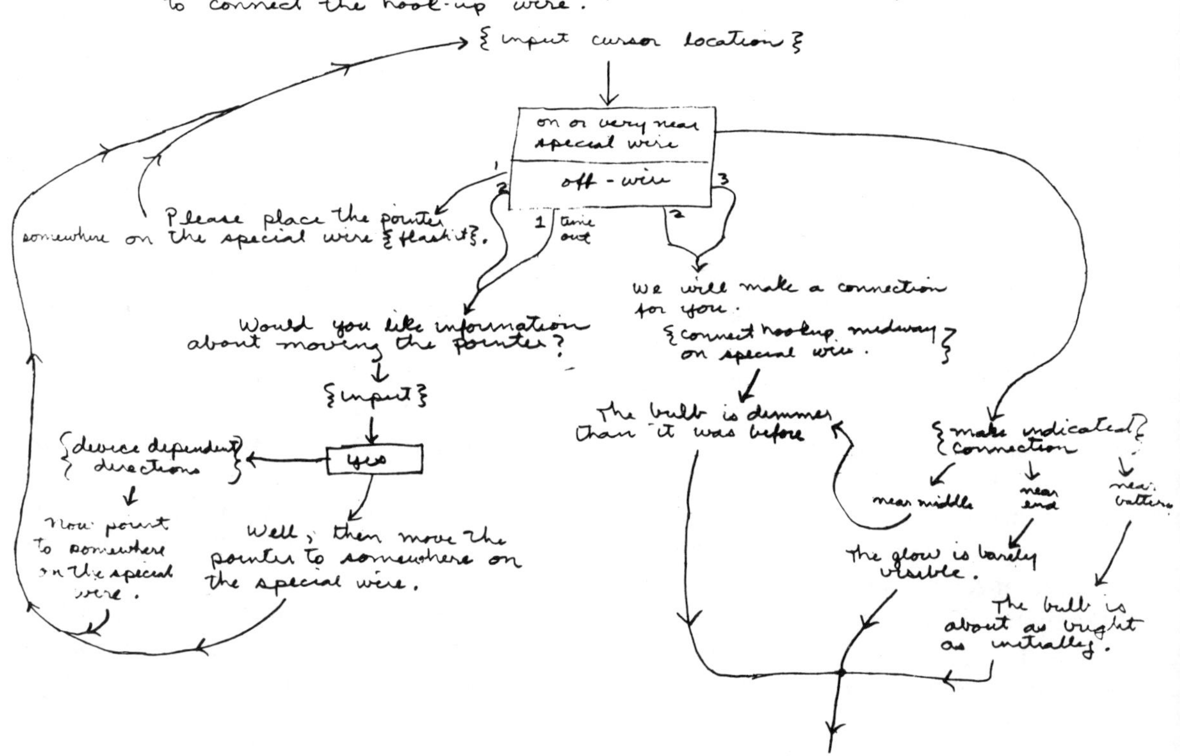

FIGURE 6-16 Pedagogical Flowchart for a Recent Dialog

This flowchart, from our recent unit on batteries and bulbs, contains a variety of things. First, it shows the text to be written out to students. It also shows sketches of what is to be drawn at a particular point. The rough flowchart also shows the logic involved in responding to student input. Note that a variety of possibilities are examined. It is not important to read the individual details; this flowchart is messy, typical of those that are produced. Our purpose is to show how the process goes. Additional extensive instructions are given to the programmer (in curley brackets) about how the material is to be displayed, particularly with elaborate interweaving of text and graphics as is often the case.

A third possibility is the use of a facility that prompts the instructor, sitting at a display, for the various pieces of the dialog that will be necessary, like the Scholar-Teach system, the DITRAN system developed by Noah Sherman at the Lawrence Hall of Science at Berkeley, the Utah system, and PLANET. The facilities available in such systems are a limited subset of the full possibilities, so material prepared this way does not use the full capabilities of the computer to aid learning. So authors do not have full freedom in designing material in such a procedure.

My own strong preference is for the second way, using teacher-oriented flowcharts. This approach removes teachers from the computer details and allows them maximum freedom to do what they want to do within the program without worrying about how to do it. It enables the instructor to interact with a variety of specialized helpers, secretaries, graphic designers, and programmers, who will be responsible for the implementation details.

The learning program, the dialog, must be entered in the machine. Since dialogs are to be used on interactive systems, either timesharing or stand-alone, it is advisable to use the often-powerful editing capabilities of such systems to assist in the preparation of the dialog material. Therefore, on-line entering and correcting of programs is very desirable except where it is ruled out by financial considerations or by system unreliability.

A good individual for typing the text is the trained secretary, rather than a programmer, student, or teacher. A vast amount of time must be spent in typing the material, since much of it is the text to be shown to the student. It is not difficult to train secretaries to use computers and to work in well-designed programming languages and editing systems.

We have paid increasing attention to the problem of screen design, how the material is to appear on the screen. This includes the placement of text and pictorial material as well as timing considerations. Another type of individual is often best to do this, a person who has training in design in the sense of industrial or applied design. The process resembles that of magazine layout, but the tools are somewhat different. If this procedure is to be followed, a collection of on-line, interactive graphic aid tools must be developed and maintained. This issue will receive further attention.

Style

To be doctrinaire about style is unwise, even more so than in the rest of this discussion, because style is individualistic. Dialogs should not always be in the same style; different people have different ways of learning.

One tendency is to approach the preparation of student-computer dialogs as if writing a text or paper or giving a lecture. But the difficulties and the opportunities are greater with dialog material, so this approach is not likely to succeed; the style of the dialog should reflect these differences, both advantages and difficulties. Most of the concern with a text is the "mainline," the right way of handling the developing material. Usually only one mainline is considered, although occasionally alternate proofs may be given. A dialog may include multiple mainlines, to react to different ways the student may proceed.

The dialog writer should also expend great energy and effort in sections that never appear in texts and lectures—wrong approaches, mistakes to which the dialog should respond in some reasonable way, remedial assistance for a student who is having mathematical difficulty. If a computer-student dialog is to prove valuable, it will need to be much more responsive to student needs than a static book. This means that the non-mainline sequences are extremely important for the dialog; typical students are likely to be in these areas of the program much of the time, so they deserve utmost care.

Dialogs should resemble conversations. The name "dialog" suggests the model of the student conversing with the teacher in the office; the teacher asks questions designed to help students learn the material or responds to the students' questions. We cannot fully realize with the computer the model of the office conversation; some people have even objected to trying to make a computer dialog resemble a student-teacher discussion. However, it is possible to follow this model. We are slowly becoming more skillful at creating such dialogs.

The model of human dialog suggests that computer dialog style, in a literary sense, should be more like a conversation and less like a book. Talking is less formal than writing and often more redundant. Humor and light touches are desirable and welcome, although not everybody agrees as to what is humorous! Informal vocabulary and structure, as opposed to elaborately structured sentences, is desirable. While some people talk in long and involved sentences of learned articles, this is rare even among college instructors! It is wise to avoid the "in" phrases of the moment, because they date rapidly. Other style considerations are like those employed in any good prose.

Another disputed issue, with little empirical evidence, is the question of the use of a first person style. Should the computer say "I" or "we?" Most dialogs developed at Irvine use the first person. Irvine students, when queried about the first person style, supported its use. More information is needed, perhaps through psychological studies, as to whether the computer should be saying "I." We used one dialog at Irvine, CONSERVE, with two branches, randomly chosen: one used the first person, one did not; no difference could be seen in student performance.

Students have a number of ways of interpreting "I" or "we" in a computer dialog. They may think of it as the authors of the program rather than the computer itself. Dialogs should identify the author or authors; this will make "I" more natural. Authors' names should appear at the beginning of a dialog. Or you can choose not to use personal pronouns.

The question of how style influences student response is undetermined. It has been suggested that relatively small changes in style in, for example, technical vocabulary, may have considerable influence on student responses, but little evidence exists. Again a randomly chosen two-branch dialog to explore this question showed little difference in student performance with altered vocabulary.

When preparing a dialog teachers should keep in mind that they have limitations in analyzing student response. A carefully organized and prepared dialog will sometimes miss the meaning of what the student is typing, even though the dialog has already been improved from past student usage. The computer is not a person, and does not have all the resources of a good teacher for dealing with the students' comments.

Largely we identify responses by string matches, looking for key words or letters in the student input. Even with elaborate care with string matches, however, we cannot react accurately to everything the student says, and we cannot currently approach the capabilities of human beings except in restricted situations and with large amounts of computer time. A good dialog can still miss about 10% of the responses. Care in how the questions are stated is valuable, but does not do the entire job. The authors try to find all the reasonable alternatives the student may use, but they will not always succeed.

This weakness indicates that a degree of humility and modesty is required in the response to student comments, particularly the comments we have been unable to analyze and we presume to be wrong. To tell the student unequivocally that he or she is wrong can be dangerous, except in environments where the response is carefully controlled by the situation, or where extremely detailed analysis of input is made. Your program may be missing an unusual variant of a right answer.

Along with this suggestion, a pedagogical point seems reasonable. A tendency exists, particularly with impatient individuals, to be scornful of students' lack of success. Abusive language or language that questions the student's intelligence is seldom desirable in a learning situation or dialog. Thus, it is not reasonable to call students "stupid" because they do not enter the response you were looking for.

A tendency to allow the technology to control the process of pedagogical design is inherent in employing technological aids to education. This trend is a mistake; teaching aims and teaching purposes should always be in the forefront in developing dialogs. Thus, in applying computers to learning, you should resist the temptation to be guided by the facilities available. Rather, the primary emphasis should be on what students are to learn and how you want to teach it, the pedagogical aspects. Ideally, authors should develop dialogs with little regard to the details of how they will be put on the machine; however, they do need background of what is possible with the computer, its strengths as a learning medium. Pedagogy should take precedence over technology in all cases.

A stylistic tendency often noticeable in new writers of computer-based teaching materials is to spend too much time "talking" to the students, accepting only trivial responses and presenting long messages. We might call this the "textbook malady" or the "lecture complaint." There are places where the student does want long messages or to interact only minimally; but a dialog that does no more than that may not be worth putting on the computer—it becomes a book. A dialog writer should involve the student differently, stimulating meaningful responses that contribute toward learning. We can have students play an active role rather than a passive role often seen in the lecture environment, one of the most important aspects of the computer as a learning mechanism.

Interesting sidelines involving much display without interaction can be made optional; thus, in a science dialog, historical discussions of the issues may not interest all students, but may interest some. Letting students choose in such situations is reasonable and increases the flexibility of the material. Similarly, a review might be optional for students who have done well, but automatic for students who have not; you can save information about performance to use in making such decisions. Auxiliary printed information can be available and students can be queried about its presence.

In many instances it is reasonable to allow students several tries at the answer. There should, however, be an eventual exit to avoid having students trapped at some point, not knowing how to get out of the trap. You can give hints, successive pieces of advice, for students not putting in the expected results or full diagnostic sequences to allow for individual differences in student background.

You can give advice tailored to particular wrong responses. For example, if you are expecting an equation and the student is not entering an equal sign or some equivalent word, then you could state that you are looking for an equation and not identifying it in the input. You may expect a formula or equation that contains certain symbols, which do not appear; you can reply with the information about what is missing. If students have only part of the answer, they can be asked to enter only the aspects missing; don't require more typing than necessary. Wrong responses may also be given special attention, particularly if the student can be led to understand why the answer is incorrect.

In examining input, a good policy is to look for only part of each key word, thus bypassing some spelling or typing problems. You might also look for likely misspellings or mistyping; this is much easier to do when you are revising the dialog. Thus, one of our dialogs recognizes PLOY for PLOT, a common typing error.

The quantity of retries and specialized advice vary from place to place within the dialog. For some important results students may need many, many attempts, but in others no more than one may be reasonable. The dialog author can spend an infinite amount of time preparing any one question in an attempt to analyze the student response. But the teacher should use judgment as to where a point of diminishing return is reached, usually a pedagogical decision. Usage with students will provide information on improving program responsiveness. The author should also be prepared for programming errors to become more of a problem as dialog complexity grows.

A detailed analysis of the student's input is not always necessary. In some situations, the program can simply accept the input and go on. Thus, you may want the student to think about the material or to have some pause between sections of the material. You may want students to make an input, intending to say the same thing no matter what is entered. Or you will, at most, give a pat on the back for a correct response.

Another situation in which the nonanalyzed input is of value is with student comments. Dialogs should usually invite comments from the student at the end; these may be too complex to allow immediate reply. Another related device useful in providing feedback as to the teaching success of the program is to ask for a long verbal description or summary of the situation studied. Thus, in a dialog involving standing waves on a string, we ask students to describe a standing wave and tell what types of standing waves are possible; if the program has worked students through the first normal mode, they can describe the second normal mode. Such a long entry, involving many lines, could not presently be analyzed in a very meaningful way, although one might still choose to respond to key words. But the teacher can examine these detailed comments, stored in a file, and determine if they indicate that most students understand the material covered. This mechanism can also be used for getting feedback to the students. A student can be asked to sign his or her questions or queries with the promise that the reply will be coming soon.

One stylistic question without universal agreement is the necessity for what the behavioral psychologists call "positive reinforcement." A view supported by many psychologists and teachers is that when students make the right response they should always be told they are right. However, others argue that we do not do this in informal conversation, and so are not willing to do it at all times.

Compromise positions exist, sometimes responding favorably to correct answers and sometimes not. I believe it should be done frequently but not all the time.

A place in dialog writing where imagination is limited is the constant need to say the same basic thing over and over, but in different ways. The typical situation is "try again," the response that the student should attempt the question at least one more time. Congratulating the student on a right answer is another similar situation, reinforcing the response. It is convenient to have facilities to vary the response in these situations.

One of the most important aspects of the dialog is the ability to respond reasonably to the wrong answers. If students say something that is wrong and you can tell them just why it is incorrect, and perhaps allow another try, then the dialog is serving an important interactive function. In thinking about the possible responses for every question, the teacher needs to consider what the student can say that is not right, and what response is reasonable. This is not necessarily easy, and some discussion with others may help; lectures and textbooks seldom take this approach. Groups of two or three in the writing process are useful in coming up with the many possibilities of incorrect responses. Good dialogs devote more of the program to responding to wrong answers than to the mainline material, sometimes dramatically more. Don't worry about how the professionals can slip by; the dialogs are written for *students* and need to be responsive to them.

No matter how detailed the analysis is on a student reply, you must be prepared for the possibility that none of your tests have succeeded; you have not been able to identify anything in the input. You must always be prepared to say something in such a case. Often students are allowed to try again after a hint. How many times they are allowed to repeat the question requires a pedagogical decision in each case. The number of tries may depend on the importance of the question, or it may be at least partially determined by resourcefulness in thinking of genuinely useful help sequences. And you must allow for the case that all the hints fail, so that the student must be told the response you have been seeking or given other aid (perhaps off the computer). You might want to note such a failure, so that you can return to this point later for this student. Or you might suggest that the student go to a text, the instructor, or another dialog.

Graphics

In early educational use, the computer had available only typewriter-like devices, so communication to and from students could only proceed through alphanumeric information. Display units with good graphic capability are now reasonable for large numbers of students. Hence, dialogs should use visual presentations as well as alphanumeric information.

We need only examine the blackboards around the universities to see the widespread use of pictorial or iconic representation of information. In addition to the more obvious graphs and curves other devices are in common use, such as underlining, putting boxes around important information, drawing arrows to show logical connection, drawing flowcharts to indicate processes, and employing varying size type faces for emphasis. Lectures or discussions also employ a simple graphic "input" device, pointing to places on the screen. All of these, and many others, are possible within a computer-student dialog, and if at all possible, should be considered by the dialog writer.

The importance of pictorial information as an alternate to alphanumeric information is great. However, teachers are not necessarily skillful in using iconic representations. On the contrary, because teachers are often the successful products of a highly verbal education, they may be less effective in using pictorial means of communication than people in other professions. Thinking about and studying these possibilities is important. The best reference in the available literature (but not oriented toward interactive computer graphics) is the book by William Huggins and Doris Entwisle[2].

The point has already been made that alternate ways exist of representing the same information or of representing slightly different aspects of the same basic situation. The use of these alternate ways enhances the educational value of the material. Students think in different ways, and an approach that will be successful with one student may not be as successful with a different student. Hence, the chances of success of the material will be greater if more modes of communication are used. Often we can display different aspects with these two modes, even if the informational content is the same. For example, compare a set of numbers with a curve.

When a curve appears on the screen, it can develop in time if this is important. The informational content of these two representations is the same. Given the set of number pairs, a person who knows about graphing could produce the curve. Nevertheless, the effect on the student is very different. If our objective is to build insight into the way planets move around the sun, the visual information is probably much more effective. On the other hand, if we need detailed information abut a particular position for astronomical or other purposes, the table of numbers might be more valuable. This is a simple example, but the ideas are repeated in a great many different situations. Visual information is more useful in developing insight into the nature of the physical world. This is no accident, but is a common property of pictorial ways of representing either realizable or unrealizable physical phenomena.

Another important aspect of graphics in learning situations is the motivational impact of pictorial material, if this material is well designed. If a large corporation develops an advertisement for a magazine, that advertisement is almost always a carefully prepared combination of graphic and alphanumeric material. It would be cheaper to produce such ads without any pictorial material and cheaper not to use colors; but the corporations are well aware of the movitational aspects of well-designed graphic material and so rely heavily on these factors. In education we are often not so wise in dealing with the motivational issues: we have much to learn.

In thinking about graphics with the computer, it is important to realize the dynamic nature of what is happening, the control over time that we do not have in a printed page. The position of someone developing computer dialogs is more like that of a filmmaker than that of a textbook illustrator. The textbook picture is there all at once, seen fully as soon as the student looks at it. The information referred to in the text must be keyed to the picture. For example, in geometrical proofs in textbooks, letters are attached to points on the diagram and the text refers to these letters.

These techniques are not needed in a dynamic environment where an interplay between alphanumeric and graphic information, with suitable delays, can take place. Hence, when a line is mentioned, that line, after a brief pause to allow the eye to shift from alphanumerics to graphics, is drawn. Elements of the picture already on the screen can be reinforced by flashing them, by encircling them, by using color, or with some other graphic device. The teacher can reflect the student's input, so that new pieces of the picture can depend on how the student is responding either graphically or alphanumerically.

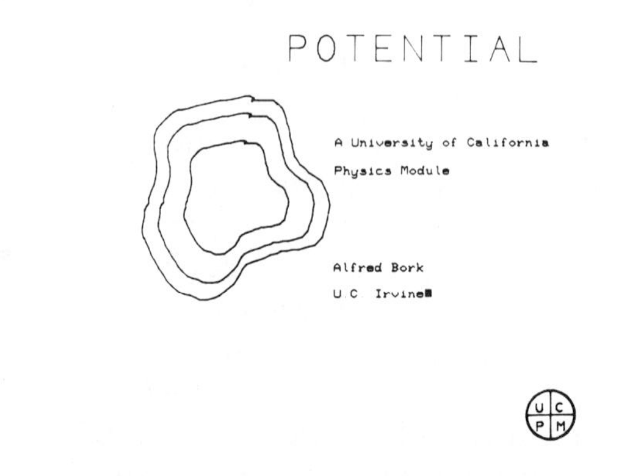

FIGURE 6-17 Title Page for POTENTIAL

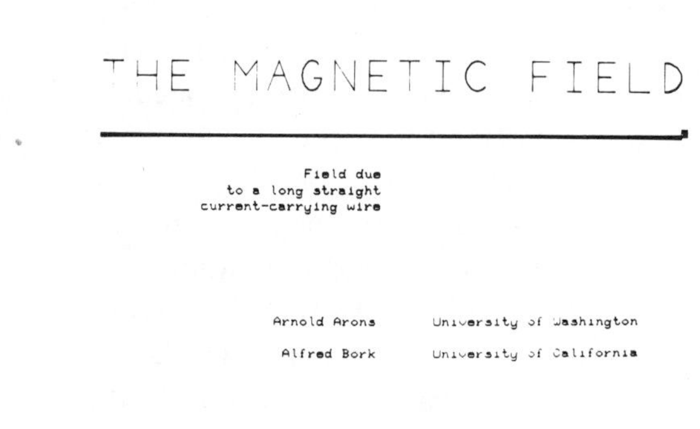

FIGURE 6-18 Title Page for MFIELD

Some devices not normally thought of as graphic are possible on graphic displays, but not on alphanumeric displays. Some of these have already been suggested. One is the occasional use of larger letters for titling or to emphasize a particular point. Graphic letters of any size, form, or orientation can be drawn. Figures 6-17 and 6-18 make some use of large letters.

Suppose that the wire is coming directly out of the screen.

We won't show the rest of the apparatus

Assume the current is coming out of the screen

Convention

current out of the screen -
tip of approaching arrow
current into the screen -
tail of receding arrow

return to continue

FIGURE 6-19 MFIELD, Setting Graphic Conventions, Not Showing Order of Display

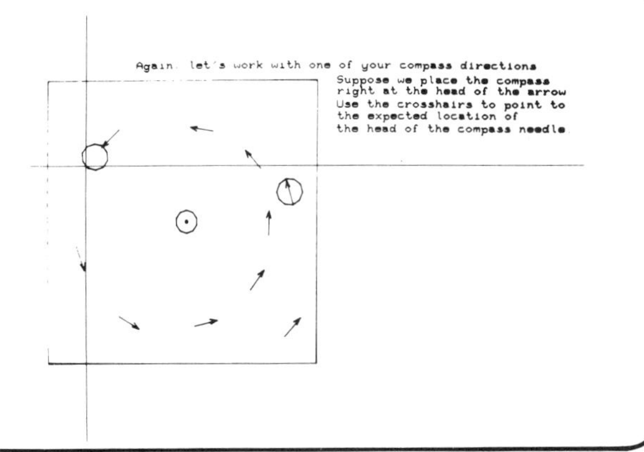

Again, let's work with one of your compass directions
Suppose we place the compass
right at the head of the arrow
Use the crosshairs to point to
the expected location of
the head of the compass needle.

FIGURE 6-20 Dialog MFIELD, A Small Experimental Simulation

Another "graphics" idea is the careful arrangement of the alphanumeric information, avoiding the tyranny of the left-hand margin and seeking more interesting layout on the paper; the text can be broken with spaces and other appropriate information to assist the student in understanding what is happening. Figures 6-19 and 6-20, taken from MFIELD indicate the variety that is possible.

Further graphic devices are flashing or blinking of text or putting text in bold.

If the Greek alphabet, or other special symbols, are needed and the display has only the standard ASCII set, these characters can be drawn. The use of this capability from the standpoint of students may depend upon what special software and other facilities have been developed to aid the student. Other devices provide alternate characters in the character set.

Although time control, the insertion of delays in the presentation, is not strictly a graphic feature, it is almost essential in the graphic environment to allow time for eye movement. It can also play an important role in the alphanumeric aspects of what is happening. Thus, the computer can stop at the end of a sentence to allow the student to read that sentence; it can even pause briefly at places where a speaker would pause briefly to emphasize the meaning of the sentences and can follow such natural rhythms as pausing after an equal sign before writing the rest of the equation.

We can increase the readability of the material by the way the alphanumeric information is handled on the paper or on the display screen. Although some details can be left to the designer, some of it must be carefully supervised by the instructor. One aspect is the way lines are divided on the screen, and the use of possible delays after natural phrases in the lines. For example, we could write:

Problems. Please
Try again.

However, this is a much less natural way of stating it than the following:

Problems.
Please try again.

This can extend not only to the sentence level, but to phrases within a sentence as in these "bad" and "good" examples:

The kinetic energy before and
after collision
is conserved.

The kinetic energy before and after collision
is
conserved.

Or the items can, for emphasis, be right justified.

One may not want to write all material in this fashion, but important items that need to be emphasized or essential items that the student must read might be put into this form.

A related aspect is *where* the material appears on the screen. All older computer-aided learning material started each line at the left-hand margin. Newer approaches allow the user to *place* material on the screen, and thus make a more interesting and visually exciting display. This too serves to emphasize the verbal messages contained in the materials.

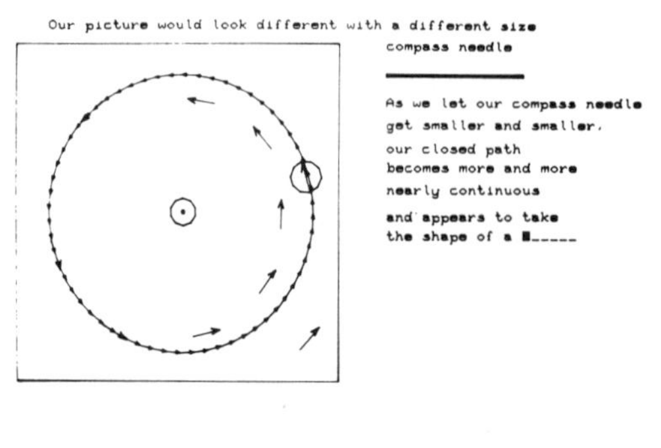

FIGURE 6-21 MFIELD, Working Toward Field-Line Concept

So far, our discussions referred to the ability of computer displays to draw pictures as part of a learning dialog. A second important aspect is graphic input, entering graphic information. This facility provides an alternate mode for student input, as in Figure 6-21.

Typically, input capabilities are still limited, but nevertheless valuable. You should inquire about what capabilities are available in your situation and see examples of running programs that use graphic input. With graphics, perhaps more than in any other area of developing dialogs, the examination of a series of well-working dialogs employing graphics will be very useful in providing ideas.

The typical inexpensive graphic input available is a pointing device, allowing students to point to a given area on the screen. The student might point to a location on a curve and the computer might respond with the coordinates of that point or it might enlarge the region around the point or some similar approach.

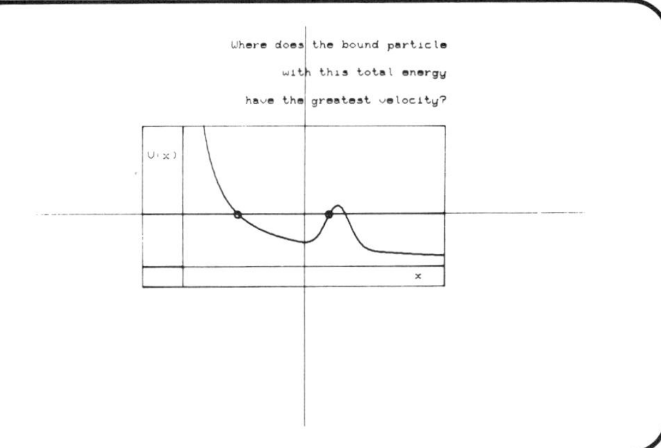

Where does the bound particle
with this total energy
have the greatest velocity?
x

FIGURE 6-22 Part of an On-Line Quiz, POT, Showing the Use of Crosshairs

Students might be asked to locate an object. Figure 6-22 shows a pointing example in one of the Irvine dialogs, POT.

More elaborate graphic capabilities may be available, such as a light pen or table, which allow free-form input of curves in a convenient manner. However, these are still rare with large-scale student use.

One of the advantages of graphic input is the mode of input; the student is so often typing information, so the possibility of an alternate way of communicating with the computer provides some relief and variability in the program.

How is the teacher, the developer of the dialog, to convey graphic intents to the computer or to some intermediary such as a programmer or graphic designer? The system will vary from place to place. The coding of graphic material is even more of a specialist's task than the coding of alphanumeric material for a variety of reasons. One difficulty is the task of carefully interweaving graphic and alphanumeric information on the same screen, so that the graphics do not overwrite alphanumeric information, and such that the total effect is pleasing to the student.

If the facilities are available for working through programmers, the author can proceed by means of drawing pictures directly within flowcharts, showing how the screen is to look for graphic output, with some verbal information on the chart describing these pictures. If parts of the pictures appear at different times, interwoven with textual information, this can be indicated in at least two ways. One possibility is to number the components of alphanumeric and numeric information, showing the programmer the order in which they are to appear; another possibility is to make use of pens of different colors and color code the drawing along with the alphanumeric information. Both of these techniques have been successfully used at Irvine. With graphic input, the job is to describe what decisions should be taken in the program for different choices of graphic input. These can be described in the instructor's own language, with the task of implementing the details left to the programmer. All this assumes that programmers are available to assist the teacher. If not, the author is dependent upon the graphic capabilities of the particular language and has no recourse but to learn how to use these effectively.

A recent development is the use of on-line programs where the graphic and alphanumeric information can be described by pointing to the places on the screen desired, entering the information in convenient ways and rearranging the components, again by pointing or by changing size or orientation, until the display takes the desired form. These programs then write the code necessary to produce the display just formulated.

Such a facility can be used by the programmer in implementing an instructor's needs as indicated by diagrams or can be used directly by the instructor. The possibility of involving a graphic designer in the process is also one that should be considered; as mentioned, this mode of working is not too different from that normally employed by graphic designers.

The software available for this in Irvine is available in APL and is known as DPL.

Let us follow an example of the use of this software to give something of the flavor. First, the problem is to design a title page that identifies material that is associated with the Educational Technology Center at Irvine. First in Figure 6-23, the designer specifies that he wants some large letters. Note that this object has a name, *A*.

FIGURE 6-23 DPL, An APL Workspace, Creates Large Letters

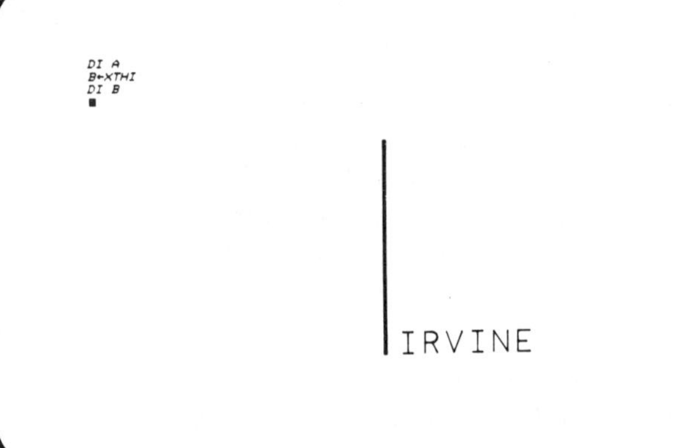

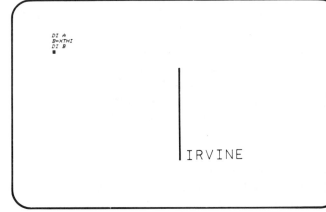

FIGURE 6-24 DPL, Addition of a Thick Line

Figure 6-24 shows the next stage in the process, putting into the diagram a thick, vertical line identified by the variable *B*.

The designer now wishes to put in some text saying "Educational Technology Center" and wishes this text to be right justified. In Figure 6-25, we see the text being entered. It is initially entered left justified, since right justification is not possible until the entire message is in.

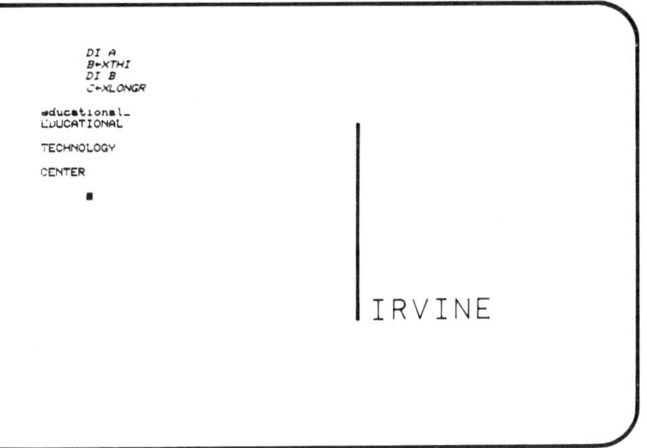

FIGURE 6-25 DPL, Adding Some Text

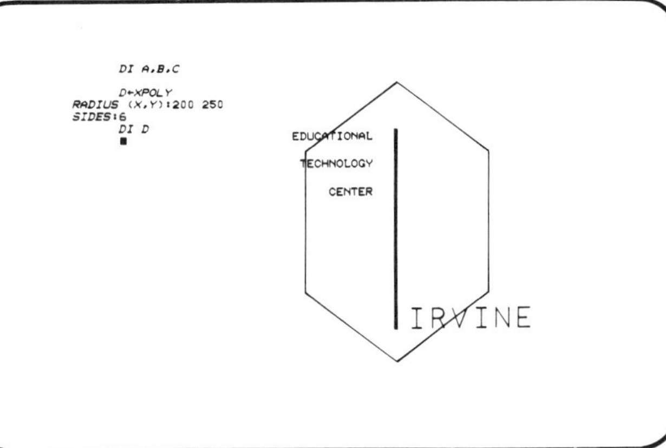

FIGURE 6-26 DPL, Placing the Elements and Adding a Polygon

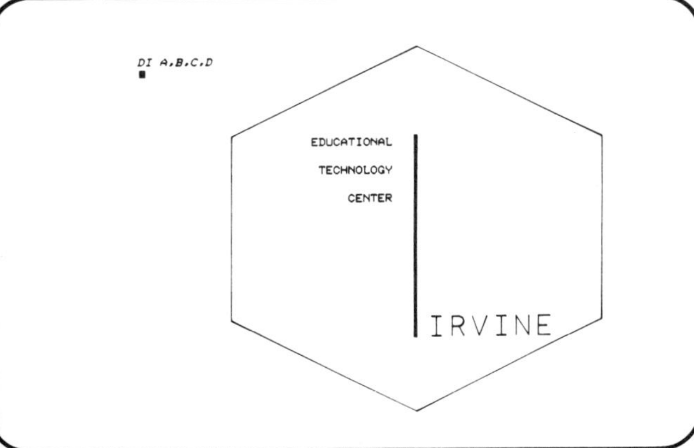

FIGURE 6-27 DPL, The Polygon Adjusted for Appropriate Size

In Figure 6-26, "Educational Technology Center" has been moved to its correct position, and we are now experimenting with drawing a polygon around the entire figure. The initial polygon, as can be seen, is too small.

We now expand the polygon until it is visually in the desired form as seen finally in Figure 6-27.

Feedback

Feedback from student use of dialogs is important in improving dialogs for later groups of students. This is, indeed, one of the main hopes for producing dialogs that will be effective learning devices. Dialogs as initially written may have only limited success in dealing with student response, so feedback and rewriting are critical in producing programs adaptable to individual student performance.

The question of what feedback is wanted from student use of the dialog, and how the feedback is to be used, should be carefully considered in advance. The dialog should be consciously planned to generate the kind of information useful for analyzing students' responses, so that this information can serve to improve the next version. You should be careful not to bury yourself under too much information; select information that is relevant to improving the dialog.

In the computer dialogs developed at Irvine, we have found it reasonable not to save all student responses, because with large student usage too much would be obtained to be analyzed successfully. What is usually helpful in improving the conversation are the responses that the program was unable to analyze.

Some of these responses may be right answers, but answers that your matching program was too crude to find. Others may give further suggestions as to what students are likely to say that is wrong, and that should be immediately commented on. The saved responses may also indicate areas that are weak and need to be extended, because very few students are able to respond reasonably; or they may indicate ambiguous terminology in the question being put to the student or a poor stylistic approach. They can even indicate that the student's use of the English language is at variance with the teacher's! In saving responses, it is essential to store information identifying the student who entered them. Thus, some insight into the problems of the dialog may be obtained by watching the progress of individual students.

Authors should also consider whether they want to keep a numerical record of performance during the dialog—how many things the student got right, which areas were employed. Again, it is important to give thought in advance as to what information should be gathered during the student performance and how that information is going to be analyzed.

The author needs access to convenient sorting programs in handling these responses, sorting both on the location within the program at which the input was obtained and on the inputs associated with each student. The result with a large class will be extensive; with sorted output the author can effectively set to work on the next, and better, generation of the dialog.

LIMITATIONS OF APL AS A LANGUAGE FOR STUDENT-COMPUTER DIALOGS

I have long been an enthusiast for APL as a student programming language, particularly for Science and Engineering students. The only competitor I see is Pascal. APL's power and elegance, particularly in handling groups of numbers and characters, is worth teaching to students at a very early stage in their programming careers. We teach APL in introductory Physics courses to freshmen students, although the computer we use allows a wide choice of programming languages. We emphasize the early use of APL graphics. (This topic was discussed at length in Chapter 2 of this book in "APL as a Language for Interactive Computer Graphics.")

Nevertheless, APL, in most of its variants, has severe limitations for preparing student-computer dialogs, programs written by the instructor to aid student learning in some subject area. APL has been used in this vein, and some excellent material has been written. My neighbors at Orange Coast and Golden West Colleges have exploited well the educational potentialities of APL.

However, APL, in spite of its virtues, is inadequate for large-scale dialog preparation. I would like to state the limitations. Many computer-based learning sub-languages have been developed in APL; the limitations are also inherent in those sub-languages.

We have developed a large body of computer-student dialogs with support from the National Science Foundation, the Fund for the Improvement of Postsecondary Education, and the University of California. These dialogs are now actively in use at the University of California, Irvine.

However, these dialogs were not written in APL! Our earlier material was programmed in opportunistic ways, allowing us to use any computer resources that seemed to get the job done. The procedure is driven by pedagogical needs, rather than by details of computer hardware or software. It has produced about 75 dialogs in a variety of areas of Physics and Mathematics as well as other areas. During the past several years we have worked in Pascal. My comments about APL are based, therefore, on practical experience with developing elaborate dialogs and using them with large numbers of students.

APL would not allow things that we are already doing with students in current dialogs, which we would be loathe to give up. Hence, I am raising serious questions about the ultimate suitability of APL for such applications.

Implementations

Unfortunately, issues will be clouded by different implementations of APL. While we previously could think of APL as a monolithic system, variants of APL are now available. Some of this discussion will apply to some dialects but not others. Even on IBM machines, two APL implementations are in use, the Scientific Timesharing APL Plus and the IBM program product.

As I progress, I will not try to relate my discussion to particular implementations of APL. All the problems occur with some common implementation, many of them holding in the dominant one, the IBM program product.

Program Size

The student dialogs we run at Irvine are assembled or compiled code, reasonably compact. Some are over 100,000 words long. When the teacher designs very simple material, the programs tend to be short. As the teacher's horizon as to what is possible expands, and he or she develops material that is more and more interactive, programs quickly become very long. This length is a direct result of pedagogical needs. Our most effective dialogs, as measured by student demand and other activities, are long.

We do not allow timesharing for personal computer access to 100,000 words of fast memory, so the programs must make use of an overlay structure, a paging facility, or segmentation facilities. In our older teaching activities we chose the first. Typically our students have 20K words of fast memory. They are not aware that pieces are being pulled in as required. The programs are organized so as to minimize such swapping. With the personal computers we now use, most of the programs reside on the floppy discs at any one time.

Thus, the typical dialog is much larger than a typical APL workspace. Some systems allow variable length workspaces and dynamic paging, but at some cost to overhead. The ability to chain workspaces, to call in a new workspace within a function, is available in some APL implementations, and this would solve part of the problem, but not all; the passing of large amounts of variables and data between the different sections would often be necessary. In an overlay facility we have complete control of just what pieces are in core at a particular time, so this data could stay in core. But loading a new APL workspace, within a function, if allowed, wipes out all previous data. Programmed COPY, calling in functions within an APL function, is available in at least one implementation, and so could help; but it is not ideal.

Thus, APL in its present versions does not support well the long programs that are often the eventual outcome of computer-student dialogs, after a history of evolution of these through successive generations of students. This is a very serious problem.

Error Control

Student-computer dialogs are not only large, but are also complicated programs; sometimes, with the best of intentions, error situations occur. Since the dialogs allow many different paths through the material, they cannot, as with any complicated program, be completely debugged. Even dialogs that we have had running for years, used with large numbers of students, still have occasional problems. This is not surprising; even the oldest FORTRAN compilers still find new difficulties in peculiar situations.

The typical APL system gives a standard message when an error occurs, an APL system message, rather than one specified by the author of the dialog. Then the program is aborted! There is nothing more devastating to an English student than to be told "WS FULL." Unless someone is around to help, the student is completely lost. A full dialog system should allow the user complete control over error situations of all types; the teacher should be able to specify what happens with each type of error. Sometimes recovery, or at least restart, may be possible. Error messages, when necessary, should be specifiable by the teacher preparing the program.

A few types of APL allow users to control error messages, allowing them to send errors to routines which analyze the errors and take action appropriate to the situation. But many do not, and so this presents another problem for dialog usage.

It is also desirable to record, for the developer's use, the information about the type and location of the error. I will return to this problem when I discuss the situation with regard to files.

Interpretive Overhead

One of APL's strong points for introductory student use is that it is an interpretive system that gives quick interaction. However, this same feature can be a handicap. This is particularly the case when the dialogs involve types of calculations that are inherently expensive in APL, because they do not fit naturally into array structures, such as the solutions to differential equations. Contrary to popular belief, many of our dialogs require extensive calculation.

We picked one of our dialogs, MOTION, which involves much computation, and put parts of it (not the complete dialog) in APL to study this effect. We found that it was no longer an interactive program in APL, much less interactive than the original dialog. The interpretive overhead was too great in sequences involving extensive calculation. This is one of our most widely used dialogs.

Calculational overhead depends on the nature of the calculation. APL would be quite competitive if the process could be programmed as an array-structured operation; but in some cases our experience shows that it is not competitive. A learning computational APL program may well be almost impossible to use with many students in a busy environment. Some types of APL can get around this problem by having these major calculational endeavors executed from tight code within an APL program, somehow introduced into the APL workspace. But most types of APL do not allow such interaction with other computer software, and such an approach invites problems in transferring to other machines.

Graphic Capabilities

Our dialogs are heavily dependent on graphics. This is the wave of the future in the use of the computer in the educational environment, particularly with the new home and personal computer.

The Tektronix 4013 is a common display for timesharing APL graphics. Tektronix provides graphics functions for most APL systems. This may be suitable for some use. However, our experience shows that this software is too slow for the extensive plotting activities needed in our dialogs. Most types of APL do not have internal graphics, and so have limitations in dialog usage in a graphics environment. Such limitations are likely to be of increasing importance in the future. The issue does not arise with personal computers—there is, at present, apparently no graphic APL stand-alone computer.

Files

It is often not realized how extensive the file requirements are in a full-scale, computer-student dialog system. Files are used for a variety of purposes:

1. Keeping records as to what dialogs are used and for how long

2. Keeping information about poorly handled responses

3. Keeping information about errors that develop in programs

4. Keeping restart information so the student can come back at a later time

5. Keeping information about what has happened in a dialog to be used within another dialog

6. Keeping information about use of facilities in a dialog.

Much of this is critical; thus, the selected storing of responses is the main information needed to improve programs in successive generations.

The files quickly become very large when systems are used with large numbers of students. Files with thousands of records are typical in our timesharing usage. Most of this information is essential for a full learning system.

While most variants of APL read and write files, these are usually limited and do not allow the APL programmer full range of access to the file capabilities in a large modern computer. They may not allow the various types of files available within the system. Thus, in storing restart information, a keyed or index file is convenient, while for other uses a sequential or consecutive file may be desirable.

More file handling while running these programs goes on than one might suspect, and so efficiency is important as well as the ability to do things. The system also needs protection against loss of files and mechanisms for recreating files that allow as little as possible to be lost. Most current APL file systems do only part of this job.

Efficient Use of Hardware

The way APL handles strings is often not the most efficient way possible on the machine. This has to do with the generality of the APL operators and ease of implementation. Thus, many machines have very powerful byte manipulating facilities at the hardware level, single instructions that allow the user to say whether a collection of bytes occurs in some larger string. But many do not use such hardware instructions, and therefore do byte matching by much more inefficient schemes. There are places in our programs where hundreds of such string matches may be made on an individual student input, to be responsive to the student. Hence, this could become a major factor.

Final Comments

I should make clear once more that I am making these comments in the way of constructive criticism. I realize that useful material has been and will continue to be written in APL. Nevertheless, users should be aware of its long-range limitations, and realize that in some situations other software is much better than APL for the preparation of such dialogs. The problems are very different from those of student programming. The programming effort, for dialogs, may be relatively small compared to the use the program gets, so such factors as execution efficiency become more important than factors of ease of initial programming.

STUDENT-COMPUTER DIALOGS WITHOUT SPECIAL-PURPOSE LANGUAGES

Introduction

By a student-computer dialog, I mean a "conversation" between a student and an instructor, through a computer display. The computer is "talking" with the student, either asking questions and waiting for answers or responding to requests from the student. The model for a student-computer dialog is what goes on between the student and the instructor in the instructor's office. We cannot hope to obtain this flexibility with current computer techniques, with sizable numbers of students, but we can approach a reasonably good approximation, particularly if very skilled teachers are responsible for preparing the dialog. In areas where the computational skills of the computer are important, we can offer resources not available to the instructor in such office conversations.

Proceedings of the Conference on Computers in the Undergraduate Curriculum, Number 6.

Standard Approach

A typical way this problem has been attacked in the past is to develop a special-purpose language for preparing such dialogs. Dozens of such languages have been developed, although few have had wide-scale acceptance. The original language to attain wide usage was Coursewriter, developed by IBM at Yorktown Heights. Coursewriter is still in existence on IBM computers and on a variety of other systems such as Hewlett-Packard. Other examples of such special languages are PLANIT, PILOT, and DITRAN. Perhaps the most extensive language of this kind is Tutor, from the PLATO Project at the University of Illinois.

Alternate Approach

An alternative to developing special languages is to work within existing languages and to extend these languages to make them easier to use in preparing dialogs. There is nothing new about this approach—dozens of attempts have taken this or related directions—but this approach has achieved far less publicity than the special purpose languages.

Indeed one document unfortunately attempted to define "hardcore CAI" as something that was written in a special-purpose "CAI" language. The student running the dialog may not know anything about the language facility in which the dialog was prepared; many dialogs currently in use could have been written in many languages including the standard all-purpose languages. So the software is not a basis for classification.

Advantages exist in working within available languages. First, these languages exist and survive because they are powerful languages at least for some purposes. Facilities these languages include would need to be present in any fully developed dialog language, and so would have to be duplicated. Thus, computational facilities such as those in ALGOL, PL/1, or Pascal would be required in many dialogs. Special-purpose languages could provide these facilities by allowing "exits" or hooks to general purpose facilities, and many languages allow this. But working directly within general purpose languages gives another way of attaining these necessary facilities.

Another distinct advantage of working with existing languages is that we can mold the facilities required on pedagogical demand, rather than through theoretical arguments on language design or the way things should be taught. Most general-purpose languages can define procedures for widely used routines. Thus, this approach can allow authors from varied backgrounds to create different kinds of learning materials. Then these programs can compete in the educational marketplace. New facilities can be added to meet author demands.

Furthermore, general-purpose languages usually allow access to all the resources of the computer, while special languages often restrict such resources. Thus, the ability to use very long programs may not be possible in such special software, but this facility or one equivalent to it will be important for developing very large dialogs. Further, because there is no single "language," no fixed pedagogical style is imposed on course authors; existing CAI languages often were developed for a particular pedagogical approach, a predetermined view of how to use the computer in learning. A more general set of facilities does not restrict the author with regard to teaching styles but allows individual teachers to proceed in ways that seem reasonable to them.

Some disadvantages and problems exist in using general-purpose languages for dialogs. The first serious question is just how we tack the new facilities, needed for an efficient dialog authoring process, onto an existing language. The mechanisms in the available language may be clumsy; procedure calls may not be flexible, and the verb CALL (FORTRAN) is unpleasant. Some languages, such as many forms of BASIC, contain very crude subroutining mechanisms. Furthermore, these extensions may not be easy to transport from one machine to another; so the movement of materials to new environments may not be an easy task.

The Irvine Dialog Approach

As indicated, working with existing powerful languages allows many variants. For the remainder of this article, I describe the variants in software and authoring employed at Irvine.

First, our critical beginning point is with teaching materials, produced by competent teachers. The idea is that software development does not precede the development of learning sequences, but *follows* such development. Thus, competent teachers write the dialogs first, in a form that is not language-dependent, and then we develop whatever new software facilities are necessary for getting those dialogs running. The older facilities developed for previous programs will typically still be useful, and many programs will not demand new facilities. But on the other hand, some programs may require extensive new software. This turning about of the usual direction (first languages, then courseware) with special-purpose languages emphasizes that our primary purpose is the development of learning materials, not the development of languages.

We want to make use of all the facilities on a general-purpose computer. That is, we do not want to restrict ourselves to a subset of the possibilities on the machine.

In view of these objectives, we began dialog preparation at Irvine in two general-purpose languages. The first language was METASYMBOL, the assembly language on our Sigma 7. The second was the well-known general-purpose scientific language, FORTRAN. The extension mechanism in the assembly language was the macro. All of these have English language command names. Our policy was to have few arguments in the macro. New macros were written only in response to pedagogical demand.

We began, about 1978, to move our authoring capabilities to Pascal, the variant developed in the University of California, San Diego. All of our current developmental work is now in Pascal. The Pascal procedures provide the extension mechanism; we have developed much underlying software in the form of procedures.

Conclusions

I present an alternative to the development of a special-purpose language for student-computer dialogs and examine possibilities for the future. A system of this kind is effective for generating highly interactive material valuable for students in the learning process.

LARGE-SCALE PRODUCTION AND DISTRIBUTION OF COMPUTER-AIDED LEARNING MODULES

Abstract

This article reviews the problems and possibilities concerning *large-scale* use of computer-aided learning materials. It is concerned with the organizations that might be involved in this activity and with the process of production of the materials. The discussion is based on the work of the Educational Technology Center and the Physics Computer Development Project at the University of California, Irvine, over the last 12 years, and the work of other groups.

Various phases of this work at Irvine have been supported by the National Science Foundation, the Fund for the Improvement of Post Secondary Education, and the University of California. Discussions with many colleagues have contributed to my thoughts.

Development of a New Learning Technology

The use of a computer as a learning aid is new. Initial work occurred in the 1950's. As with any new way of learning, we needed a period of developmental activity to understand the potentialities and role of a powerful new learning medium.

This development of the computer as an aid in learning has taken place much more rapidly than with older learning technologies. Over 200 years elapsed between the invention of printing and the wide-scale use of textbooks in formal institutions of higher education.

Much earlier work in using the computer in education was carried out by individuals or by small groups, a cottage industry stage. The question of how the materials were to be widely distributed was correctly not the primary focus. We were learning how to use the new tool, how it could be employed to aid learning. Distribution has nevertheless taken place in this period, much of it in the nature of sending individual programs to friends or people who heard about the materials at meetings. Because of the wide variety of computers and operating systems, the movement of materials to other machines, particularly complex material, has not been a simple task. Indeed, very often an inverse correlation exists between the complexity and usefulness of the materials in learning and the ease of transfer to other computers; simpler materials only have been widely transported.

Some organizations concerned with distribution have been formed; the major example of this kind is CONDUIT, established with support from the National Science Foundation. CONDUIT's review process has two stages: an initial pedagogical review and then a review as to transferability to many computers. CONDUIT assures its clients that the programs will run on almost any computer; so they can transfer only the simpler materials. Nevertheless, CONDUIT has a well tested and very useful collection of learning facilities. Furthermore, CONDUIT has established that, even at the level of a few modules rather than fully developed courses, demand for material employing the computer is present. CONDUIT has been further handicapped, again because of transportability in distributing graphic materials, although consideration is now being given to that direction. The primary delivery medium during this exploratory period has been the large timesharing system. Recent CONDUIT developments in using personal computers are moving away from transportability in the sense just discussed.

Other factors have prevented wide-scale use of the computer as a learning device. The Educom conference of 1972, *Factors Inhibiting the Use of Computers in Instruction*, considered many such factors. Of particular interest are the lack of good materials and the difficulties of supplying at reasonable cost enough hardware capabilities in many school locations, particularly for large beginning classes where the computer has potential for a great improvement over the current educational situation. Most present college and university computer systems could not support the additional burden of large use in many beginning classes.

Production Phase

As a new technology evolves and as people become more experienced in its use, new possibilities arise concerning the widespread use of that technology. The computer as a new way of learning is an exciting new direction with great potential for improving education. It has gone through a maturation period where we have learned more about its capabilities and learned more about the preparation of material.

We are now at the stage where the development of computer hardware soon will allow large-scale use of computer-aided learning material. I am referring to the very rapid decrease in cost and increase in capability of the computer. Large-scale integration (LSI) and related technologies have led to price declines which, compared to almost any other product in our time, are astounding. In recent years fast memory has gone down by a factor of 2 in cost each year; such memory is also becoming more compact. Putting this another way, each year we are able to put twice as much memory on a single chip. The cost of the central processing unit has also declined to the point where literally only pennies are involved for sophisticated devices. All the projections are for long and continued decrease in cost and increase in capability; a 30% decrease each year is a frequently used estimate.

Another factor that will further reduce cost, mass production, is just beginning to appear. Up until now, computers—while widespread in business, government, industry, and universities—have not been mass produced. The newly developed personal computer market, plus increased use elsewhere, will change that situation drastically. We can expect sales, within several years, on the order of millions of computers in the home market. Thus, units will be produced in volume never attained before, and so we will see further price reductions. One way of understanding this situation is to look inside the average graphic display of today and the average color television set. There is no question that the color television set is a much more complex device electronically; but its cost is approximately one-tenth that of the corresponding graphic display. The difference is volume production.

The most likely student delivery systems are personal computers, very occasionally interconnecting through local networks. Already respectable systems are available for about $5,000. The home systems at $1,000 are a bit too primitive to support many of our current good examples of learning materials, but in a very few years we can confidently expect that they too will be sufficient. Newer home systems offer such educational advantages as color and voice output.

An important distinction should be understood. The small systems being suggested as the delivery systems are the systems actually used by students. This is to be distinguished from the production system, the computers on which the material is developed. Up until the present, almost all developments have proceeded by using the same machine for both production and delivery. Often it was the only machine available. But this is unlikely in the future. I will discuss the requirements for production systems in a later part of this paper.

It should be stressed explicitly that I do not believe that timesharing systems—large or small—will be the principal educational delivery mode of the future. The reasons for this are expanded in Chapter 7 of this book, "Personal Computers in Learning" and "The Role of Personal Computer Systems in Education."

The personal computers—stand-alone systems—are a natural evolution of modern technology. They also provide very distinct advantages for computer-aided learning material. They are fast becoming so inexpensive that the question of what computer a particular piece of software runs on will soon be of little importance. If a piece of learning material is to be employed widely in a particular environment, then it will be possible to acquire the computer along with the curriculum material for that environment. Indeed, the hardware may soon be the smaller of the costs involved. So previous marketing strategies need to be rethought and modified.

Very low entry-level cost is possible with personal computers. A school that may eventually require half a dozen devices for a specific application could first buy one, to experiment with the material and see whether it was suitable for the local environment. No longer would a purchase of major equipment be necessary, as with today's timesharing systems.

Aspects of communication are still valuable in some learning situations. So the stand-alone systems might occasionally communicate with each other or with some large or small central system, perhaps another personal computer. Communication would take place only a small fraction of the time, and communication costs would not be a major cost factor.

Organizations

What organizations can we expect to be involved in the production and distribution of computer-aided learning modules? Will the same organization do both? What are the advantages and disadvantages of each type of organization?

The following discussion provides tentative answers to these questions. While I list a variety of organizations, the intent is not to imply that the ones mentioned are in any sense exclusive. We can expect different types of organizations to play major roles, not a single type.

Computer and Peripheral Vendors

One natural organization to enter this field is one that already manufactures and/or sells computers or associated equipment. We already have an existing example of this type, with Control Data marketing the PLATO system developed at the University of Illinois. There has, even with conventional computer systems, always been some educational software available, if only from their user program libraries.

Natural reasons exist for computer vendors being involved in this area. They are already acquainted with the problems of marketing both hardware and software in a wide variety of areas. Furthermore, software more and more becomes the ingredient that sells computers. As computers become more widespread and as more application software in all areas including education are developed, users will often choose hardware because of the materials available on that system.

In spite of these factors, the computer vendors, with the exception of Control Data, have not moved quickly into this market. Many of them, although pushed more and more into software, only carry on such development reluctantly. Furthermore, they are accustomed to in-house software. As will be indicated, much of the learning material will be done partially by people outside the organization. Further, computer companies do not have extensive background in marketing strictly educational products.

Some companies that might be expected to enter this area have also had unfortunate previous experiences. For example, IBM, with development of the 1500 system, unsuccessfully promoted the computer as a learning device. Because of this, IBM is not quick to re-enter this market, even though circumstances have changed vastly since the days of the 1500.

Major computer companies have viewed education as a very minor component of the total market. While they may see possibilities of much more wide-scale computer use in this market, their past experiences make them more suspicious than some other companies might be.

My own experience in discussing these issues with computer companies leads me to believe that many will be reluctant to proceed in this direction, even given the advantages. Furthermore, at least some vendors will be ambivalent about producing hardware for the home market, and so perhaps cut themselves off from the educational material in that direction. But others will be attracted by the very large potential market.

Distributors of Educational Materials

Companies already concerned with textbooks, films, audio-tutorial, and other learning aids might view the computer in learning as a natural extension of their current products. Hence, such companies represent one of the most promising sources for production and distribution of computer-aided learning material.

The major advantage is that the marketing organization, one that already deals with the expected audience, is already in place. Thus, a company such as McGraw-Hill is already selling books and other educational materials to a very wide range of schools and has salespeople in the field. Such companies attend and display at the national educational meetings. While the marketing tasks with current materials are not identical to the marketing tasks with computer-aided materials, considerable overlap is present.

Furthermore, publishers have some insight into production mechanisms that will be valuable for the computer. This topic will be discussed in more detail.

However, textbook publishers may be reluctant to go into a new venture, a direction very different from their traditional materials, in spite of the similarities. The technology is unfamiliar, often frightening. Some textbook companies will meet the situation simply by refusing to admit that the computer is going to become an important device in learning situations. Others are moving toward computer materials, and many companies are watching the developing situation closely.

It seems very likely that many current textbook publishers will produce computer-aided learning material. Some have already announced their interest. The textbook publishers are proceeding with caution, based primarily on their economic problems of several years ago. So I would not expect that all textbook publishers would move rapidly into this new market.

New Companies

Another possibility is the creation of special companies for either the production and/or distribution of computer learning material. Several of these companies have already come into existence, and we can expect more to appear.

Such companies are usually begun by people who already have a strong stake in developing computer materials, often coming out of projects that were university-based and supported by federal funding agencies. Perhaps the most well known such organization is Computer Curriculum Corporation in Palo Alto. It followed from the work of Patrick Suppes in developing elementary drill and practice materials at Stanford University. These materials and related later products are marketed, primarily to elementary and high schools. CCC, as it is often called, leases a turnkey system which provides access only to the Suppes material. The computer is not usable as a general-purpose machine as it normally is in university environments. While controversies exist in educational circles about the necessity or advisability of sizable amounts of practice of this type, statistics based on extensive usage show that compared to the conventional modes of teaching drill-and-practice computer material is very effective, particularly with weaker students or those with poor backgrounds. Further evaluative studies are underway.

Another company of this kind that came into existence initially as a nonprofit corporation is WICAT. WICAT was formed by Victor Bunderson and Dustin Heuston. It is an outgrowth of Bunderson's work with the TICCIT system. Unlike CCC, it did not start with a large body of marketable material, and so has had, to assure survival, to seek projects in areas other than strictly the production of computer materials.

Another offshoot of TICCIT, Courseware, Incorporated, has been engaged both in research in this area and in the development of training materials for the armed services and industry.

University Organizations

Many existing studies on production of computer-based materials have taken place in university environments. So a number of universities have groups that are knowledgeable about the modes of efficient production. So it is not surprising that universities may play some continuing role in these activities.

Universities, on the other hand, are not known for their capabilities in distribution of any types of learning materials. There are some exceptions to this. For example, extension services in some university campuses are involved in production and distribution of course materials, sometimes at the full course level. These organizations are dependent on outside funding to obtain support for development. In some cases they already have well worked out marketing and distribution strategies. The extension program at the University of California, San Diego, is a good example.

The advantage, particularly in thinking of university-level computer material, of having the universities play a major role in production and distribution is that the materials come under greater control of university faculty than they do with the typical commercial arrangement. University faculty have occasionally been able to band together for their interests, and provide a superior service to that available through standard commercial services. I am thinking particularly of the insurance available through TIAA, an organization formed as a co-operative venture of universities all over the country. Perhaps organizations of this kind will also develop for computer-based learning materials.

Computer Stores

One of the most interesting phenomena of the last few years has been the rapid rise of stores that sell small computers, either in a kit or assembled. There are now over 1,000 such stores in the United States, and the number is growing rapidly. Some of these stores are chains, while others are individual stores; Computerland, for example, has over 100 stores. Large companies are also moving in this direction, setting up such chains of stores themselves.

The primary markets of these stores have been the hobbyist market, oriented toward people who wish to put together their own computers from kits, and the personal computer market for those interested in inexpensive but useful devices either for business or the home.

Computer stores quickly discovered a demand for programming material, particularly of the game type. There is also a growing interest in educational materials, so they will serve as a possible distribution mechanism, although probably not a production mechanism.

There will be severe problems. Some of the machines being sold are quite small machines, not capable of running much of the computer-aided learning materials that have been developed. The programs sold so far are mostly in BASIC, not a powerful language for sophisticated material. While some of these factors are undoubtedly going to change, there will be limitations in the type and complexity of material that will be distributed through this source.

Existing Stores

Another possibility, again with primary emphasis on distribution, is to sell computer-based learning materials through other types of stores. Textbook outlets are the traditional distribution mechanisms for the textbook companies.

Such stores might, as materials of this kind become more widely used, see this as a viable market also, particularly if stimulated by faculty and student demand.

Other types of stores might also be involved. Radio Shack is already distributing its computers and associated software through its extensive chain of stores. Some home systems are currently available in department stores, and again limited educational software is already available through these stores. In both specialty stores and department stores, with the restrictions to limited software, the same kinds of problems are likely to develop as already mentioned in the discussion of computer stores.

As the machines sold to the home market quickly become more powerful, and as the market expands rapidly, sizable amounts of more and more sophisticated educational material will be generated for those machines; simply because of market size, commercial endeavors will see prospects of interesting markets. As the machines become faster and more sophisticated, with varieties of languages and more and better storage, the educational programs will grow in sophistication.

National Centers

An influential study was conducted several years ago by the Carnegie Commission on Higher Education, "The Fourth Revolution—Instructional Technology in Higher Education"[3]. The study suggested that one way to assure effective production and distribution of the materials of modern technology as they apply to education, including computers, was to establish national centers that would be federally funded or perhaps funded from income after some initial period. These centers would have production and distribution as their sole task. While these centers would cooperate, they would also have considerable independence. Seven such centers were suggested, and the report was even bold enough to contain a map showing possible locations.

The report described these centers as having large timesharing systems available as part of the distribution mechanism. However, the technology has changed rapidly since then. As a producer of materials and as a distributor of materials for stand-alone systems all over the country, they would seem to be an effective mechanism.

No such centers have been established. The sizable funding required is one reason why the centers have not been formed. During the period just after they were proposed there was an increasing concentration of funds in several large projects, and after that a temporary diminishing of the funds available for computer-based education. Now the swing is in the other direction, and again there is interest in the promotion of such national centers, including those having a strong research component as well as those having a strong developmental component. In recent Congressional hearings, such national centers were mentioned on several occasions, and this mention drew favorable responses from the Congressional staff and others.

Open Universities

The final type of organizational structure for production and distribution to be discussed is that modeled on the very successful learning-at-a-distance establishment in Great Britain, The Open University. While The Open University is a relatively new organization, it has already established itself as an effective and economical way to develop and provide learning[4].

While The Open University is, to some extent, an extension of the idea of the correspondence school, with the addition of video, it goes far beyond this beginning. A major strength of The Open University is in curriculum development. Preparation of an Open University course is no small task. On the order of a million dollars can be spent developing just a single course. Course teams are assembled, and they work together for about 18 months to generate the course. A variety of learning media are produced, integrated together in a total course. The Open University can afford to spend this much in producing a course, because costs for the use of the course material are relatively small compared to traditional universities that must support a large physical plant and a teaching faculty.

The Open University in Great Britain, at the present time, does not make extensive use of computers as an aid to learning. While some computer capabilities are available, and limited computer materials have been developed for some courses, the broad structures of The Open University were set down before inexpensive, personal computers were available. This balance is difficult to change within the present Open University, although consideration is being given to systems such as Viewdata and other computer systems.

A newly established Open University, perhaps in the United States, would be in a position to make better use of modern technology. Such a learning-at-a-distance university would not be inexpensive to start. Curriculum development in this country might be more expensive than in England, and so an individual course, carefully developed, might cost more than one million dollars. To start an Open University, hundreds of courses are needed. Such costs spread over a number of years are not beyond the possibility of federal support.

The Open University development of courses is one of the most rational to be found. All media are considered, and each is used to contribute to the learning process. The course is not the work of one or two people but of a whole group contributing to the activity.

From many points of view, such an Open University organization would be the most desirable way of creating new computer-aided learning material. I am assuming that these courses would be used not only in the learning-at-a-distance environment provided by The Open University, but they, or at least parts of them, would often also be useful in traditional educational settings. In particular, for our interests, the computer material would fit in with a full range of other kinds of learning experiences, used where appropriate. This way of proceeding would be desirable from the standpoint of developing computer-aided learning modules, in addition to the many other attractive features that such a learning system has for bringing education to a much wider range of people. In Great Britain the university was initially called the University of the Second Chance. While it did not entirely draw the type of people expected, nevertheless it has provided educational capability to many people who could not otherwise have obtained it, and would do so to an even greater extent in the United States.

The Production Process

The following discussion of the production process is much influenced by our work at the University of California, Irvine, during the last 12 years. I begin by reviewing some existing models for developing instructional material, both computer and noncomputer, and the I outline possible major future directions to pursue for efficient large-scale production processes.

Existing Models of Developing Computer Materials for Learning

In developing materials intended for learning, we can look at how the materials have been developed so far in that area and also seek models outside the immediate developmental area.

Many of the learning materials developed for the computer have been produced with a particular strategy. Indeed, many people assume, unfortunately, that this strategy is the only one possible. The strategy was developed in the early Coursewriter days, by IBM, but was continued at the University of Illinois in the PLATO project.

The first stage of this approach, which I will call the "Coursewriter strategy," is the development of an authoring language. Great stress is put on the simplicity of the authoring language and its ability to be learned quickly and used accurately by people with very little previous programming background. Coursewriter, developed by IBM, was the first such language to gain widespread prominence. Since then, many other authoring languages have been developed with this point of view; among these are PLANIT, PILOT, ASET, DECAL, and Tutor.

After the language is available, the next stage is to find teachers interested in preparing material. Teachers are given a quick course in how to use the language, a lecture course or a course using the computer to aid in learning the language. Typically the messier details of the language are not taught; the teacher learns only enough to get started in the preparation of materials. The person begins to write materials, using the language capabilities just learned. In some cases the teacher may also have had some instruction in pedegogical techniques. The point to emphasize is that with the Coursewriter strategy, one person does both the design of the materials and the programming and debugging of the programs implementing the design.

The difficulties with this strategy arise from several sources. First, authors are often not knowledgeable, as indicated, about programming techniques generally. So their use of the programming language is often naive. Even worse, in the rush of generating some initial material, the teacher will usually have learned only a beginning fragment of the language. Initial material is likely to be extremely simple, not because the teacher thinks it should be that way for instructional reasons, but because that is all the person knows how to do, using the language capabilities mastered at this point! So such a person writes trivial—often useless—material. If a person stays with the system and becomes more proficient in the language, then these initial shortcomings will be overcome. The best material on such systems as PLATO have come from people who have spent years learning the capabilities and becoming more and more sophisticated in their use. By this time the initial group of people has very much diminished.

Another style of approach in the preparation of computer-based materials is reflected in the TICCIT project. Teams were formed to produce the material. These teams had not only subject matter specialists involved but also had educational technologists. Some of the people who worked with such teams claimed that the educational technologists were the dominant element in decision-making on the teams, but I have no direct experience.

The TICCIT activity was based on a predetermined logical structure, designed by educational psychologists. This structure, referred to as learner control, allowed the student to access a set of maps which structured the area, and offered such facilities as "help," "practice," and "rule." Thus, only certain types of computer-aided material were possible. Subject matter experts are restricted as to what they can do.

The use of fixed logic is not retricted to TICCIT. The technique has often been adopted, with simplified logic, as a mode for producing large quantities of materials. The idea is to develop one or several "templates," fixed logic structures, and then fill in the blanks in these templates. Such approaches are often interactive, with the instructor inputting to a program that queries as to what is to happen. Ditran, Scholar-Teacher, and IDF are examples. Although frequently reinvented, this approach has not produced sizable amounts of material, and it has tended to lead to stilted material.

Recent Control Data Corporation work with the PLATO system has stressed instructional design; the tactic is to offer the prospective writer an intensive on-line course in this direction. Any extremely good classroom teacher can quickly be driven away by too much emphasis on instructional design. While any large-scale curriculum effort must have strong influence from this direction, there is a limit beyond which one cannot go and still maintain the interests of the best people in the subject matter field. But this procedure has produced good material.

Models in Textbook Production

Perhaps the most widely used example of a production system for producing educational materials, one that has been around for a long time, is that found in the textbook industry. While systems for producing films, audiotape material, and other media-oriented materials differ in details, they follow much the same outlines as the production of textbooks. The example is interesting because textbooks are the result of an earlier technological development, the printing press.

The textbook typically starts with an author or group of authors. The authors will be self-appointed, coming to the publishers with an outline or even some written material, or the authors may be approached by the publisher. Discussion about what is to be done, with outlines of the topics to be discussed, leads to a contract between the authors and the publisher. Market research may be conducted. The financial basis is typically the payment of royalties, with advances; in a few cases a fixed fee is involved.

The authors then proceed to write the book. What is produced is a manuscript, conforming to standards set up by the publishers but with the pedagogical control of content residing primarily with the author. (The publisher may require features thought to be important in marketing.) Several drafts may be developed, with editors associated with the publisher, and outside consultants, making suggestions. These suggestions may be about content, based on the publisher's and reviewers' views of the successful market, or may be suggestions made on the basis of style, learning questions, or other similar details. Textbook publishers are very much influenced by the existing successful products in the area, particularly in recent years.

After a manuscript is agreed upon by both the authors and the publisher, the manuscript then enters a production stage. At this stage, the author, while offering advice occasionally and being called upon for proofreading, plays a minor role. People working for the publishers become the focus of activity. An early necessity will be to prepare the pictorial information, usually done by artists working for the publisher with the pictures being checked by the author. Photographers may contribute other visual material. Decisions need to be made on typography—the type of paper, the margins, the type font, and many other similar decisions. In these decisions, the author may be consulted, but usually plays a minor role; designers working for the publishers are the decision makers.

The next important worker is the typesetter, using one of many different available processes selected by the publisher for this task. The typesetters may or may not be internal to the publisher. Finally printing and binding are the last important stage in the production process. Few publishers have their own printing facilities, so typically this activity is contracted out to an organization established for this purpose.

Production of computer modules is not identical with the production of books. Enough features are similar, however, to lead us to look carefully at an established model such as the book model as a guide for the production of computer materials.

One aspect of book production is abundantly clear—the type of equipment the publisher needs or must hire from others is entirely different from the type of equipment that the user of the book needs. More and more specialized types of equipment, typesetting and printing equipment, have been developed in connection with the production process. Indeed, it was the existence of the printing press that made it possible for the book to become a widely used learning medium.

In the early days of the development of computer materials, a tacit assumption was made that whatever computer was used for developing the materials would also be the computer that was used for student use of the materials. Typically only one computer was available at a given institution, and so any development at that institution assumed the same machine would later be used by students. Even today this is common. Yet an analysis of the features needed for student use, and the features needed for development of materials, would indicate that far more powerful machine capabilities will be useful in the second connection than in the first. The notion of one machine for both development and delivery is no longer a necessary assumption.

The book model gives useful clues in structuring a direction for the computer. In the next several sections, this article outlines a possible production method. Many of the features of this process have been well tested at Irvine, while others would come in with large-scale production. I begin by distinguishing between the authoring process and the production process, in a way similar to that in textbook production.

The Author's Role

Almost all viable learning material in existence starts with competent teachers. A book may be written by a single individual. An entire course, such as those developed in The Open University, may involve a large group. Teachers in the pedagogical design group should be experienced in the subject matter area and should have dealt directly with students learning the type of material to be presented in computer dialogs. They may work with specialists in instructional design or media. Since the computer material is interactive, with the student playing as active a role as possible in learning, it is desirable to have teachers who normally work with small groups of students in a Socratic mode. Thus, a person who teaches only through large lectures or through the writing of textbooks, may have handicaps in writing computer dialogs. A teacher who frequently interacts with students in a one-to-one situation, with the student playing an important role, is likely to be the best dialog writer.

It is important that persons preparing modules have spent many hours running existing dialogs that exploit the computer fully. Some of this time should be with a knowledgeable person commenting on what is happening. Understanding of what is possible in the medium is a critical aspect, and experience is a good way to gain this knowledge. It is not necessary, however, that the person should be experienced with computers or with computer programming. Indeed, we have found that some of our best materials are generated by excellent teachers with no previous computer experience. If a person has such experience, he or she begins to be concerned with what is possible to program. If this experience is limited, then the material will often be more limited than necessary.

An ideal person to develop interactive computer dialogs is one who frequently works with students in the office, much of the time in a Socratic fashion. This means that the teacher is continually asking the student questions to bring the student to understand the material. Some people teach this way in discussion groups too, and again this is valuable experience for writing computer dialogs. If the experience is recent, and in the area being considered in the dialog, that is all to the good. In writing aids for students having difficulty with particular problems, it is best to write soon after the instructor has had many conversations with such students, helping them overcome their handicaps. The instructor then knows what troubles are likely to arise and is prepared to cope with them.

The analog of a conversation with students is a good one to keep in mind during development, but it has at least one misleading aspect. In a single conversation with a single student a particular path is followed. In the computer material many paths are needed, many different directions in which students can move. Each student should receive unique material, personalized to the problems of that student. The usefulness of the material, particularly with these weaker students who need it the most, will be very much determined by how effective these various learning modes are, how individualized to the needs of a particular group of learners.

Because of this need for multi-branching conversations, we have found that it is best to prepare computer dialogs in groups of two or three authors, working together in every session. The quality of materials produced this way is better than the quality produced by any one of the authors. There is a handicap—more expensive man hours are involved in production than would be involved if a single person did it. But the improvement in quality warrants this increased cost. Groups of more than three or four often turn out to be unwieldy, with discussions and arguments on critical points occupying so much of the time that relatively little is written. This may depend on how well the individuals get along together within the group.

It is important for at least one of the members of the group to have had experience in previous writing of dialogs. If this is the case, then novice members can begin to work directly with such a person in preparing materials. The initial writing sessions become a workshop, with the new person learning the mechanism by engaging in it.

Another mechanism for starting people without previous experience is the use of a one- or two-day workshop. There are various directions for such workshops. The following outline is for a two-day workshop that members of our project at Irvine have given at many locations.

The critical part of the workshop is the group preparation of material. This can be followed by individuals or smaller groups preparing materials. In such a group preparation, with a sizable workshop, the rule of "no more than three in a group" is violated; the intent is not to produce material but rather to illustrate the process of producing materials. In such a workshop group, the leader will often need to keep a firm hand, pushing material in certain directions by fiat to make progress. The suggestion of just which material is to be prepared can come from the group or from the instructor; it should reflect common interest and backgrounds in the group. Thus, in a group of university

First Day		**Second Day**	
9:00–10:00	Review of projects developing computer-based educational material	9:00–10:30	Authoring of computer-based learning material—Group
10:00–10:30	Questions and short break	10:30–11:00	Questions and short break
10:30–12:00	Modes of computer usage in education	11:00–12:00	Further on-line demonstrations
1:30–2:30	On-line demonstrations	1:30–3:30	Preparing materials—Group
2:30–3:30	Modes of teaching	3:30–4:30	Questions and break
3:30–4:30	The computer in courses	4:00–5:00	Future directions for computers in instruction
8:00–10:00	Additional on-line demonstrations		

professors with mixed backgrounds, one can often work on high school material in illustrating the authoring process.

An important issue is what the "product" of a group of teachers preparing a computer dialog is to be. This product is analogous to the manuscript of a book, the entity that is to guide the publisher in production decisions. At Irvine we prepare dialogs in a loose flowchart format. This format specifies in detail what messages are to be displayed to the student, what pictures are to be drawn, and how the student reponses are to be analyzed, including all the branching decisions. No formal flowcharting capability is needed or even desired. We do not teach authors standard flowcharting symbols, because these are designed for other purposes. Rather, the activity should be presented to teachers as a specification of the pedagogical logic to be followed. Examples of previously produced scripts are useful.

The process of preparing such flowcharts, including suggestions to the authors, is described in more detail in information available from our project. The author may want to specify in the flowchart various timing considerations, including the order in which graphic and alphanumeric elements are drawn, the delays between these elements, the rate of text output, and special delays for emphasis or readability. They may also want to specify how the material is to be placed on the screen, either detailed or partial specifications, by drawing sketches of the screen or by descriptions. This last point is up to the individual authors; some authors may find that they have no desire and/or ability to specify precisely such visual details, while others will see such choices as ones that they wish to make. We will describe further the question of visual details in considering the production process of the group producing the material.

The arrangements with authors in the future are likely to be similar to the arrangements with book publishers, with some royalty basis, although fixed fees are also possible. The Control Data Corporation procedure with PLATO has been to pay royalties contingent on the number of times the program is used. This is not feasible in an environment where the individuals are running on personal (stand-alone) systems, where it is difficult to gather such data. In any case, it may not be worth the expense entailed. It would seem that the standard model of the book—the number of units sold—is more likely to be successful. Many aspects of this issue need further discussion and trial use.

Production Process—Editorial

The publisher does not accept a book manuscript from the author and immediately publish it. The proposed book is likely to go through several stages of refinement. At least two different processes are involved. The manuscript is sent out for review, often several times. Reviewers are chosen by the publisher to give insight into what needs to be changed for the intended market. The publisher employs editors who make extensive suggestions concerning the book, both style and content. This editorial role has assumed increased importance in recent years. It is often driven by marketing studies.

This description of the editorial process for books emphasizes that editorial work on the computer dialog in flowchart form may be required before the material is ready to be produced. With the computer dialog, the process of editorial work is much more uncertain. This aspect is not a fully explored area in the production process. The language—the messages that are to be displayed to the students—can be edited in the usual fashion. What contribution is the editor to make in logic, the analysis of student input, and the movement in different directions depending on that analysis? Should editorial work be done before or after the program is running or both? These questions can be answered only with additional experience.

It is possible to edit the flowchart. But it takes a knowledgeable individual, with experience in developing computer dialogs similar to the authors. We have edited material at Irvine, but we do not believe that the process is, as yet, completely understood.

Some companies and individuals have restricted the logic allowed to the author to make the editorial work easier for other purposes. This is an unfortunate choice, leading to material of poorer quality. The best present procedure is to restrict the amount of editorial work done at the flowchart stage, depending more on the competence of the authors than is currently true with book production. As we gain experience, the editorial possibilities will evolve. Furthermore, there is another stage, after initial implementation, where additional correctional activity is both possible and desirable, a stage often missing from book production. At this time editorial changes can be more easily made than at the flowchart stage, as the material is "visible" in the form to be used by students.

Another aspect of the editorial work that still remains a problem is that of how "long" in several different senses, the final program will be. We can ask how much memory will be required, or we can ask about the average student use. Our current methods of estimating are not accurate, probably not as accurate as with book production. Even there some uncertainties exist, and perhaps they will be acceptable in the early stages of large-scale computer production.

Production Process—Design

Computer dialogs are a mixure of graphic and alphanumeric information on the screen. The placement of this material on the screen can have a large effect on its ability to aid students. Hence, a critical stage in the production process is that of visual design of the material, its structure as it is to appear to the student.

Early computer material often ignored this issue. It treated the screen as if it were a page in a book, following much the same conventions used there. There are many differences from the book situation.

Perhaps the principal difference is that blank space, while costly in a book, is *free* on the screen of a computer display! So one can make the choice of how much material appears on a particular screen on different criteria than with books.

Books often make choices that do not follow the best design standards. Of all educational materials produced in printed form, perhaps only the printed materials from The Open University have worried consistently about how the appearance of the material on the page will affect student learning. The products and papers of The Open University are a valuable source of information in considering the visual aspects of computer material. Many important issues, such as readability, are involved.

Who is to lay out the screen display? The authors may choose to give at least partial indications of the way things should look on the screen. Some authors will have considerable skill in this direction and will be able to offer excellent guidance. Other authors are not likely to have useful ideas.

The publisher needs people with very good design background and with instructional interests who can see the value of various ways of placing material on the screen. The same type of person who works with layout in books, magazines, or ads on television will probably be useful for this, provided that person also has the necessary instructional background. Thus, someone from a practical arts background, such as industrial design or typography, with a strong interest in aiding learning, might be the best person for the task.

Once we are convinced of the importance of screen design and consider the question of what sort of individual should be involved in this activity, we can make reasonable decisions about the working environment for this person. First, since things look different on paper than they do on the screen, the primary environment needs to be the screen itself, the surface or surfaces on which the student is eventually to use the material. (Perhaps several such "screens" should be considered in the design stage, given the different target machines that may eventually be used by students as technology progresses.)

Capabilities should allow the designer to behave as closely as possible to the way the designer ordinarily behaves, choosing a variety of pictorial treatments, placing graphic and alphanumeric objects where they are desired, moving them around, changing their size and orientation, locating the text material with choice over such things as bold, flashing, font choices, left or right justification, centering, subscripts, superscripts, special symbols.

Our project at Irvine has developed such design software since 1974, letting the designer work in a natural environment. This initial facility is described briefly at the beginning of this chapter, and in detail in documents available from the Educational Technology Center. This software also writes files or code; when the designer has everything as desired on the screen, the computer is instructed to write the code or file that will produce such a display. In many of our recent programs, over 85% of the number of actual lines of code are written by the computer itself, with guidance from designers. An alternative would be to store the display information in files, easily retrievable and modifiable at a later time. More recently we have designed new software for this task on personal computers.

If code is written, the program could be adapted so the code produced can be in one of the many different languages. An alternate possibility is to produce files. Since the code or file writing will be the final stage of the program, new drivers can easily be prepared for a new target machine. Furthermore, the pictorial and alphanumeric information is easily edited, so that if at some later time some changes are to be made in the display, they can be made with the same type of capabilities that were employed for the initial material.

Production Process—Programming

Although the code generators just described will write almost all the code or files to generate text and graphics materials on the screen, there still remains special graphics and logic. This logic can become very complex, particularly if the authors, as is desirable, are given no constraints on the material they can prepare other than pedagogical constraints.

Some of the necessary work may be routine coding activities. Thus, if all that is needed in a particular response is to look for half a dozen different things that the student might be saying and go off in two or three different directions, then the coding task is easy. Much more complex sequences occur in the best available current dialogs. Furthermore, particularly in the sciences, numerical computations may be required within the program to check a student's response, particularly when problem generators, with random choices at run time, are involved, or for other purposes such as learning simulations. Graphic output may depend on internal calculations based on randomly chosen or student-supplied data.

The task suggested was in mind when languages such as Coursewriter, Tutor, or PILOT were developed. They have the capability of analyzing student input and doing the computational work required (with Coursewriter in its initial form computational capabilities were limited).

First, let us discuss the computational situation. The computations required are often standard numerical computations, the type that many languages are capable of handling. This raises the possibility of doing these computations within a standard, well understood language suitable for numerical computation. Many such languages are in existence. In our earlier work at Irvine, all computation was done within FORTRAN subroutines, added to code obtained in other ways. Recently we have worked for this and other purposes with Pascal. If we do not know in advance just which numerical capabilities will be needed, it is necessary to duplicate almost all the capabilities that exist in the common higher-level languages if we are to embed these facilities within some special-purpose

"CAI" language. On the other hand, in a versatile system, one may be able to use a higher level language as just indicated.

The other side of the story, the analysis of student input, is essentially a string processing plus control activity. The logic can be complicated, and one may want to look for several things in a given student input, exclude several things, inspect order, or keep and use information on earlier performance.

At least one language was developed for such string processing, SNOBOL. It is interesting to note that SNOBOL has almost never been used for computer-aided learning. At Irvine we originally handled this part of the code by macro-based structure, writing new macros as our requirements grew more complex. Recently Pascal has been the basis of our activities.

An important consideration for language choice is that the code will often need to be modified by people other than those who initially wrote it. At several stages it will be highly desirable or necessary to make modifications in the program; these stages are discussed in the next section. The ease of these modifications may be critical in the effectiveness of the authoring system. Furthermore, student usage will often suggest drastic changes in the approach, and these too will have to be accommodated in modification of the original code. Unfortunately many existing CAI systems have been too inflexible, making it unnecessarily difficult to make the required changes. The ability to revise the original program efficiently, often year after year, is an important aspect of the production system.

A very much related question is the initial ease of programming, including debugging activities. As computer dialogs are long, complex programs, we want to provide those who are developing the programs with a rich computer editor and with excellent facilities for debugging. As far as possible the code should be self-documenting to aid both the initial programmer and those who will see the code later in the revision process. Powerful control structures are also believed to reduce the likelihood of error in complex programs.

Most of the items described in the last two paragraphs will be recognized as simply the necessities of high-level systems programming generally. The recent work on such coding, the emphasis on structured programming, is important to us in determining what language capabilities we might pursue. The code to be produced is in some ways as complex as many systems programs, and so we can follow the lessons learned there.

In recent years, most systems coding has been done in variants of two languages, ALGOL and PL/1. So I am prompted to ask whether we can easily implant a CAI capability within a higher-level language of this power. The answer clearly is "yes." This direction is the most promising for future authoring language capabilities.

In the early days of development, such an approach, using a powerful language suitable for systems programming, was not the wisest, because the production process was not developed. Many individuals did both the pedagogical material and the coding, and so the complexities of elaborate language might not have been a good choice. Furthermore, some time was needed to learn which CAI capabilities were critical for this development. Now, however, a higher-level language approach, with added capabilities, would be the wisest direction, particularly when we consider large-scale production.

The details of describing fully the added language capabilities for computer-aided learning go beyond the purposes of this paper. The emphasis must be on interfacing with the author-produced flowcharts and on efficient production and modification of the dialog code.

Production Process—Early Revision

As soon as materials are in an initial running form, the author, editor, artist, and programmer (perhaps more, perhaps fewer people) should run the program together a number of times. Many changes are suggested by such a preview. The material as it appears on the screen does not conform entirely with the view the authors had when it was written. Timing, delays between successive alphanumeric passages or between graphics and alphanumeric, can be adjusted so that the pauses are reasonable. All parties should feel free to make changes at this time, and the overhead for adding these changes should be relatively small, as mentioned in the last section.

It is desirable for a prototype group of students to run the material, after the authors and others have been involved in the revision process. When such prototype use goes on, it is critical to gather data systematically. If the production system is a timesharing system, or has some central data machine, gathering of data is simple. If the students are running on the eventual target stand-alone machines, not connected to anything else, additional thought must be given to collecting information.

Many improvements can be made at this stage. Questions that seem clear to the authors and the editors are not clear to the students, because of differences in their perception of the English language. Authors may not have taken into account all the possible reasonable responses to a question, wrong as well as right. Usage with a sizable group of students will quickly reveal such shortcomings, and the programs can be modified. Several stages of prototype use may be necessary or desirable.

Production Process—Duplication

We now come to a stage analogous to printing with textbooks, the duplication of the material into many copies. The first question is what the medium is to be. A magnetic medium would seem to be a current choice. The flexible or floppy disc, with its sizable capacity, is the best present possibility. With cheaper units, such as the home computers, voice-type magnetic cassette units are common, but unreliable; floppy units are coming down in price and will probably soon be competitive. A full-size standard floppy holds about 250,000 characters, and so is capable of containing a sizable amount of lesson material; newer floppies hold more. Another mode for the programs for large-scale distribution may be the read-only storage unit of some type, plugged into the device. Such storage is coming down rapidly in price, as seen by its use even in relatively inexpensive programmable calculators. At a later stage such newer technology as the videodisc may well turn out to be the most practical means of duplication, particularly where slides, audio, and moving sequences are part of the learning material.

A major issue in connection with duplication is the question of making certain that only the company itself, as far as possible, is engaged in the duplication process. That is, we do not want every user to duplicate the materials, thus cutting down on potential sales. Magnetic media are easy to duplicate. One strategy is to have each machine have a built-in serial number at the hardware level, accessible through the code and to sell materials that assume the particular machine. Another possibility is to sell materials in scrambled form, with decoding devices. Legal constraints would be employed, as with other educational material. These suggestions do not exhaust the situation, but are enough to show what is possible.

Production Process—Marketing and Distribution

Marketing and distribution activities, including advertising, will probably take place somewhat the same way that they do in the book industry. The fact that this is a new product may require newer tactics initially, tactics designed not only to convince people of the particular teaching material that is to be sold but also the validity of this learning process, unfamiliar to many teachers. When sizable amounts of good material are available, this does not seem to be a difficult problem.

SINGLE VERSUS MULTIPLE AUTHORSHIP OF COMPUTER-AIDED LEARNING DIALOGS

In considering the production of computer-based teaching material, it seems critical to consider the question of whether individual modules in a series will be written by one author (the usual practice) or whether two or perhaps three individuals will be involved in the same modules. Each of these approaches has some advantages and disadvantages; the purpose of this article is to look at these pluses and minuses and arrive at a rational position.

Matters of individual taste are also involved. That is, an individual developer, by reason of a personal style, may choose to work entirely alone, while another developer may prefer to work in a group.

Unfortunately, little hard evidence can be found one way or another. Development of computer-based teaching materials has proceeded mostly on an *ad hoc* basis, with competent individuals producing more. However, considerable experience is now available.

AEDS Monitor, vol. 1, no. 7, 8, 9.

Much early material employing the computer for learning was prepared by a single individual. Thus, much of the material written in early Coursewriter or Tutor was the work of one person. We might call this use of one author the "naive" assumption: without giving much thought to the matter, many people would work alone.

The vast majority of the materials developed at Irvine have been developed with a multiple author strategy. An examination, for example, of our recent list of computer dialogs shows only about five have been developed by a single individual. Often three or four people are involved. There are few examples where more people were involved, except in dialogs where different groups develop different parts of the dialog.

Perhaps the major exception to this tendency to two or three authors was FIELD, an introduction to electrostatics developed at a workshop involving University of California faculty on other campuses. Initially, it was intended simply as a group example of how to develop such material. But, it has turned into a very useful piece of learning material. But even here, additional sections beyond the initial work were done by two people. (See Chapter 4, pages 135–140, for more details.)

The majority view within the project has been that computer-aided learning material is best developed with two or three people involved. Such small interacting groups, it is believed, can produce better material than would be produced by a single individual. This is true, particularly with regard to developing sequences for the weak student and to recognizing the various forms in which responses are likely to come from students. Experience shows that the final product is not one that would be written by the individual writers working alone.

The process in such groups is highly interactive. Each person brings unique teaching and learning experiences to the group. Often the view that converges from the heated discussions which frequently arise is different from that held initially by the individuals. Thus, in considering student responses to a question, the interaction enriches the response analysis.

It is not clear that several authors work any slower (or faster), however, than an individual author. Not enough data are available and probably the results might differ for different groups. The natural conjecture is that multiple authorship involves more person hours to create a given amount of material. But it is likely that less revision will be necessary with group-prepared computer dialogs, after the material is used with students. So a greater investment in people at the pedagogical design stage might lead to less resources needed for revision. Furthermore, if several people are responsible for the revision process (individual writers and the series editor, if any), the revision itself also benefits from this additional input.

Another important aspect of group development is that it makes possible the involvement of people with extremely valuable teaching experience, but no direct computer-based experience. Thus, the work we have done in connection with such outstanding teachers as Arnold Arons, from the Physics Department at the University of Washington, would probably not have been possible if we had insisted that teachers develop the material alone. Arons spent several short periods with us, writing many extensive dialogs. Working with people who had already prepared material, he was able to bring his unique contributions to our work. So a combination of talent sometimes is possible with this multiple authorship arrangement which is not possible without it.

Any discussion of production of computer-aided learning materials should consider not only current, limited experimental production, but should also look toward a period of a few years from now when such learning materials will be generated in increasing volume. For such large-scale production we need to think more about a full production system.

A disadvantage in a formal production system involving multiple authored dialogs is that either the individual authors will receive smaller royalties or the publisher will be making larger royalty payments for that module. Similarly, the advance on royalties might be larger. Some of this larger advance might be recouped at the revision stage in programming costs, as indicated above, but it would be unrealistic to think that all of it would be. On the other hand, the advances on royalties would eventually come out of the author's later royalties if the series is successful, while the additional programming time that the publisher would need to put into the revision process will be a nonvanishing cost.

Whether the increased quality of the materials will have any noticeable effect on the sales is difficult to predict, but it might have some effect.

In conclusion, I would recommend the multiple author strategy. I would also recommend that the publisher pay the full royalty to each of the authors involved in a multiple-authored dialog.

References

1. George Polya, *How to Solve It* (New York: Doubleday & Company, Inc., 1957).

2. William Huggins and Doris Entwisle, *Iconic Communication: An Annotated Bibliography* (Baltimore: Johns Hopkins Press, 1974).

3. The Carnegie Commission on Higher Education, *The Fourth Revolution—Instructional Technology in Higher Education* (New York: McGraw-Hill, Inc., 1972).

4. Walter Perry, *The Open University* (San Francisco: Jossey-Bass, 1977).

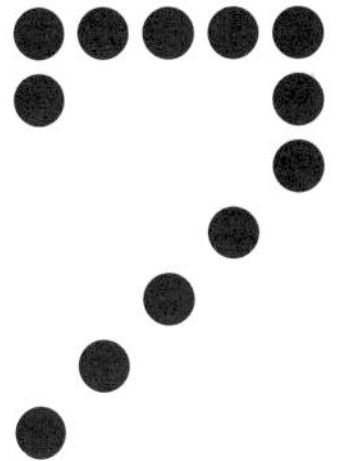

The Future

TRANSFERABILITY OF COMPUTER-BASED LEARNING MATERIALS

An important issue for developers of computer-based learning materials is the one of transferability to other computers and to other locations beyond the location at which the initial material was developed. Much discussion goes on about this problem, informally and in the literature, but much of this discussion appears to be based on simplistic solutions that do not examine the full range of transferability problems. The present article takes a broad viewpoint with regard to such transferability, delineating factors that are often overlooked because only a piece of the total problem is considered.

Two Dichotomies

This discussion of transferability is based on two dichotomies, important in a comprehensive view of the problems and prospects for transferability of computer-based learning materials.

The first distinction is that of a short-range versus a long-range point of view. Are we considering immediately transferring materials within, say, the current year or are we discussing a more long-range prospect, the eventual widespread use of the materials over many years? Although I am treating this distinction between immediate and future transfer as a dichotomy, it is a continuum. It will be convenient nevertheless to make this separation.

A second important distinction to be made concerning transferability is between the computer-related aspects and those aspects associated with innovative learning and teaching. The first aspect is concerned with the technical problems of getting the materials operational on systems *Y*, *Z*, and *Q* after having been developed on system *X*. The second aspect concerns the problems facing any new learning and teaching materials when those materials are spread beyond the institutions in which they are initially developed. Solving the first problem by no means solves the second. Thus, it is possible that the materials may run successfully on a particular computer system, but that no teachers or students at that institution will use them.

These two dimensions are independent. We can perhaps best illustrate the situation by plotting them along separate axes as follows:

Now	Future	
B	*D*	Social Aspects
A	*C*	Computer Aspects

As the diagram indicates, we have four separate problems to discuss: Problem *A* involves short-range computer aspects; Problem *B* involves short-range innovative teaching aspects; Problem *C* involves long-range computer aspects; and Problem *D* involves long-range innovative teaching aspects. Tactics that may be good for one of these categories may *not* be good for another! A full discussion must take into account all of these possibilities.

I consider each category separately, both in terms of our present state of development and in terms of the difficulties and problems associated with them. I shall also point out limitations in certain cases brought about by focusing too heavily on one or the other aspect of transferability.

Short-Range Computer Aspects

Most of the current concern of transferability falls in this category. Probably the best example of a careful treatment of the problems in this area is seen in the activities of CONDUIT.

One "standard" solution to the problem of short-range computer aspects is to write in a standardized form of most commonly available languages. This, for example, was the tactic taken by the Computers in the Undergraduate Science Curriculum in England. Another possibility is to prepare the material in several commonly available languages. John Merrill's book, *Using Computers in Physics*[1], uses both FORTRAN and BASIC, and *Introductory Computer-Based Mechanics II*[2], available through CONDUIT, presents each program in FORTRAN, BASIC, APL, and Pascal.

Two difficulties present themselves with regard to this standard language approach. First, very few languages have effective standards. Perhaps the most standardized language is FORTRAN. Here, in addition to the ANSI standard, a more restricted standard is available as defined by a program-checking program developed at Bell Laboratories, the PFORT standard. This standard is employed by CONDUIT for FORTRAN. If a FORTRAN program satisfies PFORT and does not run on a particular FORTRAN, that FORTRAN is likely to be rather peculiar.

The standardization problems with BASIC are considerably more confused. Existing forms of BASIC, even from a single vendor, differ greatly. Such terms as "standard BASIC," or, more commonly, "Dartmouth BASIC," although extremely widely used, turn out to have almost no meaning. Almost every BASIC is called "Dartmouth BASIC," yet as the Dartmouth developers point out, almost no other BASIC is compatible with current Dartmouth BASIC. For some years a committee has been at work on a standard for BASIC; the proposed full standard is quite different from any existing BASIC. CONDUIT has also commissioned studies in this area, and a group in England has also developed such a minimal standard.

APL initially exhibited a much higher degree of standardization. For a while there *was* only one APL, the IBM program product. Almost all later forms of APL have included this substantial portion as a subset, so it served as a *de facto* standard. But beyond this level, forms of APL have begun to diverge considerably. A standards committee has been formed.

Pascal is relatively standardized, due in large part to the influences of the initial implementation. A standards committee is now at work.

These language factors become even less satisfactory with regard to ease of transferability when we consider graphic capabilities. Each displayer personal computer demands different graphic code. Several incompatible graphic additions to APL have been designed. The BASIC standards have proposed graphic additions to BASIC, not yet implemented in most systems. Even UCSD Pascal, easily moved from machine to machine, becomes less transportable when graphics are involved. Because graphic capabilities are extremely important—almost essential in most areas of computer-based learning material—graphic transportability problems are serious.

Another aspect comes in when considering standard languages, the inefficiency of the code. Thus, if we write APL graphic code so it works on *everybody's* APL, as does Tektronix, this is achieved only at the expense of efficiency, often nontrivial. While this inefficiency may not be an important factor if the materials are only run with a few students, it can be disastrous with usage in large classes.

For the individual who is concerned with what will run on many other current systems in relatively brief periods of time, these issues of languages are important. As the programs become more and more responsive to student needs, and so more complex, and as they resort to more and more exotic languages, the work associated with moving them to another system becomes greater. It is significant that the programs CONDUIT distributes thus far are *simpler* materials.

But a completely different side to the question, the use of standard languages as a technique for achieving compatability, must be considered. An individual project that decides in favor of a particular standard language for all of its materials may automatically *cut off* many of the pedagogical options available to it.

Thus, someone writing in a form of BASIC supportable on a great many different machines will avoid string inputs, even though pedagogically desirable in the situation. Furthermore, a BASIC user seeking wide transferability for learning materials will avoid files or overlays, since these facilities are likely to differ from system to system; thus, the programs will be relatively short, not the longer programs that exemplify some of the most interesting material available today.

I have visited a number of projects where, if one raises the question of "Why don't you do so and so?" the answer is typically an answer that depends on features of the language rather than on pedagogical choice. In these cases the desire for transportability is an important limiting factor in the quality of the materials.

I want to summarize my views on this issue with a statistical statement that does not necessarily apply to individual programs but is generally applicable. It should be considered that I am looking at the short-range point of view, and the computer aspects only. Here is the statement that I will call Bork's First Rule:

THE MORE SYSTEMS THE COMPUTER-BASED MATERIALS CAN RUN ON, THE LESS INTERESTING PEDAGOGICALLY THE MATERIALS ARE.

Short-Range Innovative Teaching Aspects

Just because materials can "run" at a given school is no guarantee that students will see them in classes or have any access to them at all. Faculty who know that these materials are available may choose not to employ them; many teachers who *might* use them may not even know of their existence. The problems are similar to the difficulties that we find generally when we move a new teaching idea from its original developer to a completely unrelated environment. Some additional problems appear, because the computer resources available may be limited; further, accounting procedures or shortages of facilities may make it difficult for students to access the necessary computer resources. No schools currently have the resources for widespread utilization of the computer in learning.

One major problem in this area is that of instructors learning whether available materials are suitable for their course, or whether they are reliable. The CONDUIT review system is one mechanism for solving the problem of reliability. Materials under consideration, after a preliminary screening, are sent out to several reviewers; so only materials that are technically sound and pedagogically useful will be recommended. CONDUIT advertises their availability and serves as a source. Instructors will still want to look at the materials to see how well they fit into their course structure. If printed materials contain only a few programs, no particular problems are presented. MicroSift is also working in this direction.

If the materials are interactive computer dialogs, the difficulties can be greater. Because such materials are not easy to transport in the technical (computer) sense, CONDUIT does not as yet review them, although it is changing this policy as it considers personal computers. Further, while the instructor can easily browse through a book under consideration as a text, it may be more difficult to do this with a long and involved computer program, offering many different tracks for students. The design of some programs is more conducive to browsing than others, particularly if some aspects of learner control are present; but in general the instructor has difficulty examining dialog materials.

Many of the problems of short-range innovative teaching aspects are political and sociological, needing very different mechanisms to solve them than the problems associated with the computer aspects. Often, learning materials are put on a computer by the computer facility, under the assumption that faculty and students will then flock to use them. But they may not even know of the *existence* of the material! If the faculty members in the academic area were not involved in advance in the decision to place the materials on the computer, the chances of widespread use are markedly lower. Our experience with sending our materials to other institutions with similar equipment, where the computer aspects of transferability are much reduced, shows that it is almost essential, if we are to see use, to involve teachers in the decision to make the dialogs available.

One interesting approach to ease the types of problems just discussed is seen in the CALCHEM project in Britain, a chemistry project based primarily at Leeds University. Although most of the dialogs were written in two or three locations, about a dozen other institutions were involved in the committee running the project as a whole. Hence, chemists from many schools feel they have some stake in the output. This tactic should ease the transferability to these new sites.

Much work needs to be done here, much of it not particularly unique to the computer situation. We need to study in more detail the factors that inhibit the transfer of successful innovative learning ideas of all types, including those associated with computers.

Long-Range Computer Aspects

When we change the focus from short-range to long-range aspects, the problems and prospects become entirely different. Past discussions have often ignored these long-range aspects. But from the standpoint of eventually using computers in many learning situations, they are by far the most important. So the developer of such products should be very concerned with these long-range aspects.

Here we need to look at some hardware/software futures for computers, because that affects what is possible. The most important feature of modern computer technology is the very rapid current development: computers are becoming more powerful and less expensive. These developments suggest different computer systems for the future than current ones. All of our existing learning materials are running on obsolete machines. From this point of view the question of transfering materials *immediately* to machine *X* becomes then less important, particularly for the developer of computer-based learning materials who looks to the future.

At least two hardware futures for computers are projected at the moment. One involves larger and larger networks so that more and more student stations are accessing the same CPU or a group of CPUs. Donald Bitzer, Director of the PLATO project, has suggested construction of a million-terminal network, with 200 interconnected CPUs and communication supported by satellites. The present ARPA net, and its commercial offshoots, furnish other examples of networking.

A second future possibility is based on a different view of the computer universe, one that is dominated by the evolving microprocessor and its later descendants. Today's terminal is tomorrow's computer. Such stand-alone personal systems function by themselves, with full computing capabilities, without connection to a large central computer, although they might occasionally connect to another computer for such specialized purposes as massive calculations, accessing a rapidly changing centralized data base, or record-keeping. As these systems function primarily stand-alone, they would *not* be limited to current communication speeds and so allow full animation, impossible in a communication-limited environment. Other aspects of modern technology, such as the home videodisc system, might become important components of such systems.

We do need to worry about effective delivery systems that allow us to carry out all the functions that a modern teaching system will need. Such a system should have full multimedia capability, color, high-speed graphics, and at least audio output capability.

No matter which future we look at, one fact is clear: future systems will cost much less than current systems cost. Projections indicate that, because of our increasing capabilities with computer technology, computer costs will continue to decline over a long period of time. Hence, we can expect the computer systems of the future, for education and otherwise, to be cheaper and cheaper.

This leads me to Bork's Second Rule:

WHEN WE CONSIDER THE LONG-RANGE POINT OF VIEW, *NO* COMPUTER ASPECTS OF TRANSFERABILITY ARE IMPORTANT.

That is, the technology itself, with its ever-increasing effectiveness, will obviate the problems of machine transferability. If the massive networking system happens, then of course the programs will be available on any one of the million terminals. If stand-alone systems become extremely widespread and dominant, much more so than current computers, the materials can be written for such widely available systems. Furthermore, the possibilities of microprogrammability and inexpensive CPUs mean that even code written for different machines may be able to run on a variety of machines. A single machine could have CPUs matching the institution's sets of different computers or could emulate in microcode a wide variety of machines.

As materials are improved, and thus in greater national demand, stronger emphasis will be directed toward making them more available. Hence, marketing of computer-based materials will also aid in solving problems of long-range transportability. People will purchase machines just to run a particular learning package.

So the massive problems of transferability that appear with regard to the short-range technical aspects all vanish in the long range. From a long-range point of view, we do not need to put large efforts in this direction except to insure the type of hardware that will make the transferability possible.

A corollary, based on the first "rule," is that many things prepared with short-range computer transferability in mind will be too restricted to survive far into the future. Only the best current materials, using a wide range of capabilities, are likely to be usable in the future.

Long-Range Innovative Learning Aspects

This category presents some of the most interesting problems. Unlike other categories, it is not entirely independent of what has gone before. Some of the techniques involved in dealing with short-range teaching aspects also will be useful in considering the more long-range ones, particularly those that involve the political and sociological problems of widespread computer use.

The question of how these future materials should be marketed is very important. As already indicated, most current materials are produced in a "cottage industry" format. We need to develop much more careful production and marketing facilities, including the provision of royalties as an incentive to authors. Commercial distribution methods will be vital, just as they are for books and other learning materials.

Any consideration of this aspect needs to consider the development of new types of courses made *possible* by the existence of the computer. It also needs to consider new modes of education, where the formal school is replaced by other mechanisms such as The Open University in Britain or through extension in the public libraries or homes.

From the long-range point of view, we can expect the computer will not be a passive teaching device, but will contribute to a vital restructuring of our educational systems.

PERSONAL COMPUTERS IN LEARNING

With Stephen Franklin

This article acquaints the reader with the *personal computer,* with emphasis on the computer as an aid in the learning process. We consider the types of hardware available and software related to educational uses, offering advice to those just entering this area.

The Computer in Learning

We begin by emphasizing that the personal computer is, first and foremost, a *computer*. Thus, much of what has been learned about learning via computers, in classroom use and a variety of research projects in the past few years, is applicable to the personal computer. While there are differences between personal computers and their larger cousins, these differences do not necessarily make larger systems better tools for learning. Indeed, personal computers have distinct advantages as components of environments for learning. In Chapter 6 ("Large-Scale Production and Distribution of Computer-Aided Learning Modules"), it was argued that the personal computer will very likely become the dominant mode of educational *delivery*, taking over that role from the now popular timesharing computer. This article concentrates primarily on such delivery systems, and so has relatively little to say about the (more complex) production systems.

From: *Educational Technology*, October 1979

What is a Personal Computer?

The literature offers a variety of definitions of personal computers. The emphasis is that the computer is not built into an apparatus for one specific purpose, but it is a *general-purpose* machine, conceivably programmable by the user. The personal computer can work primarily *alone*. Although a personal computer may occasionally connect to a remote machine, it is primarily designed for "stand-alone" use. Unlike a timesharing system, it typically does all of its processing locally, where the user is situated.

It is important to distinguish between the personal computer and hobbyist computers. We might compare the computer hobbyist to the person who is engaged in amateur radio activities. The primary interest is in the hardware or software itself, and so such things as kits or units that can be plugged in easily become important aspects. The hobbyist is interested more in using the computer than in the uses of the computer. On the other hand, the personal computer user's primary concern is the *tasks* a computer can do. In the case that we are considering, the task is to aid learning. The user of the personal computer is not likely to be acquainted with soldering irons, wiring diagrams, boards, chips, buses, or even registers, pointers, and disc handlers.

The Ingredients of a Personal Computer

This section is intended for the computer novice. All personal computers will have a central processing unit (CPU), the part that carries out the logical decisions and calculations that are the hallmark of any computer. Typically, these units will be microprocessor chips, using the recently developed large-scale integration (LSI) technology. About half a dozen such chips account for the vast bulk of all personal computers. There is much talk about which of these central processing chips are 8-bit chips and which (the newer ones) are 16-bit chips. But from the viewpoint of the educational user, except for variance in speed, this issue is often of little consequence.

The second universal ingredient of all personal computers is fast primary memory, also usually based on chip technology. Information is usually retained only so long as power is supplied to the memory. The important variable is the amount of fast memory. In typical personal computers, this can go from 4,000 characters (bytes) to perhaps 64,000 characters. For extensive learning use, minimal systems are inadequate. The trend, given rapidly decreasing memory costs, is toward systems with more memory. Newer central processing units allow more memory.

Personal computers in education are likely to have keyboards resembling typewriters. (In a few cases, the keys are arranged alphabetically.) There is considerable variation in keyboard layout. Typically, the keyboard will have some keys not on a typewriter. There will often be keys marked "escape" and "break," which send special signals—not characters—used differently in different systems. Another possible key is "control." "Control" works as an additional "shift," producing a series of codes that are different from the usual letters and numbers and can be employed for various purposes in programs.

A third component is the display, the screen on which information is viewed by the user. (While older computers had devices that produced paper copy, this is an add-on in inexpensive personal computers.) Some current systems use a home television set for display. In other units, the computer has a built-in television set, sometimes disguised.

For a valid educational system, the screen should be capable of displaying both alphanumeric information and pictorial or graphic information. Text displays vary as to how many characters fill a line and how many lines fill the screen. Too few characters can be a handicap in many situations, including numerous educational applications.

Various special treatments of the characters may be present, differing in different systems in terms of the hardware capability and what is supported by software. It may be possible to flash, blink, or oscillate a word or phrase independently of the rest of the text, in each case to draw emphasis to it. Or, it may be possible to redefine the character set.

Graphic capabilities are essential for educational applications. While older systems often did not have these capabilities, practically all the recent personal computers do provide graphics. Many systems provide only "character graphics," that is, special characters that are small pictures or pieces of pictures (e.g., a slanted line segment). This type of "graphics" is crude, limiting, and inadequate for many of the simplest applications. "True" graphics involve subdividing displays into rectangular grids of greater resolution than that provided by character location. Here the first major issue is resolution. It is difficult to give hard-and-fast rules on resolution requirements for educational activities. Relatively minimal resolution, perhaps 150 points by 250 points, will do for most educational applications, although a few things would be enhanced by better resolution. Another interesting capability is the ability to "turn on" a full complex picture rather than drawing it line by line.

A number of other issues are of increasing interest in connection with the display screen. It may be possible to selectively erase pieces of curves or alphanumeric material rapidly. This capability is rapidly becoming essential in educational applications, although one can sometimes survive without it. Another issue is whether color capabilities are provided and, if so, how many colors and how they are controlled. It seems likely too that color will be an important component of educational systems in the future and will soon be regarded as indispensable. The difference in cost between personal computing systems offering color and those not offering color is minimal.

The final ingredient of any widely used personal computer as an educational delivery system is a mass storage device. Early machines typically had standard tape cassettes. But these are inadequate, because of the inaccuracies associated with them (particularly when used on machines other than the writing machine) and because of their slow access speeds. It is difficult to use cassettes for storing a large program, where it is not clear what data or computer code will be needed next in fast memory.

A much more successful device at the present time is the flexible or floppy disc. A standard floppy disc stores approximately 250,000 characters and can access any point on the disc in a fraction of a second. While disc drives are currently more expensive than cassette units, they are declining in price. Newer approaches to this technology allow floppy disc systems with one million bytes, and various developments with even more storage of a transportable type will soon be available. Thus, in the immediate future it is likely that the floppy disc, and perhaps its later relatives, will be the main mechanism for distributing computer-based learning materials.

Another possible technology, already used in hand-held calculators, is the plug-in module of read-only storage. In the Exidy Sorcerer, the Texas Instruments computers, and the Atari, such modules are currently being used; similar facilities are available for the home television game systems (evolving into more general-purpose personal computers).

Future Hardware

A number of interesting developments, while not yet practical, are looming on the horizon. This section discusses these developments briefly. Anyone looking at this area should be acquainted with not only the current hardware but likely future prospects.

One of the most interesting possibilities, but one with many problems and little experience, is the use of optical videodisc systems in combination with computers. These will allow storage and access to a wide variety of visual and other media including stationary pictures and video sequences, all under control of the computer program.

Voice output is already practical as seen by the fact that it is present in a home device selling for under $50.00, Texas Instruments' Speak and Spell. A variety of techniques is possible. But full voice output facilities are still uncommon in systems available for instructional purposes.

Voice input is a more delicate issue. Although there has been a sizable amount of research on analyzing speech, these systems are not practical for inexpensive systems. Predictions differ as to when such systems will be readily available.

Somewhat related to the question of voice input is the possibility of brain waves as input. This possibility was mentioned in an interesting speculation about the future of education in George Leonard's book, *Education and Ecstasy*[3], discussed later in this chapter. Research laboratories are showing some success in recognizing "vocabulary" through brain waves. The problem is not too different from the problem of recognizing speech; both are pattern recognition activities on complex waveforms.

Several systems already support a different type of audio output, music of quite decent quality. Computer music has a long history on larger systems and is an excellent way of expanding people's imagination about what a computer is "good for."

Personal Computers as Development Systems

While our emphasis has been on delivery systems for computer-based learning, we need to say something about hardware for developmental systems.

Additional capabilities are needed for development. First, a single disc drive is not adequate. Further, we will require a hard copy device in the developmental stage.

Going beyond this, we can ask whether the personal computer, acting alone, will be (particularly when one reaches large-scale production) an effective mechanism for developing the types of materials we are considering. The answer is probably *no*. One needs many of the capabilities of a larger system in such activity. Hence, it is likely that development will take place in a distributed environment with both personal computers and central machines. The central computer will be for massive storage of programs and other information, for management, for early testing of the material, and for resources beyond the capabilities of individual machines. It may be another central computer, with more storage.

However, at the present time, a properly equipped personal computer may be an effective developmental tool. As long as production is at a relatively small level, as it is at present, these tactics will be effective.

System-Supplied Software

By system software, we refer to the programs typically delivered with the machine as distinct from the software, to be described in the next section, that is particularly needed for computer-based learning activities. Such system software includes a wide variety of supplied components.

It is difficult to distinguish fully between software for delivery systems and software for production systems. Two strategies are possible with regard to production. The first is that one can produce material in a language also available on smaller delivery systems. The second possibility is that translators can take the materials developed and translate them into whatever facilities are needed for the target delivery systems. We will discuss primarily the first possibility, but it is not clear which will eventually become dominant.

A brief study of the current personal computer market shows a great variety of different systems. The language of most inexpensive current systems is BASIC. We regard BASIC as inadequate for developing computer-based learning materials, in its present forms on personal machines. Hence, our focus in this section will be on language capabilities other than BASIC.

A brief mention should be made of several common operating systems, although none of these will be discussed in detail. The first of these, which has assumed a very important role in the hobby market, is CP/M. Another system is Mini Unix, a version of the Unix system designed for small computers. A third system, available only for Digital Equipment Corporation hardware, is RT-11. Its expense makes it difficult to use with large numbers of personal computers.

The system to be described in more detail is that which we regard as the best at the present time for a personal computer developmental system and easily used for delivery. The system is the UCSD Pascal developed at the University of California, San Diego, by Kenneth Bowles and his colleagues. It runs on most widely available microprocessors. The system that we have been using at Irvine is the Terak 8510/a; the system is available on the Apple II personal computer. Western Digital makes a microcomputer designed to run the UCSD Pascal system. Texas Instruments has also announced the availability of UCSD Pascal.

Pascal is a newly developed language that takes into account recent ideas about structured programming, designed to lead to more efficient programming, fewer errors, and easier revision. There is some evidence that this promise is fulfilled with languages such as Pascal. Pascal is widely used for systems programming activity, another complex programming task. The development of Ada within the Department of Defense makes it seem likely that a Pascal-like language will become dominant in this area.

UCSD Pascal extends the capabilities of Pascal in two directions that are critical for computer-aided learning. The first is the provision of character strings as a built-in type. Since these programs depend primarily on analysis of student input, this is an important consideration. The second important aspect of UCSD Pascal, not available in most forms of Pascal, is the provision of graphic capabilities. We have already argued that graphics is essential in learning.

The UCSD Pascal system includes a screen-oriented editor and a filing system to manage the floppy disc. A command line is always present at the top of the screen. This line tells you which systems are accessible from the current location, making the system a relatively simple one to learn.

The editor deserves special attention. It is a very convenient way of manipulating either a program or a documentation file, providing capabilities similar to those in good word processing systems. Further details about the system are available from the San Diego group or from SofTech.

Finally, we should mention what may be the principal advantage of the UCSD system: it enables one to write materials that can easily be moved from one system to another, by providing a portable operating system. Previous attempts at portability have focused on languages. Since most sophisticated educational programs require features or capabilities that are not, strictly speaking, part of a programming language (e.g., external files), strict program portability means writing simple programs. More complex programs make assumptions about the operating system that are not true in other systems, and the programs are not easily portable.

Software for Computer-Assisted Learning

Various capabilities beyond the bare programming languages are needed to program computer-aided learning material efficiently. This section discusses these capabilities.

The most essential capability, beyond those of programming languages, is the *screen design* capability, the ability to construct information interactively on the screen. This refers to both the text and to the pictorial material. The authors or graphic designers should have complete control over the appearance of the screen. While early computer-aided learning material treated the screen as the page of a book, this approach limits the developer unnecessarily and unwisely. Visual appearance can have a considerable effect on the student, particularly in such problems as easing the reading difficulties often characteristic of contemporary students. The software needed can be learned quickly by a good applied artist or a graphic designer. The designer should be able to create ingredients, pictorial and text, move them around the screen, locate them, and in some cases change their size, and then ask the computer to present the material that way to the student. This capability has nothing to do with the program logic, provided at a later stage by programmers. But it does contain much of what passes for code, carrying out perhaps 75% of the actual number of lines in a program in our present material. Descriptions of our current (timesharing) system are available.

Our timesharing system was developed for graphic displays that did not allow selective erase. Hence, the new system we are developing for personal computers has many capabilities not possible in the older system. Already available is an extensive capability for controlling the text on the screen. Various areas on the screen, called textports, can be defined, many at one time. Within these areas, the computer formats the textual material in ways specified by the designer or programmer. Thus, the designer can ask for the material within a particular textport to be right-justified. The text will be automatically placed within the "window" when the program is run. The designer can specify various scrolling conditions, allowing continual writing within a particular port.

A major advantage of the textport system is the role it can play in transporting materials to other personal computers. Instead of having to reformat all the vast amounts of alphanumeric information within the program, it will only be necessary to change the definition of the textports in most situations.

Additional capabilities to carry out the common functions involved in computer-based learning activities will also be required. These procedures will be similar to those already available in many existing computer-based learning systems, so they will not be discussed further. They should fit naturally into the language environment in which they are developed.

Advice

This section offers some advice to someone just starting in this area. Some of the points will be repetitions but are included for emphasis.

1. *Develop and Keep Long-Range Goals*. Given the rapidly evolving technology and the changing nature of the market, any development that only looks at short-range activities will be in difficulty.

2. *Be Imaginative*. Don't be confined by what has been done before or premature concern about how to do some things.

3. *Work in Groups and with Other Groups if Possible*. The problem is a large problem, and one that is likely to be able to make a more significant impact if individual workers join together into

sizable groups, either formally or informally. Different people have different ways of presenting materials, anticipating different student reactions, and allowing a richness and breadth of outlook few individuals can match.

4. *Don't Start at Square One.* Investigate what has already been done in this area, what has already been learned. People in the area seem particularly prone to beginning all over again. Some of the "newer" materials for home use in arithmetic on personal computers go back to the earliest days of computers in education.

5. *Consider Pedagogical Problems Independent of Programming Problems.* Avoid the "rush to code." Good material involves careful planning and educational design. Writing the actual code is a much later and less demanding step, if the proper groundwork is laid. The first question is "*What* is to be done?" not "How can it be programmed?"

6. *Revise.* Plan to revise your work. This means, among other things, paying great attention to documentation on all levels, from choice of identifiers and key words to descriptions of what the materials, uses, and objectives are.

7. *Avoid BASIC.* Although many present systems are BASIC-only systems, we have already expressed our serious qualms about BASIC as a language for developing complex material, computer-based or any other. Different types of BASIC differ widely. While the BASIC being proposed by the BASIC standards committee would alleviate some of the problems, it is not at all clear which personal computers will follow these quite different BASIC rules.

8. *Avoid Today's Minimal Systems.* The problem with working with a minimal system today is that, given the rapid advance of the technology, it will be a completely outmoded system in 1 or 2 years. Hence, a developer needs to be looking ahead, asking about the minimal systems a few years ahead.

9. *Avoid Tape Cassette-Based Systems.* The principal issues are unreliability and lack of true random access.

THE EDUCATIONAL POSSIBILITIES OF INTELLIGENT VIDEODISCS

A possible form of an educational system combining the home videodisc with computer technology is outlined in this article, particularly with regard to the way it could be utilized in learning environments. We review the advantages and problems with current uses of computers in education and how these could be solved with the proposed new intelligent videodisc.

Computers are now used relatively little as learning devices, in spite of considerable discussion about the topic. But during the next 25 years, we will see a transition to greater usage of computers, until they become one of the dominant modes of learning. This article presents one possible mode of evolution, based on the use of the intelligent videodisc.

The intelligent videodisc is an intimate blend of two technologies. One is the technology behind the home videodisc, such as that developed by Philips and MCA. Information is recorded in a plastic disc, within grooves, and this information is read by a laser or other light source.

(Other technologies, using other means of reading, are less suitable to this application.) The second technology is current computer technology, particularly large-scale integration and newer logic and storage media. The intelligent videodisc combines both technologies, with the computer driving the videodisc. The videodisc will be randomly accessible, and the "information" of various types will be obtainable at any moment during the interaction. The device will be self-contained; when a student turns it on, the computer program will immediately be in control and will start the lesson.

Current Advantages of Computers in Instruction

To set the stage for a discussion of how such an intelligent videodisc might be employed in future educational learning systems, I begin by reviewing the present advantages the computer has in assisting students in learning.

The first advantage, not always realized, is the *level of interaction* possible. The distinction is between an active medium, with students constantly interacting while learning, and a passive medium, with students reading or being told something but making no active contribution of their own. The typical passive mode is the lecture, where it is impractical for students to interrupt to any great extent; the lecture continues on its own pace independent of what is happening in the minds of listening students. Not all current computer-based modules display a high level of interaction, with students as active participants, but the best show the inherent possibilities.

Closely related is *individualizing education*, particularly in large group environments. The book looks the same to every student who uses it. Some individualization can come with a programmed text. The computer allows individualization impossible or difficult to achieve with printed media, lecture, or videotape, reacting to individual backgrounds, previously acquired knowledge, and desires of individual students. Such individualization is available if the individual student interacts with an instructor, but in a large class environment, the instructor cannot spend many hours a week with each student.

A third advantage is that the computer can be a creator of experiences. Particularly in higher education, the student has little direct experience relative to the material studied. A typical example would be a beginning student in Quantum Mechanics, where the experimental evidence is far from everyday experience. Simulations on the computer can create a rich range of experiences, and so give students the same ability to learn on the basis of experience that they had in elementary school.

We can also furnish for the student an intimate blend of learning and testing materials, again in a way characteristic of the interaction between individual students and faculty. The testing can be prescriptive, determining what is necessary for the student in the next stage of learning.

The computer can also be a powerful aid in learning problem-solving capabilities, both through the use of programming languages, and therefore more sophisticated and more interesting problems, and also through direct teaching of problem-solving skills. Among scientists and engineers, problem-solving is often the major educational objective.

Finally, the computer can contribute toward record-keeping and course management with very large numbers of students, nontrivial problems even today.

Current Problems of Computers in Instruction

Surveying present computer-based learning activities suggests problems that would need to be overcome with any future systems, such as the intelligent videodisc system.

The major current problem is the lack of good learning materials in many academic areas. The problem is found at all levels. Hence, the questions of how we are to generate such materials is pressing and immediate.

Related to this is the lack of good marketing mechanisms. We cannot expect large numbers of people to generate computer-based learning modules unless an active way of getting them into the hands of large numbers of students is available. Although one very successful marketing effort at the elementary level has taken place (Patrick Suppes' drill-and-practice materials) and although Control Data is marketing PLATO material, we still have much to learn about how to market computer-based learning material.

A third, and again related factor, is that very few locations can deliver computer-based learning materials to students on a large-scale basis. Typically in higher education, the universities own or lease the computer systems that students use. But very few universities are now equipped for more than token use of the computer in education. You can see this quickly in an example. At the University of California, Irvine, in the fall quarter of 1976, we employed in the Physics 3A course 6,700 terminal hours in a 10-week quarter. Remember that this is just a single course! Few universities are in a position to provide even one course of this type for students. If we were to ask how many universities could be teaching dozens of courses at this level, the answer would be none! So even if much good material were already developed, and even if we had good marketing procedures, the problem of delivery would be with the universities.

Another current problem is the lack of widespread skills in developing such material. As with any new media, we can only slowly and carefully, with much experimentation, learn what is effective. We are currently in the process of gaining such experience; the material produced in the last few years is superior in effective use of the medium than the material produced 10 years ago. But the process has far to go. Much of our best current material will look crude in 10 years. Practice and experience are essential.

Although recently most of the leaders in developing computer-based educational material have extensively used graphics capability, arguing that it is essential in educational environments, we still have poor graphics capabilities. Very few current systems provide a full range of color, and very few provide a high level of animation. Very few provide the graphics of surfaces, as opposed to the graphics of lines. Color, full animation, and surfaces are all possible within current technology, but their costs have prevented even tentative explorations of wide usage for learning. Such explorations are essential to work toward future materials, where these limitations will certainly be overcome.

Most computer-based learning systems of today do not use a full range of media. Thus, while some systems show slides and others have had audio facilities available, we are only beginning to achieve the combination of all these plus videodisc facilities in a well-engineered, easily maintainable unit. Based on student response at a given point, a computer-based learning program should be able to show a video sequence and perhaps repeat sections of that sequence if later testing shows students have not achieved the desired learning objectives.

Solutions Through the Intelligent Videodisc

The videodisc, plus the rapidly developing computer technology, offers a feasible route to solving the problems raised above, and therefore to much wider use of the computer as an educational device.

The system that I have in mind would be primarily a stand-alone system, one that contains within the same "box" a processing unit, fast memory, some writeable slower memory, and the videodisc. The videodisc would be a source of slides, audio sequences, video sequences, and computer code, all randomly accessible under the control of the computer program. The discs are inexpensive, and as they will be almost indestructible and difficult to duplicate, they will offer reasonable ways of distributing and selling.

I would expect the production of the learning materials that go on the disc would occur in several centers around the country, perhaps in competition with each other. Research indicates that a more structured way of production, involving a variety of talents—pedagogical, educational, psychological, graphic, and programming—are essential in producing the best material (see Chapter 6). These production centers might rely on timesharing systems, or some variant of them, since the material must be very well tested before it can be pressed into the fixed form of a videodisc.

We would expect too that marketing groups would develop. Some of these might come out of conventional book publishing activities, since they are already familiar with the educational market. But new types of distribution companies may become dominant. We would expect royalty mechanisms based on amount of usage or sales.

Although the intelligent videodisc will operate primarily in the stand-alone environment, it would have the capability of tying into other machines for particular purposes through telephone lines or advanced communication procedures. A variety of needs, not handled by the local computational capability, could be satisfied. If, for example, the student is to receive credit for work performed, even if the system is in the home or in a public library, some mechanism must exist for recording progress on performance criteria tests in the material. Individual students may require guidance based on progress relative to other students through this material, material that might be dynamic and therefore could not be put on any one disc. There might be need to access rapidly changing or extremely large data bases, data bases available on a central machine. There might be need occasionally for massive computational capability beyond that available at the local level.

Examples of Learning Discs

In sketching examples of videodiscs that might be marketed, I confine my attention to beginning Physics, as this is an area well known to me. Similar discs and ideas would be applicable to other areas; the reader will undoubtedly imagine possibilities for his or her own area beyond those suggested.

First, we would expect a long series of full multimedia learning modules covering the beginning course, an extension of the best current computer-based instructional material. These would be at a variety of levels and would make different assumptions about mathematical backgrounds of students. These assumptions would not be known to the students; internal prescriptive testing would lead to decisions, rather than questions of whether students had "credit" for previous courses.

The environment in which these learning discs would be employed would be such that students given credit for a *particular* beginning Physics course would not all study the same material. We are already experimenting at Irvine successfully with a multi-track beginning Physics course, with students having choice of content. We can provide this freedom because of the availability of different types of computer-based learning modules. I would expect the videodisc strategies to allow a great expansion in such individualization of content toward the interests of the individual student.

Some of the discs will contain testing procedures, an intimate blend of checking and learning as suggested. These discs would determine objectives the student cannot handle, and give immediate and specific help. If credit was desired, these tests would be recorded by access to a central record-keeping machine.

Some of the discs will also "contain" standard books, perhaps all the texts and auxiliary Physics books available. Books are still valuable learning resources for many students.

The computer would enable us to improve books as currently available. First, the book-disc could contain a better index, one that cross references a large collection of Physics books rather than a single Physics book. Since individual videodiscs in the current format hold up to 50,000 "pages," such multi-book indexing would become very useful. ("Page" on the videodisc is not equivalent to book page because of resolution problems.) Other materials besides the books themselves might be built in, such as sections relating to the notation or units used in different books. Color diagrams could replace the usual ones found in ordinary books. The student could have greater control over the reading process than is now possible.

Another type of videodisc for the Physics course might have slides and video sequences of the *phenomena* of physics, providing the student with a rich background of phenomena appropriate to a theory to be considered. The fact that physical theories, or all scientific theories, arise out of experience is something that needs to be constantly stressed with students.

Some of the discs might be "enrichment" discs, bringing in a wide variety of related phenomena not directly concerned with the student's direct progress toward the objectives of the course, but allowing individualized study for students with interests in those directions. Thus, we would expect that a Physics course might have such material concerning the structure, discovery, and sociology of scientific knowledge, and might also build collections of interesting but usually unmentioned phenomena.

Related to this, but in a more structured way, would be videodiscs that provide students with structured experiences based on computer simulations. The beginning Physics student has not seen planets move around single suns, or around binary stars, because these experiences are not accessible in the everyday world. The student has not seen systems move in phase space. Such experiences, controllable worlds, are easily generated through computer simulation; they lead to a much richer range of experiences for the student.

Physics students can also use computing itself, in the form of writing programs to study physical problems, as an important aid in the study of physics. Here the computer is being used as an intellectual tool, an expander of intellect, enabling the student to study more realistic and difficult problems and to more quickly see the full power of the laws of physics. Thus, one disc might have on it Pascal or APL, complete with learning sequences to help the student learn the language, and testing sequences (with diagnostic aid) to check whether the knowledge acquired is adequate. So the intelligent videodisc could be employed in the traditional computer problem-solving mode within the Physics course.

Schools?

These intelligent videodisc systems might be in the home, public libraries, or other widely available facilities. Today most education below adult education, public school and higher education, takes place in formally organized and geographically concentrated organizations.

However, such educational successes as The Open University of Britain already indicate the possibility for decentralizing parts of the educational process. The intelligent videodisc will make *possible* a greater degree of decentralization. Hence, the question of whether this decentralization is a useful one, or whether we should still maintain schools, at least to some degree, will be an important issue to be resolved in the next 25 years. Schools in their present form may not survive in the future.

THE INTELLIGENT VIDEODISC

The combination of the small personal computer and the optical videodisc, with suitable interface, presents the educational community with major new possibilities and challenges. Although prototype projects involving hardware and curriculum development are already started, they only address a very small range of learning possibilities, and they will not provide enough experience on which to base a production system for producing sizable amounts of learning material. Previous experience with either film production or computer-based learning production can be important in furnishing the necessary background and providing the basic materials. A major question for the future concerns media choice. For some situations, the computer alone will be the delivery system of choice. For others, the intelligent videodisc will be important. Economic factors will play a role in this decision.

Third International Learning Technology Congress and Exposition, SALT.

About 7 years ago, when I first saw early demonstrations of early optical videodisc systems, I was heavily engaged in extensive development of a wide range of computer-aided learning material. A limitation of such material was that it could not call upon, except in rather crude and difficult ways, a full range of multimedia learning capabilities such as films, slides, and sound. When I saw the videodisc, I realized that it offered the possibility of providing such a range of media. At that point, I coined the term "intelligent videodisc" to represent the intimate combination of the videodisc and the computer, combined to provide an effective educational delivery system for a wide range of students.

Now, a number of years later, the possibilities of such a combination are being widely discussed, and all over the world a number of active projects are proceeding to develop the initial materials using this capability. The intelligent videodisc presents us, I will argue, with great promises and great difficulties. It will be many years before we are in a position to fully use the technology, and in the present article I hope to show you why this is the case. I will assume familiarity with the general notion of the videodisc, which has been discussed in the preceding article.

Some review of the videodisc's major features, however, is desirable. We can view the videodisc from either a technical or a pedagogical point of view. The important technical features are:

1. The storage of a large amount of information on the disc;

2. A variety of types of information, including video sequences, slides, audio, and computer code;

3. The possibility of rapid random accessibility for any of these segments;

4. An inexpensive medium, less expensive than magnetic tape.

I do not wish to imply that all the problems have been overcome in placing these media together on a single disc. In particular, problems with combining computer code with the other media still need to be solved.

The most important pedagogical feature of the videodisc has already been mentioned: it allows us to bring in all the learning media, allowing us to pick the best possibilities for each student and for each situation. The major contribution of the computer component is interaction. The intelligent videodisc can provide a medium every bit as interactive as that provided by the best current material that employs the computer alone.

Incorrect Approaches

The intelligent videodisc can be used in a wide variety of ways. Certain modes of using the disc debase the possibilities, and perhaps even could freeze us into unfortunate choices and so affect later uses of such systems. Many possible errors are ones that have already been made with computers or with other new learning media as they have been introduced.

The first problem with any new medium is that people tend to produce materials that are imitations of those produced with older learning media, with minor variants and additions. We see many examples of computer-aided learning that are like books, with only occasional use of the basic interactive capabilities of the computer and with no use of the dynamic capabilities of the computer with regard to such aspects as text and pictorial display. Perhaps this is only natural. We are all prisoners of our past efforts, particularly when these efforts have been successful in the arena in which they were developed. One example of a poor imitation of older media is to repeat lectures in newer media, such as films or on computer displays. This can be done in a variety of forms. The film, for example, can just show a lecture, or it can show a "blackboard" with someone talking. Unfortunately, many learning films are of this "talking head" on the screen; we still have a highly imitative medium. We can allow students to review a particular section as often as possible, but most of the interactive capabilities of the computer are lost in a lecture-type presentation.

Another incorrect approach to learning materials is to place technological considerations first. There is a great tendency to do this, since many of the developers are fundamentally technologists and only secondarily educators. It is easier to specify and build hardware and software than it is to tackle the tough problems of providing the best possible learning environment. So it is not surprising that often technology will dominate. But this is the wrong approach. We should always begin with the learning problems and allow the authoring team the greatest possible freedom in coping with these problems. Authors of computer-based material or intelligent videodisc materials must not be put in a straight-jacket, with only limited capabilities, but should be given almost complete freedom.

Another possible incorrect approach is that of ignoring one of the two capabilities, computer or videodisc. Thus, it is possible to produce video material with a minor overlay of computer, or to produce computer material with a minor overlay of the visual medium added. In some situations, this may be the best approach, but such a tactic often represents the limitations of developers, the types of background they have had.

Finally, a major problem is that an approach may well be an unreasonable or incorrect approach because it is underfunded. Many of the present projects are underfunded in terms of the tasks they should be carrying out.

Possible Reasonable Approaches

What can we say in a more positive vein? We have already laid the groundwork in discussing incorrect approaches to producing intelligent videodisc material.

The first important lesson is that we should put our emphasis on the learning situation, starting with real learning problems and considering the possibility of *all* media to aid in their solution. The question of media choice is still a difficult one, as I will comment later. The computer plus the videodisc—the intelligent videodisc—may not be the best choice or in many cases will not be the only choice. If we begin with learning problems, we will not freeze ourselves into an unfortunate media choice at the very beginning of the operation.

In the design of good material for the intelligent videodisc we will need *more* than an individual designer. In the cottage industry stage that has characterized much in the early development of computer-based learning material, often a single individual carried out the entire operation. But in the present situation, too many skills are involved to expect any one individual to be excellent in all of them. We must involve good teachers, screen designers, film designers, photographers, editors, programmers, and evaluators if we are to produce highly usable material. Thus, we need a team approach, a group of people working together at each stage. Even at the pedagogical stage, we believe it is not reasonable to assign this to a single individual. Rather the experiences of a group of individuals, typically two or three in our case, need to be pooled to produce highly effective modules for a wide range of students.

The team approach is not new. We see it exemplified in major curriculum development efforts around the world. The most impressive is that at The Open University in England. While one might quibble with what they have done (and they have certainly not produced any intelligent videodisc material), the general strategies and the scale of effort conducted at The Open University seem highly appropriate to the task we are considering. Other good examples also exist. In this country, the University of Mid-America engages in the full production process needed for good intelligent videodisc materials.

An efficient production system, one that will produce extremely good material at the least possible cost, is a critical aspect. To some extent we could also compare the process to that used in producing books, where again a production system involving many individuals from the author through typesetters, printers, etc., is necessary in the process.

The production team can start in many ways. One possibility is to begin with existing, extremely good computer-based learning material. In this situation, the design team would then ask where visual information—slides and films—or audio information, would improve the learning situation for students. It appears that none of the existing projects is taking this point of view. It should be expected to produce highly interactive material, if the initial computer material is good. So such an approach has great promise, particularly for computer material that has been well evaluated.

The contrary approach begins with extremely good visual material. Unfortunately, the standards of design of many educational films and video materials have very poor visual quality. Only occasionally have the great filmmakers been involved with educational material. Yet good materials that have proved effective for students do exist. These can then be chopped apart and fitted into a computer-based learning sequence which allows their interactive use. The added computer sequences can query students as to what they are learning at each stage, perhaps with small on-line tests, and will provide alternate learning sequences for those people for whom the visual information alone is inadequate. This is the approach taken at WICAT, where an existing biology film was the basis. Robert Fuller's activity at the University of Nebraska is making use of such effective physics teaching materials as the Tacoma Narrows Bridge film loop.

Finally, the obvious next possibility is the full approach, where we design both the visual and interactive computer materials from the beginning as part of the same design process. The process of carrying out a fully competent job here would be a more difficult one. It would involve the costs of producing extremely good film material that one has in the best educational films, and so would not be inexpensive. This approach is an important one to pursue.

Problems to be Considered

We are a long way from producing the best material that we will eventually be able to produce for the intelligent videodisc. Many major problems are still to be overcome. Some of these are the more obvious technical problems already referred to, but the most important and interesting problems are related to pedagogical aspects. It is those problems that I will now consider.

First, we need more research. Several types of research are needed. We need fundamental research into the learning process, research that is independent of a particular learning medium. We have a number of competing theories in the literature today about how learning takes place, and none of these theories gives a complete view of the learning process. Nevertheless, some of these approaches are proving to be extremely fruitful. For example, the insights provided in modern cognitive psychology in understanding the manipulation of material within the brain in terms of models of the information is important. Another important set of insights comes from the study of developmental stages in progress and the resulting effect it has on such factors as providing a wide range of experience for students to learn. A third set of insights comes from the mastery learning enthusiasts, insights that insist that detailed feedback for each student is critical.

In addition, we need media-oriented research on the unique capabilities of such learning media as the videodisc and the computer. As mentioned, we tend to use these media without too much thought in ways that are similar to the older media, but they are very different media.

As an example of the differences, I consider one problem: how the material is to appear on the screen of an intelligent videodisc. I discuss the material stored in computer code form, but similar considerations apply to other visual components. The computer screen is *not* a page of a book. It differs in many ways from a book. For example, blank space on a computer screen is free and can be used as a pedagogical element. In a book, blank space costs money. The book has no timing considerations. When the page is turned, the full page stares at the student. We can control the time in many different ways on the screen, providing a dynamic reading medium which we could never do in any other form until the advent of the modern computer. We still do not understand all the factors involved, and much research is needed even in such a specialized area as this.

The unsettled commercial situation again presents problems, although of a different nature from those discussed. We already have a number of competing videodisc systems on the market, and we do not have anyone yet marketing a full combination of the computer plus videodisc (although we might expect that DISCOVISION ASSOCIATES formed by MCA and IBM might have products in that direction). One of the videodiscs that may be a major contender in the home market, the RCA system, may not be usable as an intelligent videodisc. It has a needle that rides on the groove, making rapid random access unlikely. The wear on such a system may make it an expensive medium. Optical systems, although related, are to some extent incompatible with each other. Thus, the MCA system, the Magnavision (Philips) system, the Thompson CSF system, and the Ardev system are by no means identical.

A problem with any new medium is that little practical experience is available in instructional design employing such a medium. Naturally this experience must be gained slowly, with many attempts. Thus, although we have been developing computer-based material for 20 years, it is only recently that we are beginning to gain the experience that leads to effective production systems. Unfortunately, the lack of such practical experience can become extremely limiting, restricting greatly what can happen. Many proposed authoring systems do not allow the full range of capability in the medium, but restrict the medium in ways that are unfavorable in terms of the possible results.

Little experience in developing materials and therefore little material developed implies that we have very little student experience in using such material. Using material with a few students in very selected environments with the developers present and consciously or unconsciously offering aid is very different from full formative and summative evaluation of the material with widespread student use. Even with computer-based learning sequences, with their much longer period of development, relatively few full-scale classes in the United States or anywhere in the world routinely make heavy use of computer-based learning material. Recently I put together a session describing such courses at a meeting of the Association for Computing Machinery, with courses at Irvine (Physics), University of California, San Diego (Computer Science), and Stanford (Logic). But there are not many other examples of full-scale courses, and so even there student experience is limited. With intelligent videodiscs, it is almost nil. I am unhappy about proceeding to full-scale production without extensive student experience. Developers of material have often been wrong in the past; it is the students who keep us honest.

Finally, we still have little reliable information about the effective choice of delivery system. It seems only reasonable that the intelligent videodisc system will not always be the system of choice of a particular application. Rather, we would expect the media choice to be application and student-dependent with choices differing in different situations. In many places in science education, for example, little would be gained by adding the visual medium. In these situations the computer alone, a cheaper delivery system than the intelligent videodisc, would probably be a better choice. On the other hand, I can conceive of situations where the visual information does play an important role. For example, many areas of biology, where one can see things that are not available to the naked eye through instrumentation or through changing time scales, offer interesting possibilities. With students who are in the concrete operational stage, we would expect too that real life examples, video sequences of actual phenomena, would play an important role in materials, and so we would need both the computer and the videodisc. As with many of the other problems raised, the final need is for greater experience and based on this effective ways of choosing appropriate media.

The Future

Each of the problems discussed suggests routes we need to explore for the future. But we may not have time to explore carefully all these routes. The press of developments may overtake us and force us into precipitous choices, choices that will have long-range effects on the educational system.

We are moving into an entirely new educational system. During the next 25 years we will see changes not only in the typical delivery of educational material but in the nature of the institutions that we refer to as schools. The major mechanism for this change will be the computer, sometimes alone, sometimes in combination with the videodisc.

One problem is that there is so little vision at the present as to what would be a *desirable* future. We cannot expect to move toward effective futures without consideration of what we would like an educational system to do. Some efforts of this kind exist, but far too little.

The critical factor in determining this development will be that of the entry of large companies or government-supported institutions into the production and distribution of computer-based learning materials or intelligent videodisc learning materials. This still is perhaps 5 years away, although it is difficult to say exactly. Many companies are interested, and some are already actively working. With the entry of many large companies at a sizable level, our freedom of choice is likely to be very much restricted. They will determine later directions.

The possibilities for improving the educational system are great, but we have a long way to go. Our future is not necessarily a bright one.

THE EXTENDED UNIVERSITY VIA COMPUTERS

A survey article by Albert J. Morris, "An Overview of the Extended University," appeared in *T.H.E. Journal*[4]. This article dealt with an important topic and gave a report on efforts undertaken so far. But it was too restrictive, precluding computer-based technology. It did not treat sufficiently the major problems associated with the use of television technology in the extended university environment. Computers in this environment, along with various other technologies, are dismissed in a sentence or two. My purpose is to argue that computers are highly relevant to the extended university, and so cannot be neglected in future planning.

The Open University in England is one of the most well carried out and successful extended universities. As I understand it, The Open University's problems with funding have to do with the fact that far more students would like to be involved in The Open University than can be accommodated. The experience of The Open University indicates that television is a smaller component of the students' studying time than was expected. The programs are broadcast over BBC, and are offered several times. But the student must be at the television set during one of the times when the program is given—there is no way of seeing it at the student's request. This violates one of the criteria for an extended university: allowing for individualized and self-paced instruction. There can be self-paced instruction only when the material is available precisely when the student needs it.

Reprinted by permission of *T.H.E. Journal*, vol. 3, no. 2.

This problem of limited availability is not restricted to The Open University; it is likely to be a major problem in any program that relies very heavily on television. The only delivery modes allowing TV to be employed at student demand are the videotape and videodisc.

The Future

It is critical to project ahead when thinking about possible forms of extended universities. We are not talking about an institution to be established tomorrow, although some extended universities already exist or are being developed. If we want to analyze the potentialities, we must leap ahead 5 to 10 years in technology, making reasonable estimates based on current technology.

The costs of developing effective materials are nontrivial, and they demand considerable expertise. For example, in The Open University it takes a year of work, by a sizable course team, and hundreds of thousand of dollars, to develop a single course. The results, The Open University courses, are good—I consider their course material, with some exceptions, superior to those produced in conventional modes. The sizable effort needed to produce extended university material also suggests a long time scale in thinking about extended universities, and emphasizes that we need reasonable assumptions about the future. It also argues that, because of the high developmental cost, we should set our sights high.

Computers Versus Television

Let me now compare computers and television as teaching media generally. I admit that I am biased toward computer usage, although I certainly would not rule out any learning facility.

The first question concerns cost. Here it is extremely important to look to the future as suggested. At the present time, we could argue the relative costs of television-based and computer-based learning environments. As with many other aspects of educational cost, the argument might depend on just how one did the bookkeeping. But it is entirely clear that in the quite near future the cost argument will favor the computer. Computing is the *only* technology for assisting learning that is currently *declining* rapidly in cost; all others are increasing. It is estimated that computer costs will decline by a factor of 10 over the next 7 years, and one sees even more striking predictions. Further, capabilities will increase. For example, an article by Gerald G. Smith [5] says: "Computer processes already can serve the necessary functions but will become still more powerful and considerably less expensive. Terminals able to accept voice commands, speak clearly, alter the input and output languages, accept touch signals, brief case size, will also be introduced within our decade." A new and very interesting piece of technology is available for television, the home videodisc systems; I will have more to say about those later. The computer will soon be competitive with *any* teaching media, no matter how the bookkeeping is done.

One difficulty in older attempts at using the computer in education was the lack of graphics. Here television was superior, because it could use the important components of learning that depend on visual imagery. But new student displays now make graphics practical in all educational environments. Furthermore, graphic displays are within the range of costs that do not make them prohibitive in learning applications with large groups.

One current handicap with computers is the relative lack of experience in employing computers in the learning environment. Television technology has been around longer than computers. It still plays a very minute role in higher education, probably no more than the role already played by the newer technology of computers. But it is true that we are only slowly learning to use computers effectively, and that more effort in this direction is required.

An important advantage of the computer is the potential flexibility of delivery. Unlike the situation described with broadcast television, the computer-based material is available at any hour of the day or night. Our records of usage of such materials at Irvine show very strikingly that often students are working in the small hours of the morning, a time that we usually do not think of a university as functioning, but a possibility we want to allow in a self-paced environment. If suitable home stations or stand-alone systems were widely available—and they do not seem very far away—the computer materials could be accessed from any home at any time. Hence, they could meet a great variety of student scheduling. Self-pacing is an important component of the extended university environment, and the computer provides an excellent self-paced delivery system.

The *major* advantage for computers is that they are an *active* medium as opposed to a *passive* medium. While a very limited amount of interaction could be built into a television program—pauses while the student tries to formulate a response, for example—the medium has nothing like the possibilities for interaction that the best computer-based learning materials are already exhibiting. A computer dialog can be extremely responsive to the needs and background of individual students, presenting a different learning experience for each person employing the program. Where students go is dependent on previous responses through the program, and perhaps in other programs too. Not all of our current computer material realizes these possibilities of individualization, but we are beginning to become more skilled in the process of developing such interactive student-computer dialogs. This issue, active learning medium versus passive learning medium, is the strongest single point in the present argument.

A Future Delivery System

Up to now I have compared computers with television as a learning medium, with particular reference to the extended university situation. Now I would like to discuss what an effective computer-based delivery system of the future might look like. I do not regard these requirements as insurmountable; they all can be met in a relatively brief period of time, from 5 to 10 years.

First, although I have argued the relative merits of computers, learning environments should provide students with all media; the developers of the material should decide which media to use in particular situations. Often a multimedia approach, with alternate modes of learning available, will be desirable, given different learning styles of students. We would like the approach to be highly individualized. Thus, a series of slides might be valuable for a certain student but not another. Or a videotape might be needed only in very few situations. All the common media, including video-based as well as computer-based media, should be available in learning systems of the future, in a form usable by any student. The full capabilities of computer-based learning should be readily available.

One problem that plagues both television and computer material at the present moment is that neither possesses all the mechanisms associated with the publishing of books. We need a publishing mode, with royalties available to authors, rival developments so that materials can compete in the marketplace, and marketing organizations. Whatever gadgets are built for education, the question of how the material is to be published and marketed is an important issue.

The devices of the future need to be inexpensive, particularly if they are going to become, as I would like, very common and highly accessible. These learning aids should be available in schools, in libraries, and, in the not-too-distant future, in homes. Hence, the individual devices cannot cost much.

These systems should provide full graphic capability, including full color. One thing that television has taught us is the importance of iconics in the learning process. Unfortunately we are still weak in learning how to use these nonverbal modes of education, but further experience will lead to better materials.

Realization

The system described in the above paragraph, a computer-based graphic system providing full multimedia access, is already possible. The rise of microcomputer and large-scale integrated circuitry technology has meant that it is possible to build computers at far lower cost, and in much less space. Individual stand-alone devices now have sophisticated computing power, but not the degree of sophistication and power that I am proposing. The field is developing rapidly and there is no doubt that it will continue vigorously.

This does not satisfy the multimedia requirements, however. How are we to bring other media, such as slides and television, into the computer-based system? The home videodiscs present a clear possibility. Although the videodisc was conceived primarily for home entertainment, or as a cheaper alternative to video cassettes, its potentialities in education are much greater. We could store on a single disc many video sequences, of arbitrary length, slides, audio sequences, and, even more important, *computer code* that would direct an elaborate individualized learning experience for students. This student experience would bring in video materials and other media just where they are necessary, giving individualized multimedia aid.

The discs also provide the publishable medium that is required. The production of the discs, the technology involved, is mostly understood. They can be marketed in the usual fashion, and are not expensive. They are difficult to pirate, since making such discs involves large equipment. Conventional book publishers or similarly organized concerns could handle this market, since it would not be too different from present book publishing once sizable numbers of systems are available.

Such intelligent videodisc systems, combining in one device computer capability and the videodisc, are not going to appear immediately. Neither technology is quite at the point that we need, but both are moving in the desired direction.

Systems of this kind are a much more interesting prospect for effective extended universities than purely television-based systems.

GEORGE LEONARD'S VIEW OF THE COMPUTER IN EDUCATION

Workers developing educational materials using the computer can, and often do, simply start where they are, with whatever equipment they can acquire, and chip away at courses.

However, effective long-range plans must be much more systematic and detailed. We can distinguish readily between short-range goals—what we are immediately trying to do with present projects—and long-range goals. Long-range goals can be formulated only if we decide how the future should be shaped. Individuals with strong views about the future, with powerful ideas about the role computers should play in education 20 or 25 years from now, can offer guidance and may well influence the future; a prophecy of this kind can be a self-fulfilling prophecy.

Relatively few people have attempted to view the future of computers in education. Developers who continue working where they are, with the equipment they have on hand, often become fierce defenders of that equipment, arguing its merits, rather than, perhaps more rationally, striving to improve it.

Science fiction has offered views of a computerized future that mention educational aspects, in such works as Arthur C. Clarke's *The City and the Stars*[6]. Often the views presented in such literature are hostile. For example, the computer-teacher in Zamatien's *We* [7] aids in dehumanizing the society.

George Leonard's *Education and Ecstasy*[8], shows a positive and extremely interesting view of the role computers may play in learning. This view is almost unknown to today's developers of learning materials employing the computer. Like all predictions, this must be taken with a grain of salt; Leonard suggests as much in the introduction to the two chapters of the book that will concern us. One of my friends has characterized the passages as romantic. I believe, nevertheless, that they do represent an interesting view of the future, even if time should prove them not entirely accurate.

Leonard's book combines two seemingly unrelated trends in modern society: the encounter group philosophy of such establishments as Esalen, and Skinnerian approaches to learning, particularly those involving the computer. In earlier didactic chapters, he brings these possibilities together while criticizing education as it exists today.

The main interest in *Education and Ecstasy* is in the chapters that portray a school of the year 2001. The description uses the fictional guise of a visit by parents to the school to watch the progress of their children. We get a panoramic view of the learning acitvity, and we see the overall "philosophy" underlying the school.

The learning structure pictured is completely dependent on the computer, and would be impossible without advanced technology. The computer technology depicted is graphic, employing large three-dimensional color pictures and sound, in addition to alphanumeric interactions.

The main arena for the knowledge-based forms of education is the Basics Dome. Students enter and leave freely; the school is unscheduled, stressing that students do not appear for "classes" at any particular time; there are no classes!

The students are 3 to 10 years old. After age 10, people are expected to know all the "basic" information, including Calculus! Since the time is free, enormous thought has to be given to motivational issues, so the students will want to do the necessary tasks, rather than be coerced to do them as is often the situation in schools today.

The educational view presented, the free learning view, is a natural extension of the self-paced or Keller plan ideas that are now coming into practice, with much more emphasis given to complete freedom from scheduling, and with the material much more highly individualized than at present.

Students entering the Basics Dome see a circular ring of computer consoles around the outer wall. Each has a keyboard, allowing access to all human symbols, not just the ASCII or APL set. The technology for allowing access to all symbols is available, but the standard displays today deny us this feature. Each student has headphones for audio messages. The display is a large three-dimensional hologramic display in full color. The displays touch each other at the edges, so that the room has a continuous band of pictorial information. This touching is more than simply physical; the computer is clever enough to have the displays interact, and information may spread over more than one display, moving and contracting. Furthermore, displays will have in their intermediate areas related aspects of what students at each of the stations are doing.

Students are identified to the computer by means of an electronic identification device, which they attach to the chair. This device also does queueing. The computer has complete records of students' efforts, so whenever students resume work it is ready. A session starts with review and then moves on to new items. The individual sessions are not long.

A sample session of language learning is sketched. As one would expect, this is difficult to do, and while, interesting, is perhaps one of the weaker features of the chapter. Writers about the future often have this problem. It is easier to imagine the overall structure than to delineate concrete details. This sketch is done much better in this book than in B. F. Skinner's *Walden Two*[9], where a great discrepancy separates the glowing philosophy and the mundane details.

Graphics play a vital role. Almost all of the current major educational developmental projects in the United States are graphics based. I regard it as an historical accident that earlier terminals were nongraphic, forcing users of the computer in learning situations to begin with nonpictorial formats. The role of pictures is well established in all educational processes, in a variety of levels. We could even argue that extensive nongraphic developmental work is a waste of time today. The future of computers in education will almost certainly be highly pictorial, allowing teachers to access to important nonverbal learning techniques.

The learning environment in *Education and Ecstasy* is a computer-managed environment, with the computer knowing the educational progress of each student and making judgments based on this knowledge within the learning material. Each student has a highly individualized learning sequence. This is a long-standing goal for computers in education, even though it remains difficult to achieve. We are now beginning to see systems that do this, systems where extensive memory of students' efforts and achievement both on and off the computer, is accessible to the program.

At least two aspects of the technology pictured are beyond anything possible today (and probably beyond what will be available in 2001). The first, in active use in the schools we visit, is the use of brain wave information within the learning dialogs. The headset that brings the sound also picks up brain patterns, allowing the computer to determine what the student is absorbing, whether the material needs to be reviewed, whether the program can accelerate.

The second advanced technological innovation, more radical and "criticized" by the "conservative" school director, involves direct brain manipulation, bypassing the senses entirely. The details are vague and it is not clear if the criticism is tongue-in-cheek or is the usual resistance to new educational developments. Contemporary readers are almost certain to approach this with apprehension; such future possibilities have been the subject of frightening fictional presentations, such as John Hersey's *The Child Buyer*[10]. It seems unlikely that any such technique would be in use in 25 years.

I hope I have encouraged at least some of you to read the book, which includes many more details.

How realistic is this view of the future? What alternative patterns are plausible? Alternative views have been expressed, both the view that the picture presented is much too radical a change to occur in 25 years and the view that changes will be much more drastic than those suggested. The notion that educational change occurs only slowly is ingrained, and does seem to have empirical basis. The vested interests in maintaining the system as it is are powerful. So desirable educational change is not rapid.

On the other hand, we are in a period of very rapid change in computer technology. Computers are becoming more economical while everything else is increasing in cost, promising that highly computerized educational systems will come into widespread use in the 1990's. Economic considerations alone will be an important factor in pressing for such change, provided viable materials can be developed in sufficient time.

This last factor, the existence of the pedagogical and programming skills discussed in *Education and Ecstasy*, is much more questionable than the hardware. None of our current computer-based education projects show such sophistication in computer use in educational situations, although many projects are striving to use computers more effectively. We still have a long way to go.

Even the hardware aspect is not entirely clear. The environment projected is a timesharing environment, with the central computer holding the record capabilities. There is probably local processing at the displays. Except for record-keeping and large data bases, future use will not be in the timesharing mode, but will tend toward sophisticated stand-alone machines. A striking aspect of recent technology has been the development of more compact computers. We have now many competing "computer-on-a-chip" assemblies which can be put together to form systems. This development of microcomputer technology will continue with units becoming cheaper, faster, and easier to assemble.

To think of today's personal computers is misleading. The power of such systems in the near future will be more comparable to that of very large contemporary computers, even though these systems will be largely self-contained and stand-alone. Modern video-based technology will, I believe, have great ramifications too; it also suggests the possibility of very powerful local processing. The local processor can drive displays without timesharing limitations, and interactive computer graphics can overcome the limitations of a 1200 baud connection.

George Leonard's view of the future is only one of many. But such speculation, such description of ideal future conditions in a broad and sweeping sense, is important for developers of computer-based material. It is easy to become frozen in the hardware and technology available at the moment, and so waste years of time preparing materials that will be obsolete when they are finished. Perhaps nowhere is the future shock phenomenon likely to be more important than in areas touched by the computer, because of the very rapid advances. Whether or not you accept George's Leonard's possibility, the need for thinking and speculation about the future is important for all of us.

INTERACTIVE LEARNING: MILLIKAN LECTURE, AMERICAN ASSOCIATION OF PHYSICS TEACHERS, LONDON, ONTARIO, JUNE, 1978

We are at the onset of a major revolution in education, a revolution unparalleled since the invention of the printing press. The computer will be the instrument of this revolution. Although we are at the very beginning—the computer as a learning device in current classes is, compared with all other learning modes, almost nonexistent—the pace will pick up rapidly over the next 15 years. By the year 2000, the major way of learning at all levels and in almost all subject areas will be through the interactive use of computers.

I do not intend to offer any full discussion of this impending revolution. Many of the factors involved go far beyond the question of computing. I will review those factors briefly.

Our colleges and universities will be drawing from 15% fewer high school graduates in 1985 than they did in 1975. Because of the development of a variety of alternate modes of education, the formal institutions of higher education—our institutions—will predictably be enrolling a smaller percentage of the high school graduates in 1985 than they are today. So enrollments will drop significantly. The demographic factors are not uniform across the country. In the U.S., the northeast and north central regions will sustain the greatest impact.

Coupled with decreasing numbers of high school graduates will be a shift in the nature of our student population. Harold L. Hodgkinson, at a conference on general education held by the University of California and the California State University and Colleges systems, commented that our students will soon be "older, poorer, and blacker" than our present students. Thus, many of the students will not be our "traditional" students, but will be students that Patricia Cross designates as "new" students[11]. These students are often very poorly served by our current strategies in higher education. Their presence will demand changes. Finally, universities all over the country are in trouble with the public, with increasing pressure to reduce the cost of education. Particularly in times of

The American Journal of Physics, vol. 47, no. 1.

economic difficulty, universities are increasingly vulnerable to this unfavorable political-social climate.

These factors will combine with the rise of the computer as an inexpensive and effective learning device, to bring about tremendous changes in our instructional institutions. These changes will not always be ones that we like. I will discuss briefly the types of change at the end of my comments. We can look forward to an exciting and demanding period.

Any view of radical changes in education should begin by asking some fundamental questions, with the hope of influencing these changes. What kinds of learning opportunities should we ideally provide to students in our university environment, particularly within our Physics courses? I will begin with such considerations. From this basis, I review the problems with our current courses. Then I discuss the role of the computer in the learning process with emphasis on the future.

What Should Education Be?

All of us come into our teaching experiences as the highly successful products of the existing education system. But I do not wish to start with what we do now but rather with an ideal view of the situation.

One way to begin is to consider education historically. If we go back very far in human experience, we see that most learning must have taken place as individuals interacted with the environment, generalizing on the basis of that interaction, or with individuals interacting with other people. The emphasis should be on the word "individual." The notion of formal learning situations is relatively new in human history.

This early learning was rich in experiences. We can get some view of it by noting a place in our society where it still happens, early childhood education. There education is often a natural outgrowth of play. Kenneth Eble, in *The Perfect Education*[12], queries this way: "Where does education begin? Surely it begins in play and continues in play for all of our lives." Play is a way of gathering, under highly motivating circumstances, a variety of experiences, possibly even focused experiences. An experiential base is a vital ingredient in the learning process.

Much of this information is visual. George Nelson, in *How to See*[13], discusses visual literacy, asking, ". . . how does it happen that young children, all of whom quite naturally absorb great quantities of visual information, grow up to be visually illiterate? The answer, as far as I can make out, is that this early capability is simply beaten out of them by the educational process."

One critical aspect of play is that it is always an active process. The child or the adult, engaging in games for learning or for pleasure, is playing an active role, constantly interacting with the environment and manipulating the environment. We cannot play passively!

The experiences of play are unique experiences for each individual. Each child does different things to the environment and obtains different results, even in group situations. Individuals do not play at a single fixed pace. We do not have to think long about play to see the instructional usefulness of those features just enumerated: experience, the active role of the student, and the individualization of the experience for each student. Most contemporary learning theorists, coming from a variety of approaches would see these as critical components. We see the same factors in the learning activities of primitive societies.

Although we often look upon the development of written language as a very positive step in human history, and in education, not everyone agrees. Plato, for example, in a story in one of the dialogs, describes the invention of writing as a catastrophe in human history, killing the oral tradition and killing mental training in remembering. In Plato's letter to the relatives and friends of Dion, he comments: ". . . every man of worth, when dealing with matters of worth, will be far from exposing them to ill feeling and misunderstanding among men by committing them to writing . . . if one sees written treatises composed by anyone . . . these are not for that man the things of most worth, if he is a man of worth. . . ." However, most of us would feel that writing was a major advance.

A new mode of learning came into prominence in Greek times, seen in its best form in the Socratic dialogs in the works of Plato. To some extent this interactive process, the dialog, was a formalization of early learning by interacting with others. The "teacher" played a special role. The teacher did not tell things but rather tried through a series of carefully formulated questions to lead the student to understanding. Eble[14] comments about this process as follows: "The Socratic method, dialectic, is one of the inheritances from the classical past that is essential to maintaining the dynamics of learning. Basically it is a method of arriving at a firm answer to a series of focusing questions that rests on an even more basic assumption that thought must be exercised in order to develop. It also implies that answers to questions are best arrived at through this strenuous kind of questioning."

In Greek times, the lecture also became prominent. Plato did not think highly of this idea, but it has become almost a dominant educational delivery mode.

The invention of the textbook was also a critical moment in education. Here, we go back to the introduction of printing in the west. It is significant, in thinking about our current scale of development, that 200 years elapsed between the invention of the printing press and the extensive use of textbooks within formal institutions of education.

Many of these "recent" educational innovations occurred not so much because of their educational desirability but rather as responses to the increasing problems of educating very large numbers of people. The notion of one-to-one student-teacher interaction still is held in great esteem, but this type of interaction, Socratic or otherwise, is seldom realizable given the millions of students in schools and universities.

We can approach the question of what education should be in many directions other than historical. For example, we can examine courses to determine their deep objectives. I am not thinking of the objectives in the sense of specifying carefully for each individual unit just what the student is to learn—a necessary development in any rational curriculum organization—but rather our hidden agenda.

One way to seek deep objectives is to see what is tested. The vast majority of the testing in science courses is based on problem-solving. The ability to increase the student's problem-solving skills is the major hidden agenda in science teaching, one of the abilities we hope students will retain from our courses long after they have forgotten particular statements of physics.

Another underlying objective guides many courses in the sciences. We are very much concerned in teaching not simply the details by the methodologies of how we arrived at these details. Knowledge for most of us is not archival but, rather, is evolving. We hope to foster the growth of people who will be able to further this evolution in the next generation. We hope to show students too that these methods are relevant outside the formal study of science.

Problems with Our Current Situation

I suspect that many of you are beginning to feel uncomfortable by the ideal description I have just given of what is "good" in education. The difficulty is clear. Most of our courses are far from the ideal learning situation. The vast majority of Physics courses at the present time are lecture-based courses, often lectures to very large groups. Physics is not unique; this situation prevails in most academic areas.

Reasonable experimental evidence indicates that the lecture, while having advantages with regard to motivation and role modeling, conveys information poorly. But our courses do not seem to take this evidence into account. Given scientists' commitment to the empirical process, it seems ironic that they are so unlikely, in a statistical sense, to pay attention to research on how learning takes place. I do not want to claim that this research is always marvelous. As a whole it is of poor quality. Nevertheless, we cannot as scientists dismiss all of it just because some is poor.

Another characteristic feature of the contemporary situation is the dominance of the published textbook. Only a few books account for most of the courses in each discipline. This by itself is not an objectionable idea. Certainly reading is one of the major ways to learn, although many of our students have difficulty learning this way. But the textbook situation in the last several years has taken on an unhealthy complexion, one that has been little noted within the academic community. Standard publishers tend to refuse to publish a textbook that departs even in minor ways from the existing successful textbooks. How many new textbooks do you see published that do not use "SI" units? How many new textbooks introduce significantly different ways of approaching the subject area? How many textbooks recognize the existence of the computer? How many textbooks discuss topics different from all the others? In all these cases the answer is "very few."

Conservatism among textbook publishers is a recent development. In the past they have published books that were very radical for their own times, such as Sears and Zemansky and Halliday and Resnick. How ironic it is that these previously radical books are now a major deterrent to new ideas in the teaching of Physics! The difficulty arises from several factors. The declining economic situation in the textbook industry a few years ago made publishers much more cautious. They moved into a "marketing" strategy with study of "successful" books and with extensive surveys sent out in advance asking what the content should be. Such surveys yield a least common denominator; any idea not accepted by most current teachers will be excised from the eventual book. We cannot expect books generated out of surveys to develop radically new ideas.

Hence, the current method of publishing textbooks is antithetical to cultivating exciting new approaches. We need to bring this problem to the attention of the commercial textbook industry. Perhaps we will have to resort to models such as the Teachers Insurance Annuity Association (TIAA) in insurance, with universities banding together to form profit or nonprofit corporations to fill the void left by the commercial publishers' abdication.

Another difficulty in our current situation is the meager resources we provide for students to learn problem-solving. I have already noted that problem-solving, as judged by how we test students, is a major component of our courses.

Our method of teaching problem-solving in most courses is a "follow me" approach, with examples of solved problems in books or similar examples displayed by instructors or teaching assistants on the blackboard. In most cases, students do not see the solution of problems, but only the polished product of the solution, the building with the scaffolding removed. Everything happens magically, in exactly the right progression. Students working at home later discover that their problems do not work out in this neat logical fashion! This is no surprise to us. We know that the solutions to problems are not typically neat and logical at first. No clear presentation of the process of solving problems exists in most of our courses.

This type of information, however, does exist. In a variety of books, such as George Polya's *How to Solve It*[15], explicit heuristic strategies for problem solving are developed. But very few of our courses expose students to these strategies.

Many of our courses use primarily passive learning methods through lectures and books, most often keeping students within a fixed pace rather than letting them proceed at their own rate. Physics has pioneered in the use of variable-paced techniques. But these techniques are still in relatively little use in spite of research supporting them, summarized in articles in the *American Journal of Physics*[16]. Again, the problem is not with our "good" students, who can be counted on to go beyond the required material, but rather with the majority of students.

Another problem with our courses is that they are too verbal, too restricted to teaching people to repeat material. While this is a successful mode with some students, it is a barrier to others. Many faculty members have difficulty recognizing this problem, because they are highly verbal. But many students require more visual or other aids in the learning process, aids that are not stressed in our learning materials. The new students of the future will require still more nonverbal learning modes.

This situation is particularly bad in courses such as the physical science survey. This course, often taught to prospective teachers, gives a false impression about what science is all about; rather, it perpetrates the notion that science is a miscellaneous collection of odd pieces of information, "revealed" information not to be questioned. Given the number of elementary teachers who have had such courses it is not surprising that they misrepresent science when they teach it in the elementary schools. This is a major national problem, demanding our attention.

The notion of where terms in a scientific theory come from, how they are connected with experience, the notion of overall structure of scientific theory, the notion of scientific models and how they are used, and the notion of operational definitions and the relations of terms to experience are missing from many courses.

Many of us are aware of a newly discovered problem that plagues our current courses. Typically, we have assumed that our students are all capable of abstract or formal reasoning. But recent extensive experimentation, reported in the *American Journal of Physics*, and elsewhere, indicates that many of our students are still deficient in important characteristics of formal reasoning[17]. Yet almost all of our courses assume such capability on the part of the students. Thus, we are in the unfortunate position of teaching courses that are inherently unreachable by perhaps a third of our students in those courses.

I could go on; I have not covered all the ills of American education. I refer everybody interested to the many insightful papers of Arnold Arons for a fuller discussion[18].

What Can We Do with Computers?

Does the computer represent learning modes that will overcome some kinds of problems that I have emphasized? How is the computer to offer us anything new? One way to approach the problem is to talk about all the different ways in which the computer can be employed within the learning process. There is not a single unique way, but a whole variety of ways, bearing on different aspects of some of the problems just identified.

I should like to make it clear immediately that I do not consider all current uses of computers in education as progressive or even as pointing to useful future directions. Much of the existing computer material is less than impressive. As with any new and powerful learning medium, we are at an early stage of learning how to use the medium.

Yet we have made and continue to make progress in a variety of modes of computer use. We are beginning to understand both the process of how to use computers effectively in education and the process of producing effective course materials.

I do not consider that the current equipment in our schools is the equipment that large-scale delivery of computer-based learning materials will use. Although many of us are now running on timesharing systems, the new generation of stand-alone equipment and the elegant products of the large-scale integration technology will become more and more the dominant delivery mode. While timesharing systems will still continue in modified forms to have some use in education, most future use will be primarily with systems in which all or almost all of the processing takes place at the device itself.

I will review briefly some of the modes in which computers can be used and some of the advantages of the computer as a learning device.

Interactive Learning

You might guess from the title chosen for this article that the most valuable aspect of the computer in education is that it allows us to make learning interactive, with students constantly cast as particpants in the process rather than as spectators. Psychologists agree that the best feedback comes immediately after the event.

Jeremy Anglin[19] comments on Jerome Bruner's view of education: ". . .The acquisition of knowledge, be it the recognition of a pattern, the attainment of a concept, the solution of a problem, or the development of a scientific theory, is an active process. The individual...should be regarded as an active participant in the knowledge getting process...."

In many lecture situations the students are passive. In some reading of textbooks, particularly with students with weak backgrounds, the process is also one of passively letting the textbook information "flow" into the individual. Good interactive computer programs can provide a very different environment. As soon as a small amount of information is given to the student, the program can begin to ask questions. With skillfully written programs, the process can be a dialog in the full sense of the word. The student is not conversing with the computer but rather with the authors of the material. The authors of the material are creating not a single dialog but a whole collection of such dialogs, conversations with each student. Visual information should play a critical role in this "conversation" if we are to serve the needs of all students. The sequence in Figures 7-1 to 7-4 is from the help sequence for the PROJECTILE quiz.

Individualization

In the computer dialogs just described each student response can be analyzed. Different actions can be taken depending on the exact student input. Cumulative records of student performance in that session, and even previous sessions, can be maintained and used to affect the flow of the learning sequences. A student who does not learn with a particular approach can be presented with alternate learning materials. The learning experience for each student can be unique, tailored to the needs, desires, and moods of that student.

This individualization is a humanization of education, compared to what typically happens in the large lecture situation. There the process is fundamentally the same for every student, a mass production system. With the computer, each student can have a unique learning experience (Figure 7-5 to 7-8).

Experience

I stressed earlier the role of experience in initial learning. Robert Karplus suggests that experience is the first stage of the learning cycle. But when a student enters the university, experiences directly relevant to the learning situation are not typically available. Here a new mode of computer use becomes important. It can amplify everyday experiences. The computer can create worlds that are not available in convenient form for students to play with and explore. Thus, we can create realms of experience with the hope of enriching the formal learning environment to follow and with the hope of

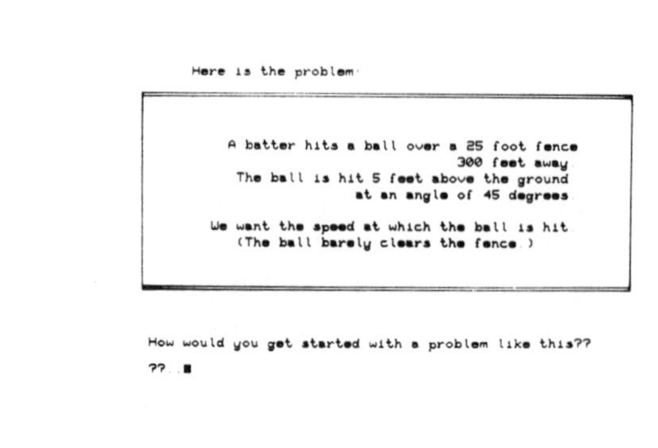

FIGURE 7-1 Introduction to PROJECTILE Help Sequence

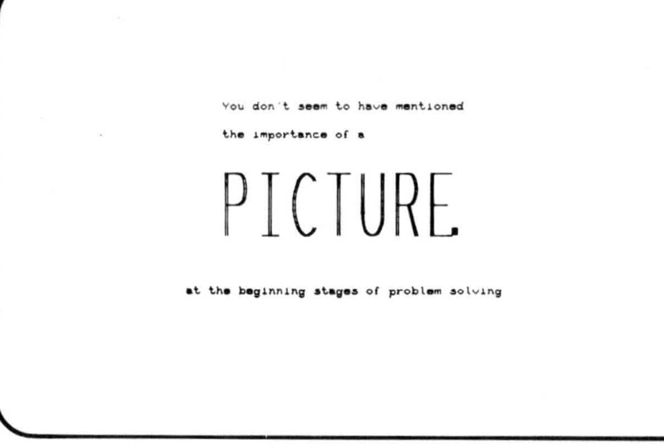

FIGURE 7-2 PROJECTILE—One Reply to a Response in Figure 7-1

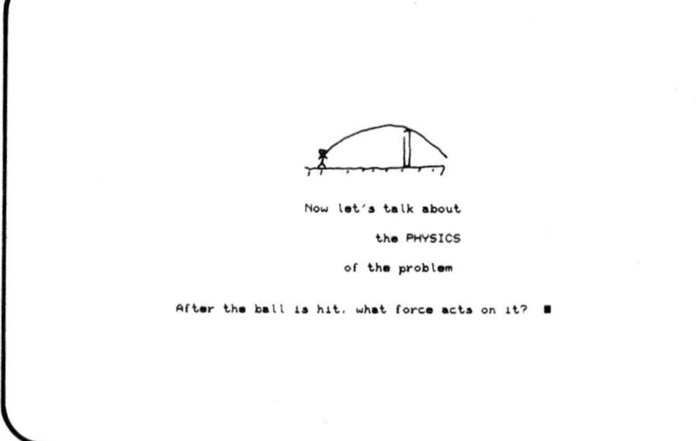

FIGURE 7-3 PROJECTILE Help Sequence

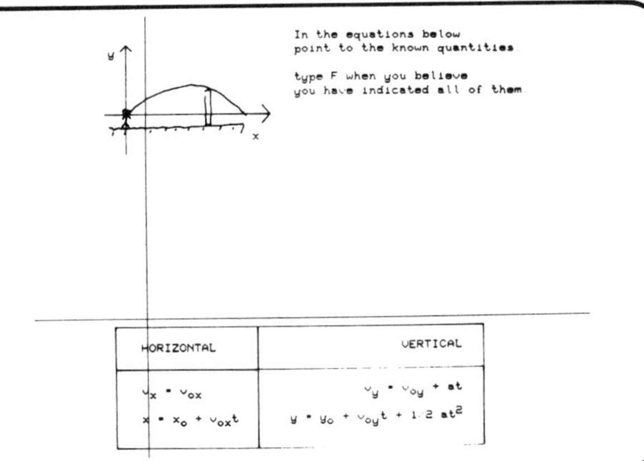

FIGURE 7-4 PROJECTILE Help Sequence—Student Showing What Values Are Known

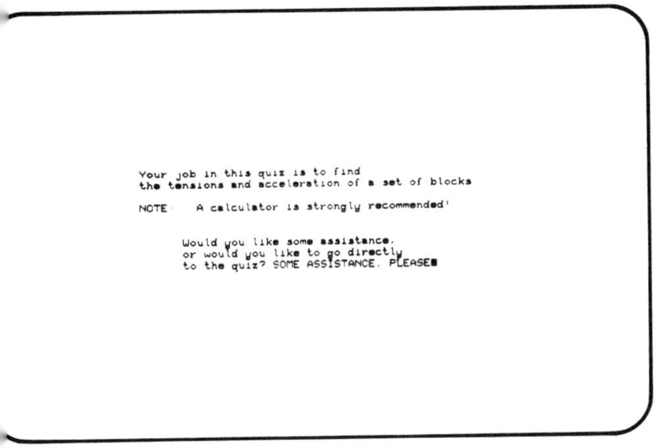

Your job in this quiz is to find
the tensions and acceleration of a set of blocks

NOTE: A calculator is strongly recommended!

Would you like some assistance,
or would you like to go directly
to the quiz? SOME ASSISTANCE, PLEASE

FIGURE 7-5 The Quiz NEWT—Student Requests the Help Sequence

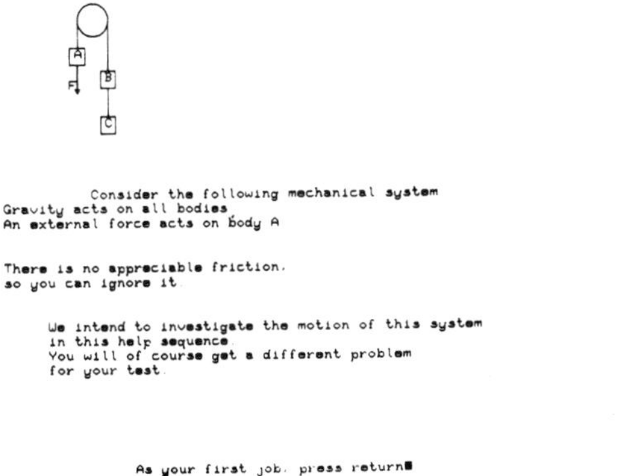

FIGURE 7-6 Beginning of the Help Sequence in NEWT

building up student insight and intuition about the physical processes that are later to be described by mathematical details (see Figures 7-9 and 7-10).

A typical example of such material, illustrated in this book, is the use of electric field plotting to give insight into the way static electric fields, or later changing electric fields, behave. Visual representations of field lines and of equipotential surfaces can give students, through a structured set of experiences, a view of the way charges lead to fields that is not obtainable by working with formulae or differential equations.

As with all play material, something is needed beyond the play. Our early experiences with this material at Irvine indicated that while faculty were often extremely interested in our controllable worlds, only the more motivated students, a small fraction of the total class, made active use of them. It was a classic example of material that was attractive to the teacher but not attractive to many of the students. We have better success if we provide a structured learning situation, in which students have a least some guidance as to what kind of play is reasonable—the kind of thing you might say happens in nursery school. This can be provided either directly within the dialog or in separate written material. We also work to give students some explicit way of seeing whether they have indeed understood what we hoped they would understand with this play. For example, with electric field lines we have available an on-line quiz, determining whether students can "read" the field diagrams and have picked up the ideas we would like to be understood.

Intellectual Tool

So far the type of computer usage we have been observing is one in which students interact with programs prepared by others for some specific pedagogical purpose. But programming itself is increasingly a fundamental skill in modern society.

Even more importantly, programming can often lead to new and powerful ways of approaching a subject. For example, if students are in a position to write programs, they can be brought much sooner to understanding the laws of motion as differential equations. Many of our beginning courses present the laws of motion as purely algebraic structures, in terms of the kinds of problems the students can work. Yet we know from intermediate and advanced courses that the real power in these laws is in their use as differential equations. The fact that they are not discussed in the beginning level is due to the mathematical difficulty involved. But the computer, through simple numerical treatment, allows an "end run" around these difficulties. This particular subject has been very well discussed in the literature, in noncomputer form in *The Feynman Lectures in Physics* and by many others (Arthur Luehrmann, Herbert Peckham, John Merrill, and myself to mention only a few). Materials are available through CONDUIT, at the Computer Center of the University of Iowa.

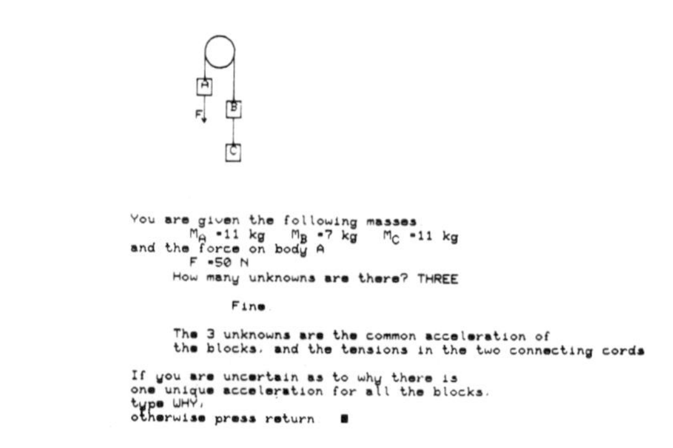

FIGURE 7-7 Further Details of NEWT Help Sequence

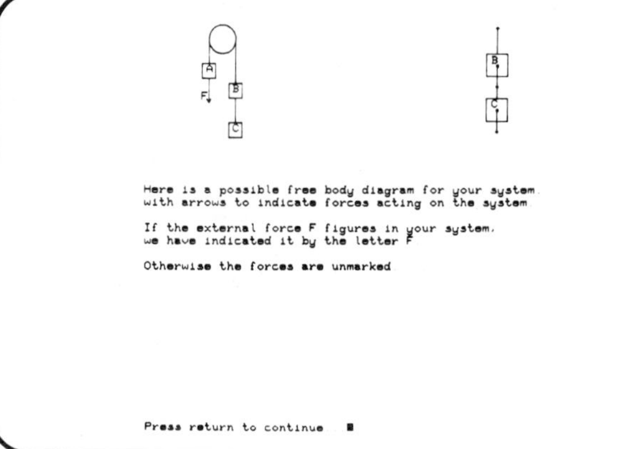

FIGURE 7-8 NEWT Help Sequence, Continued

One of the advantages of this approach is that students grow up feeling that the computer is a natural tool to use in a variety of areas. Such a tool will become as important as reading, writing, and arithmetic in the future. As with any learning tool we want to introduce it to students in such a way that they will use it in reasonable and proper ways.

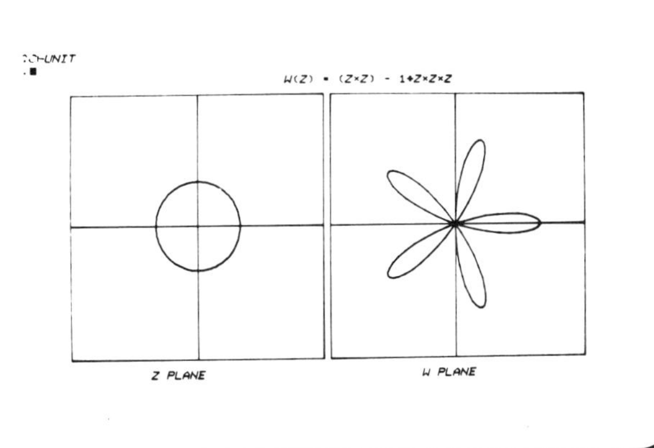

FIGURE 7-9 Conformal Mapping in an APL Workspace

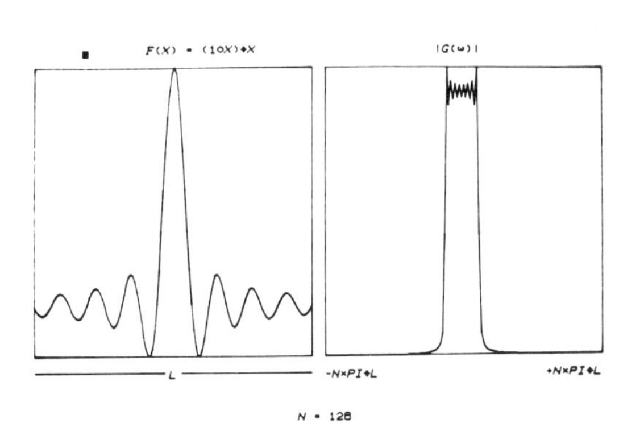

FIGURE 7-10 Fast Fourier Transform in APL

Student Control of Pacing

Do all students learn at the same rate? Do all students spend the same amount of time in the learning process? These are not entirely settled research questions. But there is evidence that the answer to both questions is "no." The typical courses of today force everyone to move at essentially the same pace, not allowing for individual differences. The midquarter exam comes for everyone at exactly the same time. No allowance is made for students to move at different rates through the material, perhaps reviewing learning sequences where necessary.

The computer is not a necessary component for variable student pacing. Indeed, most variable paced systems such as the Personalized System of Instruction (PSI) have not used computers. But the computer makes individualized pacing convenient and commercially practical.

One of the advantages of variable pacing is that it allows for students with very different backgrounds. Thus, if remedial materials are available, students may be referred to those materials and may spend several weeks with such materials before continuing with the mainline materials. Such students are typically lost in our current courses, although some help possibilities may be available in learning resource centers. The computer can provide a much more flexible set of alternatives.

Time and Sequence Control

Related to the student's ability to be able to control movement through the material is the ability to control the sequence of flow of material within a learning sequence and to control timing of presentation.

In a film, the filmmaker constantly decides on timing. Pauses will be inserted to allow students to absorb a particular idea. This is in contrast with what happens when one turns the page of a book, where the entire material is spread out in front of the reader. There is no control over the order in which the material on the page is seen by the student and no control over the timing within that order.

The computer more closely resembles the film or, with another analogy, the development of material on the blackboard in a good lecture. The sequence and timing are under program control, and can be modified on student request. The dialog can move back and forth between alphanumeric material and graphic material.

Delays between such material can allow time for human concentration and reaction. Within alphanumeric material we can stop at the end of a sentence, allowing time for reading. We can come back and reinforce ideas by various graphic approaches, such as underlining, making words flash, and encircling words.

Student Control Over Content

In a typical education situation, every student sees almost the same content in a course. The only difference is in such things as term papers or special projects. Thus, the main learning outlines fail to take into account any individual preferences or any differences in background. Because the computer can provide a great variety of interactive learning experiences and can provide management capabilities, there is no reason why students cannot be allowed a variety of choices.

The implication is not that the student could simply do anything. The instructor can still control the types of sequencing that are possible. But within these constraints students can be allowed considerable flexibility. In one of our courses we specified six different tracks through the quarter, based on two sets of materials.

Testing as a Learning Mode

One of the newest and most exciting roles of the computer is in an intimate combination of testing and learning. This kind of use is of particular interest in a self-paced environment based on mastery learning, such as with the Personalized System of Instruction. Patricia Cross in *Accent on Learning*[20] comments that "Mastery learning is a revolutionary concept that lies at the heart of the new teaching strategies. Simply stated, mastery learning permits all students to learn to the same high degree of achievement regardless of time period. Traditional education, on the other hand, permits the level of attainment to vary while the amount of time is perceived as a constant across the group of learners."

In a traditional course, tests play several roles. They furnish an input to the grading system, typically and unfortunately a norm-based grading system that compares students with other students rather than determining just what they have learned. In a PSI environment, the tests are competency-based with students obtaining feedback as to just which of the objectives in the unit needs further study before they can progress to the next unit. The emphasis moves away from the evaluation to aiding students in learning.

The computer as a medium for tests allows us to go much further than this. Students can be reinforced immediately when an answer is correct not only by being told that the answer is good but by auxiliary construction or review of the problem. A wrong answer can not only be identified immediately as wrong, but in many cases it is possible to determine just why the answer was wrong and to offer immediate learning sequences to the student dealing with that precise problem. It will be seen that such an experience is an intimate blend of testing and teaching. In terms of student learning, this mode of computer use, although new, is one of the most powerful and promising. We can provide immediate and precisely formulated feedback, offering direct aid to students.

A variety of techniques can be used to make each exam unique, yet each testing for the same objective. Our physics tests, developed primarily by Steven Franklin, Joseph Marasco, and myself, illustrate the tremendous power of such procedures. Figures 7-11 to 7-14 show some examples.

Management

If students are taking tests on-line, this leads naturally to the notion that the computer can also maintain class records. In a large class environment, keeping accurate records and allowing students to check that no errors occur is a nontrivial problem. In our own department we have a half-time secretary whose major occupation is to maintain records, primarily for the big beginning courses. Faculty members too put considerable amounts of time into this process, and no one would claim that this is the most productive use of their time.

The computer is a very powerful information-gathering and handling device. The exams write results directly into an on-line data base; other items not covered with on-line exams can be entered into the same data base. Feedback can be provided to both students and instructors as to what is happening, what problems are developing, and which students need aid.

Communication

Another use of the computer in classes is as an additional mode of communication, beyond the traditional ones usually available. The computer can drive an electronic mail system, with the instructor broadcasting messages to the students, the students sending queries to the instructor, and the instructor replying to such queries. In my own large courses, this mode has assumed increasing importance. Typically I answer about 15 computer letters per night from my home terminal while running a large course.

Any way of increasing communication between the teacher and the student is desirable. Electronic mail does not replace personal contact—presumably the instructor will still have office hours and will meet with individual students—but it does offer another significant channel of communication.

Personal Factors

The computer has no prejudices. All of us are subject to inherent prejudices, often at the subconscious level. These unconscious personal feelings present in all of us may well affect our students. Many of us, for example, are consciously or unconsciously supporters of the better students, those most "like" us, and so tending to have our sympathy. The problems of students struggling to learn a particular piece of material are difficult for many instructors. Even the best teachers with the most devotion to the vast majority of students may occasionally tire of such problems.

Some students may prefer to deal with the learning material in an impersonal way, rather than to come into the faculty member's office.

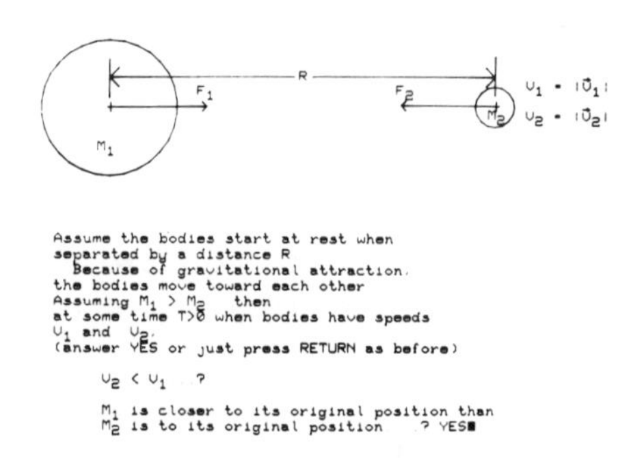

FIGURE 7-11 Early Problem in the Quiz TWOBODY

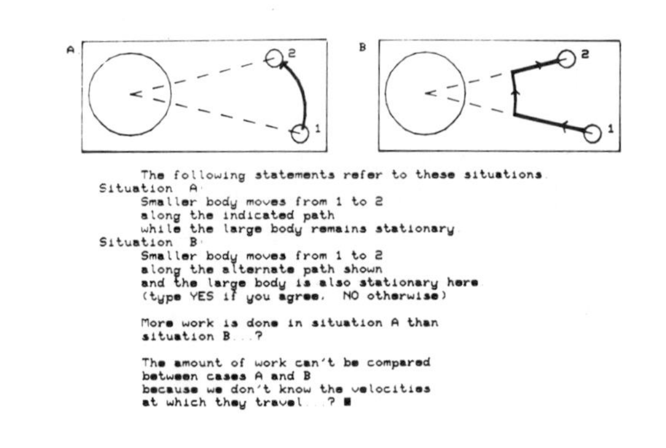

FIGURE 7-12 Another Problem in TWOBODY, Illustrating Concealed Multiple Choice

Production and Distribution

I only touch on important issues concerning widespread availability. At the present time, production of computer learning materials is almost at the cottage industry stage, with the individuals producing and sending a few copies to friends. Journals, such as the *American Journal of Physics*, have aided in wider distribution. New organizations, such as CONDUIT, have been set up by the National Science Foundation for this purpose. But so far these activities have only scratched the surface.

Fundamental to widespread use of computer learning materials are more structured ways of producing and distributing the materials. Efficient production demands that we examine carefully the process of production and distribution, setting up centers with particular expertise in this direction.

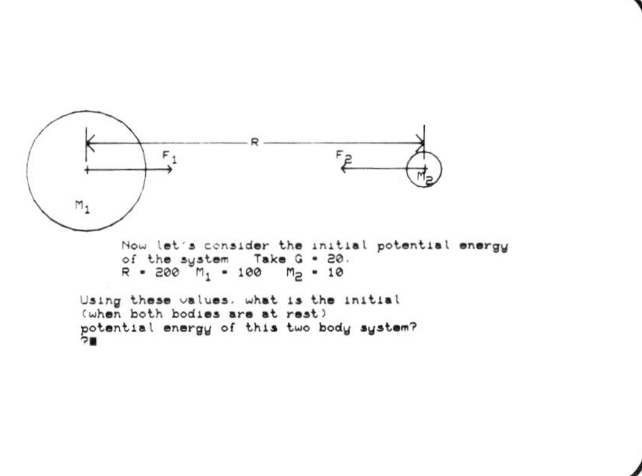

R
F_1
F_2
M_1
M_2
Now let's consider the initial potential energy
of the system Take G = 20.
R = 200 M_1 = 100 M_2 = 10
Using these values, what is the initial
(when both bodies are at rest)
potential energy of this two body system?
?■

FIGURE 7-13 TWOBODY, Beginning of a Sequence of Numerical Questions

Summarizing our results to this point we have

	Separation	Total Energy	Potential Energy
Initial	200	-100	-100
Final	100	■	-200

Now fill in the missing entry

FIGURE 7-14 TWOBODY, Further Details on the Numerical Question

These centers may be within universities or may be within commercial organizations. National centers were first proposed in the Carnegie Commission report of about 5 years ago, *The Fourth Revolution—Instructional Technology in Higher Education*[21]. In the report, seven such centers are suggested. No such centers have yet developed, but they still seem an attractive possibility.

What types of firms will be involved? Perhaps they will be the traditional book publishers. Perhaps they will be computer vendors. Perhaps they will be special companies, profit or nonprofit, formed paticularly for the distribution of such materials. Within the elementary level a very successful company already exists, Computer Curriculum Corporation steered by Patrick Suppes. Perhaps universities will become the producers and distributors of these new types of curriculum materials.

Production methods for these materials must take into account the variety of tasks. The pedagogical specification of the materials is a different task from that of programming them to run on a particular machine and requires different talents. Graphic and instructional designers must also play an important role in the process. Programs must be easily modifiable over a considerable period of time, as experience is gained with direct student usage.

Institutional Changes

I have already suggested that institutional changes are likely to be drastic because of the demographic factor, the changing nature of our student body, increasing legislative and public control, and occasional economic depressions. I realize the inertia of the system, but I believe these factors will be sufficient to overcome this inertia. The computer will offer us our best approach to coping during this difficult period.

We already see signs of this change in our current institutions. Patricia Cross (in *Individualizing the System*, edited by Dyckman W. Vermilye[22]) comments, "By the year 2000 an instructional revolution will have changed higher education in fundamental ways. Signs of that revolution have already appeared."

We can expect more self-paced courses, more emphasis on mastery learning. Furthermore, we can expect more emphasis on self-paced curricula in which the curriculum is not tied in with fixed time constraints with courses beginning only at the beginning of the semester, but rather is adapted to individual students. There is no reason, given the computer environment possible now, why a student cannot start a course at any time, subject to any desired constraints. The self-paced curriculum may lead to the final destruction of perhaps the single most sacred feature of American universities, the four-year degree. New attitudes will be generated with regard to grading, with more emphasis on competency-based grading. The question of credit, and similarly degrees or other marks of achievement, may well be brought into question also. In all of these developments the computer will play an important role in suggesting solutions, with computer use steadily becoming larger.

Perhaps the most exciting development in institutional change will be the rise of entirely new kinds of institutions, ones that depart from our traditional patterns of education. They will compete with traditional institutions for the limited number of students available.

The most exciting example, although with little use of computers so far, is The Open University in Great Britain. In its first 6 years of operation, The Open University received over 250,000 applicants and registered about 74,000 students. In 1975, the total cost per student including governmental funds and student fees was about £369 (about $500) a year. The Open University is effective in terms of its learning procedures and very cost-effective compared to our traditional universities. The emphasis is very much on the development of course materials, and much less expensive delivery systems are featured. Thus, the university has no student "campus" with many expensive buildings. Rather, students work primarily in their homes and in scattered learning centers all over the country. Some aspects of The Open University are probably not appropriate in our hemisphere, but we have much to learn from this exciting educational experience.

Central to learning is the creation of an environment particularly conducive to the area involved. Seymour Papert, at MIT, likes to compare two situations for learning French. One is that of the typical high school course in French in our schools. Learning to speak French in this environment is often a difficult process; not all students are successful. Yet in France all young children learn to speak French! Can we create such an environment for physics, a Physics Land? That is the challenge before us!

What Can We Do?

What is our role, as educators, in this process? First, as Physics teachers, we are, among all the faculty in higher education because of our own technical training, the group in perhaps the best position to advise and help administrators and faculty colleagues in understanding the pressures for change. We can aid in creating changes that lead to healthy educational environments rather than to unhealthy environments.

Many of us hope to play major roles in the development of computer-based learning materials, the new and exciting materials the computer will make possible. We can work with the companies that may be involved in either the production or the sale of these new types of materials, particularly in the early uncertain period. We can exhibit materials to our faculty colleagues to show that the computer is not a frightening device at all, but rather is one that has great potential for improving learning.

Like many uncertain futures this future can be both terrifying and exciting. It is terrifying because we cannot see all the possibilities that will develop in the troubled period of the 1980's. It is exciting because we stand at one of the great moments in the history of education.

References

1. John Merrill, *Using Computers in Physics* (Boston: Houghton Mifflin Company, 1976).

2. *Introductory Computer-Based Mechanics II*, CONDUIT, Iowa City, Iowa.

3. George Leonard, *Education and Ecstasy* (New York: Delacorte Press, 1968).

4. Albert Morris, "An Overview of the Extended University," *T.H.E. Journal.*

5. Gerald G. Smith, *T.H.E. Journal*, September 1975.

6. Arthur Clarke, *The City and the Stars* (New York: Harcourt, 1956).

7. Eugenii Zamatien, *We* (New York: Viking Press, 1972).

8. George Leonard, *Education and Ecstasy* (New York: Delacorte Press, 1968).

9. B. F. Skinner, *Walden Two* (New York: The Macmillan Company, 1948).

10. John Hersey, *The Child Buyer* (New York: Alfred A. Knopf, Inc., 1960).

11. K. Patricia Cross, *Beyond the Open Door: New Students for Higher Education* (San Francisco: Jossey-Bass, 1971).

12. Kenneth Eble, *The Perfect Education* (New York: The Macmillan Company, 1966), p. 5.

13. George Nelson, *How to See* (Boston: Little, Brown and Company, 1977).

14. Kenneth Eble, *The Perfect Education* (New York: The Macmillan Company, 1966), p. 71.

15. George Polya, *How to Solve It* (New York: Doubleday & Company, Inc., 1957).

16. Thomas Taveggia, "Personalized Instruction: A Summary of Comparative Research, 1967–1974," *American Journal of Physics*, Vol. 44, No. 11, (November 1976).

17. Robert Carplus et al., "Proportional Reasoning and Control of Variables in Seven Countries," AESOP Report ID-25, Lawrence Hall of Science, Berkeley, California, 1975.

J.W. McKinnon and J. Renner, "Are Colleges Concerned with Intellectual Development?," *American Journal of Physics*, Vol. 39, p. 1047.

Robert Bauman, "Applicability of Piagetian Theory to College Teaching," *Journal of College Science Teaching* (November, 1976).

18. Arnold Arons, "Cultivating the Capacity for Formal Reasoning: Objectives and Procedures in an Introductory Science Course," *American Journal of Physics*, Vol. 44, p. 834 (1976).

Arnold Arons and Robert Carplus, "Implications of Accumulating Data on Intellectual Development," *Journal of College Science Teaching* (January, 1972).

19. Jerome Bruner, *Beyond the Information Given — Studies in the Psychology of Knowing,* ed. Jeremy Anglin (New York: W.W. Norton, 1973), p. 397.

20. K. Patricia Cross, *Accent on Learning* (San Francisco: Jossey-Bass, 1976), p. 11.

21. The Carnegie Commission on Higher Education, *The Fourth Revolution—Instructional Technology in Higher Education* (New York: McGraw-Hill, Inc., 1972).

22. K. Patricia Cross, "The Instructional Revolution," in Dyckman W. Vermilye, ed., *Individualizing the System* (San Francisco: Jossey-Bass, 1976) p. 51.